RADIATION SOUNDS

RADIATION SOUNDS

MARSHALLESE
MUSIC AND
NUCLEAR SILENCES   JESSICA A. SCHWARTZ

DUKE UNIVERSITY PRESS / DURHAM AND LONDON / 2021

© 2021 Jessica A. Schwartz
This work is licensed under a Creative Commons Attribution-NonCommercial 4.0 International License.
Printed and bound by CPI Group (UK) Ltd, Croydon, CR0 4YY
Designed by Matthew Tauch
Typeset in Alegreya and Archivo by Westchester Publishing Services

Library of Congress Cataloging-in-Publication Data
Names: Schwartz, Jessica. author.
Title: Radiation sounds : Marshallese music and nuclear silences / Jessica A. Schwartz.
Description: Durham : Duke University Press, 2021. | Includes bibliographical references and index.
Identifiers: LCCN 2021005879 (print) | LCCN 2021005880 (ebook) ISBN 9781478013686 (hardcover)
ISBN 9781478014614 (paperback)
ISBN 9781478021919 (ebook)
ISBN 9781478091813 (ebook other)
Subjects: LCSH: Music—Political aspects—Marshall Islands—History—20th century. | Music—Marshall Islands—History and criticism. | Marshallese—Music—History and criticism. | Music—Marshall Islands—History and criticism. | Radiation—Health aspects—Marshall Islands. | Nuclear weapons—Marshall Islands—Testing. | Marshall Islands—Foreign relations—United States. | United States—Foreign relations—Marshall Islands. | BISAC: MUSIC / Ethnomusicology | HISTORY / Oceania Classification: LCC ML3917.M37 S38 2021 (print) | LCC ML3917.M37 (ebook) | DDC 780.9968/3—dc23
LC record available at https://lccn.loc.gov/2021005879
LC ebook record available at https://lccn.loc.gov/2021005880

Cover art: Uranium-235 Atom Model. Science History Images / Alamy Stock Photo.

This book is freely available in an open access edition thanks to TOME (Toward an Open Monograph Ecosystem)—a collaboration of the Association of American Universities, the Association of University Presses, and the Association of Research Libraries—and the generous support of Arcadia, a charitable fund of Lisbet Rausing and Peter Baldwin, and the UCLA Library. Learn more at the TOME website, available at: openmonographs.org.

YOKWE YUK LIJON, MAY YOU REST IN PEACE.

You, and so many others, deserved so much better.

This is dedicated to all my friends, mentors,

and interlocutors in the Republic

of the Marshall Islands,

whose voices resonate

as the spirit of

perseverance.

ACKNOWLEDGMENTS ix

Introduction: "It Was the Sound That Terrified Us"

1

CHAPTER ONE

Radioactive Citizenship: Voices of the Nation

41

CHAPTER TWO

Precarious Harmonies

83

CHAPTER THREE

MORIBA: "Everything Is in God's Hands"

131

CHAPTER FOUR

Uwaañañ (Spirited Noise)

170

CHAPTER FIVE

Anemkwōj

211

NOTES 253 / BIBLIOGRAPHY 273 / INDEX 287

ACKNOWLEDGMENTS

There have been so many absolutely amazing people who have been the impetus behind this project and truly facilitated its development that it is nearly impossible to list everyone individually. To the Rongelapese and Bikinian communities, I am deeply grateful, as I am to so many wonderful people, both Marshallese and US American, who resided in the RMI during my ethnographic work. Hermi, Grace, Lemeyo, Abacca, and all the members of *Iju in Eañ*, your commitments to each other, your culture, your homeland, and your invitation to let me participate with your group, as well as your acceptance of my commitments to learning about Marshallese musical culture and the nuclear issues, cannot be paralleled. I hope to learn so much more from you all. And to Talien and the Ejit community, thank you for letting me stay at your house and on your land, and inviting me to the practices, to church, and to other community festivities. Again, I can't begin to communicate how much I have learned from you.

While this is by no means an exhaustive list, I must also sincerely thank Alson Kelen and family, *Irooj* Mike Kabua, *Irooj* Imata Kabua, the Kwajalein aḷaps, Fred Pedro, Eddie Enos, Dean Langinbelik, Mayor James Matayoshi, Senator Tomaki Juda, Councilman Hinton Johnson, Mayor John Kaiko and family, Jack Niedenthal, Glenn Alcalay, Holly Barker, Neijon Edwards, Pastor Percy Benjamin, Peterson Jibas, Mary Silk and the CMI Nuclear Institute, Ingrid Ahlgren, Peter Rudiak-Gould, the Fisher family, the Utter family, Scott Stege, Tina Stege, Mark Stege, Andrea Helkena, Ben Kiluwe, Risen Philips, Telbwe Alik, Jai Lewis, and the Majuro Cooperative High School graduating class of 2012. And to my interlocutors, my friends, who have since departed—Lijon Eknilang MacDonald, Shirley Langinbelik, Senator Tony deBrum, Deacon Johnny Johnson, Willie Mwekto, Larry Edwards, and Alkinta Kilma—I am grateful for the time we spent together. With each conversation, my perspective broadened in ways I could have never imagined. My appreciation cannot be expressed in words alone, but I will offer three: *Kom lukuum emmol*.

I also want to extend a special thanks to my editor, Ken Wissoker, for being enthusiastic about this project from our first meeting and a source of continued encouragement throughout the process. Thank you to Joshua Gutterman Tranen, the entire production team, and the anonymous readers who compelled my work in new, exciting directions from its nascency.

Thank you to the rich intellectual communities at New York University and Columbia University, where I was fortunate to spend my graduate and postdoctoral years, respectively. Thank you to my wonderful mentors who engaged with these ideas in their earliest state and trusted that an exploration of "resonances of the atomic age" in the US and the Marshall Islands was worth their investments: Jairo Moreno, Suzanne G. Cusick, J. Martin Daughtry (and father, Don Daughtry), David Samuels, Ana María Ochoa Gautier, and Michael Beckerman. To Aaron Fox, Kevin Fellezs, Ellie Hisama, César Colón-Montijo, Amy Cimini, Andrew Burgard, Michael Gallope, Jenny Olivia Johnson, Stephen Smith, Siv Brun Lie, Alex Ness, Adam Mirza, Emily Wilbourne, Clara Latham, Benjamin Tausig, Michael Birenbaum Quintero, Gavin Steingo, John Melillo, and Nick Kirby for being part of this journey. And to my musical accomplices in New York City—Krishanti and Erin of Lady Bits—and in Los Angeles—Jez and Nancy of GRLA.

Thank you to my colleagues at UCLA's Musicology Department, past and present, for welcoming me and being so incredibly supportive of this work: Olivia Bloechl, Nina Eidsheim, Cesar Favila, Robert Fink, Mark Kligman, Raymond Knapp, Elisabeth Le Guin, Tamara Levitz, David MacFayden, Mitchell Morris, Catherine Provenzano, Shana Redmond, and Elizabeth Upton. Thank you to the graduate students for thought-provoking engagements and to the entire Herb Alpert School of Music community. Additionally, thank you to Rachel Lee, Elizabeth DeLoughrey, Keith Camacho, Lisa Cartwright, Marianne Constable, Laura Kunreuther, and Judy Tzu-Chun Wu for reading through and providing insightful comments on the manuscript.

Thank you to everyone at the Marshallese Educational Initiative, past and present, including Carmen Chong-Gum, Faith Laukon and Nixon Jibas (and family), Benetick Kabua Maddison, and Carlnis Jerry. And to April Brown ("ED"), a super special thanks goes out to you for reading through and making comments, edits, and revisions to the manuscript. HLVS!

Thank you, Bandit—my always companion.

And thank you to my family—my unceasingly supportive dad (who taught me the meaning of "never give up"), my mom (who encouraged my love of music), Julie and Ryan, Uncle Danny, Aunt Mara, Uncle Al, Lauren and Jeff Cohen, Rosy and Adelina, Michael and Maxwell Charenzo Schwartz-Polk.

Earlier versions of parts or portions of this book have appeared in the *Journal of Transnational American Studies*, the *Journal of Interdisciplinary Voice Studies*, *Shima Journal*, *Music and Politics*, *The Oxford Handbook of Music and Disability Studies*, *American Quarterly*, and *Women and Music*.

This research was assisted by a Dissertation Completion Fellowship, which is part of the Andrew W. Mellon / American Council of Learned Societies Early Career Fellowship Program.

INTRODUCTION

"IT WAS THE SOUND THAT TERRIFIED US"

On March 1, 1954, the United States detonated its most powerful thermonuclear weapon, code-named "Castle Bravo," at Bikini Atoll in the Marshall Islands. Situated to the southeast of Bikini, the populations of Rongelap Atoll, including people residing on Ailingnae and Utrik Atolls, watched in confusion as the sun seemed to rise in the west. On Utrik, Rijen Michael, eighteen years old at the time of the explosion, was startled from his sleep by women talking about the incident, the *baam*, with a great concern that it was the "end of the world."[1] Yostimi Compaj, born in 1942 in the midst of World War II, retains sensory imprints of the bomb as well: "First, there was a great light that came to the island [Utrik]. It was beautiful, with shades of pink like the early-morning light."[2] The stunning visual display was caused by Bravo's radioactive mushroom cloud, which rose into the stratosphere to an altitude of more than 115,000 feet and spread 70 to 100 miles in diameter in under ten minutes. Eventually, the pattern of fallout expanded over 7,000 square miles.[3]

As the cloud plumed higher into the atmosphere, a shock wave and resonant boom prompted screams from frightened children on Rongelap. Molly, a Rongelapese woman who was fourteen years old at the time, explained that people were frightened by the "loud sound [that] shook the ground" and caused the thatched houses to shake.[4] Rijen described this same loud rumble that reached Utrik as *iñurñur*, the Marshallese onomatopoeic word that describes an array of unpleasant noises (groan, moan, rumble, growl, grunt). As Yostimi explained, "After [the sky changed colors], there was a great sound, and it was the sound that terrified us. We ran to the church then because we didn't know what it was, because the sound was so loud when the bomb fell."[5] Aruko Bobo, who was living on Rongelap, described how "the air around us was split open by an awful noise. I cannot describe what it was like. It felt like thunder, but the force from the noise was so strong that we could actually feel it. It was like the air was alive. . . . Everything was crazy."[6]

Later that day the wind carried irradiated coral dust from three completely vaporized islets at Bikini Atoll to the east and covered the atolls of Rongelap, Ailingnae, Rongerik, and Utrik.[7] However, the island populations had no explanation for why white flakes began to fall on what had been a clear, albeit unusual, morning. On the atolls of Ailingnae and Rongelap, children played in the fallout because they thought it was snow.[8] They "tasted it" and "rubbed it in their eyes."[9] Women recall that their scalps burned and their hair fell out in large chunks. Men, women, and children became violently ill and ran into the lagoon for respite, but they could not sense that the water was dangerously radioactive.[10]

The confusion of the islanders only grew as Americans came to survey the islands and departed without giving the residents clear directions or explanations in regards to the unusual event. Magistrate John Anjain stated that by the afternoon of March 2 (thirty-six hours after the explosion), two US officials came to Rongelap "to inspect the damage done by the bomb," but in their short survey that lasted less than an hour, "they left without telling anyone that the food, water, and other things were harmful to human beings."[11] Forty-eight hours after the Bravo detonation, after much fear and bewilderment, the US military came with a ship and seaplane to evacuate the Rongelapese. They commanded the Rongelapese to strip off their clothes and to leave all their possessions on the island. Scared, humiliated, and sick with radiation poisoning, the Rongelapese obeyed, and they followed the Americans onto a naval ship. The Utrikese, treated similarly, were evacuated on the same naval ship, and both communities were taken to Kwajalein Atoll; other atoll populations that received radioactive fallout, such as nearby Ailuk and Likiep, were not evacuated. The Rongelapese and Utrikese became part of a classified study on the effects of radiation on human subjects, code-named Project 4.1, without their consent.[12]

Meanwhile, halfway across the world in the Bronx, New York, Jimmy Keyes, first tenor of the African American doo-wop band the Chords, and his bandmates were sitting around watching television when they became captivated by footage of the early atomic explosions that took place at Bikini

Atoll. The group began to throw around an idea: "Wouldn't it be amazing to sound something so awesome in a song?"[13] Shortly thereafter, the Chords composed a song with two explosive syllables at the core; they took the street vernacular popular in the postwar atomic milieu "boom" and added "sh," on the upbeat, to give an anticipatory silence that they perceived as constitutive of how the bomb's explosion sounded so powerful. Although the poetic refrain could be classified as an onomatopoeia, the influential song, "Sh-boom (Life Could Be a Dream)," is often noted as being one of the first to employ nonsense syllables in the style that is now characteristic of doo-wop. Recorded on March 15, 1954, it was the first song by an R&B group in the 1950s to place in the top ten of the Billboard pop charts (reaching number nine), making it a "crossover success" in the racially segregated music industry. "Sh-Boom" is also considered one of the first, if not the first, rock 'n' roll song, as popularized by the cover of the White Canadian group the Crew Cuts. Considered a more "sanitized," "traditional" version, the Crew Cuts' version went to number one on the Billboard charts after the band appeared on the *Ed Sullivan Show*. It highlights a string of "nonsense syllables" from the opening "hey nonny ding dong" rather than the powerful refrain with which the Chords' version opens: "Life could be a dream, life could be a dream. Doo doo, doo doo, sh-boom."[14]

While doing research on a genealogy of punk through rock 'n' roll, I read Richard Aquila's article "Sh'Boom; or, How Early Rock & Roll Taught Us to Stop Worrying and Love the Bomb" (1997), which included Keyes's story about watching television with his group, which he had told to CNN in 1994. American popular music was instrumental in the domestication of the military, such as harmonizing the bomb and giving it a human voice, which disconnects people from the realities of nuclear weapons testing and persists in American pop music today. Contextualized by Aquila's article, "Sh-Boom" compelled a question: do Marshallese have "bomb songs"? I spoke with the US American-Bikini Atoll liaison (and former Peace Corps volunteer) Jack Niedenthal, who told me that Marshallese have many songs dealing with "the bomb," and he encouraged me to come to the Marshall Islands where I could hear firsthand the impact of US nuclear weapons testing from those who live it.

From 2008 to 2010, I conducted ethnographic work in the Republic of the Marshall Islands (RMI), which is an autonomous nation-state in the north-central Pacific that includes twenty-nine atolls (twenty-four are inhabited) and five islands.[15] I stayed on Majuro Atoll, the capital, and I was fortunate to speak with a range of people from a number of the atolls. At this moment the Rongelapese are in flux, and they live in Mejato Island (Kwajalein Atoll), Majuro Atoll, and various locations in the United States. Some Rongelapese were preparing to move back to Rongelap, but many government leaders and Rongelapese elders are concerned about safety, for cleanup efforts focused only on the main island and not on the more than sixty other islands that make up the atoll.[16] The Bikinians are displaced for the foreseeable future because of the persistence of radiation on their atoll after US cleanup efforts failed to make any portion of their atoll safe for human habitation. Much of the population of Kwajalein also remains displaced after being removed by the US military, which continues to use their atoll to test nuclear delivery systems.

Over the course of my two years in the Marshall Islands, I would often ask Marshallese from different atolls "Did the Americans ever tell you what they were doing?" My question referred to the sixty-seven nuclear tests conducted by the United States from 1946 through 1958, the forcible relocations, and medical examinations. The programs were shrouded in secrecy; information about the tests conducted on Marshallese bodies and their lands remains classified. One Rongelapese woman's response was a long silence accompanied by a head shake, which seemed to indicate that her answer was "no," reinforcing much of what I had been told. This silence is resounded in spaces that hang at the end of questions unanswered to this day by the US Department of Energy (DOE) and appeals denied by the US Supreme Court. These questions resound stylistic influences of American vernacular musics, such as country music and Protestant hymns, and in the Rongelapese song "*Kajjitok in Aō Nan Kew Kiio*" ("These Are My Questions for You Now, Still"), which was composed in 2008 after the exclusion of the Rongelapese and Utrikese women from the official meeting between the DOE and the RMI government.

These sonic fragments are part of the intricate, unequal, and unevenly developed relationship between the United States and the RMI. They attest to the highly controlled yet dynamic boundary between sound and silence that continues to be an essential component of our relationship to nuclear weaponry and its devastating global consequences. Global nuclear culture, as an aural culture, developed around the radically inaudible phenomenon of nuclear weapons and created, in a literal sense, new and vital roles for listening and hearing—in short, new aesthetic sensibilities to hear the inaudible: the consequences at the explosive core of what has been called the "unthinkable" parameters of nuclear war and its "insensible" radioactive aftermath. The radical reconfiguration of what can and cannot be perceived sensorially has produced new listening practices attuned to hearing what has been rendered unhearable: silence itself, such as the literal silence of governmental agencies that guard information on atomic energy research and the unheard-of effects of nuclear weapons explosions.[17]

This book addresses the United States and the Marshall Islands as configuring a politics of silence and sound that emerged during the production of global nuclear culture: the socio-sonic practices, including but not limited to music produced while living under US nuclear hegemony, the material dimensions of this existence, and the discursive formations mediating this existence. More specifically, I stress the need to understand nuclear culture as a sonic culture by examining the radical reconfiguration of what could and could not be sensorially perceived.[18] The aural uniquely elucidates complexities of the United States and Marshall Islands' strategic interconnectedness and also the relative cultural shifts that were specific to both countries' geopolitical positions within a general nuclear culture. A focus on the aural within the larger synesthetic field is important in this discussion because of the conspicuous manipulation of silence that I argue has characterized the construction of global nuclear culture. To more thoroughly probe the relationship between the lacunae in our present understanding of nuclear issues and the role of post-Bravo sensorial and expressive modalities, I account for the imbrication of neocolonial and gendered violence in the production of scientific nuclear knowledge from 1946 onward, which depended on the legally sanctioned silencing of humans as "restricted data." Within global nuclear culture, the scientific harnessing and the bureaucratic withholding of information pertinent to nuclear power depended on official sanctions of silence and secrecy. In dealing with such communicative obstructions, writers on atomic culture have woven the nonsonorous into varied analytics of this postwar culture that dismiss the sonic, affective dimensions of global nuclear culture and highlight the culture of secrecy without framing it theoretically.[19] Further, global nuclear culture and its manifestations across various scales of human life and activity were coconstituted by another field of audition that has been generally overlooked in nuclear culture: a specifically musical one. Musical texts, performances, and listening practices illuminate the cultural task of making the "nonsonorous sonorous."[20]

Radiation Sounds chronicles seventy-five years of a Marshallese musical repertoire that emerged in response to the deleterious effects of US nuclear militarism. These songs archive significant changes in both American and Marshallese musical thought regarding the perception of sounds as well as silences and the reorganization of their transformative potential through music making, music circulation, and musical practice. Marshallese singing practices, and in particular notions of the throat, draw on vital religious, cultural, and political nodes to make US nuclear violences sensible and intelligible. Through Marshallese singers' words, stories, and performance aesthetics, this study details how music yields insight into the role of expressive culture in mitigating the damages of a persistent nuclear legacy that, at various scales, continues to play out in secrecy and silence. From laments to Christmas songfest competitions, the Marshallese musically and textually evoke the consequences of nuclear hegemony: forced exile, gendered and cultural violence, and the inscription of "insensible" radiation into bodies as heard, for example, in precarious harmonies composed of irradiated women's voices.[21] I value these songs in terms of the labor of making radiation sound and consider them to be important political, social, and healing work both for Marshallese and for a rigorous evaluation of US history.

This book traces how Marshallese singers politicize musical texture—or the sensible arrangement of voices, bodies, and information—to form new communities, solidarities, and the possibilities for new subjectivities to emerge. Drawing on the language of harmony, or musical characteristics that refer to the general order, ideal community, and means for conflict resolution, I show how nuclear culture instanced the redefinition of societal relations and a new world order based on the United States leading the West (the "free world").[22] The bomb and its radioactive aftermath were portrayed as transformative, democratizing instruments that manifested "peace and democracy," as well as prosperity, shifting the once militant, colonial power of Japan to an effeminized, peaceful ally and then making the Marshall Islands, once Japan's labor colony and gateway to the Pacific, America's atomic frontier.[23] I trace this history from World War II through the contemporary political milieu, unpacking shifts in the sensorial grounds increasingly marked by modern warfare through key songs that speak to strategic dematerialization and dematrilinealization, including the severing of female lineage and land-based political agency, through incarcerations, incinerations, and incorporations that aimed to neutralize potentially defiant groups and dissenting histories.

According to Teresia K. Teaiwa, an I-Kiribati and American poet and academic, "The literature on the history and politics of Micronesia is deafeningly silent on women. Colonialism is responsible for the long suppression and dispersion of women's voices; it is also deaf to the sound of women's voices." She writes that colonial power functioned on "the divide and rule principle, the first exercise of which occurs in relation to native women and men. Alienating one half of the native population—the women—from deliberations facilitates the process of colonization and administration." Teaiwa stresses how "the perpetrators of colonialism made a grave mistake in failing to recognize the power of women."[24] I find that sonic histories of the senses are crucial, particularly as a methodological tool to better understand the ways in which the bomb and radiation are part of a *longue durée* of processes through which women and colonized persons have been rendered insensible and unreasonable by removal from their ancestral homelands and, in the case of nuclear redress, from Western law. I concentrate on the gendering of humans in their separation from nonhumans as two constitutive breaks of nuclear colonialism. I am particularly interested in how nuclear colonizing processes, which created a gateway for the militarized development of Kwajalein and democratic political development of the nation, have been gendered.

Positioned within the Pacific Indigenous rights movement, the aural aesthetically amplifies the conditions of possibility within global underdevelopment and crisis as bound by imperial ideologies. Thinking through the vocal techniques and timbral capacities of the coded female and male voices and bodies performing in political spaces, I consider the unheard or underacknowledged women's wartime musical roles, including their political voices in these productions as part of a gendered representation that is intelligible to Western notions of the public/private spheres and diplomacy but that silences the matrilineal kinship system. This speaks to the gendered and racialized violence at the core of environmental injustice and rights-based remediation. At times the policy and productions assumed to counter environmental inequity reproduce stereotypical gendered or racialized (ethnic and Indigenous) representations of precarity and strength. Women have always been involved in ways of reading the tenor of the atollscape and participating in politics, sonorously and otherwise, yet as this book shows, their gendered and sexualized labor, bodies, and lives were dispossessed from their means of political authority and employed in the service of nuclear colonialism. Singers' voices can be heard in decolonial context, such that their voice crossings challenge the socio-categorical rigors that stream them into disempowered oppositional binaries. These movements resound what Teaiwa terms "fluidarity," the solidarity of intercultural (nonwhitestreamed) feminisms, and also a generation of Native Pacific scholars who address, in various ways, gender and gendering issues in the context of colonialism.[25] I listen to voice crossings, and drawing from anarchic and Indigenous feminisms but also incorporating other nonwhitestreamed, queer theoretical models that value unlearning normative ways of reading or listening, I contemplate the value, beauty, and strength in the equivocal, particularly in ways that can intervene in the staunch installations of the nuclear superpower.

This book unfolds in five chapters, following my introductory discussion of its theoretical contributions. *Radiation Sounds* is an inquiry into the politics of harmony that focuses on songs which detail a musico-poetics and politics of radiogenic decay and Indigenous survival. I listen to the contested terms of how the RMI came to be harmonized into the global system in spite of—and because of—the extant and unsettled nuclear issues, and how Marshallese citizens protest their inclusion into the international system and exclusion from nuclear justice. I argue that to better hear the limits of voice and democracy, listening to voice(lessness) produced by the contested space of harmony is crucial. Chapter 1 delves into the sonic history of US nuclear testing in the Pacific that provided the grounds for promises of postwar "global harmony." Listening to the instrumentalization of radiation, I explore how the United States staged and circulated Marshallese voices in American geopolitical memory and engendered a national public vocality predicated on contracts and contrasts.

Chapters 2 through 5 focus on the political histories and musical activism of specific groups that have been marginalized because of nuclear testing, masculine militarism, and the neocolonial system of harmonization. Each chapter emphasizes how Marshallese reappropriate the "scenes of [their nuclear] subjection" as they were staged in the American global media, their Indigenous humanity depreciated.[26] Focusing on a sense-based politics of harmony, or how Marshallese pair Western concepts of harmony, as an agreement—a contract—with their notions of harmony in terms of the collective spirit that moves through the collective throats or seats of souls of (non)humans, these chapters develop a sonic politics of indigeneity that resounds the consequences of Bravo through the embodied throats and resonant voices of those people attuned to its still-present transmutations in their bodies and the lands they call home. Chapter 2 focuses on the gendered labor of petitioning for health and declassification in Rongelapese women's "musical petitions." Chapter 3 shares how Bikinians compile a national nuclear repertoire comprised of a double vocality to challenge the overdetermination of the US–RMI court-based relationship. Chapter 4 contemplates Bikinian spirited noisiness in terms of gendered protections. Chapter 5 documents the life of Ebeye and the struggles of the Kwajalein landowners through resistant practices of "homecoming songs." In each chapter, singers recuperate ancestral memories of embodied knowledge and place naming, which reemplaces maternal and matrilineal epistemological orientations to a militarized land.

The introduction unfolds in three main sections. First, I position the (in)sensible and politics through a framework that I call "global harmony," in which I theorize US nuclear incorporation of the Marshall Islands through militarized and mediated violences (e.g., mass mediations, voice leadings, nuclear listenings, vaporizations) and offer a genealogy of colonial silences during the juridico-political effacement of nuclear violences through the international politics of reconciliation at the foundations of the Compact of Free Association (hereafter "COFA" or "Compact"). I read systemic breaks through Marshallese songs that I hear in terms of a musical poetics of the bomb through cracked, broken soundings that resound multiple harmonies through the destabilization of a dominant harmony. Second, I draw on Marshallese concepts to consider how singers instrumentalize their voices in rerouting vocal currencies (energies) from the "rational" musical system and "rational" political system (representational) to Marshallese embodied currencies of their homeland that is radioactive and from which they are displaced. Such political work can be read in terms of a sonic politics of indigeneity, whereby singers' throats move voices to navigate cracked interconnections among the various communities severed by the bomb (and militarism). Third, I share how these songs can be considered in terms of remediation, which is a recursive methodology, and focus on the repairing of societal relations.[27] Remediation is the concept that helps me navigate the first and second theoretical interventions; it helps shift the frames and filters through which radiation is deemed (in)sensible by listening, such that what is presumed to be known about voice, the human, peace, harmony, democracy, and ultimately justice—and their practices—is unsettled.

GLOBAL HARMONY

The Marshall Islands were used as a nuclear staging ground for the production of US Atomic Age diplomacy, which promised global harmony built upon the principles of democracy, personal freedom, and political liberty. Such staging bolstered the cold war liberal consensus, which was a blueprint and goal of US foreign policy; it was a cultural project that disseminated the West as normative and also provided an ideological hierarchical model of opposition. The cold war consensus was based on the proposition that America was to provide military force to ensure national security and promote freedom worldwide as well as international containment of communism and spread of capitalism and democracy.[28] This consensus, which was so pervasive that it was often not perceived as an ideology but simply as "common sense," has also been considered in terms of "global harmony," which was a trope used by US architects of the cold war, domestic and international (although the project of global harmonization and American expansionism disrupts any neat binaries between domestic and international).[29] Global harmony can be approached in terms of an ideal and in terms of reified neocolonial relations based on geopolitical social theory conceptualized by the United States—the architects of the "new world order"—as they considered immigration, decolonization, and media presence following World War II.[30]

An example is *One World or None* (1946), the first "atomic scare" film that was released the same year as Operation Crossroads commenced at Bikini Atoll just a year after the devastation of Hiroshima and Nagasaki, which was credited with ending World War II and with the US victory.[31] The film gives an overview of the advances of weapons of war, each with increasing devastation, to show the exponential scale of damage that nuclear weapons can incur. Sponsored by the (US) National Committee on Atomic Information, the film proposed the solution that would suit its geopolitical aims—namely, that nations should align with the United States and join the United Nations, which was recognized as an international peacekeeping organization said to promote security and cooperation between nations and to act as "a center for *harmonizing* the actions of nations."[32] RMI sovereignty, within this context of harmonization, depends on nuclear militarism and moralized notions of harmony. Resistance to such totalizing harmonization requires the ongoing amplification of both the relational Western harmony and Indigenous (dis)harmony through which breaks resound challenges to "one world or none" as defined by the United States. Read as a critique of the individuated voice through the politicization of harmony, singers engage their Indigenous sensibilities to perform a politics of (dis)placed indigeneity that unsettles the genre of Indigenous voice and challenge the denial of Native subjectivity.

Post–World War II geopolitical relations draw from Western intellectual history shaped by Pythagorean notions of the harmony of the spheres, a mode of universalist thought and universal justice that Pythagoras believed might be enabled by "harmonizing" unlike spirits or rationalizing them, dividing them, such as the staging of place-based and gendered binaries in democratization. In order to decolonize harmony and listen to hear the labor of the negative, it is important to trace harmonizing and democratizing genealogies as modernizing. As Patty O'Brien writes, European men posited the Native Pacific women as their opposite given the distance from Europe.[33] Staging Native Pacific women as occupying the private or domestic sphere without political voice, eighteenth-century Enlightenment leaders theorized that European men were the only rational persons entitled to "universal suffrage," the vote and voice in the public sphere, which began a historical narrative and scientific treatments of the world that have proved disastrous for those positioned outside of legal and political voice. The Enlightenment also saw the theorization of the development of European tonal harmony from the "common practice period" that aligns with European colonialism and scientific rationality, particularly through the sense of hearing that affirms ratio-based proportions through movement and later becomes fixed in written ratios.[34] Harmonic universalism applies "Pythagorean" musical theory, which claims the "intervals of the Greek diatonic scales were more 'natural' than other scales," in an extension of Enlightenment philosopher and mathematician Marin Mersenne's theory of "physical universalism." The latter "linked the sounds of nature, inanimate objects, animals, children, and women with non-European people and their music." Mersenne's laws of harmony, or the correct placement and positioning of sounds within a musical system or social system, "formed the basis for European cross-cultural thought for the next two centuries."[35] The law and politics of harmonic universalism, even though debunked, were powerful missionary-colonial organizational tools that shaped postwar global configurations through US developmental means that positioned the Pacific, which has been characterized as "opposite" of European culture, as the site of the most devastating thermonuclear tests.

Historically, singing has been a point of connection for Marshallese and Americans; it has been used in diplomacy between the commoners and customary elites (chiefs/*iroij*) working in cooperation with colonial authorities. Protestant missionaries from the Boston-based American Board of Commissioners for Foreign Missions (ABCFM) arrived in the mid-nineteenth century and were the first foreigners to have a sustained relationship with Marshallese. Hymn singing provided a way to connect in the face of language and cultural barriers. Euro-American Protestant songs also assuaged tensions with the German political administration of the atolls (mainly for the copra trade) and offered a new expressive construct for the commoner class to sonically contest its position in the fixed customary hierarchy. Tonal harmony is an art form, or model for sensorial education and attunement to an abstraction of the Western systems that Marshallese learned as they became part of the newly formed working class (from the power base). As Christian gender separations were taught through role assignments, soprano, alto, tenor, and bass (SATB) voice registers that produced and were produced by harmony amplified gendered separations. Many are adamant that although they had their own vocal patterns, they did not have "bars," "measures," "scales," "notes," "lines," "rests," or "keys" before the missionaries arrived. The missionary structures, such as physical arrangements in boarding schools and churches, arranged bodies, yet these prescriptive biopolitical mechanisms arranged sensibilities through written material in books, such as the Bible and the *Bok in Al* (hymnbook), which were cognate with colonial law. The shift from collective sense making through place-based, generational attunements to collective sense making from the eye to the ear, where the ear becomes directed to and through the eye, created a means of sensorial or feelingful familiarity that the US government capitalized on. When US troops returned in 1945, they sang hymns with the Marshallese, who were grateful that the war was over and viewed the Americans as liberators, a role that the United States embraced as it set out to remake Marshallese sociopolitical systems in its own image.

The universalized trope of voice and voicelessness pervades human rights discourses and legal cases. In the wake of the two world wars and with a revived emphasis on newly configured ("post-1945") human rights and postcolonial self-determination, voice has been upheld as a preeminent "gift" from the United States and as an intervention that combats voicelessness, particularly in undemocratic, undeveloped countries. The moralized Christian rhetorical conflation of harmony with humanity and voice with the human seemingly justified the salvation, liberation, and overcoming narratives emphasized by the victor superpower that can intervene and reroute voice as capital currency through transitional justice and networked neocolonial pressures (investments). Drawing on Western intellectual history that positions the speaking voice as requisite actualization of the person or the political human—namely, the human who counts as human (has rights)—Jessica Taylor offers that "to speak (and to hear the voice) is to be human."[36] Musicological studies of harmony and counterpoint recognize how the musical rationalization of voices was a means to normalize the rationalization of bodies through colonial legal structures and the modern state that secures national voice through citizen-subject voice. Ana María Ochoa Gautier explains that the voice is central to such governance because it is viewed as a productive site to distinguish "the human from the nonhuman."[37]

The perceived and instrumentalized malleability of the voice—that it can be used to separate and relate the (non)human and the potentiality for prejudicial rights therein—evidences a powerful complex that operates as a dividing line between the redressable and the unredressable when it comes to postwar and post–cold war pathways to self-determination and sovereignty through the jurisdiction of the United States. This complex is the constitution of voice, which includes an effacement of disempowering violences to subdue colonized Native populations through their (non)-human and sex-based (gender-assignment) separations, both of which can be made to resonate in the singing voice because of acoustical semantics surrounding register, intonation, and contour, for example, when attached to meaningful words. Yet these techniques are part of musical harmony and thus an array of "vocal anthropotechnologies" that have been deployed in the service of "directing the human animal in becoming man," such as musical notation, diction, orthography, and various means of training and dissemination.[38] The legal concept of the person is thus intimately related with the sonorities of the persona: the voice. Marshallese radiation songs wield senselessness by placing it on center stage and making it sensible. Here, voicelessness is also voice because it is staged and amplified by musical, even harmonious, boundaries. Decolonizing critique inheres in pivoting listeners from voiced notes and rests to re-fusals of voice(lessness).

Marshallese often credit ABCFM missionaries in terms of bringing "harmony" and "peace" to the archipelago in a complex, moralized salvation narrative that rehearses a Pacific Atomic Age diplomacy and solidarity through the importation of Western culture and White-supremacist, paternalistic savior culture. Historicizing affective alliance across different socio-natures is an important part of this project, especially with regards to the partitioning of the collective *through harmony*. I aim to provide an analytic corrective to earlier theories of "affective alliance" deriving from cultural studies approaches to popular music, which do not take cultural or historical embodied dispositions of affectivity into consideration.[39] There is the tendency to dehistoricize, naturalize, or universalize affective capacity; the openness is historically mediated. Structures of affective alliance or taken-for-granted nature cosmopolitics, I argue, maintain the structures through which hegemony is reproduced (e.g., the body articulated to the senses, spatialized place). It is crucial to review the operations of power and medial structures through which affective alliance comes to be felt as real and personal, such as colonial structures of appropriation, from antinuclear protests to book-based abstractions.

Following Olivia Bloechl's application of Dipesh Chakrabarty's work to a postcolonial musicology, I read music history—through musical harmony—as an "imperious code" that evinces how the senses are codified through musical entrainment and how representative voices come to be heard.[40] These practices participate in capitalist and democratic entrainments that founded the moralized force of nuclear worlding.[41] Singing afforded colonized populations, specifically underrepresented women and commoners, diplomatic voice (even in an informal capacity). Yet hearing the singing voice in the context of an individual, or modern, voice is limited by the human-centric musical framework that amplifies voice in the first place. Voice can be code for self-determination, particularly within the bounds of the nation-state and its citizenry. The making of Marshallese radiation communities' voice-and-voiceless interplay—from their minoritized positions through which they became representatives in US nuclear mediations from the postwar to today)—can be read along the lines of post–cold war liberalism. Following Lisa Lowe's work on "modern liberalism" and the violences that subtend it, I explore how the emergence of the RMI voices and voicelessness (as a matter of unfulfilled promises of political participation) manifested. Moreover, I trace the impossibility of liberal, representative democracy, as the promise of political participation and exercise of voice, to manifest as such within the constitutionally bound nation-state. "By modern liberalism," Lowe refers to "the narration of political emancipation through citizenship in the state, the promise of economic freedom in the development of wage labor and exchange markets, and the conferring of civilization to human persons educated in aesthetic and national culture—in each case unifying particularity, difference, or locality through universal concepts of reason and community."[42] The overcoming narrative (coming to voice) is based on affective alliances and formative dependencies. The tensions between the atoll polities and the RMI that play out in voice(lessness) evince how singers challenge the overcoming narrative while they also pursue hegemonic redress. US nuclear testing—the myth of the American Enlightenment—was premised on the debasement of Marshallese as unable to overcome the war—and come to self-determined voice—without US developmental democracy; this provided a foil for the military presence in the region, which is a message on which the Truman administration worked with mainstream media to disseminate.[43]

After being zoned as "strategic" by the United Nations as part of the US Trust Territory of the Pacific Islands (TTPI) from 1947 through 1986, the Marshall Islands became constitutionally independent on May 1, 1979. The RMI, headed by Iroijlaplap (paramount chief) and President Amata Kabua, then became a sovereign nation in 1986 after the signing of the COFA with the United States. With the terms set by the COFA, RMI citizens were given the ability to move, live, and work in the United States without a visa. The RMI was also afforded US military "security" and "protections" and access to funding opportunities, and the United States received the benefit of strategic denial, military use, and other stipulations concerning RMI international relations. Through the COFA, the United States was able to avoid accountability and waive settlements for damages for the populations of Marshallese that it deemed outside the officially demarcated radiation-affected zone.[44] Although the entire archipelago is downwind from the nuclear detonation sites, only four atolls—Enewetak, Rongelap, Utrik, and Bikini—were included in Section 177 of the COFA, which deals with claims for nuclear damages, even though bills have been proposed and supported to include additional atolls. Out of the twenty-four inhabited atolls, seven voted against the COFA: Bikini, Rongelap, Kwajalein, Ebon, Jaluit, Mili, and Wotje, all of which "had direct experiences with Americans, and histories of direct opposition to Amata Kabua."[45]

Section 177 outlined the US's "full and final settlement of past, present, and future" claims to nuclear damages in an espousal clause, and a Nuclear Claims Tribunal (NCT) was established for the RMI to oversee the process of awarding claims. However, US government documents declassified in the 1990s showed that Marshallese were unknowingly used as human test subjects in Project 4.1 and that the effects of the tests were much more widespread than previously known. Realizing that funds would not cover NCT awards and given this newly declassified information, the RMI government petitioned the US government for additional compensation in 2000. The Changed Circumstances Petition (CCP) was the only legal means the Marshallese were afforded concerning the "personal injuries" and "property damages" as well as health issues that persist because of radiation as defined in the language of the COFA. Although the Marshallese used this legal remedy to request additional funding if compensation provided was deemed "manifestly inadequate," their petition was judged by the US Congress as a political matter, which takes it outside the law (as a legal question), and the petition was rejected in 2004. A major turning point for Marshallese with whom I spoke was the signing of the amended COFA in 2003 (COFA II) that went into effect in 2004, which they felt lessened their chances of resubmitting the CCP. Funding for the NCT ran out in 2009. The nation, and in particular those communities that desperately wanted and needed to receive the awards from the NCT, were still trying to find legal recourse.

Others are concerned about the RMI's inability to be a free or independent nation if the RMI cannot control its relations with other nations or have its own voice, or vote, in international affairs. In 2007 the UN Declaration on the Rights of Indigenous Persons was approved overwhelmingly by the General Assembly. However, the United States was one of four nations that initially rejected the vote. Eleven nations abstained, Ukraine and ten Pacific nations that were absent from the assembly, including the RMI, even though the majority of the nation is Indigenous. Similarly, in 1985 the RMI, along with the Federated States of Micronesia and Palau, did not sign the Treaty of Rarotonga, also known as the South Pacific Nuclear Free Zone Treaty, and in 2017 the RMI, along with the nine nuclear weapons nations, refused to sign the Treaty on the Prohibition of Nuclear Weapons. This most recent refusal of the RMI and internal groups, such as Bikinians, to voice their support was responded to by antinuclear activists and organizations with disbelief and outrage. Yet all these examples share how the RMI nation-state, and therefore to varying degrees the COFA minority groups' voices and votes, are constrained by COFA with affective dimensions of hopeful trust and anxious threat woven into the political, economic, and military dimensions of the compact. Marshallese political diplomacy takes on an aesthetics of subversion, weaving in and out of global harmony in voice-and-vote–based abstentions that can be read along the lines of "equivocality" or "equal voices" that demand a flexibility, which is often moralized negatively as ambiguity.

These examples complicate the political articulation of the nation-state, the voice, and identity to self-determination, which can uphold notions of the fixed individual as means of movements rather than relationality. The modern nation-state functions on the concept of self-determination, individual will, and agency, enabling the rise of state-sanctioned, morally legitimized militarism and the spread of violence (of one voice) as protection (of the many), which is germane to representation. The celebration of self-determination, as progress, needs to be treated with a critical ear. This book complicates a statement by legal scholar Upendra Baxi: "The modern idea of human rights, which sought to civilize and conquer, [is in contrast to] 'the 'contemporary' human rights paradigm . . . [that] is based on the premise of radical self-determination. Self-determination insists that every human has a right to *voice*. . . ."[46] The entanglement of the nation-state's legal existence, through which citizens are entitled to voice, is based on the political legitimacy of violence that protects self-determination. This networked protection of self-determined voice is procured through the normalization of protection as weaponized division (militarized boundaries, nuclear politics) to uphold the imaginary of a stable identity. And with it, the harmonizing or unifying work of the United Nations, for example, seeks to promote cooperative negotiation as made possible by self-determination, even though self-determination is based on divisive violences.

Radiation Sounds proposes plural harmonies and challenges notions of individualized voice, which is listened to through fragmented modern sensibilities and through its capacities to produce musical harmony. Rather, by recognizing the institutional work of prescriptive texture that divides and leads voices to confine resonance's composure rather than enable it to be felt as potentiality, the significance of state-sanctioned—and therefore precarious—human rights tied to individual voice (as something given that can be taken back) and the historically changing constitution of the human, as person, is illuminated. For those particularly in minoritized positions, the state can decide to limit movement in a wealth of ways, based on the "common good," harmony, or consensus: privatization, domestication, and segregation, to name a few. This book's repertoire of songs and performances routes (dis)harmony, as the ebb and flow of voices, through unheard material process of lived embodiments of US state-sponsored radiogenic violence, experimentation, and disenfranchisement. The threads of these histories, and of assumptions about what it means to be a human that are forcibly mapped onto bodies in "civilizing" and "development" projects, are woven with vocal fry and frayed edges of harmonic tapestries that challenge neatly bound notions of state-based self-determination and the representational limits of voice and modern media. These limits are explored through musical reifications of politics and the (in)sensible, according to the nuclear project constitutive of globalizing modernity, capitalism, and democracy (global protest).

POLITICS AND THE (IN)SENSIBLE

Radiation, we are often told, is insensible. The ways in which radiation is made sensible to some subjects yield insight into the complex processes of classification that undergird global capitalism and representative democracy. Nuclear classifications are based on the production of nuclear knowledge, the definition of nuclear damages, and the scope of remediation. Radiation provided the means to instrumentalize social classifications predicated on racialized, classed, gendered, sexualized, and age-based differences, as well as human and nonhuman differences, in the service of efficient, exclusive procedural organizations in which US representatives would speak with and listen to some subjects only (male, politically elite, human). Songs mark the silencing of some voices in the service of the sounding of others. This book examines the consequences of these fraught aural hierarchies to contribute to conversations that show how racism, sexism, and classism—along with ableism—are constitutive means of global capitalism and (nuclear) colonialism. The intermediary-based networks comprise differently positioned lives and voices in geopolitical arrangements of laboring, reporting, and ruling bodies in what I am calling global harmony.[47]

Radiation, a "physical force" and "symbol" of neocolonial domination, is one of the ways in which the RMI is united and divided.[48] RMI constitutional independence, nation building, and national memory have been mobilized, in part, around Bravo. An index of the nuclear "unthinkable," Bravo has been considered "the worst radiological disaster in history" for its global spread of fallout, prompting calls to make sense of the insensible presence of ionizing radiation.[49] The sensible is an embodied disposition particular to historically situated subjects. Following Jacques Rancière, I understand aesthetics, politics, performance, and (shifts in) the sensible as crucially interconnected. I consider how singers challenge both meaning and the grounds of meaning through what Rancière calls the "distribution of the sensible," which he explains as the "system of self-evident facts of sense perception that simultaneously discloses the existence of something in common" and delimits "the respective parts and positions within" that commonality.[50] Drawing on Rancière's work, Gavin Steingo writes that "music doubles reality" by being of and surpassing the limits of reality; he explains that *"music is the very name of this separation*—a separation that requires a very particular sensory apparatus and a very particular set of operations carried out through that apparatus" between that which is and is not (yet) sensible in ways that play with the in-common by breaking with particular positions endemic to the musical or sensible commons.[51]

The modes of making Bravo sensible, such as "Sh-Boom" or "*Kajjitok*," are themselves affectively charged moral discourses that are meant to orient us in particular ways to the things named in the lyrical content. Placed together, the bomb can be positioned as a pivotal event bookended by the nuclear silences (sh-boom-sh). The relational retrograde can be approached through sonic-temporal overlays of the "sh" surrounding the bomb as *prior* and *aftermath* that become absorbed by the mediated treatment of the bomb, which was and continues to be a consistent normalized reminder of national security. "Sh-boom" and "*Kajjitok*" offer different perspectives and sensibilities, but they can both be read through the modern representational, intersectional positions and intersensorial relational processes. The temporal dimension of musical performance gives shape to the ways in which radiation has been rendered sensible to particular subjects and in the making of new subjectivities. "Sh-Boom" epitomizes the anticipatory silences of the nuclear threat and the interruptive refrains that, like broadcast alerts, remind Americans of the nuclear threat. "*Kajjitok*" reverses this, offering a retrograde of explosive silences interwoven with the vocalized material aftermath of the bomb (boom-sh).

In this section I draw up a contrast between the Americanized disposition of (voice) leading roles and nuclear listening practices through the making of nuclear silences, which compels (Marshallese) cracked, broken soundings. US cultural hegemony fashions nuclear incorporation (global harmonization) by normalizing an aurality around identity-based voice leading that is related to citizenship and rights, freedoms, and democratic participation, and nuclear listening, which is an aural disposition to which US mainland and Americanized listening subjects are entrained in ways that trivialize, celebrate, and fetishize the bomb. Nuclear listening is an attunement in which civil defense and pop culture created spaces where the bomb could be seen and heard spectacularly as democratic development because these spaces were subtended by the undemocratic US government classified archives, which upheld notions of scientific rationality and unequally resourced colonized populations and were available only to US Americans with clearances.[52] For example, "sh-boom" could be repeated as a playful "nonsense" vocable, whereas studies depicting radiation's effects on humans were kept sealed. In fact, there are countless American popular songs from the immediate postwar through the present that map the explosive, horrifying power of the bomb onto certain bodies, tethering an optics of the nuclear spectacle to an acoustical dismissal of Native subjectivity.

The staging of the nuclear spectacle has been explored as civil defense theatrical "stages of emergency" extended to homeland security's affective "theater of operations."[53] Histories of the atomic bomb often make the visual primary in ways that reinforce the nuclear spectacle as object of contemplation. This divides rather than redraws political communities that experienced nuclear silences as preempting the explosive event, enabling them to develop survival strategies within the reconstitution of the social order. For example, the awe-inspiring, billowing image of the mushroom cloud has been framed to erase the horrific consequences of nuclear weaponry, effectively creating what art historian Peter Hales has coined the "atomic sublime."[54] Touted as massively destructive and presented as aesthetically pleasing, the atomic bomb was often pictured in its splendid aftermath as mushroom cloud plumage, like the setting sun, spreading over mythically vacant lands either in the US desert or the South Pacific, conjuring impressionistic associations with the American frontier imaginary. According to Rod Edmond, complex "western representations of the Pacific were to form important chapters in the history of the Enlightenment and Romanticism, of nineteenth-century Christianity, science and social theory, of modern painting, anthropology and popular culture."[55]

An aim of this book is to provincialize the bomb by sharing how Marshallese musical form breaks the totalizing narratives of postwar living or overcoming that is endemic to the Enlightenment historical narrative.[56] Scenes of urban destruction were linked with a migration from the pluralistic, ethnically diverse cities to the suburbs by the growing middle class and a privatization that stood in contrast to communist ideology.[57] These spectacles, which aesthetically rendered settled land disposable, also helped justify the geopolitical acquisitions of the United States, a cold war superpower that maintained an "exceptionalist" narrative of progress. Surviving urban ruination promised—even necessitated—conquering and expanding the modern frontier: the West, the Pacific, and ultimately outer space. Postwar conditions of economic advancement, technoscientific development, and militarization thus shaped the broader cold war sensorium: the grounds on which the nuclear threat was perceived as real. "The goal," Joseph Masco writes, "as one top-secret study put it in 1956, was an 'emotional adaptation' of the citizenry to nuclear crisis, a program of 'psychological defense' aimed at 'feelings' that would unify the nation in the face of apocalyptic everyday threat."[58] Citizens were taught that survival was possible if they learned the correct skills and purchased the proper goods.

The US government understood it needed to boost the economy affectively and production-wise through what economist Joseph Schumpeter called "creative destruction," which was considered generative to capitalism.[59] Music and aurality mediate sensible and temporal unfoldings in ways that enable radioactive generativity as means of belonging, which I call *radioactive citizenship*. Radioactive citizenship is societal positioning or agency afforded through harmonizing the bomb. Specifically, in this context I write about the voice-based mediations that draw on acoustical signifiers of the bomb and mentions of radiation as the insidious force of nuclear weaponry. Radioactive citizenship can be situated in the US government's Federal Civil Defense Administration (FCDA) programming, which was the first national alert-based media-communications effort of its kind. The FCDA was heavily based on sound design because of the available technologies that would make people aware of the nuclear threat, such as air-raid sirens and the radio.

US Americans learned about the bomb, were taught to anticipate the bomb, and, perhaps most importantly, were taught how to survive the bomb by experiencing sounds that trained people to be civil defenders and fostered certain feelings and attitudes. The act of listening in the Atomic Age was a mechanism of survival; it made people more reliant on music as a dimension of temporal survival. Public-service announcements, exemplified by the popular slogan "Listen and learn, civil defense is common sense," are echoed today in the Department of Homeland Security's "If you see something, say something." Broadcast alerts communicated that the public's survival depended on the development of particular aural skills, honing what I have elsewhere called "the hypervigilant ear" and "nuclear listening" because they kept people attuned to the US government and corporate radio, which defined the parameters of listening. Still today, a repertoire of "bomb songs" with even more codified military sounds circulates across playlists in gendered formation, which I address later and elsewhere. Importantly, for now these sounds are subtended by the silences that have come to be normalized as part of wartime, cold war, and (inter)national security.

"Silence means security" was an American slogan coined during World War II as the nation began to formulate its role as a world power. During this period, atomic weaponry was being developed in a top-secret milieu. With the Manhattan Project and consequent cold war and arms race, national security was more tightly linked with secrecy as both domestic and foreign policy. The US government developed a complex "secrecy system" to withhold information from the American public and its adversaries regarding the magnitude of the bomb's destructive capabilities. The Atomic Energy Act of 1946 defined a new legal term, "restricted data," that made any utterance, mention, or rumor of restricted data until their declassification a violation of the law. "Restricted data" extended to all speech acts and continues to be enforced today, ostensibly protecting the arms of the nation over freedom of speech. Given the limits of logocentric voice, it's important to move beyond the speech-based aspects of censorship or the censoring of voices and consider how voices themselves can be heard as the dividing line or the doubling of worlds: the means of production and the product of harmony. I understand "the voice" both as a disciplined production articulated to liberal humanized agency and political sociality through which Marshallese singers can share their stories, and I also understand the disciplinary processes through which individuated voices are produced as silencing mechanisms of the militarized state that is upheld as protective.

Nuclear silences are the excesses of what can be heard and thus listened to through US modern mediated hearings that create cores and peripheries, insides and outsides, in which the latter is incorporated into the former. The US imagination of Marshallese peoples, particularly the "isolated" atoll groups who were geographically farthest from missionary "civilizing" institutions and colonial administrative bases, as subhuman, savage, and uncivilized in ways that rendered them unable to feel, sense, and think or know as much as US Americans has been devastating. Radiation, in the United States, is aligned with a particular moral orientation articulated to modern progress, as Rebecca M. Herzig details in *Suffering for Science*. As Linda Tuhiwai Smith discusses in *Decolonizing Methodologies*, *research* is one of the dirtiest words to Native communities because it conjures up abuses for the "good of mankind." Displaced and taken as test subjects, Marshallese became subject to sensorial effacement on multiple levels, from modernization and the fragmentation of the senses to being subject to examinations and other means of sensorial commodification and rationalization through which "memory as a metasense" or "memory of the senses" became incrementally denigrated.[60] This was complicated by the notion that radiation is "insensible," which restricted Marshallese from perceptual sense and meaningful sense, such that meaningful sense is often rendered in the form of severance, decay, and the "sensible" settler culture as a means of communication and appeal. As Herzig writes, "Without sensibility there is no right. A being without sensibility can suffer no wrong." Through their human subjectivation to radiogenic experimentation, some Marshallese groups became part of the Americanized culture of "sacrifice" (of their Indigenous lands and lives) in ways that would afford them agency, selfhood, personhood, and ultimately possession of voice via state sovereignty.[61]

Nuclear silences impede Indigenous movements: place-based temporalities and sensibilities, which manifest in the "near inaudibilities" in musical form. I follow Eugenie Brinkema's "critique of silence" in which she writes that "the violence of silence is to being, in order to render that kinetic stillness; the violence of near inaudibility is to form, sustaining the pressure of a duration—creating that 'space of time' for the sensation of extreme quiet to manifest."[62] In theorizing a broader nuclear aurality and global interconnectedness, I demonstrate how silence emerged as the paradigmatic Atomic Age sensibility and was instrumental in controlling bodies and information in both the United States and the Marshall Islands. I refer to nuclear silences as metaphorical, regulatory, and actual, although it is important to consider the interrelatedness of the three broad categories. Metaphorical silences are those silences that are, for example, symbolic of regulatory and actual silences, the traumatic internalizations—and therefore incommunicable dimensions—of nuclear damages and rhetorical silences; they are pressures through which the "sense of voice" forms, such as the pregnant pauses throughout an interrogation or singers' cry breaks. These silences manifest as expressive "non-sense" or "noises" that disrupt the law (language). Regulatory silences are the laws that restrict or prohibit speech, enforce policies of isolation, and protect classifications. These juridical and political matters that control information also control bodies: not just what they can say but also with whom they can talk and where they can go. The actual, or physical and material, silences result from forcible violence that renders a "kinetic stillness" of life, such as the vaporization of islands, forcible removals that separate sites of memory, and radiogenic disease and biomedical procedures that shift anatomies and cause damage to vocal cords, creating the physical inability to sing, speak, or make sound.[63]

Through the use of radiation aligned with total salvation and total destruction, the United States aimed to "[control] sensory difference" in stages of modernization, development, and nuclear incorporation. In *Ways of Sensing*, Howes and Classen point out that "societies have customarily made use of three basic methods for dealing with threatening differences (whether deemed to be physical, ideological or cultural in nature): containment, elimination, and assimilation."[64] The dismissal of Native sensibilities and severance of commensal communities are instruments of the anesthetics of empire and the disenchantment of modernity. It is steeped in colonial relations in which Indigenous persons are denied personhood and rights precisely through the denial of perceptual acuity and the ability to feel pain, creating the justifications for abuses, such as violence toward women and Indigenous persons, in ways that would get them to become "civilized" or "developed" and thus become "sensible." Such practices of the withholding of the means of consent through the denial of the sensible participate in what Patrick Wolfe calls the settler colonial "logic of elimination" that eradicates Native populations through various mechanisms, such as outright genocide, the destruction of heritage and Indigenous culture through guilt and shame, emphasis on a discourse of loss, and the debilitation of Indigenous agency through restrictions on mobility: physical and social.[65] J. Kēhaulani Kauanui focuses on Wolfe's designation that settler colonialism is a "structure, not an event," and shows how biopolitical controls and governmentality often normalize these structures of genocidal incorporation, meaning incorporation of the human to labor for the colonial power by mass extinction (genocide and assimilation) of "the native as native."[66]

Following authors such as Adriana Cavarero, Amanda Weidman, Ochoa Gautier, and Rancière, who understand the voice in terms of the sensible (and its distribution), I explore the material entanglements of voices of humans and nonhumans (machines, technologies) in more-than-human communities that speak to relational silences embedded in the politics of voice emergent in the nuclear age.[67] I present a robust counterpoint of listening and sensorial orientations to voices that re-fuse voice leading techniques within the prescriptive (neo)colonial system of harmony. These voices accrue resistant power, I suggest, when we listen to them as decolonial dissonances, dissonances that cannot be resolved within structures that mediate and resolve discord in the service of a teleological, linear history, be it of sounds or of bodies to which sounds become (problematically) attached as identity rather than relational network. Decolonial dissonances are vocal spacings that counterbalance technological determinism, Atomic Age diplomacy, governmental secrecy, and scientific objectification that have anesthetized agentive relationalities and upheld acoustic barriers in the historical present, which in turn structure archives that produce intellectual trajectories, bodies of knowledge, and political ecologies.[68]

BROKEN SOUNDINGS: A SONIC POLITICS OF INDIGENEITY

Global harmony can be read as a metaphor for the organized modern system. Sonic abstractions of global harmony (one world or none, global nuclear culture) can be heard in songs shaped by the formal rigors of musical harmony. Marshallese singers often use the figure of harmony and performances of harmony to amplify multiple ontologies that take shape as discord with the dominant "global" system, or the US political arrangement of Americanized cultural boundaries—including the limitations of voice-based identity as agency—in hierarchical configurations endemic to global capitalism. I consider how Marshallese songs challenge the sensible, structural underpinning of US American systems that categorically deny them hearings. To redirect auditors' listening, Marshallese generate musical dissensus, "the essence of politics . . . [as] the demonstration (manifestation) of a gap in the sensible itself." Rancière considers politics to be a break with the logic of a system wherein a few rule over the democratic masses. He writes about "the efficacy of *dissensus*, which is not a designation of conflict as such, but is a specific type thereof, a conflict between *sense* and *sense*. Dissensus is a conflict between sensory perception and a way of making sense of it, or between several sensory regimes and/or bodies."[69] I trace how Marshallese vocality and musicality respond relationally to the modernizing global phenomenon of nuclear silences as gaps in present-day nuclear knowledge, by first framing the issue within the nuclear context and rooting it in an exploration of these meaningful practices, conceptions of the body/senses as relational pathways, and notions of the social and political, all of which renders indistinguishable questions of health, politics, and intergenerational survival as felt and thought.[70]

Public performances that draw from Indigenous, customary colonial, and contemporary cosmopolitan modes of expressivity are vital for political groups, such as women's groups, Four Atolls polities, and Kwajalein political representatives, to redraw protective boundaries that can resist and participate in neocolonial incorporation. Through these counternarratives, or what I read as a sonic politics of indigeneity, Marshallese singers employ Indigenous epistemologies and modern reading practices *as complementary and interlocking*. Marshallese Indigenous values have been their survival mechanisms. Values of togetherness (*ippān doon*) and complementarity challenge fragmentary practices, such as divisiveness and individualism. Amid the violence wrought by masculinized militarism, Marshallese emphasize listening to matrilineal resonances, which are nonbinary composites of maternal mixing, in the vibrant, interlocking communications of more-than-human communities. Here, currency accrues through an understanding of how to listen to hear the movements of the land and lineage in directional movements (rumblings) of nonhumans, which augment or diminish the throat in its vocal capacities. Although Marshallese singers structure their musical outreach with Western musical harmony (a pitch-based system that abstracts, disembodies, and universalizes voices), the singers share the invasiveness of radiation as a musical system of resonant displacements that unfolds through timbral harmonies (internal intonation through poetics/onomatopoeia) that share the exhaustion of embodied voice—as muscular motions and memory—in singers' performances of the labor of making radiation sound that is realized through Indigenous ways of making sense.[71]

Pacific histories, Tongan scholar Epeli Hau'ofa remarked, cannot be understood without "knowing how to read our landscapes (and seascapes)."[72] Alternative ways of reading, or literacies, have become an important aspect of study in critical Indigenous, settler colonial, and Native Pacific cultural studies.[73] Contributing to these fields' investments in alternative literacies, I explore how Marshallese music structures dissonances felt by the extant presence of radiation as it circulates through the lives, lands, and futurities of Marshallese. The disembodied voice produced through the pitch-based Western musical system links to patriarchal networks through which currency flows; the matriline, the mother-son relation, and the lineage are empowered with attention to the throat, for timbral singing is felt in and resonates through the throat, and it attunes singers to nonhuman-human relations through the personalized realization of the nonhuman sounds that the person communicates. I listen to hear how singers and poets creatively interweave multiple readings from Indigenous place-based value concepts, which I explore in terms of "currency," that ground the atollic movements, including throat- and atoll-based voices that resonate alphabetic text from literature to law to medicine to Bible passages; here, singers' voices "produce different relations between words, the kinds of things that they designate and the kinds of practices they empower," such as recollections of Marshallese matrilineal, spiritual, and communal modes of protection, strength, and security that have been devalued by the United States, submerged by radiogenic violence, and placed outside of legal protections.[74]

Marshallese have an onomatopoeic sound for the explosion of the bomb: *erūp*. The word, spelled *erub* in certain instances, translates to "broken." It is used as a meaningful acronym for the Four Atolls designated in Section 177, ERUB: Enewetak, Rongelap, Utrik, Bikini. It is one of the breaks that is sutured into the formation of the nation-state, evincing unequal violences that forcibly pushed those atolls that were deemed the most distant from Western civilization into the center of global development. The break is central to the legal project through which Marshallese democratic voices have been entrained. As anthropologist Stuart Kirsch contends, "The Nuclear Claims Tribunal, which provides compensation for damage and loss, obligates communities to demonstrate a break with the past. . . . Marshallese claims about culture loss are influenced by the legal processes through which they are adjudicated."[75] These affective social spaces are of critical importance in examining musical performance and circulation as an alternative to, and perhaps critique of, the NCT and the US Supreme Court, which rely on certain modes of speech and voiced appeals to perform loss as intelligible. The political, social, and economic breaks tether or interlock with bomb songs from anywhere (e.g., "Sh-Boom") that, when engaged, can resonate the ongoing presence of radiation within durative structural racism, sexism, ableism (value placed on modern, corporate sensibilities), and other modalities of policing bodies as investments in maintaining the flow of privatized resources.

Theorists often read modern frameworks through discontinuity. While Marshallese musical breaks can be read as resounding such discontinuity (under modernization), it is important to listen beyond or in excess of modernizing frameworks that focus on the break (in ways that orient toward hegemonic assimilation). By relistening to Marshallese harmonic breaks in the context of a sonic politics of indigeneity, we can hear harmonic breaks as opening up sites of hearing that are not foreclosed upon by modern sensibilities but rather become pathways to Marshallese Indigenous values. For example, looking at Walter Benjamin and Ernst Bloch's take on modernity, C. Nadia Seremetakis writes that they only "looked to discordant objects, experiences of discontinuity, and cultural zones of non-contemporaneity in everyday social practices as containing interruptive possibilities in relation to the dominant myth of the continuum. . . . They tended to ignore or undervalue the extent to which particular cultures and social strata had developed their own indigenous, self-reflexive practices which cultivated break, rupture, discontinuity, and alterity in modern life."[76] Taking Marshallese sounds of the break and bomb as metaphorical and literal sound structure provides alternative frameworks to harmonic form as dominant mediation and entrainment of sensibilities. These resonant entrainments can be heard in terms of the interrupted break that materializes a sharing of the throat as a sharing of the labor, perhaps in interlocking gesture to continue sharing these stories. As Laurie Stras writes, "The disrupted voice conveys meaning before it conveys language . . . it is indicative of passions, suffering. . . . We hear it, too, as the result of labor—the physical trace of an agent working on the body, a measure of the body's cumulative experience" of forces: pressures and time.[77]

Kathryn Geurts writes that "a culture's sensory order is one of the first and most basic elements of *making ourselves human*."[78] Whereas scholarly reflection upon radiation has favored visuality rather than audibility—the eye rather than the ear, for example—this project works at the cross-sensorial: the crossing of the senses or the transmutation of the atomic flash of light and sonic boom to the "slow violence" that unfolds over a latency period where the effects of radiation cannot be perceived until after several cycles of cell mutation and organic attenuation.[79] These effects are observed over time; they are the compiled questions of sisters, the collective ennui of a group, the patterns of illness, the change in taste of food, the shrinking of plants, and the shifts in movement—for example, of movements of plants and animals, documented in song and compared and critically assessed. The movements away from health and agency are composed into visceral and audible phenomena—into sounds—that hum subversively in ways that permit them to go uncensored and remain unclassified. Working across the senses, I consider how radiogenic damages are registered (and communicated) as a host of uneasy, disjointed, and dispirited feelings. In this way the five senses, and in particular the ear and the eye, lag in registering the impacts of radiation, as do the classifications of diseases catalogued in Western medicine.

These songs, which assume care and accountability, amplify silent gestures to the thyroid, the biopolitical scars (eugenic scars) alongside gendered vocal parts in musical harmony. *Radiation Sounds* registers how Marshallese singers gesture to their (fragmented) body parts and disentangling (fragmented) voices, which are connected to radiation and removal. In particular, Marshallese return to their throats, which are approached as the center or seat of the soul, akin in ways to the metaphor of the heart in the West, and as the seat of the emotions. Unlike Western musical thought, which frames the voice as sounding an individual's deepest emotions, aligning voice more broadly with a person's identity and metaphorically with an individual's agency, the voice in Marshallese thought is one's "sound": it is the sonic component of the throat complex and speaks to a larger network based on conviviality and lineage (which is directly related to the land and the mother). The ability or inability to express emotions depends on an entire social network, knowledge of a lineage, and a "healthy throat," which comes from communality. Rather than the individual animating the musical voice, it is the musical voice that animates the person, primarily because the musical voice is itself a mnemonic device for summoning an entire heritage and therefore realm of knowledge concerning how to live and engage with others. Moreover, unlike the voice, the timbre-resonant throat cannot be overdetermined according to a Marshallese *jabokonnan* (proverb): "We reach and understand the sea, but not the throat (heart) of human beings."[80]

I theorize singers' throat-based, interconnected knowledge through an "erūp epistemology," or ways of knowing displacements—expropriative abstractions, severances, and damaging fissures—that mark systemic fissuring of Marshallese interconnected Indigenous bodies. Musical weaving can be understood in terms of "re-fusals." These re-fusals take shape through alternative sites of strength in which communal forms of empowerment gesture to new denuclearizing subjectivities and solidarities. Musical refusals are performances that (1) refuse or reject the dominant system's hegemony; (2) re-fuse or rewire, reroute, currents and flows (attentions and movements); and (3) sonically weave what Americanized listeners might consider musical re-fuse or "excess" of the sound-based musical representation system. Seremetakis reminds readers that performances must be understood beyond the representational system: "*Performance is not 'performative'*—the instantiation of a pre-existing code." Performance has the potential to make that which was imperceptible perceptible, like radiation songs can make radioactive "decay" heard through the song's composite temporal processes. "It is a *poesis*," she writes, "the making of something out of that which was previously experientially and culturally unmarked or even null and void."[81] Victor Shklovsky coined the term *defamiliarization* to address the ways in which "poetic devices" were used to "[counteract] the tendency of our minds to get used to everything, including ways of speaking and writing," such that people "no longer notice anything—a condition of deadened perception."[82] In order to "(re)educate the senses" in "bodily learning," defamiliarizing techniques are needed to "break . . . conventions" and "help reinvigorate" singers *and* listeners in "unexpected" ways, thus engendering communities of sense through which radiation and the means of its harmonization (e.g., COFA, CCP, Christian culture) can be perceived in a musico-poetics of neocolonial (radioactive) decay; so too can Indigenous regeneration be perceived anew.[83]

Although democratic promises of equality and freedom circulated, Marshallese have reflected on the layered breaks they must use their embodied voices to remediate, which demands repairing the severed throat as well. Prior to the US and Japanese imperial powers, which displaced Marshallese en masse and promoted patrilineal inheritance, the throat was understood as the seat of the soul and emotions where Marshallese connect (or feel the lack of interconnectedness) with the matrilineal bodies and lands. It was also the *seat of reason*.[84] The severance of "reason" from the embodied, emotional lives of Marshallese shows how the making of "irrational," "insensible," and "unreasonable" people happens. Marshallese sensorial locations of reason (interconnections) were stripped and severed from emotional cues through the imposition of modern rational systems that exclude and efface Marshallese relational being, or "memory of the senses," as matters of life, death, survival, and health: to detect radiation, to develop voice, for protection, for security, for remediation. In doing so, doctors, scientists, and politicians who had access to "reasons" for why Marshallese felt tired after taking medicine, to the duration of their removal, and to the dangers of radiation (as well as its presence in the immediate moment) would often restrict these reasons from Marshallese sensibilities and therefore processual embodiment, engendering "emotional management" as the displacement of reason, articulated to irrationality and insensibility that further dehumanized Marshallese and rendered them subject to nuclear, political, and state-legitimized violent processes of removals, experimentation, and withholding of information, data, and explanation.

REMEDIATION

Radiation Sounds is interested in remediation in terms of health and healing. Marshallese restage their nuclear history in ways that hold the United States accountable for the modern history of decay as a temporal genre that dispossesses Marshallese of their ancestral homelands and lifeways. By listening to Marshallese radiogenic poetics of decay as a component of larger processes of Marshallese regenerative grounds, Marshallese radiation songs resound remedial efforts; they are remediations of nuclear history, and they are remedial insofar as they are crucial to health and healing in terms of outreach and singing, as vibrational practices of *bōro wōt juon* (one throat only). Rather than resistance in terms of oppositional conflict, remediation challenges the consensual through the dissensual. Music offers a stage to hear reparative investments that Marshallese nuclear communities have made to their health and healing as well as to national, transnational, and international politics. Here, Marshallese singers break with conventional notions of remediation tied explicitly to the environment and point to their throats, and thus the severed collective, intimating the nuclear subjectivation as the stage for isolation-making in the severance of humans and nonhumans. The Marshallese word for health—*ājmour*—offers a poetics of movement with complementary phonemes "āj" (weave) and "mour" (life) that speak to Indigenous temporal sovereignty in terms of nonmodern temporalities as orientations, the forging of pathways, and navigational wayfinding in excess of (radioactive) decay.[85] Moreover, weaving is a practice that is gendered female, since women often plait in the Marshall Islands. Thinking about remediation in terms of ājmour symbolizes the weaving of life resonant through Marshallese matrilineal voices that has persisted throughout the gendered, transcorporeal violence of the nuclear project. It is a poesis, a making of the not yet known and felt.

I use the term *remediation* in three distinct, albeit correlated ways. First, I address biopolitical and biomedical remediation. Second, re-mediation suggests passing through more than one media. And, third, remediation refers to the contradistinction to quarantine/segregation, which recalls the problematic division between environment and people. In the first case, musical outreach, an extension of voices as potential for relational hearing spaces, frames sensorial conflict, musical dissensus that might easily be assumed within the biopolitical structures of surveillance. Songs are instances through which sonic cues recall the medical care and state-sponsored remediation, post-Bravo, through which human subjects were created through experimentation. Given that DOE medical care persists, so too do opportunities for neocolonial extractions and dismemberments. Songs re-mediate, as instances for the mediation (yet again) of Marshallese voices and bodies that have already been "remediated" in the American geopolitical memory. Singing displaces or unsettles them from the classifications to which they have been subject.

Marshallese ERUB singers perform multiple (dis)identifications that are critical of the boundaries within which they have been placed and instrumentalize symbolic materials to connect with dominant and minoritized communities. Drawing on José Muñoz's concept of disidentification as a "performative mode of tactical recognition that various minoritarian subjects employ in an effort to resist the oppressive and normalizing discourse of dominant ideology," I explore the ways in which Marshallese collectivize through indexical ambiguity and (dis)identification through multiple meanings, which enable them to move between onto-political identifications and socialities that match the movements of the song and meanings.[86] For example, pointing to the bōrō wōt juon can speak to Christian, US, and UN appeals to unification as well as the Indigenous survival mechanism of ippān doon as togetherness, specifically in more-than-human communities of which radiation has become profitable, as part of the survivor-victim (antinuclear) protest complex, and devastating (in the making of nuclear survivors and victims).

Second, re-mediation is by definition that which passes through more than one media. Marshallese embodied voices are sites of multisensorial interconnections and outreach. Marshallese songs re-mediate nuclear histories in excess of the secular sensibilities of the spectacle, the ear, eye, and hand—and the modern fragmented senses—through the collective throat. The re-mediation of nuclear histories and of nuclearization, individualization and modernization, via the Marshallese throat are recursive processes, creating interruptive breaks when the frame of harmony is too limited for the vocal apparatuses—the throat as aural sphere of singers and audiences—which cannot bear the weight. This book also re-mediates nuclear histories, therefore, by listening to these interruptions and tracing them through the cognate stories, drawing connections and shifting sensible orientations through the performances to amplify the disconnects of nuclear silences and nuclear listening. To return to Teaiwa's work, re-mediation draws on the interweaving of the feminine voices to push back on the colonial alienation of women. Marshallese singers return to more than one media, the univocal sovereign, and listen to their place-naming practices and other emplaced and embodied rituals of hearing together equivocally in political deliberations. Centering the throat (bōro wōt juon) in this respect is a crucial way of thinking "sensory democracy" for it reveals the voicelessness and other embodied damages to be systemic.

Attention to Marshallese cosmological narratives, particularly those mapped onto modern RMI political narratives, can be read for how voice comes to pass through more than one media and offer regenerative possibilities for hearing the breadth of injury and scale of reparative needs. Such remedial readings disrupt political archives in which nuclear history-telling retains its masculine, individualistic tenor. RMI political narratives often center on (male) chiefly characters and actions that draw explanatory power from Marshallese legendary figures. This is particularly true with the tendency to focus on US-RMI relations, specifically around imperial violence and modernization, with the trickster (L'Etao) and the virtuous chief (Jebrọ) as symbolic embodiments of the US and RMI governance, respectively. Working from the political representation (voices) of these figures, as sons, to their mothers offers insight into what the stories tell us in terms of positional situation in supporting the communal, intergenerational strength of the matriline (Indigenous futurities) since their voices are never about the individual character alone. His movements are afforded by his mother and by extension her relation within the cosmological network. According to Marshallese cosmology, as explained by Phillip McArthur, there are three female figures who possess three different sources of power. The name of the eldest sister is Lijenbwe, or "woman (*li*) from/of (*jen*) the divination knot (*bwe*), derives the power of divination (*bubu*), and it is from her descendants that the highest-ranking matriclans originated. . . ."[87] The middle sister is Lōktañūr, "the primal matriarch who instituted the high chief title," and whose story describes "the way the legitimate course of authority comes through obedience to one's mother."[88] Lōktañūr, the weaver of the first canoe sail, has twelve sons who engage in a canoe race to become the first chief of the Marshall Islands. Lōktañūr asks each son if they will give her a ride across the lagoon. Since she is carrying a large bundle, her sons fear that she will slow them down, and they all deny her—with the exception of her youngest son, Jebrọ. Her bundle turns out to be the first sail and harnesses the winds and waves, empowering Jebro to win the race and become the chief. As chief, he is entrusted to always respect, or carry the "weight" of, his mother as lineage and the land, which function as the animate means of his political voice (winds, waves, currents).

Today, Lōktañūr and Jebrọ continue to direct Marshallese; they are guiding constellations. The youngest sister is Limejokedad, or "woman (*li*) who (*me*) is dirty (*jokeded*), [and] gives birth to the so-called 'trickster' figure, L'Etao."[89] L'Etao is the figure of modernity and the United States. As I explore, the toxification and ruination of the land through modern war seemingly rebirths the trickster in his return to the atolls in which the sounds of war become echoed through the bombs and their violent aftermath. L'Etao's voice, according to the *Marshallese-English Dictionary*, translates to the Echo.[90] The Echo, or the voice of modernity, is associated with the disembodied male figure in Western intellectual history and also the embodiment of individualism (since his voice is the only one that is individualized and given a proper name) that is aligned with mastery over the senses (trickery) rather than a deeply rooted (and routed) engagement (care for) the growth of the community. To pass through more than one media is to critique the liberal notion of the individual and the individual voice mapped onto an essentialized identity in ways that challenge reproductive essentialisms articulated to the isolated figure of the "mother" or "son" as well as humancentric time, which becomes extended through the written word.[91]

Marshallese (Indigenous Pacific Islander) concepts of historical spacetime are rooted in and routed through the ancestral atoll, where *m̧wilal̦* (depth) has accrued through the contributions of the ancestors over time to help continue the *bwij* (lineage, primarily matrilineal) and *jowi* (maternal clan) and so take care of the land.[92] Marshallese are connected to their ancestors through the land inherited through their *bwij*, from which the word *bwijen* (umbilical cord) comes. The intense connection of the maternal, or feminine, cords that bind the atoll chains can be called "atoll umbilicals" and, by extension, ainikien umbilicals that "sound" the ancestral land.[93] Ainikien fibers of the atoll umbilicals are interwoven for the health (*ājmour*, meaning "weaving of life") of Marshallese societal organization and culture, which are extensions of the feminine voice, considered the "the ultimate authority" in customary practice and archived in cosmology. Extending this relation to the atollscapes can extend the analyses of equivocality further in terms of what radiation has severed, creating empowering networks from re-fusing the severed nodes by way of the feminine voice within the atollscape. Atoll umbilicals can be in tension with the cable umbilicals or modern media lines through which Western sovereignty produces envoiced, individualized subjects whose sociality is mass mediated.

Equivocality is a methodology to hear multiple ontologies and systemic complexes without deference to the dominant system, such that Indigenous poetics and politics of convivial valuation, which the bomb has injured but not fully destroyed, resonate and provide direction. The collective singular throat materializes sonic histories informed by seascape epistemologies and the weaving of atoll and cable umbilicals. With attention to the throat as nexus of the collective currencies, Marshallese interconnected ways of being, doing, and respecting can take on vocal currency. Here, as Ochoa Gautier writes, "The voice [can be] understood [in excess of] that which represent[s] . . . identity. Instead, the voice manifest[s] or enable[s] the capacity to move between states of multiplicity or unity where a single person can envoice multiple beings and where collective singing . . . can manifest a unity in which the collective is understood as expressing the singular." Within this singularity, she continues, "Different living entities or musical instruments voice the breath of life . . . , and where culture is understood 'as an on-going act of creation' rather than 'the distillation of a set of abstract ideals. . . .'"⁹⁴ These regenerative practices of equivocality move through multiple media and bodies in ways that network against the isolated and the fragmentary, as well as the dismemberments that emphasize the modern form of the break (as distinguished from the break as knowing, or navigating through displacements). As Creek poet Joy Harjo, the first Native American US poet laureate, has explained, "There is no separation between poetry, the stories and events that link them, or the music that holds all together, just as there is no separation between human, animal, plants, sky, and earth."⁹⁵ Marshallese music therefore cannot be defined but rather appreciated in terms of musicality, as the movements of life, that share reasons (of the throat) and meaningful frameworks *to appreciate timbral or personal connection with(in) the world and a nuclear reality in which we are all implicated.*

Finally, Marshallese musical remediation restages the myth of segregation and quarantine in two senses. First, there is the myth of the island as isolated, and second there is the myth of toxic segregation in which toxicity can be confined and not harm people, such that a large dome was placed over nuclear waste (Runit Dome on Enewetak Atoll), or that only four atolls were impacted by nuclear fallout and the larger radioactive culture.⁹⁶ Moreover, Elizabeth DeLoughrey has written extensively on the attempts to contain radiation, as part of the larger Cold War containment culture, through radiation ecosystems ecologies.⁹⁷ These developments created significant media that structures how the world is perceived and materials are treated, yet they are often premised on affective dimensions, such as fears of contamination and desires for purification. By emphasizing the deleterious impacts of the culture of global radioactive citizenship and the specificities of how it maps onto individual polities, countries, and regions in global harmony, I aim to dispel such myths through Marshallese music and sensibilities that resound interconnectedness rather than classified and contained.

By musically recalling their homelands with attention to the disrupted reciprocity of the throat, Marshallese singers unravel the falsehood of island-based isolation and quarantine as something that is geographically "natural." Land, separated from generational knowledge embodied through language and ways of doing and making, is central to Indigenous struggles for justice. Listening to Marshallese voices that resonate the work of the throat, which is considered unreachable yet connected to the living land via the soul, is crucial in hearing damages and possible means of remediation. As Wilfred Kendall shared, "Land speaks of your being, essence, reason for living. You relate to the world in terms of land [that] provides for your present, future, and future needs. . . . You cannot put enough value on land. . . . How do you put a value on something that people consider as a living thing that is part of your soul?"[98] Glen Coulthard calls a way of knowing through "reciprocal relations" with the land "grounded normativity," which is "a place-based foundation of Indigenous decolonial thought and practice . . . the modalities of Indigenous land-connected practices and longstanding experiential knowledge that inform and structure [Indigenous] ethical engagements with the world and our relations with human and nonhuman others over time."[99] In this respect, the role of listening to the voice to hear the connectivity of the throat can be appreciated in terms of remediation of "Indigenous decolonial thought and practice" that move through the many media of the atollscapes.

Second, Marshallese singers contest the myth of the clean slate, the empty space, and the isolated place in which toxic radioactivity can be dumped without consequence. By directing attention to the throats, or hearts of the matter (the material that has decayed because of US nuclear waste and military dumping), Marshallese singers refocus attention. Marshallese remix and remediate nonviolent protests drawn from transnational inspiration: sing-ins, sail-ins, and radiophonic attunements to RMI history are all occupations of the terrains once occupied by the US as a territorial possession. Karin Ingersoll develops the concept of "seascape epistemology" to reemplace Indigenous knowledge of oceanic connectivity and fluidity, which cannot be occupied, dominated, or exploited.[100] The Marshallese "atollscape" or "aelōñ" epistemology structures an understanding of how to move through and make sense of the world. An atollscape epistemology, like a seascape epistemology, is about interconnectedness and interdependence. *Aelōñ* can be translated to "the currents and everything above them" (*ae*—currents, *lōn*—what is above, such as the dry land and sky).[101] The Marshallese word for sound, *ainikien*, combines the root words *aini* (like *ae*, "current," "to gather and circulate") and *kien* ("rules"). Ainikien is about knowing one's place within an interconnected world, specifically in terms of the rhythms afforded by the mother and her connective cords: not just the umbilical cord but also the vocal cords, the currents in the air and sea that flow in and out in breath and move the waves (sound, oceanic). Voices are the vibrational, acoustical movements routed through "atoll umbilicals," or the nourishing threads, waves, and currents of Marshallese navigational sensibilities that network the archipelago via circulations, gatherings, and distributions (vocal currency).[102]

The military culture is part of Marshallese culture, as well, and what Brian Massumi has called a "politics of affect" can be nuanced with a deeper theorization of how remediation of nuclear histories through Marshallese senses can reposition American alert-based culture of civil defense and contemporary emergency thinking in ways that have contributed to the masculinizing of the atollscape such that there exists a COFA-based "affective alliance."[103] Remedial efforts can again displace such emergency thinking through the restorative, reflective rest or break. A remediation of "affective alliance" and moral pressure shifts our "ethical listening" not only to "political listening" but from the rational listening centered in text-notation (tones, pitches) to the reasonable listening that treats interconnectedness of the (non)human animate spirit as crucial in political decisions (timbral relationality). This repositioning of listening, as a remedial practice of staged affective alliance, speaks as well to the "remediation [as] a citational operation that colonizes the residual media regime to redress the failed utopian promises and violence of that regime," such as the means of harmony via the construct of the representative voice predicated on the break between land and human complementarity and gender complementarity (as well as who can speak for whom).[104] Since the US nuclear project was premised on democratic and capitalist expansionism that are foregrounded by human activities, these breaks necessitate remedial listening practices to hear the interconnected world.

Radiation sounds, I argue, can be heard in the vocal interplays in songs (lyrics) that gesture to embodied acoustical silences as nuclear silences because it has become necessary for the human to "speak" for the "nonhuman," as it were, and "make decisions." Radiation is one modality of energetic transference that has its own currency or temporal, space-time movements (lifetime). Writing about the literary "counter-canon" to representations of the Pacific that sustain environmental racism wrought by French nuclearization and US bombing in the Pacific, Dina El Dessouky conveys the ways in which Indigenous Hawaiian activists and writers "coarticulate [their] indigenous bodies and island places, advocating the fundamental, interrelated, and equal rights of both human and nonhuman ecological communities."[105] Listening to radiation songs with an ear toward voice-based *equality* in the interrelatedness of "human and nonhuman ecological communities" (and acoustical sounds and silences) as harmonies comprising more-than-human communities can attune us to more-than-human temporalities and the limits of human-centric time in modern systems (such as the law) that promulgate inequality (e.g., COFA,

CCP). I read Dessouky's analytic as helpful in putting forth a decolonial notion of "sensory democracy" that emphasizes the ways in which nuclear injustice manifests through representational limits that cannot be voiced in modern institutions.

I expand upon Andrew Dobson's concept of sensory democracy that he traces by focusing on listening in deliberative democracy to hearing as a means of resonant potentiality in being guided through voicelessness or detours away from meaning making by communities whose ontologies can be assumed through proprietary sense making (reading practices of their worlds). Dobson proposes the concept of "apophatic listening," in which a listener suspends judgment and listens quietly such that an eventual guided means of listening and reciprocity between speaker and listener unfolds.[106] Apophatic listening seems crucial for "agonistic cosmopolitics," or contested ways of ordering the world through which negotiations can be made when all ways of ordering the world (socio-natures) are looked at as legitimate such that their impacts are parsed. Here, Anders Blok follows Latour's notion that cosmopolitics is the forging of a world "in common" that is not dependent on human actors in a nature-culture duality but rather recognizes (non)human relations in governance systems and their scientific foundations, which are built on antidemocratic platforms in our contemporary moment and academic institutional structure through the division of the sciences, social sciences, and humanities.[107] Latour's notion of the in-common world that takes into account nonhumans through the merging of politics and science by way of those authorized to speak, as it were, echoes Dobson's intervention in ways that underscore the exclusion of marginalized, minoritized subject positions that are unable to be represented within modern, rational institutions in full.

The US military-industrial-academic complex has participated in exclusionary practices in the name of democracy and global harmony. This book traces Marshallese musical memories of some of these systemic disqualifications through medical, environmental, and educational institutions as they resonate viscerally and intergenerationally. As I conclude my introductory framework, and writing from my position in music and the humanities, I want to underscore the importance of remediation in projects and programs that actively aim to "trouble and divest" democracy "from its Western, capitalist desires" such that it "can be reimagined as a viable concept for both critical and indigenous forms of education."[108] As we move toward global humanities, augmenting cold war identity-based studies programs, this critique of global harmony as institutionalized world making, I hope, contributes to the ways in which music, sound, and voice studies take shape in and across the environmental humanities, medical or health humanities, and digital humanities, especially when considering who and what get excised from which interdisciplinary programs and "intersectional" frameworks because of nondominant (systemically silenced) means and modes of relating.[109] A more-than-human-humanities approach must engage Indigenous understandings of entangled relationality expressed and taught by Indigenous scholars that challenge the normalizing of democratic, academic, and capitalist ableism that have participated in colonial, eugenic practices.[110] Sensory democracy, as a framework, rejects those filters of "ability" and "voice" as given while respecting their systemic power in the academy as well as the capitalist and democratic system. This is, more broadly, a call to respect and to listen across political boundaries and representational mass mediation and uniform programming. Participation through disidentification and detours can express limits, incommensurabilities, injustices, and inequalities that manifest from systemic inclusion, or governance, as remediation or reparation that has required severances, cuts, and fragmentations. Songs, compositions, and other formal modes of communication become ways to "voice" and demarcate a being-and-beyond the voice that materializes in the formal projections of minoritized bodies themselves shaped through normative justiciable projections that require nonhegemonic remediations. In radiation songs, it is the perseverance of the sense of the throat—the collective and communal spirit—amidst the waves of imperial violence that evinces the persistence of the soul, the living land, and those who refuse the nuclear silencing of their knowledges and their futurities.

If the social contract of global harmony is predicated on nuclear ruins and, more specifically, Indigenous ruins as subjects of nuclear colonialism, meaning the contested grounds over which masculine militaries battle for geopolitical control, then these songs share their refusals—rejections and reweavings—of how history can play out. Marshallese singers challenge any clear division between the public and private realms because their spiritual being and becomings through the collective throat are both and neither. On the one hand, they have been forcibly rendered public, where musical gestures amplify human rights discourses in terms of survivor and victimhood that connect the Marshallese with larger networks of historically subjugated communities made vulnerable by global power inequalities. The knowledge that the Marshallese throat can never be overdetermined affords the vocal currency (ainikien) that carries and circulates "radiation sounds" because it is based on reciprocal relations rooted in and routed through (dis)placed, embodied Indigenous sensibilities. Drawing on a sonic politics of indigeneity, singers demand answers and maintain spaces in which the US as neocolonial power must be answerable, while upholding the vital processes of matrilineal Indigenous futurities predicted by the ancestors who, like the singers, continue to weave life.

CHAPTER ONE

RADIOACTIVE CITIZENSHIP

VOICES OF THE NATION

Tropical rain blanketed Rita Village, Majuro Atoll's easternmost village of the main island, as I waited for a taxi. Standing just a couple hundred feet from the palm-tree-lined and shrub-lined edge of sloped earth that led to the coral reef, connecting the vast Pacific Ocean with Majuro lagoon, the only sounds I could hear along with the wind, rain, and lapping waves were crickets chirping and the hollow echoes of home radios tuned to V7AB, the national radio station and one of the few with enough broadcast strength to reach Rita Village. Eight o'clock on this December evening felt more like midnight as I made my way from Ejit Island to the residences near the Majuro Cooperative School in Delap Village. A streetlight briefly illuminated a rusted four-door sedan that looped around the dead-end road, where palm trees and foliage sat atop a six-foot-high slope of rocks that gave way to the reef. The taxi radio was playing, but it was not V7AB. The song was a slow rock number with a reggae inflection, but I didn't pay much attention, and the signal was relatively weak, yielding moments of light static. Then I heard the lyrics boom from a bass male vocalist: "Marshall Islands government, what have you done? American government, what have you done? We can rock, we can roll, but we can't do [*inaudible*] in the Marshall Islands. Marshall Islands government, what have you done? American government, what have you done? There's something wrong with the [*inaudible*] system."

As the taxi wound its way to Majuro Cooperative School, the song ended. We pulled up to the gate that separated the surrounding community, mostly of *ri-jerbal* (workers), from the private school where many of the islands' elite were educated. The conversation died down again as I began to speak. "Thank you," I said to the driver as I handed him an American one-dollar bill. "What was the name of the song?" I asked in English as he handed me two quarters in return. He replied in English, "What song?" with a confused expression. "The song that was on the radio," I added, "with the words 'Marshall Islands government, what have you done?'" The taxi driver shook his head, and he raised his eyebrows under a furrowed brow, which let me know that, regardless of the reason, our conversation was over. The man to my right was waiting with the door slightly ajar, preventing rain from entering the vehicle. My quick farewell was met with a collective "good night."

As I asked my interlocutors about the song—reciting the lyrics, humming the melody, describing the situation, most everyone thought it was one song in particular: "CCP," which is the acronym for the Changed Circumstances Petition. The CCP was part of the first Compact of Free Association (COFA) in 1986, and after the US government rejected the CCP, some Marshallese groups, such as the Kwajalein landowners, believed that their chance to appeal to the US Congress was gone. However, the song "CCP" is neither the "Marshallese/American government" song, nor is it titled "CCP."

The song known as "CCP" is actually titled "Compact II," and the lyrics were penned by Fred Pedro and Alkinta Kilma, a team of radio station founders in Majuro, specifically for the political radio station, V7EMON, which translates to V7 "good," articulating the moral sentiment of what was, at the time, the development of an oppositional party in support of two politicians, Senators Tony deBrum and Iroij Imata Kabua (also the former president). The music was composed and performed by a popular Marshallese rock band, Sunrise Lip, from Kwajalein Atoll, home of the US military base and the other urban hub. The story, which paints a bleak image akin to urban deindustrialization, is a musically upbeat take on the tune of "Bad Moon Rising" (1969) performed by Credence Clearwater Revival. Written by American singer-songwriter John Fogerty, "Bad Moon Rising" was inspired by a hurricane in a film and is about an imminent apocalypse, which many take to be about the Vietnam War or the nuclear arms race. The song protests the 2004 renewal of the US-RMI Compact of Free Association. As the singers offer, "Today, they're saying Compact II . . . a big word [concept] for us." The message draws on a politics of affective media education, particularly when the singers remind the population to "be on the watch," drawing on the familiar alert-based oppositional politics of radiophonic broadcasts that attuned listeners to be "alert today, alive tomorrow" in the United States concerning the Soviet Union or the "see something, say something" broadcasts of Homeland Security. Through the radio, which is central in the RMI's public sphere, those who disseminate the "news" or "word on the street" of the amended COFA signing affectively attune listeners to their perspectives, creating an auditive voice-over, by which I refer to the use of radiophonic listening to shape voices, or votes, in the modern mediatized society.

The RMI and US governments participated in creating or sustaining a broken system, one that allowed for the radio station on which the song that told of systemic disrepair, a radio station that was just a couple of hundred feet from the taxi, to collapse into static on a rainy night; this system is, I argue, the voice itself that emerges from a damaged apparatus or one that is not rooted in or routed through Marshallese lands or denies women's voices and the feminine voice (nonbinary, nonhuman) to be heard. Reflecting on the line "We can rock, we can roll, but we can't do ___ in the Marshall Islands," the breaking of the system, the relational voice that is the American and Marshallese relations of power, is not so much an epistemological question as it is an ontological condition of the US nuclear-military power complex that has immobilized some groups or dismembered some parts of the body politic while enabling other components, such as the voices that sing rock 'n' roll, to experience seemingly unfettered freedoms, but individualized freedoms that have discounted the ways in which Marshallese move.

"Compact II" is part of radioactive citizenship, which is a form of postwar belonging in which people harness the bomb (nuclear culture) to be heard on the radio or other means through which the representative voice is broadcast. With the Americanization of global media and military culture, radioactive citizenship takes on different contours in localized places, depending on the particular group's relation with the United States and (nuclear) militarization. In the RMI, radioactive citizenship marks a decisive self-determined, decolonial "break" with the Trust Territory of the Pacific Islands (TTPI) such that radiation, when shared through voices of the nation, can translate to power or currency for the RMI nation to progress. Through the COFA, however, the United States has maintained military power over the Marshall Islands and at the same time refused to take seriously its petitions and appeals to deal with the extant issues in ways that speak to a modernized notion of progress, which can be understood in terms of the voice of modernity, L'Etao's voice or the Echo. Nuclear silences resonate from these ungrounded echoes of the US failure to listen, and Marshallese remain voiceless because of the constraints of the law, which shape their radioactive citizenship, their belonging through the global phenomenon that is nuclear power. For example, when I arrived in the RMI, in August 2008, the US Court of Federal Claims dismissed a lawsuit filed on behalf of the people from Bikini and Enewetak who sought "just compensation" under the Fifth Amendment, also known as the "Takings Clause." Writing for the panel, Randall R. Rader stated, "In sum, this court cannot hear, let alone remedy, a wrong that is not within its power to adjudicate."[1]

The concept of radioactive citizenship is central to the dematerialized notion of voice and the normative modern disembodied male subject that (as mind) can be circulated textually and in sound recording. In short, radioactive citizenship is a mode of belonging and survival that is tied to nuclear national security through law. Political legitimacy and power come from the force of the bomb written into law, exercised verbally as a trace of the law or through the mediatized eye and ear of neocolonial subjective sensibilities. To be heard, citizens amplify empowerment through these radiophonic means and, with it, their sociopolitical positionalities. Globally, people "know" the bomb through the radioactive sphere or the mediatization of the sounds and sights of the bomb as broadcast from places such as the Marshall Islands. Marshallese radioactive citizenship, which is contoured through the technologies of the liberal voice but grounded in claims to land and knowledge of the land, treats knowledge of and claims to nuclear injury as part of land-based knowledge and land claims. In certain respects, radioactive citizenship, from the grounded sensibilities of Marshallese, mirrors Adriana Petryna's notion of "biological citizenship" that treats health as a "political issue" that "became a complex bureaucratic process by which a population attempts to secure a status as harmfully exposed and deserving compensation."[2]

"BREAK AWAY" AND NATION BUILDING

The United States justified its administration over the TTPI, the only strategic territory afforded to the military superpower, in terms of developmental democracy. US officials worked with local officials (male customary power or elite commoners) to advance a democratic framework for the country's postcolonial self-rule, also known as self-determination. Initially, the United States sought a "permanent alliance" with the Marshallese and assumed (in the early 1960s, at least) that the population would ultimately vote to become part of the United States. Decolonization was becoming a buzzword throughout the developing world, and administering (especially poorly) "colonies" did not fit well with the US self-imposed characterization as a defender of freedom and democracy in contrast to the Soviet Union. In response to a 1961 UN report that sharply criticized TTPI administration of Ebeye (see chapter 5), the Kennedy administration appointed Harvard economist Anthony Solomon to recommend actions that would shift the local rhetoric of "colonialism" to "global democratization." Solomon's report, in part, advised Kennedy to build up education, where English would be the medium of instruction and "patriotic songs and rituals" would be performed in class.[3] President Johnson also followed Solomon's recommendations, which included financing radio technology developments that authorized the Federal Communications Commission to "license qualified Micronesia radio operators to encourage young men in radio technology."[4] Throughout the 1960s and 1970s Marshallese leaders, along with their Pacific counterparts, debated issues of sovereignty and dependence.

Eventually, paramount chief Iroijlaplap Amata Kabua melded liberal democratic representation with codified customary law. Monetary compensation from US nuclear militarism, which included nuclear weapons projects, human radiation experiments, and expansion at the Kwajalein military site, such as the Strategic Defense Initiative (SDI, or "Star Wars"), which began in 1983 (the year of the plebiscite), was constitutive in the decision of the Marshallese political leaders—Amata Kabua, in particular—to pursue constitutional independence, which established a "break" with the TTPI. Iroijlaplap Kabua, the first president of the RMI, who maintained his position for seventeen years until his death in 1996, was at the helm of this break or "break away," which, along with constitutional independence and the signing of the COFA in 1986, would form the three debates that would most publically define the formation of the sovereign RMI as a self-determined nation.[5] Sebastian F. Braun writes that "part of every nationalistic program has to be the silencing of heterogeneous voices, to render the harmony—or, depending on the perspective, cacophony—of historically diverse voices into a repetitive monotone and monologue."[6] The RMI, as representative "voice" or vocal intermediary for Marshallese citizens, has been part of the "global democratization" (meaning neocolonialism) through harmonization processes of the nation-state. This RMI sovereign "voice" begins to take shape through the "Break Away."

Radio, the "Voice of the Marshall Islands," was at the center of the independence movement or "break away." In 1977 the Marshall Islands Constitutional Convention ("ConCon"), with Ruben Zackhras and Tony deBrum as the cochairs, drafted the Constitution, which established a parliamentary government (Nitijela) based on Amata Kabua's preference for a parliamentary rather than presidential model. During this period of time the figure of the "voice" emerges as a metaphor of democratic participatory politics. Laura Kunreuther examines the "figure of the voice" in Nepal's emergent liberal democracy and pays particular attention to the coconstitutive "political voice" and "intimate voice." These understandings of voice, she argues, "are important aspects of modern subjectivities" and are "intermingled with a vast media complex—newspapers, television, documentary and commercial film, radio, phones, and cell phones—through which 'the voice' is generated, circulated, and reproduced."[7] The nuclear media complex, in global capacity, has often been driven by the United States, and it became a way of depreciating Marshallese as underdeveloped people for whom the United States was doing a great favor by sharing its modern skills and democratic political system without the constant reminder of what a boon to the US economy and capitalist expansion the bomb was, as either a series of "tests" or mediated representations for most of the world.

I endeavor to show how the mediated voice-overs of US American white-male normativity "lead" Marshallese voices today in part through constraints placed on the auditor's listening and viewing practices that are distanced through the othering of Marshallese and entwined by the harmonizing, humanizing work of the bomb that during key political decisions takes on a wider expressive dimension. Radioactive citizenship is predicated on these formative breaks through which voice is withheld and then becomes the mechanism of societal re-pairing, albeit constrained through the other mass of constellated modern breaks—from the fragmented senses to statutes of limitations to socio-categorical divisions from the colonial period, such as the human, and grouping filters such as race and gender articulated to biological difference that seemingly sanction suffering and its performative connections that take shape in articulated dimensions of pain; nuclear remediation and the performances of "property damages" and "personal injury" that voice binds are part of these breaks.

Modern breaks produce the voices of the nation that promise to unite but ultimately divide. Majuro became a veritable stage for oppositional politics between Kabua's "Breakaway" party ("*jab*," vote no to "break away") and Ainikien Ri-Majol's call to stay together ("*aet*," vote yes to remain). Radio station manager for V7AB (formerly WSZO) Antari Elbōn recalled how the public debates were a turning point, producing new forms of oppositional politics (representative voicing):

> There was a big campaign going on over the radio—people were angry with each other. And I remember one time when one of the members of the other party came and broke the microphone here because the ruling majority at that time were in control of the radio station, and they would play these "breakaway songs" over and over and over again—all day long. So one of the members of the opposition came into the radio studio and broke the microphone.[8]

Elbōn's story illuminates the importance of control over the broadcast during this emergence of the Marshallese national public sphere. It also shares how the opposition went to the infrastructural apparatus of the broadcast, or the throat that resonated the voice of the ruling party, and broke one component (microphone) to destabilize the party's power. In the 1978 referendum, the Marshall Islands ultimately voted to "break away" from Micronesia and on May 1, 1979, adopted the Constitution and established the Marshall Islands as a self-governing nation.

Jorelik Tibon told me how he was concerned when he came back to Majuro and heard echoes of positions without reflections. Tibon's songs, which write of *emakūt* (movements, instability) and also share a resistance to this uncontrollable movement, are some of the first that I heard that use the trope of shaking or moving, which will come to pervade the national discourse of loss, especially in the 1980s onward with "radiation songs." His comment below suggests it was through an intersensorial modality of "hearing poison."[9] Although Tibon registered political vocality—the public debates that aimed to affectively rouse people to get their votes—as something uncomfortable, some composers were less concerned and more determined to take a stand:

> I had just returned to Majuro, and the independence movement was gaining momentum. So I heard the good and the bad from either side. And at the time, I had no political motives. But that is when I started to really seriously write songs. I think everything just caught my attention, and without really knowing what [was] good and what [was] the best direction to take, I just made some general comments that we're moving, so be aware of something in the air. Be careful about what you hear. I penned the lyrics "there is something in the air like a poison." When I say this in English, it doesn't make good music sense. But in Marshallese it does because "poison" can mean also a "lie" or some rumors that create a negative impact. So I'm saying that I am smelling something in the wind that is coming with the wind that is like this poison, poisonous . . . and I'm afraid that what I'm hearing might be also poisonous.[10]

Tibon's reflection on the distortion of the airwaves that carry poison, as an alteration of signal or information, importantly positions this "lie" not as noise but rather as the simplified sided oppositionality that enforces division and fights over claims to truth. Tibon ties Marshallese independence to the forceful coming of poisonous winds that he "smells" (or picks up on in ways similar to hearing a connective resonance) in ways that recall the postwar mythic liberation from the Japanese through atomic bombs and militarization. The force of *emakūt* are those uncontrollable movements that pull Marshallese from their culture through the mechanisms of sensorial effacement and fragmentation where what is heard is cordoned by media frameworks that orient listening to "yes" versus "no" when it comes to political decision making through "voice-overs" that limit participatory action to voice or vote. Here Democratic participation can also be read as part of the authorization of violence that has been predicated on conflict of side-based wars, wars that can be a distraction from the care and caution demanded of attentional and intentional hearing as (mis)directed listening.

The first part of this chapter shares the matrilineal disenvoicing of US stagings of the atomic frontier that afforded American mediation of nuclear weapons as part of a celebrated radioactive citizenship that in the 1950s resonated freedom alongside the American musical genre of "rock 'n' roll." As the world was being introduced to rock 'n' roll, Marshallese were being militarized in a carceral archipelago; this militarization has been part of the contrast-making constitutive of the oppositional politics that founds public vocality as well as the gendering of the voices of the nation as the disembodied male subject (linked to the Echo or reproducible text, law, the figure of sound).[11] The second part of the chapter discusses the opening of the archipelago such that Americanization could "give voice" to the country and cultivate a "strategic alliance" within global democratization, which was the euphemism for neocolonialism. I focus on the public vocality that emerges from this strategic opening and how the radio and radiation are used to give the nation-state legitimacy, or voice, such as bargaining tools for self-determination. I concentrate on the contested terms of the voices of the nation as they vie to be heard in their musical petitions to the RMI government and US representatives who will share their messages in the global public sphere.

The song "Compact II" and V7EMON, the radio station for which it was specifically composed, are part of a constellation of modern oppositional politics and assumed democratic spaces wherein citizens enact their political subjectivation as they strive to be heard in political representation.

A Marshallese government official explained the role of compensation and helplessness through which the voice is generated:

> [The nuclear] issues changed history in terms of payment . . . and also some people—maybe I am one of those who felt helpless. There is this problem that some experts say [we] are facing now, and nobody wants to deal with it, so many people feel that we're getting sicknesses, and yet what can you do? So it changed some perspectives, I think, and also people want to take that as an opportunity to probably go beyond what they know that they deserve, and maybe people also take that as a means to be heard.[12]

Radiation and the radio have been crucial components of sense making in the period of nation building, which has been, in part, about seeking remediation for the breaks that are then harmonized by the nation-states in international law. As this chapter shows, radiation becomes a marker of this process of modernization in nation building, particularly on the grounds of nuclear militarism. As a marker of modernization, radiation comprises the connective tissue that is itself the break, which is heard as, with, and through "voices."

"JINED ILO KOBO, LEEJ MAN JURI!"

In the militarized spaces of the Marshall Islands, there is no shortage of reflections on war, peace, and conflict resolution. One song I heard often was one with a refrain: *"Jined ilo Kobo, Leej man juri!"* ("Jined ilo Kobo: Our mothers forever, make peace!"). This reflected a battle cry during customary war: the chief would sound the *jilel* (conch shell), the battle would commence, and the men would call on the women to make peace or stomp out aggression, at which time the women would do so (*leej man juri*), and the men would listen. Globalization, imperialism, Americanization, modernization, and colonialism are processes that have created the conditions of possibility through which domestic violence has become a problem in the Marshall Islands, which is the message of a Women United Together in the Marshall Islands (WUTMI) 2006 educational video—a PSA—that used the trope of conventional antiphonal war to tell the story of Marshallese gendered complementarity. Told through Marshallese sonorous and political history, women protected the lands and lineage through ongoing (non)-human interlocution through which the woman came to voice the end of war and direct peace by listening to the land and lineage and the chief's needs during war. These media productions share the centrality of Marshallese women's political participation in customary practices, which has been denigrated in nuclear modernity, and they recall the force behind the chiefs: the primal chief and matriline (Jebro-Lōktañūr).

For example, WUTMI was kept off V7AB, the governmental radio station, because of perceived government hostility when the organization wanted to speak about domestic violence, and the group had to seek out a Canadian grant to purchase equipment to broadcast on its own. Only recently has WUTMI been approached by the station to conduct weekly broadcasts.[13] Nevertheless, the 2006 PSA speaks to the larger issues of matrilineal disenvoicing and the relation between the local (domestic) and global (international) in terms of militarized spaces and violences meted onto women's bodies and silencings of the feminine voice, which in turn speaks to the silencing of the land and lineage in a feedback loop.

The song "*Ioon, ioon miadi kan*" ("Upon, upon Those Watchtowers") is testament to the denigration of women's political participation under masculine powers and militarism. It shares how the feminine voice becomes constituted not only by these powers but also through domestic censorship of the composer's voice, which became her communicative lifeline after she was displaced from her land and placed in a leper colony during World War II. "*Ioon*" is one of the first songs I recorded. Two elderly women performed this "bomb song" for me, and since then I have come to appreciate the import of its listening modalities and predictive readings as crucial means of the female chief composer. Composed in 1944 by the Marshallese female chief (*leroij*) Laabo, the song documents the Indigenous population's experiences of the Japanese and American military battles during World War II that resonate through the present day, particularly on the lands of Kwajalein and in the lands and bodies of those irradiated, for constant war is constant labor for the Indigenous population.[14] As the song shares, part of this constant labor is the articulation of voice to form in ways that can share the violences to survive them.

Laabo aims to protect the land and lineage by extending her voice as a warning, perhaps, of the detriment she fears to her body and the lands: the matriline. Displaced from her homeland, Laabo fills the song with onomatopoeic lyrics that resound the crunching of jets (*iññurñur*), gunshots (*bu'm*), and bombs exploding (*edebokbok*). The poetic devices not only shape the musical material but also structure its performance. Sounding the audible markers of attack, decay, enclosure, and pressure, the singer shares an embodiment of her generational engagement with colonial and imperial violence. With each contemporary performance of the song, the singer would explain that the melody of "*Ioon, ioon miadi kan*" was Japanese, noting how Laabo wove together the musical material of the Japanese, Marshallese, and Americans to create such a powerful sonic imprint *of* war. The popularity of the song and its continued transpacific circulation among disenfranchised, diasporic Marshallese are reminders not only of the displacement and dislocation that occurred during World War II but also of militarism's impact on Marshallese everyday lives and culture today, particularly in the disenvoicing of the matriline in the formation of the nation-state.

As Senator deBrum explained, "I have heard enough of the elders saying [the song] was [composed] just before the bombing, so '44 would sound right. . . . It is important because . . . it relates the realities of war, but still allows for poetic reflections of a woman who could not have read about such attacks much less experienced an actual air raid. The lyrics will remain part of Marshallese musical history for a long, long time."[15] He speaks of the predictive import of the song in Marshallese musical history in terms of a historical document that contains Indigenous ways of reading the land, sea, and sky, and thus expresses the political legitimacy of the feminine voice as Laabo listened in her capacity as lerooj to the spirited, patterned movements of the archipelago and warnings and also as a document of how the emergent nation that was caught in the midst of the masculine militant firepower takes on the disembodied text-based voice, precisely as a matter of survival. The song is upheld as a crucial part of Marshallese music history, not least because it is through the compulsory disabling of Laabo's mobilities through war and by placing her in a leper colony, isolated, that we hear her voice. Thus, voice, as split from her being, comes as a matter of territorial dispossession as well as possession of knowledge, agency to share, and literary skills, both musical and land based.

In Marshallese customary political organization, Laabo would have the preeminent voice, meaning that the men in her clan would consult with her before making any decisions and that identities would come from her ancestral land. Also, as leroij, she would have listened for the calls during battle to "make peace" (*leej manjui*). "*Ioon*" tells of a different system of power, a new political organization where she and, by extension, Marshallese men are nearly inaudible. "*Ioon*" systematically shares the denigration of the each of the positive attributes afforded to Marshallese girls at birth: *leejmanjuri*, peacemakers who have the "power to cease the warring between brothers or any other dispute"; "*kōrā mennunak*, the traveler, literally free like a flock of flying birds, indicating that a woman has the freedom to move and marry as she wishes, unconstrained by notions of place"; and *"kōrā in wōnene,* as long as the bwij (lineage) of the woman is intact, all power, right, ownership, and authority continue through her lineage." Marshallese women are described as nurturers and mothers as *jined ilo kobo,* "weavers of society to make sure it does not unravel" *(kōrā in eoeo),* encouragers *(limaro pikpik kōlo eo,* "shake the spirit"), and *"kōrā jeltan bwij,* literally one who unravels," which speaks to the "power [of a woman] to draw [her] spouse away from loyalty to his mother."[16] Laabo imagined herself "amidst the wreckage," ultimately "between death and life" or "near death" (sick, *nañinmej*), where her voice becomes the means for life in this militarized space. This battlefield is unlike the customary sites in which women and men's voices were interlocking, and it speaks to the gendered formations of oppositional politics as well as the modern air-based sensibilities of radioactive citizenship. Crucially, deBrum told me that her family doesn't like to speak about the song because what is remembered is her leprosy rather than "the genius of the song." Here, Laabo's voice is what is listened to in ways that speak to modern medial vococentrism, yet it is important to listen to how her story, as a woman with disability mapped onto her body that prevents her song from being discussed, is cultivated through nuclear silences and resounds an endurance by those who reembody and emplace her voice in the grounded sensibilities of listening to the violence of war on the international scale and the domestic scale, through which she has also been silenced.[17]

AMERICAN ATOMIC AGE DIPLOMACY

As Gregory Dvorak reminds us, World War II was a "theater [of three] masculinities" that produced two superpowers and one emasculated "colonial site and its subjects."[18] This theater persisted in postwar gendering. Americans opted to work with men once they returned to the Marshall Islands in a triumphant show of power. After they defeated the Japanese in 1944, American troops worked to clean up the war-torn atolls with Marshallese men. Marshallese were, at first, in awe of the soldiers and the seemingly endless wealth and resources they had. As Americans treated Marshallese to cigarettes, foodstuffs, and entertainment, the US military established a civilian governing system alongside communications infrastructures that would mutually reinforce American and Marshallese postwar positionality. American Armed Forces Radio (AAFR), which had been used by the US government during the war to connect troops to imaginaries of home and infomercials that sold them products and wartime campaigns such as "security through silence," remained active at Kwajalein, unlike other World War II radio station installments that were disbanded. The preexisting infrastructure enabled Americans to broadcast programs such as *Melody Roundup* (1942–1945), which featured acts such as Tex Williams and Gene Autry.[19] Troops would share their music with Marshallese workers and those "liberated" men who were becoming part of the new political system with "nominal[ly] paid" positions that included a chief magistrate (local *iroij*), an advisory council (*alaps*), and a "scribe, tax collector, and information gatherer."[20] After an atoll had been secured, US Navy personnel nailed "large cardboard posters" to palm trees with proclamations written in English and Japanese to notify Marshallese of their intent "to leave undisturbed (within the realm of military necessity) the existing civil practices of the islands as well as the rights and customs of the inhabitants."[21] Military Governor Admiral Chester W. Nimitz touted a return to self-government and "freedom" as the military established a hierarchical and fraternal governing system. Marshallese remember how Americans prepared them for independence by teaching them the "Star Spangled Banner" and to respect the American flag as lessons in liberty.

President Truman instructed Americans to play up their moral convictions and religious connections to the Protestant missionaries, which Marshallese mirrored in return, often by singing hymns of thanks. From the beginning of the occupation Americans emphasized the practice of Christianity. As the September 1945 *National Geographic* comments, "Missionaries made friends for America. . . . Americans have had more influence [in the Marshalls] than any other people. . . . In the 1850s, the American Board of Foreign Missions in Boston spread its activities into Micronesia from Hawaii. Subsequently, they reduced the Marshallese language to writing; gave the people schools, medicines, a new religion; and brought conflicting clans to peace."[22]

The American staging of the postwar moral alliance reached new heights when US Navy Commodore Ben Wyatt reenacted the missionaries' arrival on Sunday morning with the intention of removing the Bikinians from their homelands to conduct nuclear testing. From March 1946 through August 1946, Bikini Atoll became the set for highly choreographed performances: the verbal transaction between Wyatt and the Bikinian chief "King" Juda, the Bikinians' removal from their atoll, and the first atomic tests, Crossroads Able and Baker. Media dissemination of these Hollywood-style productions reached the United States, strategically connecting the Marshall Islands and a complicated new imaginary to this new culture of mass destruction and an allied pursuit of world salvation, which is the foundation of postwar globalized radioactive citizenship.[23]

The month after the cameras stopped rolling because of Truman's Atomic Energy Act of 1946, which made all atomic information immediately classified and mention of atomic research a violation of the law, *Radio News* offered "a 'behind-the-scenes' resume [at Bikini Atoll] of history's greatest radio-electronic show featuring 20,000 instruments."[24] The Bikinians, meanwhile, removed from their lands, were given a one-way radio to listen to the Kwajalein military station, from which nuclear operations were directed. The Bikinians' relocation physically cut their ties with their homeland and their means of self-sufficiency. Dependent on the United States, they learned quickly that communication was a matter between men, and they cultivated vocal practices to improve their new diplomatic relations. Within a matter of weeks after their removal in March 1946, the once-skillful navigators began to realize that Rongerik was not an ideal place for resettlement. Although it would be two more years until they were relocated, after severe dehydration, starvation, and illness, the Bikinians had no other option but to welcome Commodore Wyatt during a visit to Rongerik in hopes that the American government would provide an alternative to their distressing situation.

Wyatt brought aerial photographs of Bikini Atoll after Operation Crossroads, the first globe that Bikinians had seen, and three books for the children, who welcomed Wyatt by singing three songs. According to Jonathan Weisgall, the first song was "My Faith Looks Up to Thee," which they sang from a missionary hymnal. Then, although none of them spoke English, they sang from memory "God Bless America" and "Good Night Ladies." In appreciation, Wyatt turned to the group and said, "Such lovely voices deserve a finer church." He promised to send some beams from Kwajalein to support one side of the community church, which was sagging.[25] Wyatt's moral evaluation of the Bikinians, which led to their material profit, was centered in his ability to police them through their singing voices. Here, harmony exists as a social promise (promissory note/gift) and framework through which Wyatt processed Indigenous noise into something appreciable (literally, that Wyatt could appreciate and invest value in their voices).

Like Wyatt's dismissal of the precarious conditions in which the Bikinians were placed on Rongerik that necessitated they sing for church beams, for example, US media (radio, newspapers, and film footage) refused to circulate the Bikinians' material conditions beyond their singing voices represented by American voice-over actors. One narrates the Bikinians' singing as recognition that they were blissfully uninterested in what the "atomic bomb means": "Out here in the peaceful Pacific, where the natives sit, in their courtesy, and in their friendliness, with their smiles, with their happiness, they aren't sure exactly what the atom bomb means, but at least they admit it . . . so you have 'You are my Sunshine' sung to you in Marshallese, perhaps the top tune of the week, you might say, out here on the tiny isle of Rongerik."[26]

The US media circulation of laughing, smiling, singing "natives" was meant, in part, to counter animal rights activists' dissent with positive images from the Marshall Islands following tests that used animals as test subjects. Angered citizens around the world (mainly from the United States and Europe) lambasted the military and President Harry Truman, who then signed the Atomic Energy Act of 1946 into law, transferring atomic oversight from military to civilian control and establishing the Atomic Energy Commission (AEC) to oversee nuclear weapons development and nuclear power management. Section 10 of the act, "Control of Information," contained the unprecedented "born secret" clause. Under the "classified at birth" clause, all information pertaining to nuclear weapons was considered "restricted data" until its official declassification.

This legal restriction on free speech created a structure wherein Bikinians were stranded on Rongerik Atoll, where they suffered from starvation, according to University of Hawai'i anthropologist Leonard Mason, who visited Rongerik in 1948. Mason's report prompted the United States to relocate the Bikinians to Kwajalein Atoll, where they lived in isolated quarters on the main island. The Bikinians were provided food, shelter, entertainment, and access to a more cosmopolitan lifestyle, although Bikinian counternarratives often stress feelings of isolation in Kwajalein's "tent city" from the other Marshallese laborers, who had been working with the US Army since war's end to build up Kwajalein as a base of operations. Later, when the Marshalls were placed under the purview of the United States as TTPI administrator by the UN in 1947, the new TTPI government decided to enlist the Bikinians in a "self-help program." The Bikinians were relocated from Kwajalein to Kili Island in 1951, a move that ultimately shaped their social organization by creating a new patrilineal system of succession from father to son as opposed to the traditional Marshallese matrilineage. This is one of the decisive moves that linked the Bikinians more with modernization and the masculine "character" of the United States. Bikini Atoll, given its geographical locale, has sparse vegetation and a calm lagoon in which to fish, unlike the more tropical Kili Island, which had no lagoon, creating a deeper dependence on US food supplies. Bikinians were incorporated through nuclear weapons testing that provided the "isolated" "clean slate" for Americans to experiment with techno-scientific instruments through which they would glean knowledge that would return to the Marshall Islands in some material, ideological, and thus hierarchical configuration of Americanized professionalization.

Radio technologies and broadcasts in Marshallese became central in the creation of affective imaginaries of Marshallese-American postwar political alliance as manifested in the political center. Moreover, this affective alliance was strengthened through the dissemination of the Marshallese vocal male professional. Young men were trained as mechanics, public speakers, and manual laborers, while education for women focused on the "domestic" arts.[27] WSZO was the first radio station broadcast from the US government's administrative center in the Marshallese language. For the inaugural ceremony in October 1953, the team chose "The Kaiser-Walzer, Op. 437 (Emperor Waltz)" by Johann Strauss II (1889), to commemorate WSZO becoming a "member station of the far-flung communications system of the Trust Territory of the Pacific Islands."[28] During the ceremony, TTPI official Maynard Neas explained that the purpose of the broadcast in the Marshallese language was to serve the Marshallese people by providing entertainment, news, and weather warnings, which had once been the purview of chiefs and persons who practiced divination. As Marshallese became dependent on American literacies and communications, the US military was testing increasingly powerful weapons without alerting the atoll populations. In *Listening Publics*, Kate Lacey explores the radio in terms of its democratic scope in the making of public spheres, political networks, and cultural communications.[29] She writes on the *"re-sounding"* of the public sphere in a representative democracy, the move from a "reading culture" to a "listening culture," which was central in the media dissemination of the bomb through which people could take part in a radioactive citizenship. As the Marshall Islands became increasingly developed through networked radiophonic and radioactive spaces, Marshallese continued to seek resource in a "grounded normativity" through which they appealed for the cessation of testing and in which they located their spirits.[30]

THE PETITION

On March 1, 1954, the Rongelapese and Utrikese were incorporated into the US nuclear program as test subjects. They were not told about this and were left for forty-eight hours on their irradiated atolls while American weathermen were evacuated within twenty-four hours. Because they were part of the nuclear program, their lives became classified as information, secret "restricted data" in Project 4.1, the "Study of Response of Human Beings Exposed to Significant Beta and Gamma Radiation Due to Fallout from High Yield Weapons."[31] Since the 1940s, the US government had been conducting studies on human responses to radiation, so the exposure of Marshallese, specifically the Rongelapese and to a lesser extent the Utrikese, was valuable to the United States as data, which meant that Americans did not consider Marshallese cultural bodies or language in their "observational data gathering." Beginning on March 8, 1954, the Project 4.1 AEC medical team—doctors and scientists under the direction of Eugene Cronkite and with strict instructions from the US government on this "Secret and Restricted Data" mission—began to examine Rongelapese and Utrikese and document their findings, such as loss of hair in 90 percent of the children and 30 percent of the adults. A month later, the doctors reported that the Rongelapese had been exposed to such lethal concentrations of radiation that they should never be exposed to radiation again throughout their lives.

The March 22, 1954, issue of *Time*, under its section "The Atom," stated that the "twenty-eight U.S. observers and 236 natives of local islands . . . [were exposed to] radiation [that was] ten times greater than scientists deem safe, but the AEC was reassuring, 'There were no burns. . . . All are reported well. After completion of the atomic tests, they will be returned to their homes.'"[32] The mediated silences increasingly stifled Marshallese who decided to take direct action and resist these nuclear silences by filing a complaint to the United Nations in the aftermath of Bravo on April 20, 1954. Their petition addressed the sociocultural, physiological, and psychological problems they identified as resulting from US nuclear weapons testing over the previous eight years, which were escalated and exacerbated by Bravo. The Marshallese, fearing the continuation and worsening of their conditions, requested the United Nations to intervene and place a ban on the US testing of nuclear weapons on their homelands.[33] The *New York Times* printed the story using the metaphorical "softness" of wording and belittling terms to minimize the atrocities contained within:

> Native leaders in the Marshall Islands . . . have sent an urgent plea to the United Nations for an end to hydrogen-bomb tests near their *tiny, scattered* Pacific atolls. In a softly worded petition to the United Nations, the Marshallese said that islanders on Rongelap and Utrōk . . . had become ill— with nausea, burns, falling hair, and "lowering of blood count." The petition from the islanders made it plain that what the islanders wanted most of all was to see the tests ended. But . . . if for the well being of all the people of the world the tests must go on, then at least all possible safety measures should be taken to protect the people of the Marshalls. [This] should include removal of people in the danger area and teaching of safety rules.[34]

In the petition the Marshallese representatives referenced the importance of land: "The Marshallese people are . . . very concerned for the increasing number of people who are being removed from their land. Land means a great deal to the Marshallese. It means more than just a place you can plant your food crops and build your houses; or a place where you can bury your dead. It is the very life of the people. Take away their land and their spirits go also."[35]

The United States issued a public statement of "deep regret" on behalf of the American government and people, but with the promise to take care of the Marshallese, nuclear testing was allowed to continue. The publicity of the complaint and international concerns led the United States to increase censorship of the occurrences taking place at the Pacific Proving Grounds. Still, to compensate for the globally negative press caused by the petition, the US government decided to move the Rongelapese from Kwajalein to Ejit Island, an island about the size of a football field, where Bikinians live today to be closer to the RMI and US governments. As with the Bikinians' coverage, military films and journalists covered the Rongelapese move, which the government promised would last only a year, until their atoll was completely safe for resettlement. Johnston and Barker comment on the move: "U.S. government reports of the relocation of the Rongelapese . . . describe the relocation as 'a modern version of the American covered wagons,' as 'natives' were transferred on covered ships loaded with their personal possessions, children, and household items."[36] A June 24, 1954, article in the *New York Times* announced, "Bomb Refugees Find New Home in the Pacific," and explained how "the 'poisoned people' have a new home," a reference to the relocation of the Rongelapese to Ejit Island (referred to as "Mejit Island") in Majuro Atoll fifteen days before. The article states that they had been under the "care" of US Navy and AEC doctors and that they would be ready to return to Rongelap in one year, although these same doctors surmised that they should never receive additional radiation.

US government officials, according to Johnston and Barker and the declassified documents they cite, were aware of the unsafe levels of radiation and moved the Rongelapese to continue to study the population in the administrative capital. The document also explained that to make sure the Natives did not easily acquire wealth, they provided them with the least assistance possible to survive. At this time, the Utrikese were returned to their homeland, where they would be visited periodically to be monitored by AEC doctors. The populations were also stigmatized; people thought they were contagious. Moreover, as visibility of the nuclear testing and ramifications swelled, the US government reduced monetary support of Marshallese, which prompted a public statement. In a July 13, 1954, *New York Times* article, Frank Midkiff, the UN Trusteeship Council governor, justified the lack of financial assistance given to Bikinians and other Marshallese as based on the Native American population, who, he said, had "developed a tendency to regard themselves as wards." The *Times* article concludes with "The road toward self-help has been made easier through the United States aid in education of native administrations, agricultural experts, and in the production of salable commodities."

MAKING BOMBS

While the United States worked on public relations marketing to frame the post-Bravo narrative, Marshallese across the archipelago who were not relocated after Bravo, particularly but not limited to the "mid-range" atoll communities of Ailuk, Likiep, and Wotje, continued to be confused by what they experienced on March 1. From varying degrees of fallout-related illnesses to noticeable shifts in health and vegetation, word about the detonation and its aftermath was making its way through the atolls in different forms. Speaking to his experience in Likiep Atoll as a child when he witnessed Bravo, deBrum explained: "The nuclear issues have contributed to the Marshallese popular musical repertoire. There is even a Marshallese nursery rhyme called '*Kōṃṃan Baaṃ*' ['Making Bombs'] from the nuclear

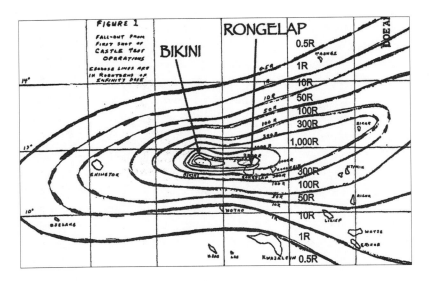

1.1 Radioactive pathways. Likiep Atoll is in the 10 rems range.

testing period. It's from Likiep. I grew up hearing it on Likiep, and I am sure that most youngsters in the Northern Marshalls will remember it."[37] Just as radiation had spread, so too did the song. (See figure 1.1.)

DeBrum was instrumental in making sure that the CCP was part of the COFA because he had lived, embodied experience with the radiogenic aftereffects of the detonations. Likiep Atoll, identified in the 10R (rems) range, was not part of Section 177, nor was Ailuk Atoll, which received, according to this representation, 50R. After the final report (1995) of the federal Advisory Committee on Human Radiation Experiments (ACHRE) was released to the RMI government in truckloads of boxes of partially declassified (partially redacted) paperwork, deBrum began combing through it with anthropologist Holly Barker to prepare evidence for the CCP. The report revealed the knowledge about the exposure of these atolls and the decision to leave the populations in place. For example, the 401 people on Ailuk Atoll, just south of Utrik, were contaminated with significant amounts of radioactive fallout that were similar to the exposure of the Utrikese. Two destroyer escort ships had been available to evacuate persons on Ailuk. However, according to Lieutenant Colonel R. A. House, "'The effort required to move the 400 inhabitants,' when weighed against potential health risks to the people of Ailuk, seemed too great, so 'it was decided not to evacuate the atoll.'"[38] Evacuation would have reduced lifetime exposure to ionizing radiation threefold. The United States created demarcations around "exposed" populations and, using the "Pacific Proving Grounds" as a laboratory, studied with earnest those populations and chose some supposedly nonexposed Marshallese for "control groups." Those in the mid-range atolls, such as Likiep Atoll, and also atolls in the southern part of the archipelago show radiological damages still uncounted and uncompensated, such as high rates of thyroid abnormalities.

Four decades before deBrum read through the paperwork, marred with thick black lines that indicated redactions on often otherwise blank pages, he already knew of the exposure. "When the teachers' training program was set up, I think the song they were supposed to be working with was [called] 'Making Farms' or 'Gardens,' but it turned up 'Making Bombs.' When it came up to the outer islands, everybody understood it as a 'making bomb song' because it was during the bomb-testing period," he said of the nuclear contamination of his community that had gone unrecognized, officially, by the United States. It was not for lack of trying on the part of deBrum and other Marshallese in direct collaboration with a handful of Americans that the United States failed to hold itself accountable for more-expansive damages and injuries that would ultimately, should they be recognized, require more compensation and perhaps a new look at the relationship between the nations and those most severely affected groups within it.

A renowned politician, deBrum contributed countless interviews to global media, sharing his time with journalists, documentarians, academics, and activists as well as other politicians. As he explained,

> For some [Marshallese, the nuclear testing] is a tremendous psychological scar, and sometimes they will just say, "Yeah, that's the case [the tests happened]," and back off because they don't want to talk about it anymore. [But even if people say they don't know], they do; they just don't want to talk about it. It's a denial, and it is interesting how long it has remained so real that the denial phase has not proceeded on to [being] something in the past. Many of the people who I grew up with in Likiep who I ask about this "Kōṃṃan baaṃ" song tell me that they don't remember. I [ask] them, "Don't you remember dancing to it?" They say [no].[39]

DeBrum's account of the silence from people he grew up with on Likiep can be read along the lines of the "hidden realities of suffering" kept hidden with "premature closure" that has written Likiep time and again out of being a nuclear-affected atoll.[40] In 2000 the RMI government petitioned the US Congress for additional compensation and was understandably devastated in 2004 when the State Department denied the claim for insufficient evidence and ruled that it had no legal obligation to provide additional compensation.[41] The RMI tried again to extend and expand coverage for those nuclear affected and get more funds for the NCT, when in 2007 it resubmitted a request for additional compensation, which was supported by New Mexico Senator Jeff Bingaman and became S. 1756 (Senate Bill 1756), titled "Republic of the Marshall Islands Supplemental Nuclear Compensation Act of 2008." In addition to requesting funds to monitor a nuclear landfill, Runit Dome, on Enewetak Atoll; vocational rehabilitation for nuclear-affected persons; and "providing eligibility for Marshall Islanders who worked at test sites to an American nuclear worker compensation law," the bill aimed to acknowledge that persons from or living in "Ailuk, Mejit, Likiep, Wotho, Wotje, and Ujelang Atolls" should receive medical supervision at least quarterly because they were also "affected by the nuclear testing program of the United States."[42] The bill made it out of committee with a recommendation for full consideration by the Senate but was never acted upon. Bingaman reintroduced the bill in 2010 and 2011, but the Senate still failed to act. The unresponsiveness of the US government and its outright denials share with us the layers of what Jill Stauffer calls "ethical loneliness," the feeling of being completely "abandoned by humanity," which is the "injustice of not being heard."[43] Being heard is not based on "ethical listening," however. This would presume that those listening—the United States—had the capacity to understand what they were hearing, which they did not. Their inability to hear was based upon the notion of modern civilization and the colonial myth of *terra nullius* ("nobody's land"), affirming that although the United States aimed to distance itself as a colonial power, nuclear colonialism is an extension or an echo of other forms of violent and legally manipulative rule.

Over the course of this nursery rhyme as told by deBrum, the musical movements become frozen through the constant motion of making bombs. The affective tension inscribed into the delivery of lyrics that tell of uncompensated (forcible) labor in the nuclear colony is set to the tune of a "Filipino planting rice song," making possible a space to hear transpacific networks forged by the transit of laboring bodies at times differentiated for services given their sexed and racial comportment. The foundational narrative is thus written into this song too. With the transpacific in mind, the permeation of multiple histories of forcible labor into the tuneful choreographies of nuclear war resonates with the congregation of the Asia-Pacific region under and, importantly, between these imperial powers. And with the foundational narrative of movements of Japanese and American empire that become mapped with the "peaceful" atomic bomb onto the terrain of northern and mid-range atolls in an uptake of the body, reflections on other uptakes, other workers, and other imperial penetrations come to the fore in the often euphemized "Seabee" births of Bikinian women in the first years of nuclear diaspora.

Kōṃṃan baaṃ, kōṃṃan baaṃ
Jillǫk jān jibboñ ñan boñ
Emetak pā emetak ne
Emetak aolep in ānbwin (kimnu)

In an aō jerata bwe jej aikuj in enta?
In ra kwōj baaṃ
In ra kwōj baaṃ in
I kinaḷnaḷ kōn

Making bombs, making bombs
Bending over from morning till night
My arms hurt, my legs ache
There is pain all over my body

Misfortune brings sadness, and for what do we suffer?
The bomb has frozen your limbs
Your limbs ache (are frozen) from the bomb
as if ants are gnawing at them from the inside

High-yield weapons destroy other yields, such as Marshallese copra, arrowroot, pandanus, and breadfruit crops. They also destroy humans' ability to tend to those crops. The echoes of the bomb (*baaṃ*) that follow the word *making* (*kōṃṃan*) mark the break, and the song lays claim to the land and its history before and after the nuclear testing. If we consider exposure as forced labor to make bombs for the United States, then there are additional claims to compensation that remain unaddressed through the continual dismissals in the courts and legislatures. The stakes of proof as (an) objective are crucial, particularly when it comes to documenting the drastically different experiences that deBrum and his peers had relative to those of the Rongelapese (see below), which have shaped the course of remedial possibilities and those of memory: "During the testing, I think it was one of the effects, I have no proof for it, but *kinaḷnaḷ* is common among students at Holy Rosary [Catholic School on Likiep]. Sometimes we would show up for school, and a lot of the kids would complain of these kinaḷnaḷ pains in their bones, and they would be administered aspirin or APC—half tablet." DeBrum refuses to let the space of hearing be overdetermined, and with the word *but* he displaces the subjective and offers the structural space of the song as media through which to back up his accounts with the evidence *in the song* that breaks its contained harmony as "the work." From his determination to remember musical and choreographic records that speak to the shift from "making gardens" to "making bombs" to his numerous political interventions, sharing the shift from the "grounded normativity" to one in which Marshallese were forced to participate in a radioactive citizenry via the nuclear colony in which they labored for the United States without compensation.

The disposability to which deBrum speaks can be heard in the ticking of the Geiger counter that met Utrikese when they returned from Kwajalein to their irradiated homeland, which sounded like "clocks" and "buzz[ers]." Yostimi Compaj located the Geiger counter sounds, which indicated radioactive hot spots, as being near natural food sources:

> After the bomb, it took three days for [the Americans] to come and see what happened on Utrik. . . . He went near the church where there was another breadfruit tree that made the sound again, so he set up another sign. The signs are still up in Utrōk today, and we didn't get rid of those. . . . The plane left, but there was no meeting held with the people, the man didn't tell us what he was doing, but us boys we went to see for ourselves, and we heard the sound made by the devices. . . . After they returned the people to Utrōk from Ebeye, Kwajalein, they told us not to eat the food, we were not allowed to eat anything, foods were brought in from Kwajalein for [us]. We were not to eat chickens, pigs, or anything made from *mokmok* [taro/arrowroot] . . . and they even killed all the pigs and the chickens and dogs. They took them and threw them away.[44]

Others added details that the island and some of their houses were full of trash. The common theme in all the statements is how little Americans valued their lives. When Americans soiled their land with radiation, disposed of their food, and trashed their homes, the message sent was one of complete disrespect and devaluation. The Geiger counter sounds reminded the northern atoll populations of the forced disposability of their lands and lives, thus their voices. The immunization of the voice, the privation of the ear, and the boundary of the human from nonhuman remove plants from the conception of losses with respect to nuclear injury as a "biological" matter. Plants become part of land as property that humans must use their voices to represent. The lack of reciprocity with plants—the intertwining of systems that has been prevented from displacements to urban centers or other isolated spaces where tending to indigenous plants is not possible—is embodied by humans. Marshallese link many illnesses with the bomb, including diabetes, whereas Western science contests any direct link. However, the link is evident when we hear it in the immunization of the voice that is claimant in courts; the courtroom, split from the sensorial worlds of Indigenous interconnectedness, speaks to the immunization of Indigenous bodies from one another—where gustatory insecurity is a eugenics of the human community via contrast making.

Contrast making, as a matter of the ear, was also prevalent in the human radiation experiments, which also created the opportunity through which US professional males became vocationally empowered. For Rongelapese who remained on Kwajalein Atoll, Geiger counter sounds would come to attune them to the insensible poison they had absorbed. One woman recalled her experiences at the US military base on Kwajalein Atoll while testifying in front of the Nuclear Claims Tribunal:

> In front of [the male Rongelapese translators] . . . , three times a day for three months, the Rongelapese women were told to undress and stand naked at the lagoon's edge. The women would cry from embarrassment and try to cover their genitals with their hands. U.S. Government officials, all men, ran Geiger counters up and down the bodies of the naked women both before and after they bathed in the lagoon. Frequently, the Geiger counters would start clicking wildly when taking readings from the hair on the women's heads and from their pubic hair. The U.S. Government workers would tell the women to soap their pubic hair again, in front of everyone, before a second reading. [The male translators] . . . tried to avert their eyes whenever possible but their presence by their naked mothers and sisters was mortifying.[45]

In addition to the racialized boundaries created through Geiger counter aural modalities, we hear how Geiger counters were an extension of the male colonial gaze or what we can call the "audition," which staged women in ways that created significant differences in their experiences of being subject to nuclear violence and violations.[46] For women, these sounding and listening practices were aligned with taboo cultural practices and shameful engagements over which they had no control. The sound of the Geiger counters clicking wildly attuned the Rongelapese women to an embodied toxicity, yet it sonorized a private experience of the irradiated female body for the public sound-scape of male doctors, making it seemingly unnecessary for anyone to ask the women about their experiences.[47] Although they functioned as translators, this created a double silence for the male intermediaries, who sustained the hierarchical nuclear listening practices and served in and as silent witness to their sisters' humiliation from which they could not protect them.

During the three-month sequestration following Bravo, Rongelapese were subject to frequent urine collections, blood injections, and transfusions along with the insensitivity of doctors who, time and again, would refuse to explain what they were doing. Women, including one woman who wanted to go by the alias "Molly," told me about the invasive gynecological examinations and other medical stagings of her community as objects of scientific inquiry rendered into intelligible means through reductive measures. Medical teams used instruments to listen in to bodies, such as the stethoscope and X-ray, probing or sounding devices that separated pulse from temperature from respiration from skin condition, creating information sets out of complex lives. By disembodying the Rongelapese symbolically as data, American nuclear colonial power incorporated them into the system of professional corporation, as biocapital to be reinvested for profit elsewhere.

Molly reflected on her experiences of isolation on the military base. Throughout this portion of our interview, she conveyed a lingering sense of disbelief in regards to the treatment of her community.

> They put us in a camp alone, and they put a fence around the camp so nobody would go out and nobody could come in. . . . I don't know why [the US government] did this, but it was a long time that we couldn't go out. . . .
>
> Sometimes I said [that] maybe we can't go out because if we eat with others, they will contract radiation from us. . . . So we just slept and walked around in our camp.
>
> Sometimes [the Americans] brought movies, and they always brought food. . . . This was the time they started to examine us because things were growing on our feet and necks, and some of our hair started to fall out. . . .[48]

The Rongelapese isolation was a regulatory mechanism that maintained the appearance that they could be contagious. Racialized and gendered fears of types of "contagious" bodies map into the women whose movements and diets are tightly controlled as part of their role as human subjects or scientific objects of study to produce and reproduce nuclear knowledge for them. The borders of the camp—the island laboratory—emulate in some respects the borders of the Marshall Islands, where, until 1968, no one could leave or enter without permission or a valid reason, according to the governing body, which deemed only Western education, military service, or medical procedure for nuclear issues admissible for travel.[49] The ACHRE report indicates that the medical program was called a "study" from the outset but that the heads of the medical team, Cronkite and Conard, "maintain[ed] the project never included nontherapeutic research."[50] However, the report notes the simultaneous therapeutic treatments and research on radiation exposure. It emphasizes that no evidence supports that Marshallese were intentionally exposed for research purposes, which is a sharp contrast to the feelings of many Marshallese. An issue of course is that once the larger system becomes broken down into parts—the military officials that set up the tests, the weathermen relaying wind patterns, the scientists looking forward to the nuclear experiment, the doctors seizing upon an opportunity—there is room in the chain to defer accountability and stress an "accidental exposure." The Marshall Islands were consistently referred to as a laboratory, but their official designation was, for all intents and purposes, the Pacific Proving Grounds.

It is in the culture of the colonial laboratory and the colony as carceral laboratory that anthropologists have noted "sensationalized racial contrast" is constructed through making "visible and accessible" colonized subjects who were processually being "trained or prepared for conversion or assimilation."[51] Molly "slept and walked around," which left her oriented to the space of the camp and open to the American foods and entertainment brought by the American personnel. Molly emphasizes food here too: "They always brought food" and contemplated that radiation poisoning might be transmitted while eating together, which speaks to the sharing of food as convivial, *bōro wōt juon*. The control of food was possibly part of the control of the Rongelapese to make sure of what went into their bodies and what came out, giving access to the intimate orificial sites. Nuclear silences, which are the lack of any pertinent information, acted as a distancing tool through which division and difference could be produced. And although these silences distanced them, the boundaries that contained them made them dependent on the United States and, importantly, on the occasional movies they were brought and the daily food regime. The administration of movies as treats, the movement of ideals on the screen when the spectator is trapped in a painful and confusing situation, creates an imaginary where the movements on screen (and the culture attached to it) becomes more preferable than the life that is lived.

I read the camp as part of postwar immunization that accompanied global democratization in the making of the voice, as a eugenics of the vocal apparatus of which orificial intimacies are part. In the postwar era the rise of global health, as explored by Kirsten Ostherr, was paralleled by "the rhetoric of contagious globalization." This rhetoric parallels the US rhetoric of "globally spreading democratic liberties," creating the dialectics of dispersal and restriction.[52] For example, these movies taught Rongelapese important aspects of American culture through manner and language that was not reciprocated by the members of the Brookhaven medical team, for they did not learn about Marshallese culture, diet, or language, which impacted their modes and methods of research. Through radio and radiation infrastructural underdevelopment, Marshallese could become listening citizens without physical copresence, which helped integrate them into geopolitical postwar hierarchies.

Gendering processes of contrast making were part of American vocational growth, predicated on US political bodies or the normative body politic. Dana Nelson writes about the institutionalization of a "national manhood" that promoted white, male professional sameness through "the scientific/medical investigations of otherness, now mobilized as 'careers.'"[53] The growth of the American middle class depended on white manhood's ability to establish difference, which was done through racial science and the medical subfield of gynecology. Radiation sounded opportunities for an emergent American middle class carried by professional patriarchs to echo itself into powerful positions. American scientists created reference indexes of human bodies based on their likenesses, which proved damaging to all "others" measured by this ideal. Radiation intake and body burden levels were calculated with the "Standard Reference Man," who was the prototypical healthy Euro-American thirty-five-year-old able-bodied male living in an urban locale with a diet and lifestyle to match. For example, the Standard Man did not spend much time sitting or sleeping on the ground in an equatorial region and consuming indigenous plants, as did Marshallese. The Standard Man did not get most of his hydration from coconut water, nor did he have a thyroid the size found in women or children (which is larger than adult males because of the need for calcium and hormone production).

While I was in Majuro, the elderly Rongelapese men were often absent or quiet, and I always wondered where they were because the women were so vivaciously present. The men were conspicuously absent during many of the public events, and they would often hang back during gatherings. The Rongelapese women would laughingly tell me that the men "weren't needed." There were a handful of men, such as Willie Mwekto and Tarines Abon, who seemed to keep company with the women on occasion. Both men contributed to the collective memory of the Rongelapese. Abon, I was told, composed the song "*LoRauut*" ("Mr. Urine"). I had read about the song in Barker's *Bravo for the Marshallese*, which stated that this is one of the few songs composed about this time on Kwajalein Atoll. Barker had collected the translated lyrics from Abacca Anjain-Maddison. When I first met with the Rongelapese women, Anjain-Maddison told me about the song, but she said that the women did not feel comfortable singing it because it was "the boys' song."[54]

Barker pinpoints the "dehumanizing" and "culturally inappropriate handling of the Rongelapese" that is conveyed through this song. She also stresses that the song gives a humorous bent to the absurdity and the extreme discomfort and confusion of being shuffled about and out in awkward positions by a string of medical professionals. The humor, Barker writes, offers laughter as catharsis for the suffering and pain caused by such traumatic encounters with doctors that get so close to the patient to almost "kiss them," sexually violate them, touch inside and out with ease, and constantly observe them and their insides with radioactive pictures or the X-ray.[55] In addition to documenting the reduction to ID cards and numbers, the final line, which speaks to the unyielding X-ray pictures, day and night, recalls much of what has previously been discussed in terms of US militarization and surveillance, creating a thorough biopolitical incorporation of Marshallese as a matter of American national security.

"*LoRauut*" is an education in perceptions of the body and the senses in a disciplinary and invasive setting. It shows how young boys encoded names with actions, using their Marshallese musical logic, and brought their worlds together in a time of confusion and upheaval. This song, which gives directions and implied statements like a navigational chant, makes the connections for them so they could move through their days with a key to their uncomfortable journeys, which they could shape in song. Like the place-names that get imbued with predictive names because of noticed patterns and get a title, Mr. Urine gets the "Mr." title (*LoRauut*). The boys are not learning their identification through the world via their engagements with place; they are learning how to cohere another world while they become scientific objects of study through it. The boys had different experiences than the girls, so it wouldn't make sense for the women to sing this song. This different experience is shown in an NBC newsreel from 1957, which along with American attention-grabbing headlines that referred to the Rongelapese as "poisoned people," contributed to their political silencing, as emphasized by their tightly controlled visibility in mainstream American media that negated the potential value in their speech or perhaps denied the possibility that they could speak at all.[56]

This video exemplifies the dehumanizing process by which Marshallese were systematically incorporated into the US fraternal order. This assimilation-structured process strips their voices of value and places them in subjugation to figures (e.g., US scientists, doctors, politicians, narrators) that model voices they are to emulate to accrue political and social value. It is exemplified by the voice-over, coded or typecast American-White-Male, narrating the examination and providing background information as the camera zooms in on the faces of the Rongelapese men:

> To the AEC Argon Labs in Chicago last week came seven men, natives of the Marshall Islands. These are fishing people—savages by our standards. John is mayor of Rongelap, which is 100 miles from Bikini . . . , so a cross section, a delegation, was brought to Chicago for testing. John as we said is a savage, but a happy amenable savage. His grandfather ran almost naked on his coral atoll. The White man brought money and religion. John knows how to read, knows about God, and is a pretty good mayor.[57]

The newsreel captures the journey of nuclear incorporation. "Savage" boys, who ran almost naked like their grandfathers, get to use that one piece of clothing (almost, not quite animals) to pivot and transform themselves by getting new "grandfather figures": the American scientists who came courtesy of the other white men who brought money, morality, and skills (to be a "pretty good mayor"). The narrator's vocal delivery stresses the excitement in the journey: "To the AEC Argon Labs," the narrator exclaims, and he aligns the words *native* and *savage* to describe "John" and his community, which is close to Bikini Atoll, and thus reinforces previous associations of the "nuclear savage." In this excerpt alone, the word *savage* is used three times for effect. The subtext offered is that John, being the "mayor," gets the privileges of being examined with a "cross section" of the population or, in more American-English civilized terms, "delegation." Note that the seven-person delegation is all male and that they all wear business suits or business casual attire until they are placed into medical garb, giving the American scientists access to their bodies. The promise of the political exists in the nuclear transaction.

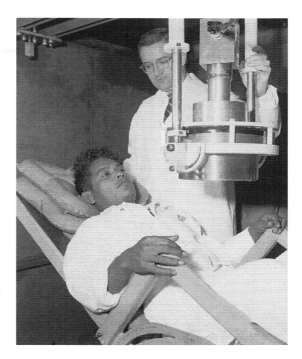

1.2 John Anjain, voiced over, constrained, and under a whole-body Geiger counter. Atomic Energy Commission Photo.

John Anjain, the magistrate, is called an "amenable savage" over a visual of him changing behind a curtain (monitored by a lab technician). The lab technician (a white male, younger than the scientists) leads him to the medical equipment in a position where he is immobilized and dominated by the Geiger counter machine and the scientist who mans it (see figure 1.2). The medical equipment that scans his body, listening for the insensible, is an extension of the adjudicative aurality enabled by a series of mediated nuclear listening rendered visually by an oscilloscope onto a screen watched by the scientists (one dot, one gamma ray). Here it is not the voice; it is the echo of American penetrative techno-science, the seeds of the bomb for which the team listens. The distance that is created through the mediation of the Geiger counter, like the stethoscope, maintains the racialized hierarchy between Anjain and the scientists. The lab assistant gets to position the machine over Anjain and thus align himself more with the "voice" (race) of the scientist.

In addition to the procedures, American mediation violated taboos, but the Americans also taught the Rongelapese men how to be viewed in subservient positions or how to "take it" like American white professional men. Anthropologist Julianne Walsh has analyzed the importance of "altitude and height" to honor, prestige, and status: "Respect for a higher status (height/status) individuals is evident in the behaviors, physical postures, and social interactions between people of various social positions. . . . Status is acknowledged and reproduced in numerous everyday interactions through these types of subtle gestures."[58] With distance comes the confused intimacy through the sexualized manner of the techno-scientific penetration of bodies, which creates an abusive intimacy. Throughout the entire newsreel the Rongelapese men do not speak, and for their services they are rewarded with "apples and other good things to eat." The narrator tells us that the men were only lent these suits and topcoats in Hawaii and that they would return them on their way back to their various atolls "in the middle of the Pacific Ocean, where hardly anybody lives."

To say that "hardly anybody" lives in the Marshall Islands, of course, denigrates the human and nonhuman bodies and their interconnections. The narrator reminds us, with this statement, just how many nuclear silences, regimes of the unsaid and unheard, went into marking Rongelapese for near-death experiences as subjects of study. In addition to a human-centric approach to what constitutes a "living body," the scientists knew that the other "bodies" in the Marshall Islands, the atoll bodies, and especially Rongelap, were contaminated. In fact, in 1956, a year prior to the newsreel, the AEC deemed the Marshall Islands to be "by far the most contaminated place in the world."[59]

Just prior to the newsreel, however, the AEC stated that the radiation levels on Rongelap Atoll were insignificant, and it opted to return the Rongelapese to their homeland. Medical tests and withheld information continued. Rongelapese now believe the United States thought they were "animals" to be tested like "guinea pigs." They were treated like humans in the nuclear colonial and capitalistic exploitative sense for their raw materials (their bodies), and in the Aristotelian sense of the political voice where they actually mattered, they were treated like animals. The terms used by the "voice-over" remind the viewers of this denigration of Marshallese with the words *hardly anybody* and *savages*. The newsreel fades as all the men walk out together, intermingled and smiling, having been through and "finished it," this experience of (momentary transformation and/as) togetherness. The two white male doctors shake hands in front of Mayor Anjain. He puts his arm up but then realizes they are shaking each other's hands only. He smiles. They continue walking. This is how nuclear incorporation works.

1.3 Handout provided to the Marshallese from the Atomic Energy Commission.

These communities' political voicelessness is not only metaphorical. As I mentioned about deBrum's "denial phase," political voicelessness can often inscribe literal voicelessness through bodies that form through repeated denials and silencings. And political voice, what is often thought to be metaphorical voice, manifests in the literal embodied voice of a historical person that speaks to the intercultural conditions of possibility for aural connectedness—voicing and listening—in the first place. The political voice, in the Americanized political milieu of the postwar, can be taken as resonances of the American "voice-over," which becomes taken on silently by the men who learn that they will be rewarded for taking it silently, as the Bikinians were rewarded for their singing voices. These seemingly pederast political relations become so because they continue to play out through the mediation of the US neocolonial domination of the RMI as perpetual caretaker and exploitative power. Naori Sakai affirms the importance of mediation to securing these fantastical roles: "We must understand how certain representations of sexual relations are appropriated by international politics and employed to consolidate power relations in colonial domination. For international, interracial, or interethnic sexuality is *not immediately* a relation of the victor and the vanquished; it becomes so only when *mediated* by the regimes of fantasy and national identification."[60] The fantasy therein is the docile Marshallese test subject through which Americans moralize their techno-scientific means of incorporation and retain a distance from those men who have yet to receive a political voice in America, even if they are "mayors" in training. This justifies the continued presence of the United States in the Marshall Islands in terms of "developing" and "training" those voices through modern infrastructures that require the tightening of the cable umbilical to American media that will continue to remind Marshallese (and other nonwhite male professionals) of their place in sounding nuclear power.

RADIATION SONGS

In 1982 the DOE (previously the AEC) provided documents to Rongelapese, Bikinians, and Enewetakese concerning radiation on their atolls. These bilingual documents (English and Marshallese) quickly circulated and gave the populations a new, nuclear-centered language, which they had heard and developed in their own languages but which was not a point of political communicative connection until after the reports were distributed.

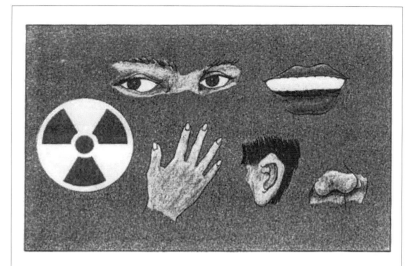

1.4 "Radiation is something we can't see, hear, taste, smell, or feel [sense]."

The Rongelapese learned that they had been living on a contaminated atoll for thirty-five years. They were given a US Defense Department Nuclear Agency publication that "contradicted the 'storyline' told and retold to us and the world over the years" and revealed to the Rongelapese that the DOE knew that the wind had shifted and was "headed for Rongelap to the east [of Bikini] . . . [but that] the decision to shoot was reaffirmed."[61] Rongelapese believed that they were given unfair treatment because the Bikinians were evacuated and they were not, which created fissures between the two groups.

The second report was the DOE publication *The Meaning of Radiation for Those in the Northern Part of the Marshall Islands That Were Surveyed in 1978*. The DOE, which first went to Majuro and then Rongelap, said the purpose was so it could make a choice about the plebiscite about to be held. However, as John Anjain stresses, the negotiations had been underway since 1969 and were "nearing completion." The images shown in figures 1.3 and 1.4

are from that publication, and it is clear that the DOE designed the book for young people rather than adults. The DOE didn't want to "burden" the Rongelapese with too much scientific detail.

The report stresses that although radiation is everywhere, the probability that it will cause harm is low. And regardless of whether it is everywhere or nowhere, radiation is insensible. There is, according to the book, no way for humans to detect it using their five modern senses, further making their survival dependent on modern media. The Rongelapese were horrified when they saw a two-page color map with one to four levels of radiation and Rongelap measured at the same level as Bikini and Enewetak. Senator Jeton Anjain gave representative voice to the distress of the Rongelapese in exile in front of the Subcommittee of Insular Affairs and International Affairs and the Committee on Interior and Insular Affairs: "From the moment the DOE Report was presented to us, the 66-page document began to overwhelm and dominate our lives." In his 1989 testimony the representative explained the decision to depart their homeland: "Fear gripped the people. We had to leave the atoll."[62] (See also chapter 2.)

Political testimony was bolstered by and produced through a political musical genre I call "radiation songs" that were composed from the early 1980s onward, which began to take on the tenor of the court cases through appellate voicings and the inclusion of reference to material evidence of problems tied to nuclear issues. These songs employ new nuclear-centered radiation languages to make sense of radiogenic complications. For example, the popular Marshallese musician Walter Laelang performed a song called "Radiation" with a pan-Pacific island feel and country twang.[63] The song works as a petition, and its compositional structure follows, remarkably, that of a trial brief with a form that can be read as sectional introduction or preliminary statement, a statement of facts, question presented/summary of argument, and overall argument outline (justification). The song can be read as an exercise in litigation and culling evidence through the modern transaction wherein pain and victimhood can be financially profitable, especially with "facts that have an emotional response or sympathetic value for the party" represented.[64] The lyrics speak to events that occurred in September 1978, when Trust Territory officials arrived to evacuate the nearly 140 Bikinians who had resettled their atoll after the US government announced it was safe for habitation a decade earlier. Despite their eagerness to return to Bikini, approximately 200 Bikinians (of 450) had spent a significant amount of time on the atoll since 1968, during which they consumed contaminated local foods. In 1975 Bikinians sued the

US government to force it to conduct a radiological survey. Information later came out that the AEC had recognized that Bikinians' urine samples showed increased levels of cesium-137 and plutonium, yet it wasn't until 1978 that the DOE publicly announced that it had found unacceptable levels of radiation at Bikini Atoll.[65]

During the evacuation some Bikinians returned to Kili, but others chose to relocate to Ejit Island in Majuro Atoll so that they could be closer to the American government. Some even negotiated with state officials to relocate to American soil in Hawaii "so that they won't be forgotten by the U.S. Government."[66] In March 1981 the Bikinians filed another lawsuit against the US government, in part for violating the Fifth Amendment by taking their lands without just compensation. Because US and Marshallese officials were negotiating terms of the COFA at the time, the court initially suspended proceedings to avoid interference, but the claims court allowed the case to move forward.[67] When the COFA vote came up in September 1983, 80 percent of Bikinians voted against it because they knew RMI sovereignty meant they could not negotiate with or file legal claims directly against the United States.

The Laura, Skate Em Lā, a string band popular on WSZO, was invited to Kili Island to play on Bikini Day. Robert, the guitar player, remembered that Bikinians paid them a decent amount of money and adorned them with dollar-bill wreaths. The dollar-bill wreath would become customary shortly thereafter in atolls that had money to give. They played a number of songs from their oeuvre, but Skate Em Lā had also written a song specifically for the celebration, "Radiation." The song is played on the radio, and it was in the film *Radio Bikini* and in other films about the Marshall Islands. Rather than have lyrics specifically about Bikini, Skate Em Lā wrote a song about the interconnectedness of the atolls. It marked Bikini as the site of the explosion (where the sun seemed to rise in the west), drawing from the Animals' "House of the Rising Sun," recomposing it with Marshallese rhythms and with a shuffle feel in the major mode. Robert discussed that he would see people in the hospital dying from radiation poisoning and he saw the changes in the land and sea. Exemplifying Marshallese narratives that speak to the expanse of nuclear damages, his observations contribute to mounting evidence that the US classification of the "four atolls" is limited (in ways that foreclose proper remediation).

Radioactive citizenship manifests as nuclear nationalism. Over the radio, people can express problems that they believe are nuclear related; songs can be sites for alternative sense-making practices outside the bounds of modern legal and scientific classifications that discipline sensibilities. Songs retain memories of US denials of radiation and memories of denials of memory. Radiation songs archive these complex processes through which radiation becomes an empty signifier and the means of democratic voicing, taking the shape of voicing (its) presence/absence or erasure from historical records. As a form of radioactive citizenship, RMI citizens' language of suffering is radiation, which is part of global harmonization in secular modernity.[68] These songs and their structural orientations that take shape through the mediated complex through which vocal subjects are produced amplify temporalities of radioactive movements and the means of dealing with them over time. In doing so, the songs recall the dissonance that founds the material sustenance of the burgeoning nation, challenging Joseph Masco's notion that the United States has invested more than any other nation in nuclear ruination as a form of nation building and "new social contract."[69]

After negotiating the COFA, President Kabua handled incoming US funding designated for the government, lease payments to the Kwajalein landowners, and nuclear compensation payments to the four atolls.[70] He used COFA funds and took loans to develop tourism and the national facade. In 1991 he also composed the current RMI anthem, "Forever Marshall Islands," which takes a decidedly supranational religious and patriarchal tone that reworks the land-based and maternal affections of the previous anthem, adopted in 1977, "Ij Iọkwe Ḷọk Aelōñ Eo Aō, Ijo Iaar Ḷotak Ie" ("I Love My Islands, Where I Was Born"). Kabua increased radiophonic expenditures, which augmented the space primarily defined by men's broadcasts and political debates in pursuits of tightly cohering the nation's attention to the centers of power. New equipment, including a 25,000-kilowatt transmitter, was purchased in 1995, making V7AB one of the most powerful radio stations in the Pacific. The station's motto shifted from the "Voice of the Marshall Islands" to "The Heartbeat of the Marshall Islands," imagining a more Western body politic with a closed circulatory system. Elbōn writes on the importance of radiophonic affective proximity to the RMI government and the "center" of the nation:

> The radio station's primary mission is to inform, to educate, and to entertain the people of the Marshall Islands. A major part of the station's role is the dissemination of information to the country, including shipping schedules, weather forecasts, early warnings, and live broadcasts of the Nitijela [Parliament] meetings, and important public events. . . . Broadcasting is

an essential function in the dissemination of a flow of substantial factual information to our people, who are widely distributed among the many islands at great distances from each other. The radio offers the most effective medium of building up our national identity with emphasis on the cultural, social, and economic fabric of the island communities.[71]

The station, which follows the governmental protocol of the current administration, has been scrutinized for being state run and sharing broadcasts of the Nitijela meetings. At times, the station has been unwilling to let women's organizations, such as WUTMI, broadcast about "sensitive issues" such as domestic violence, which is part of the international power structure of masculinizing militarization. The internalization of nuclear silences, or the censorship of what can be shared, points to the problematics of oppositional politics mapped onto human sociality that reinforce hegemonic behavioral expectations through procedures of withholding.

After receiving declassified documents in 1994 about the human radiation experiments (see chapter 2), the RMI began to work on submitting its CCP, including hosting the first Nuclear Victims' and Survivors' Remembrance Day (NVSRD) in 1998. A year later, Kessai Note, the first "elite" commoner (of Bikinian and Japanese descent), was elected RMI president with the United Democratic Party (UDP), following a tumultuous and scandal-ridden term by Kabua. Note's presidency was fiercely contested by Kabua and by Kwajalein landowners, ultimately giving rise to the Aelōñ Kein Ad (AKA) Party, which primarily represented the interests of the iroij in the Nitijela. The rivalry between Note's UDP and Kabua's AKA focused on COFA II negotiations. Kabua and the Kwajalein landowners wanted to negotiate separately with the US government. Ultimately, the Note administration signed an agreement that, over time, lessened US grants, increased RMI loans, and extended the US military lease of Kwajalein through 2066. In response, Kabua and the Kwajalein landowners refused to sign the land-use agreement, which was a requirement for the lease payments to be made.[72]

As the government changed parties, so did the broadcasting of V7AB. In May 2003, shortly after the government ratified the renewal of COFA II without waiting to hear about the fate of the CCP, V7EMON cofounder, owner, and DJ Fred Pedro left his long career in the RMI Nitijela. Pedro, along with Alkinta Kilma and Wally Milne, founded V7EMON. The station call number means "V7 good," and it draws on conservative Christian notions of democratic values, sharing the "good news" (the Gospel—traditional democratization) as a political critique of progressive democratization. In

2008 the Pacific Islands Association of Non-Governmental Organization described V7EMON as "privately owned by Pacific Media Services, a consortium of five local businessmen . . . funded by advertising and private investment, including financial support of individuals active in AKA." When I asked Pedro about the financial support the station received from individuals associated with the AKA, he explained that the station was not a "party" station insofar as it was launched to "serve the community." When you bring up political issues in a "small community," he remarked, you are seen as part of the opposition, what he called "the other side." He stressed that "we've never received pay."[73]

Pedro, like Elbōn, explained that radio is the most effective way to disseminate information, and this is based on Marshallese culture, language, and communications patterns. His impetus to begin V7EMON, he stressed, was to diversify radio content and "bring the news"—as "news" or as "music"—to Marshallese.[74] When I visited V7EMON, I watched Pedro engage in a live radio broadcast reporting translations of what he saw on the BBC. He contrasted V7AB with V7EMON, stressing that only V7EMON programmers translate world news into the Marshallese language, increasing its accessibility. The founders referred to the station as a space that "balanced" the government. "Balanced" politics at the time, for Pedro, entailed a dispersal of knowledge about the actual meaning of COFA II to Marshallese people.[75] Pedro lamented the RMI government's impetuousness concerning the ratification of the renewal and felt it had done a disservice to the nation because it had not engaged in a proper "debate" with the United States over the terms of COFA II. He added that the vote was split in the RMI government between those who supported COFA II and those who opposed it. He also explained that both COFA versions wrote out most of the wishes of the Kwajalein Atoll Cooperation (KAC), an association formed in 1981 to represent the landowners, who pushed for greater compensation (see also chapter 5).[76]

Although the nuclear-affected atolls, political representatives, and cognate atolls (e.g., Likiep and Kwajalein) clamored to make their cases for radioactive citizenship as a case of still-present albeit changed circumstances, radiation—the language of decay that signifies the splintering of the nation—seemed to hold the most hope in the public culture for the Marshallese decolonial movement. This proved tricky because the promise of the "good life" hinged on an affective attachment to and alliance with the radioactive colonizer: the United States and its interlocutor, the RMI government. Although the public language of radiation is used, many of the songs still have codes within dominant sounding systems to refuse mythico-histories that have been handed down generationally. These coded articulations of a nuclear resistance and Indigenous sounding are highly contextual and are deeply layered in neocolonial abuses. Radiation, as an empty signifier, is problematic because it shows nuclear silences to be at the core of unequal access to language, education, and resources insofar as "radiation communities" are viewed in both stigmatized ways and as "privileged."

In 2004 radiation songs from all generations flooded the capital. They shared different takes on radioactive citizenship based on mediated images of and lived relations with the US nuclear complex from their position domestically, transnationally, and globally. One elderly man, "K," a teacher and musician, shared a folk song that thanked the United States for its help while documenting the problems caused by nuclear testing. Linking his indirect appeal, K's diplomacy was routed through grounded sensibilities through which he knew of the failures of US categorical markers: the singer spoke of how he was swimming in Majuro after the bomb when the lagoon became frothy and the fish became poisonous. K also spoke of how his father and his father's friends worked at Enewetak as cleanup workers; his father died shortly after and everyone else became ill, without compensatory means to alleviate their pain.

Bands took to the air, their songs marked with questions, arguments, and historical markers of decay aligned with US imports and values. The Marshallese all-male youth group Island Rhythm recorded a song called "Bikini Atoll" that begins with an uneasy sci-fi drone and bomb sound effect. They ask "Uncle Sam" why he "dropped the bomb" by using an alternative or nineties hip-hop delivery that is set to a militaristic march underlying the Early Baroque Doctrine of Affectations era Pachelbel's Canon in D, performed "in C" on a Yamaha. The sound-bank oohs that fall in fourths and step up, and the canonic "striving" effect, recall mediated versions of this song, which resounds a bittersweet harmonic alliance that continues circularly, without voices aligning but rather echoing one another. The vocalist sings: "It is written in history that you liberated us from the Japanese, but when I look around, all I can see is that you fooled us, all the Marshallese." Drawing on Black diasporic verbal vernacular that resounds the racialization of Marshallese that has been bolstered by mediated representations, as well as a resistance to Uncle Sam as the archetype of White male leadership, Island Rhythm recalls nuclear deaths incurred by their kin in urban slang: "Rest in peace to all my homies, my countrymen and women who died of radiation."

Radiation songs encode defiant measures of Indigenous soundings that transnationally connect different expressive and communicative modes. A V7AB disc jockey gave me a Marshall Islands playlist (mix tape) burned on a CD that had a collection of songs about the Marshall Islands, including songs by Eddie Enos (see chapter 5), Skate Em Lā (see above), and Chaninway, who are popular musical performers throughout the country (and in the diaspora). The songs are about "the bomb and life in the RMI." They are all polished and have the pan-Pacific island rock, country twang feel (with the Marshallese rhythmic buoyancy) performed on Yamaha keyboards or string-band style. The CD opened with "ERUB" by Okjenlañ, which is a radiation song. The song begins with constant bomb sound effects as background noise to an a cappella lament that spells out ERUB and explains: "E-R-U-B these four atolls are broken, it's true that E-R-U-B these four atolls are broken." The breaks are codified in the signing of the COFA as are the means to make the breaks heard: through the singing voice. Although they are politically centered on the issues of the nation or the local, they draw on a transnational poetics of global radioactive citizenship, thus melding different expressive means through which to voice the (potential) power of radiation, yet these voices resonate a politics of the break, voicing the power of the aftereffects of the bomb (radiation) as voices of the nation on the radio in predominantly male timbres.

CHAPTER TWO

PRECARIOUS HARMONIES

We don't only speak about our experiences, but we sing about them. One person will write the song, and we all accept it and learn it because everybody is affected by [the radiation]. We sing on the anniversary of Bravo, at parties, at church, and especially when visitors come and they want to learn more about our experiences. The songs are happy and sad. Sad because of all the radiation that has poisoned us, but happy because when we sing the songs we remember our peaceful home of Rongelap and our ancestors, who we miss. —ABACCA ANJAIN-MADDISON, October 28, 2008

The death of Rokko Langinbelik, a former Rongelapese councilwoman and antinuclear activist, and the Rongelapese community's three phases of funerary customs structured the conditions under which I first made contact with the Rongelapese women, members of one of the Marshallese atoll populations severely affected by the US nuclear testing program and exposure to radiation from the fallout.[1] I had relied on American liaisons, such as a public advocate from the Nuclear Claims Tribunal, to introduce me to receptive members of the Marshallese nuclear-affected communities. Two months after I began fieldwork, on October 26, 2008, he sent me the following text in an email:

I spoke with former Rongelap Senator Abacca Anjain-Maddison on Friday and briefly introduced you to her, describing your dissertation fieldwork and explaining that you were teaching at [a school]. I also asked her about the funeral arrangements for former Rongelap Councilwoman Rokko Langinbelik, whose recent passing was noted in the Marshall Islands Journal. Rokko was an elementary school student living on Rongelap at the time of the Bravo test and had been very active in the "ERUB" organization (Enewetak/Rongelap/Utrik/Bikini people).

Abacca said that Rokko's body was scheduled to come out of the morgue that afternoon or Saturday and would lie in state at her house in Delap. Abacca also said that there will probably be occasion for the Rongelap people to sing some of the songs about their experiences to remember Rokko and celebrate her life and said that you may call her on her cell phone to set up a time and place to meet.[2]

The next day, I called former Rongelapese Senator Anjain-Maddison around 11:00 AM, and she explained that the actual funeral was scheduled to take place that day. She suggested I stop by the following day. After teaching sixth-grade social studies to Marshallese children, I walked through the muddy field to the faculty apartments and made phone calls to see about taking a Marshallese language class. As I hung up the phone, its shrill, generic landline ring startled me, and I grasped the receiver as I answered. Abacca warmly greeted me on the other line and told me that the funeral had been moved. She sounded as though she was busy, and so I followed her instructions to "come over now" even though I had no clear idea of how to navigate the nameless streets according to her directions: "Back road Payless. Tent, lots of chairs. The color of the house is yellow with blue trimming. Name. Rokko."

The rain continued to pour as I stepped out of the apartment. I hailed a taxi by the school playground that is situated in between the open Pacific Ocean and the Majuro Hospital and Morgue. The garbage receptacles had rusted through, spilling out medical waste that was frequented by dogs, rats, and pigs. Children would play in and around the receptacles, finding props for games. The mood of downtown Majuro was only slightly dampened by the rain, I noted, as we slowly began our way up the road lined by garbage on the side of the hospital and palm trees on the side of the houses up to the supermarket, Payless. We went past Payless on the "back road" (Oceanside), and I spotted a yellow house with blue trimming and the many chairs occupied by Marshallese women dotting the front.

After paying the dollar taxi fare, I tentatively made my way toward the women and asked where I might find Abacca. One woman pointed me to inside the house, but before I entered, a woman wearing a long white skirt and black top walked toward me and warmly introduced herself as Abacca. After greeting me, she led me inside the house and asked, "Do you speak Marshallese?" At this point I knew how to say, "I am learning to speak Marshallese" but not much more in the way of anything substantive. We walked in the house, and in the center was a coffin with Rokko's body. Plastic flowers and dollar bills adorned the casket. Women, and a few toddlers, created a circle around the coffin, their backs resting on the walls of the cinder-block house. Rokko's house turned out to be her eldest daughter, Shirley's, house. The older women were preparing for the second phase of her funeral, and they stopped braiding wreaths from towels to share some songs. The towels had flower prints on them, and Shirley later explained that they stood in for the real flowers that were traditionally used. "Too many funerals and not enough flowers," she lamented, offering an unassuming metaphor for the world out of balance.

Abacca provided mutual introductions. She went around the circle of women and explained who they were, particularly the older women, and mentioned that they had lived on Rongelap on March 1, 1954, when Bravo was detonated. Abacca told me something about each woman, and then she stopped: "And this woman, and this is the famous [composer] Lijon."[3] Abacca explained that the women had composed a song the week before to present to the Department of Energy (DOE) as a "petition." The women, Abacca elaborated, "[are] petitioning the DOE for answers to their sicknesses. They are scared that the thyroid medicines they have been taking for over fifty years are hurting their livers, their kidneys, and their emotional and mental states. They are getting sick[er]."

With Abacca's direction to sing the song, the women, still seated, filled the living room with an a cappella performance of "*Kajjitok in aō nan kwe kiiō*" ("These Are My Questions/Problems for You Now/Still"). I was amazed that I understood any amount of the song. The accomplishment was in no part to my credit because what I understood, without the translation, was part of the radiation language: the English words within the questions that created the structure of the song (e.g., aspirin, calcium). Everyone remained silent after the performance. Unlike audience participation after most songs, at which point clapping is acceptable if not welcomed, Abacca explained that for this genre, a musical petition, you do not clap. Then Lijon spoke in Marshallese, and Abacca translated: "The medicines they take for the thyroid affect their bodies and minds, and they just want to know—*they just want to know*—what the side effects really are—and please, can the DOE tell them?"

Kajjitok in aō nan kwe kiiō

Kajjitok in ao nan kwe kiiō
Komaron ke jiban ippa
bukot mejlan aban kein ao
kab ro nuku

Komaron ke uwaak io?
Etke ejjelok an *takta* ni?
Deka im jibke, im arin,
Im arji-ajin

Imaron ke bok melele
bwe en emman lomnak
Ke na imaron in
udiakak kin ao jaje?

Ewor ke baj jemlokin ao idraak?
Aspirin, calcium, uno in kirro,
Uno kan *tyroit*
Ewi waween am lomnak
problem in aō
bwe etakie na jab kiki
lo aenemman
Ewor ke baj jemlokin ao idraak?
Aspirin, calcium, uno in kirro,
Uno kan *tyroit*

Uno kein im ba kaki remaron ke
in kakure *kidney* ka ao,
komelij e ao,
im menono e ao?

These Are My Questions for You Now, Still

These are my questions for you now, still
Can you help me
find a way to untangle myself and my family
from these things that hinder us?

CHAPTER TWO

Can you answer me?
Why don't I have a dentist?
A doctor for my lungs, my kidney, and
my liver?

Can I please find meaning
so that I can find peace of mind?
Because I might go insane
not knowing.

Will there be an end to taking pills?
Aspirin, calcium, gout medicine,
Synthroid
What is your opinion
of my problems
because there are times I can't sleep
peacefully

Will there be an end to taking pills?
Aspirin, calcium, gout medicine,
Synthroid

Will these pills
damage my kidneys,
my brain,
and my heart?

I was invited back to record their songs the following day. When I arrived, I brought a human subject consent form. Abacca looked over it, and she said that I was the first person to bring such a document. Because funeral preparations were still ongoing, only five women were present; they were elderly. They took time to discuss the form with Abacca, and then they signed it. I set up my recorder and sat opposite from the women. As they were singing, their voices would weave in and out of audibility. The precarity of the women's harmonies was particularly pronounced during one song about their acoustemological experience with a Geiger counter, which "said" that radiation was "in" their bodies and their lands, confirming what they knew and forcing them to relocate, thereby defying the US wishes. In the midst of the funeral for their sister, who had shared the experience of being a DOE "human subject" without a consent form and without the presence of younger women who shared in the collectivized (not merely collective) memory and who, Abacca told me, had "better voices" because they did not have "thyroid" (operations), the elderly women shared their feminine voices positioned as human (radiation) subjects. My experience of listening to these women struggle to harmonize, or even sing for that matter, greatly shaped my research. The radiation that was forced into the lives of the Rongelapese women (and other Marshallese populations), I realized, was not only insidious and insensible, causing the need for thyroid operations and cancer treatments (introducing more radiation into their lives), but it literally reworked the musical material and formal constraints of songs. The forcible intrusion of radiation and the people who managed it (often to their detriment) had also significantly altered the expressive possibilities of this culture.[4]

MUSICAL PETITIONS, NATIONAL SECURITY, BIOETHICS

This chapter focuses on the ways in which Rongelapese women instrumentalize their singing practices to guide, to empower, and to draw attention to the injuries sustained at the level of their throats and appeal for declassification such that they can mend themselves. Western medicine views the heart as central to an individual's circulatory system, the system that is vital to an individual's health and prospects of immunity from certain diseases. A human's circulatory system is defined, by medical terms, as "closed." In Western medical thought and philosophical thought from Hobbes onward, immunity and the body are matters of an individual, and intermediaries, such as the state and inoculations, are needed to deprive the individual from the communities that might expose him or her to lethal diseases, effects, and so forth.[5] There was a sensory disconnect between cultures, given that the senses are what makes us human and the Rongelapese were treated as senseless or with only partial sense and partial voice. Rongelapese, although they asked questions about the biomedical tests done on them, were not asked for their consent, nor were they informed about the nature of the procedures. As the Advisory Committee on Human Radiation Experiments (ACHRE) stressed, "For the most part, consent for tests and treatment appears to have been neither sought nor obtained."[6]

US national security has been used to justify experimentation on and classification of Rongelapese lives, founding the bioethics through which they are expected to remain incorporated. The Rongelapese women were part of the human radiation experiments or national security that founded the bioethical guidelines that were mandated by my university (the human subject consent form); these guidelines depoliticized my relation with the Rongelapese women. The women's voice(lessness) became guidance to displace "informant" speech acts of the written in shifts that concerned the lack of consent and material violences used to incorporate the women. As such, I focus this chapter on notions of voice(lessness) as guidance in differently gendered spaces, for I occupied spaces of both women's empowerment and those historically dominated by the male figure, such as the researcher—recalling how our voices shift, depending on the relational context. The feminine voice is the voice of guidance, which emerges, I argue, in its voicelessness as well, which speaks to the lack of democracy and freedoms for movements: musical, vocal, and otherwise.

The Rongelapese women have been one group that has been marginalized and made vulnerable because they were the closest to Bravo. Whereas some of the displaced Rongelapese live in Mejatto in Kwajalein Atoll, others live in Majuro Atoll, primarily Batkan Village, which is where Lijon stayed with some of her family. The Rongelapese women collectivized in a group they called "*Iju in Eañ*" (the North Star), which is a reference to Rongelap. Lijon explained that both groups have the name in Mejatto and Majuro because from both locations they can follow the North Star, Limanman (Polaris), and find their way to Rongelap. When it comes to nuclear violence, the women remind their chiefs, politicians, and the entire audience that they are the affective force of the nation, that they embody the guiding principles of the North Star. The women resound guidance and stability through precarious harmonies; this is the stability of reclaiming of their bodies, particularly their bodies as sites of injury and of beauty, of struggle and strength, of voices that harmonize and voices that, produced through the rigors of the neocolonial harmonic system, cannot be or refuse to be harmonized. The issue has been that their musical petitions are not being listened to correctly. Petitions guide listening to spaces of hearing.

Reflecting on the dissonances created by gendered and political oppositionality (see chapter 1) in the heteropatriarchal system, a Rongelapese woman named Lemeyo asked a newspaper reporter, "How do you think a man can get his title? It comes from his mother, but now I don't know if men are systematically trying to change this. . . . Sometimes from my observations, it's like the men are pushing the women down. They belittle women and say women can't move up." This directional impress, this gendered violence through which depression happens, impinges on the bodies through which voices resonate. The Rongelapese women, as the Northern

Star, and through their voices offer direction to spaces of hearing their femininities, often in (non)human entanglements—from biomedical to Indigenous. They have been at the forefront of official Nuclear Remembrance Day activities. In this chapter I listen to how singers remediate nuclear remembrance through musical registers tied to the condition of the throat. I show how spaces wherein masculinist pressures have impinged upon their bodies as that which has decayed gendered complementarity or their notions of harmony registered in their depressed and silenced voices and *būromōj* (cut, desensitized throat, depression), and I share how they sing their fullness or harmony in communal spaces in which they relate through a feeling of togetherness in *bōro wōt juon*.

WUTMI AND *BŌRO WŌT JUON*

A few days after Rokko's funeral service, I attended another Rongelapese women's performance, which was part of a dinner concert for WUTMI (Women United Together Marshall Islands), which is a women's nonprofit that formed in 1983, the year of the UN plebiscite on the COFA. WUTMI, like the Rongelapese women's group and the Rongelapese women's collaborations with the Utrikese women, marks an important move to create spaces for women's reempowerment within the heteropatriarchal and masculine militarism through which the RMI materialized its political voice in an international milieu of political voices with the male tenor. Women's organizations and contributions to Marshallese literature, creative arts, education, and national health are vital components and interrelated to the ways in which the country deals with negative foreign imports. As chapter 1 shows, not only was a male vococentrism sculpted in US nuclear mediations and the nation-building projects of the RMI, but women were also humiliated, pushed aside, and violated in ways that remain difficult to discuss. The networked solidarity of women's organizations through which women carve spaces to be heard in national political spaces has created the space in which the first female president in the Pacific was elected in 2016 in the Marshall Islands. This is amid the poems, stories, books, songs, place-names, and other inscriptions across the archipelago that animate reminders of the mother-son connection that gives "voice" to Marshallese lineage (matrilineage).

During the WUTMI events, the Rongelapese women's performance emphasized the fullness of the feminine voice. I was even pulled into the performance by a woman who danced over, grabbed me, and pulled me to the front in the middle of their set. Completely disoriented, I just tried to move with them and listen to both older and younger women singing "*Kajjitok.*" In this performance, even if one woman's voice slightly went out, the rest of the women were there to share the responsibility of singing, and the song continued. The fullness of voice contrasted with my previous interview in which the separation of a few women from their community to sing with microphones and other mediating technologies, asking them to agree to my university's consent form (a type of depoliticization), and my guiding questions that would return to the traumatic breaks within the socio-scientific research space were conducive to hearing those breaks. And it was through hearing those breaks that I was able to listen to the communal work that the women effectuated and negotiated depending on the context. For example, at the funerary remembrance at which footage of Rokko was played along with Puff Daddy's "I'll Be Missing You" (1997), the Rongelapese women sang "*Kajjitok*" for nearly seven minutes with numerous vocal breaks, some of which seemed to be cadential until the women recouped and continued singing their questions that they have been asking—that Rokko had asked and was asking perhaps through them—and pointing to the consequential breaks, the cracks in the system that led them to that moment, namely, the moment of missing their dear, departed sister who had, at one point, held up a sign in protest of the agency to which this song was addressed: "DOE = Death on Earth."

IMPACTS OF RADIATION ON WOMEN AND CHILDREN

The US nuclear weapons testing program affected the Rongelapese women disproportionately. Women are valued as the anchors of Marshallese society, given that traditional social and land rights are matrilineal. After the nuclear testing program, a majority of the Rongelapese developed thyroid cancer and had to have their thyroids, thyroid nodules, or lymph material removed. Given that women are more susceptible to thyroid disease and cancer than are men, the change in their vocal range and timbre resulting from the surgeries was more noticeable. Gender divisions are important to social structure as well, and this is included in women's ability to sing "like a woman," more specifically in the soprano range. Marshallese from other atoll populations would hear the Rongelapese women speaking or singing and stigmatize them as *ribaaṃ* ("bombed people") or *tyroit* (a person having thyroid disease).

The demeaning terms speak to the uninformed Marshallese population that contributed to Rongelapese "experience[s] of profound humiliation, marginalization, and stigmatization as a result of their injuries and reproductive problems."[7] A non-Rongelapese man recalled a "love song" that detailed the unrequited love of the singer and his Rongelapese love interest, for the latter was "poisoned," so the singer could not become involved in a relationship. "Our radiation exposure was so embarrassing," recalled Norio Kebenli. "Whenever we went to the hospital to get any kind of care, people would always point at us; they knew who we were. Many people used to say things like 'Don't marry the Rongelapese because they are sick and your kids will be sick.' . . . The embarrassment continues today."[8] Kebenli continued to say that a number of Rongelapese youth graduated recently and would not admit to being from Rongelap. Given the importance of one's matrilineal kinship networks, this failure to admit being from Rongelap further genders the shame involved through the denial of matrilineal voice.

Vocal articulation of this suffering became increasingly difficult as the majority of the women had a number of operations on their thyroid and in some cases were forced to have the thyroid removed.[9] The surgeries affected their voices, especially because of the vulnerability of the vocal cords exposed to repeat thyroid surgeries.[10] Laurie Stras has explored vocal disfluency by "integrating both social and medical models" of disability: "In the case of the voice, the significance of vocal disruption of damage to an individual will be in proportion to his or her reliance to vocal function for daily activity, and the more significant it is, the more disabled that person may be seen in afflicted by vocal pathology."[11] Stras's work positions the damage as a matter of the individual voice and one that is all the more compromised the more one works with the voice in daily routines. She speaks to individual pathology as a matter of the self, the self within the context of the environment that produces, following the cultural-social and medical model of disability, vocal pathology via vocal disruption.

One medical study explains the development of thyroid nodules:

> Nine years after the accident [Bravo's fallout in 1954], a 12-year old Rongelap girl was found to have developed a nodule in her thyroid gland. Within the next 3 years, 15 of the 22 Rongelap people who had been under the age of 10 years at the time of exposure had developed thyroid lesions. At that time, the first thyroid nodule in an exposed Rongelap adult appeared and in 1969, 15 years after the accident, the first thyroid nodule appeared among the exposed people of Utirik [sic]. It has become clear that thyroid

2.1 Atomic Energy Commission doctor Robert A. Conard checks a woman for thyroid abnormalities, 1970, Brookhaven National Laboratory.

abnormalities—which include benign and malignant thyroid tumors and thyroid failure—are the major late effects of the radiation received by the exposed Marshallese.[12]

Thyroid surgeries and lymph-node removal can result in dry vocal cords that do not have the proper pliability to manipulate good pitch. The nerve that controls vocal-cord closing runs along the top of the thyroid gland, and it is therefore susceptible to trauma during surgical invasion. Repeat surgeries may cause laryngeal neuropathy (roaring, hoarseness, vocal/glottal fry when singing). Tumor growth and/or thyroid growth abnormality leads to surgical reception, which can tug or push on the vocal cords, leading to weakness. In addition, radiation directly to the tissue cluster alters mucus production. The altered mucus production often results in dry mouth and throat, leading to vocal inefficiency. Moreover, fibrotic process (the interruption of tissue production) leads to scarring and consequently reduction of vocal control.[13]

Victor Bond, who accompanied Eugene Cronkite on the Project 4.1 mission, told the Advisory Committee staff that the Marshallese exposed group "seemed to be perfectly healthy people [, but] we were well aware of the latent period, and that they might well become ill later." (See figure 2.1.) He followed the recognition of delayed onset of radiogenic illness with a reflection on the thyroid issues, which the Advisory Committee deemed the "most significant late effect of radiation among Marshallese," and it is one they note is particularly widespread, increasing in incidence from the northern atolls to the southern atolls, such as Jaluit, which neighbors Kili Island, where the majority of exiled Bikinians have lived since 1951.[14] Bond continued: "And quite frankly, I'm still a little embarrassed about the thyroid. [T]he dogma at the time was that the thyroid was a radio-resistant organ.... It turned out they had very large doses of iodine ... to the thyroid." Cronkite backed the statement: "There was nothing in the medical literature ... to predict that one would have a relatively high incidence of thyroid disorders."[15]

Some women became temporarily mute, and others would refrain from speaking—more specifically, singing—from fear of hearing their altered voices:

> We used to love singing! . . . Personally, I don't sing in public anymore because people stare at me. It's like we're in a constant state of puberty where our voices keep cracking.[16]
>
> After the bomb, we can't harmonize anymore. Everyone's voice is a bass, and there are no more sopranos amongst us. We have no interest in singing anymore. People make fun of us when we do and say "*Etyroit men ne*" ["That thing near you is thyroid" or "That thing of a person has a thyroid problem."][17]
>
> At the time they cut my throat, I thought they—well, I don't really know, I really can't sing anymore, but I want to sing again, but now I can't. . . . My voice won't go high anymore. Is that not from the contamination?[18]
>
> It was a while after I had the surgery that I was able to sing again, and it wasn't just my voice, but it happened with the voices of all those who had surgery on their throats. . . . I made sure to ask the doctors about it, though, to make sure they did a good job so that I would be able to sing again because that is my only talent—singing—and I needed to be able to sing again.[19]

These statements expose the resonant, embodied voice as a barometer of communal health via the collective throat (bōro wōt juon) that materializes the relational voices. Communal self-care is communal self-auscultation; it is a mode of Marshallese literacy that understands the resonant voices as processes of the interconnected (and also severed) consubstantial throat. Social balance and gender complementarity are made audible through musical harmony, yet the Rongelapese, through their nuclear journey, have been gendered and dispossessed of their Indigenous, land-based societal balance. These processes render impossible social balance and gender complementarity particularly when the voices are produced by the Western system (harmony) in the context of lyrics and performance that makes the performers attuned to such fissures. The American missionaries introduced harmony as part of a Western separation of the genders (classification) in the nineteenth century. This gendered aesthetic and moral education instilled notions of what it meant to sound and sing like a woman or man, where men ideologically occupy the ground and carry the weight in the musical and social relationship. In Marshallese culture, women are *dedo* (heavy), and it is important to carry the weight of the mother (of women) to harness the winds and waves, the breath and spirit (emotions).

To hear Rongelapese women's harmonies as precarious means the overarching structure systematizes them as precarious. Moreover, the silencing of a characteristically female vocal quality—the ability to sing as a soprano—also points to another devastating repercussion, another form of silencing, of the nuclear testing program: the severe impact of radiation on the reproductive capacity of women. And it gives us pause to recall another moment of the reduction of women to their reproductive abilities (to reproduce humans) under the missionaries, which further emplaces women into so-called domestic spheres. Prior to missionary encounters, Marshallese had, for example, their own methods of human population control because population increases affected the security and health of the entire atoll. Taking women's reproductive rights away, in our contemporary society, creates this restricted movement-as-body, freedom-as-voice reality where voice can protest those confines in which the politicized marked body is trapped (as non–Standard Man). Voice in this respect is pathological.

The US government intervened in global reproduction rights with the detonations of these megaton weapons, and closest to the core, they restricted the human-centered reproductive rights of women (as well as the reproductive rights of their matrilineage, a part of the *bwij* and the *bwijen*). After the 1954 test, many Rongelapese women had multiple miscarriages, gave birth to severely deformed babies who would die shortly after the birth, or had to undergo hysterectomies. The inability to produce offspring generates, in Jennifer Cognard-Black's terms, "the silence of lost generations and as a result, lost history."[20] Taking this statement outside of the human-centered terms we often conceive of (and in), ancestral land offers the already born humans their connections with the silenced generations, the elders and their spirits that are now trees or coral heads or rocks or birds, for example. The palpable din of nuclear silences grows increasingly loud when we also remember the intense shame and guilt women felt when they were unable to birth (healthy) children. Silence functioned as a form of cultural censorship as many women, ashamed, humiliated, and fearing stigmatization, would conceal their pain. An Utrikese woman, Minji, explained:

> After Bravo, I had many *jibun* [miscarriages], and also several of my babies who were healthy at the time they were born died before they were a year old after getting sick. Altogether, I lost four babies. My son Winton was born just one year after the bomb, and he has had two operations on his throat for thyroid cancer. I believe Winton got his sickness from me because he nursed from my breast and my milk contains poison from the bomb.[21]

The silence of the lost generations therefore becomes internalized by the women as *theirs*: their productions or reproductions that must stand in for the sounds of a healthy throat or a healthy, living child. Minji's testimony recalls the routes through which radiation passes maternally and materially. Her words also touch on the loss of the figure of the mother as protector and nurturer under nuclear colonialism that takes masculine, militaristic protection as its frame. So too do the terms of militaristic "security" and neoliberal "development" rhetoric of "self-help" and "dependency" echo through Minji's self-blame.

At the time of this writing, the Centers for Disease Control and Prevention has a specific website page for "Radiation Emergencies: Breastfeeding," which explains that radiation is passed through the breast milk and gives women information on how to accommodate breastfeeding if they have been exposed to radiation or are undergoing radiation treatments.[22] On the website, which is in English and Spanish, having access to a radio or a method of being "tuned in" is important. The RMI government did not invest in "women's health," which, under US development projects, is also marked as "exceptional" or supplementary. It has been on women to shoulder the responsibility for radiation exposure, going so far as to raise funds in the late 1990s for a mammogram machine for the national hospital, which was not supported by the government. This is part of the neoliberal regime of economic accumulation, where some voices resound over the nation while others are disenvoiced.

The system is more complex than "blame" registered as individual because corporations and the US government cannot *feel* blame; they become accountable only through punitive measures. Ultimately, the structures of feeling and expression absorbed by the women are not noticed by the United States, which created the structures and developed the nuclear weapons and made decisions to conduct experiments that made people like Minji and Winton sick. The US government gained the resources from the bomb that poisoned Minji's breast milk, but even this statement is contested by modern medical reports that often individualize cancer and other illnesses within neoliberalism through the labeling of pathology as "genetic," which, like radiation, remains insensible to most people. These are partial truths, partial declassifications of the public secret of structural inequities and the power-knowledge complexes that sustain them. There were enough resources expended on Bikini Atoll alone to preventatively move all the populations of the northern atolls.[23] However, to develop those atolls further from the "centers" of industry, to bring them in as "productive" and "reproductive" nuclear colonial subjects, they were left to mutate intergenerationally. Their voices were less than meaningful in this respect. The labor of making radiation sound is the attunement to one's interconnected body, and it is the strength of feeling that body in its compromised processes and sounding it against the so-called insensible (maternal strength, radioactive milk).

Thus, for Minji to speak her fears is power because it connects her: a "case" that might be considered a "special circumstance" (an Indigenous woman irradiated by Bravo/aftermath on an island in the middle of the Pacific) to the nuclear silences experienced, to varying degrees, by populations worldwide and persons who are tasked with imagining that cancer—or any disease—is the fault of their genetics and taking on the burden of paying for remedial work, such as radiation therapy or counseling. Medical ethnomusicology must account for the gridded soundings of neoliberal economic regimes that profit from individualized pathology or pathological individuation and striate voices through "fault lines" (blame, sounded in speech and musical systems) that become part of the expressive modalities through which "illness categories" are performed and maintained.[24] Cultural responses to these fault lines differ. For Rongelapese women, they have become cracks in the gridded surface that inspire vocal remediations. The Utrikese and Rongelapese women sang the DOE song together for the US governmental agency. The questions in the song punctuate the nuclear silences in silent relief, if only temporarily, that recognizes the "fault lines" are not caused by a dirty woman's body but rather by dirty weapons and the government that deploys them. Transposed to Marshallese sensibilities, the sounds that marked the presence of radiation were internalized as aural displacements and were personalized as embodied dissonances. If hearing allows for transformation and sensibility allows for change, the compromised female singing voice resonantly vibrated the throat, the center of the spirit, and registered the harbinger of sickness, death, and silence.[25] The injured throat was therefore used as a warning signal within the reproducible linguistic coordinates that mark loss and mnemonically allow for sensorial recovery of customary practices, dislocated but not dismembered.

OPERATION EXODUS

After being presented in 1982 with the DOE document "Meaning of Radiation in the Northern Marshall Islands" and with abnormalities at birth, miscarriages, and aberrant illnesses, such as leukemia and thyroid cancers, becoming the norm, the Rongelapese appealed to the US government for assistance with relocation. Ultimately, they were denied help. After almost thirty years living in nuclear waste and being studied as human radiation experiments (although they wouldn't find this out until 1993), on May 17, 1985, the Greenpeace environmental activist organization's *Rainbow Warrior* arrived at Rongelap Atoll on what would be its final journey: "Operation Exodus." When the *Rainbow Warrior* was stationed in the lagoon, donning a "Nuclear Free Pacific" banner, a Rongelapese boat came to greet it. Activist David Robie recalls the banner that the eleven Rongelapese were holding up—"We love the future of our kids"—while women sang the first Marshallese anthem: "I love my home island, where I was born / I will never leave it / This is my home, my only home / And it's better that I die on it."[26] The *Rainbow Warrior* helped move Rongelapese to a small island, Mejato, in the corner of Kwajalein Atoll. The US government lambasted the Rongelapese for defying its assessment of the atoll (that it was safe to inhabit) and moving away, and this information was published in the national newspaper, the *Marshall Islands Journal*, on May 3, 1985, coinciding with increasing political tensions between the United States and the RMI over the emergent COFA agreement. However, the Rongelapese saw their health as their primary concern, and they refused to return to their homeland, stressing the United States' deceptive ignorance of the pervasive illnesses in their community. The newspaper responded: "The U.S. treats Rongelap as if it doesn't exist, ignoring or covering up the problem, [Jeban Riklon, Kwajalein senator] charged: The U.S. spent billions of dollars on its nuclear testing program which contaminated his islands, but won't help them now that the problem is getting worse."[27] Even people who were not on Rongelap or nearby when Castle Bravo was detonated suffered radiation-induced illnesses. A number of women confirmed that they were away from Rongelap in 1954 but shared stories of becoming ill and having reproductive complications. Sarah, a Rongelapese woman born in the 1970s, recounted the frequency with which the doctors would visit Rongelap, collect samples, and dispose of the medical waste in the lagoon. As a child, Sarah and the other children would collect the syringes that washed ashore and play with them. She remains unclear about whether it was the waste, the contamination, or both that have caused her medical problems. Like the currents that washed the syringes to shore and carried nuclear waste to the Rongelapese, the community would harness the power of the currents: oceanic, airwave, and emotional. Their appeals enabled them to enlist Japanese scientists to determine levels of contamination, which prompted the antinuclear community to help.

The relocation was less a victory than a testament to Rongelapese self-determination. Within the Marshall Islands and the antinuclear activist community, it was publicized and made a loud statement that Rongelapese and, by extension, Marshallese were holding the United States accountable for its deceptions and damages: the United States needed to do more to help clean up the radiation from Rongelap, and the Rongelapese and other groups were motivated to curb the ramifications of nuclear phenomena. The US government did not respond enthusiastically. If relocation to Mejato in the northern part of Kwajalein Atoll was difficult, life there proved even harder. On rented land, basic resources were not available, and they had to construct their own homes. They literally were building off not much more than memories, which some documented in songs celebrating their togetherness and fortitude amid what seemed almost an unbelievable turn of events. Groups from nearby islands came to greet the Rongelapese on Mejato, and when others from around the Marshall Islands heard the news on the radio of the Rongelapese hardships, they would take the long journey from their home atolls to bring food, kerosene, lamps, soap, and other useful items. The Rongelapese would prepare food and sing songs that stressed their reasons for relocation (among others) as a gesture of gratitude, such as *"Ta in eṃōkaj aer ba"* ("What Are They Talking About?"), composed by a Rongelapese woman shortly after the community evacuated their homeland and moved to Mejato.[28]

Ta in emōkaj aer ba

I. *Ta in emōkaj aer ba*
bwe ta in ear walok
rej ba nan koj bwe jen emakūt

jen aelōñ in Rongelap
bwe ekakumkum emakit in ad
bwe ebbo ilo <u>computa</u> ej ba
"eḷap an <u>too much plu</u>,
<u>radiation</u> ippān"

II. *Ta eo in eḷap aer ba*
itok wot jen <u>177</u>
Na, oh, emakit lok
jen aelōñ in Rongelap
bwe ekakumkum emakit in ad
bwe ebbo ilo <u>computa</u> ej ba
"eḷap an <u>too much plu</u>,
<u>radiation</u> ippān"

What Are They Talking About?

I. What are they talking about?
What happened?
They say we have to move
from the island of Rongelap
because there are many dangers, we move
because the computer [Geiger counter] says
"there is too much plutonium,
irradiated within."

II. What are they talking about that is so big?
It comes from 177
I, oh, have to move
from the island of Rongelap
because there are many dangers, we move
because the computer [Geiger counter] says
"there is too much plutonium,
irradiated within."

The song begins with the marker of nuclear silences (abstracted absence): the figure of the question. The United States wanted the Rongelapese to remain on their atoll, and it discounted the Rongelapese and its own publication (the 1982 DOE report). The Geiger counter resounds the near inaudibility of radiation. The machine's voice is a sensible reminder of the Rongelapese voices that were made to sound radiation (through thyroid surgeries ten years prior). The Geiger counter thus gestures to the consubstantial *burō* (radiation within throat and land). With respect to the Geiger counter, or the "computa" ("the computer says there is too much plutonium"), an emphasis is placed on the speech of the machine. It *talks*; it "says," showing how the Geiger counter has a political voice that is more highly valued than the women with respect to their appeals for evacuation. Yet it "says" or continues to speak only when remediated by Rongelapese voices in song. In terms of evacuation and exile, silence is written into the delivery: what matters is what the computer says, not what the Rongelapese say. And if we take the limitations of language seriously and therefore posit that truth is not dependent on linguistic constructs, then this silence is in part superficial. This silence, or a gesture toward this silence, can be reemployed in the song to underscore the historical experiences that have denied Rongelapese agency, but it becomes the task of the Rongelapese to *voice* precisely that point. There is an ambiguity about where the Geiger counter locates the "plutonium"—within them or the land—and this ambiguity shares the contentious issue. Americans refused to recognize Indigenous cultural patterns and diets, making the Rongelapese consubstantial and even more susceptible to radiation intake.

The song's message would travel back with the other atoll communities, each circulation generating momentum to help the displaced community that suffered from medical complications. The circulation of a song depends on the ability to resist a melancholic stasis that results from mourning while preserving the sociopolitical function of mourning. This is of the utmost importance when we consider that the difficulties in the women's ability to pass down legends, stories, and songs rooted in the land without the sensible geographical markers have been compounded by their restricted access to their traditional means of healing. The song works with the capacities of who, or what, can speak and who or what can move.

"*Ta in emōkaj aer ba*" presents the changing circumstances of Rongelapese commitments to sounding out their relationship with their land in the three decades since Bravo. The singers perform a vocal remediation of the sounds of imperial instruments that intervene in sounding their lands through their bodies: the Geiger counter and scientific terms such as *plu* (plutonium). This sounds to the world the new destructive use value associated with the Marshall Islands, with Rongelapese bodies and lands where the last navigational school was located.[29] The symbolism of this destruction, the Indigenous agentive mobilities registered as anxious movements in "*Ta in emōkaj aer ba*," vocally remediates the song's contour with a final verse that I cannot share because it is untranslatable beyond the Rongelapese community and their singing practices of gratitude to the ancestral land. The United States and Americans like me cannot probe those depths for meaning about nuclear knowledge production. What we can hear are the radiogenic silences that, like genetic materials, mutate the formal constructs of radiation songs as generative interruptive mechanisms of near-audibility, emptying out their responsibilities of sound for us professionals while keeping the tenor, the tactile hold, on nuclear epistemologies as a petition to keep being heard.

I first came across the Rongelapese women's voiced morphologies of professionalized erasure the first time I heard "*Ta in emōkaj aer ba*," although I didn't realize that I had heard this. Following my return to Shirley's house the day after I met the Rongelap women, Abacca was present with about six women (five older women and Shirley), who were continuing the funeral preparations. They sang the first two songs softly with Abacca, who explained they would sing one more song. For about four and a half minutes, the women spoke among themselves, talking about the song with the words "*computa ej ba eḷap an too much plu*," and then they would try to harmonize. They would stop, their voices disentangling from one another, and they would try again. As four and a half minutes worked its way to five, Abacca sensed my confusion, and she explained, "Because they had thyroid operations, they are having problems with their voices. . . . But they're trying. They're trying."

The women, in the middle of preparing for their sister's funeral, had allowed me, apparently the first person to come with consent forms for "human subjects," to interrupt their daily rhythms, which Robert A. Conard also noted that he did during the early medical testing. Our modes of research, without clear returns and operations of envoicing remediations, return pain and anxiety, I believe, and the affective figure of the būromōj formalizes in the fault lines that rhythmically sever communications. Although this "trying" is a struggle, a will to have the power to communicate, and this will challenges, pushing up against the limitations of language and all other confines to articulate the Rongelapese nuclear experience, voicelessness becomes a protective mechanism to amplify exploitative listening practices of the near-inaudible, which was our context for the interview: death on Earth, what Rokko and her sisters called the DOE. When the women were fragmented, when they were isolated, when they were tired, and when they were sick, they did not have the energy to remember their painful subject roles. Bōrō wōt juon disabled any systemic resilience wherein complete silence or complete sounding was acoustically intangible, and the only vibratory relations that sustained us in the moment were the emptying out of harmony and its resonant promises.

"JUON JOTIININ" (ONE NIGHT), ARCHIPELAGIC KNOWLEDGE

By 2009, the Nuclear Claims Tribunal had run out of funding. The Marshallese who moved to Hawaii were taken off Medicaid, creating an uproar in the capital. And I found myself in a routine where every other week I would meet up with Lijon, the prolific Rongelapese singer/songwriter and antinuclear activist I had first met a year earlier. A short prayer of thanks in Marshallese and a meal always prefaced our conversations. Lijon provided lunch, which usually consisted of spaghetti (my staple offering) and fish, donuts, rice, ramen, pancakes with *jekaro* (coconut syrup), and diet sodas. We would sit on the floor or her bed as I listened to her childhood memories of Rongelap, her recent frustration with the RMI government, and her continued anger with the US government for its lack of responsiveness to the health needs of her community. Daily life away from her homeland, dependence on Western medication, and listening for answers that never seemed to come from the DOE were all reminders of the insidious violence that bolstered US nuclear hegemony and has continued to put pressure on the recently sovereign nation.

During one meal, Lijon took out some papers and presented a visual accompaniment, which became part of the musical histories she shared with me. One was a large foldout map of Rongelap Atoll so that I could see the different areas and have a better mental image when she spoke of its meaningful topographical features. Then she brought out an article by National Claims Tribunal (NCT) Public Advocate Bill Graham, an American, called "The Pursuit of Truth." The article, a collection of writings about John Anjain, the Rongelapese magistrate during Bravo, appeared in the *Marshall Islands Journal* on July 30, 2004, a month after COFA II became official. It was an obituary of sorts that concluded with Graham's statement, "Yokwe Yuk, John. May you rest in peace. You deserved so much better." Lijon pointed out the section in the article that quoted the 1957 NBC newsreel, which showed how John and his family (by extension of US logic, all Marshallese) were juxtaposed with American male laboratory scientists. She proposed that the United States treated the Rongelapese people like "guinea pigs" (a common metaphor in the community) because Americans thought of them as "savages" to be disposed, and she conveyed how seriously she takes the language that was used against her people to rationalize the brutality and violence that irrevocably altered their lives. Lijon explained to me the stakes of the words that were circulated as public rationale for an atomic archive of words (and worlds) born secret or kept. She then emphasized the importance of her words and her voice in combating this betrayal. Lijon once said, "Sometimes I wonder if our people were born to evacuate," and the idea of US nuclear incorporation as a thorough evacuation, the near-inaudible series of removals, made her comment particularly poignant.[30]

She grew up with the bomb. On March 1, 1954, she was on Ailingnae Atoll with her grandparents. It was her eighth birthday, and they were going to have a picnic that day. Lijon was one of the children who learned stories, chants, and other protected knowledge from the elders, and she also was tasked with taking care of the elders. Instead of knowledge transmission and celebration on her birthday, Lijon had memories of the bomb seared into her very being, her becoming. As a consequence of radiation exposure, Lijon has had many health complications, miscarriages, and operations on her thyroid. Of her experiences, she says, "Having suffered multiple losses when bearing children, having uncontrolled weight fluctuations, having memory loss and tight curling fingers, having nearly lost my voice, I can say that nothing is more important than having my health and my voice to sing."[31] Lijon recognized the impossible separation of having health and "a voice to sing." She previously told me that "a home without music is a sick home," and she said that when she was very sick, she stopped singing and listening to music altogether. Further, she could not sleep, and she "hated" it when people would talk. She could not process, and she was irritable. Without health she drops out from the community, she is literally *nañiñmej* (toward death, in Marshallese) and not facing life, those living around her. Lijon said that when she "got better," she slowly taught herself how to play instruments and make music again.

With Lijon, there were not many silent moments. In the span of six or seven hours, she would tell stories compiled from the materials she had gathered throughout her life's journey, including climbing trees, knowledge of medicinal massage, living and playing music in the United States, and her struggles incurred by the US violence and RMI political collusion. A self-professed "good politician," she amplified her songs with these stories, each one including lyrics that she chose to translate or not, and sometimes she would recite chants with explanation and without direct translation (for which there was none). She was scheduled to go to the United States to testify in front of Congress, but the RMI presidential impeachment had the national government tied up. "Another opportunity to share, to testify, lost," she lamented.[32] With that opportunity gone, Lijon provided the opportunity to share her songs with me.

Political testimony necessitates the informative mode because it is a matter of evidence, but the narrative mode is archived in songs that perform the work of memory (*kememej*) as a "meta-sense."[33] Lijon composed songs, such as "*Juon jotiinin*" ("One Night"), for the purposes of shaping collective memory and thus vocal remediation of fragmented temporalities, symbolized by her relationship with her homeland. The memory in the performance of the song is the memory of lost knowledge as experiential continuity. I asked Lijon to explain why she wrote the song, and she responded:

> I composed this song by myself because of the time I would sit and spend time contemplating the bomb. I realized there needed to be a song about the bombs dropped on Bikini and Enewetak because it is something I grew up with. I used to dream at night about the bomb, and in my dreams I would see the bomb drop on an island, and I would be the only one standing, with all the fire, and there weren't any people, and so I would be scared. I would awaken and cry because I was so scared, and I'd wake up because the flash of the bomb hurt my eyes. I would cry so much, and that is the reason I wrote this song.[34]

Lijon's statement demonstrates her thoughtful approach to musical composition. Like many of the respected composers, Lijon composed the songs alone after much preparation and deliberation, sometimes over years, over a lifetime. She would then share her songs with the community, and they would sing them. The songs are thus "collectively" composed insofar as they are performatively realized, but there are individual composers who know how to listen to the world and render it poetically. Here, Lijon shares the impetus as one of terror. She was traumatized by the bomb, and it returned to her at night in her dreams, precluding other visions and realizations. The nuclear silencing of her life, her future, and her health was caused by the fire that gnawed her land and the flash that hurt her eyes. The flash was a sensory resonance of the thermonuclear explosion that returned in painful shards that occluded her vision, forcing her to wake up in fear and crying. She explains that she wrote the *al in keememej* (memory song) because she would cry so much. By composing this song, the bomb exists in her memory, but it can be sung as an object of contemplation. She could collectivize and give voice, vocal remedial practices of objectification, to her community's pain.

"*Juon Jotenin*" has an additive form. There are two distinct parts that were composed at two separate times, almost a decade apart, when Lijon believed that her homeland and the memory of her homeland were slipping from the collective consciousness. The first verse is a composite of the chorus and the second verse. The chorus, which she composed while living on Majuro Atoll in 2004, followed. This was a year after COFA was amended into Compact II, and it was the fiftieth anniversary of the Bravo test, when the discourse of loss was reactivated in the service of politics. Lijon offers a mix of unique experience and the radiation language that would be intelligible in the public discourse. I have underlined the words that belong to the nuclear-centered language and make audible semantic and affective connections.

I. *Juon jọtiinin iar kiki*
im ettōñake ijo jiku im
aō lamoren,
Eo rej ṇa etan Jelaen Aelōñ,
juon āne emakelok,
Aelōñ in Bikini Atoll,
ijo U.S. *ear kōṃṃan kōmelmel ie.*

I. One night I was sleeping
on the porch of my place,
of my homeland,
They call it Jelaen Island,
it's an isolated island near
the atoll of "Bikini Atoll"
where the US conducted [nuclear] tests.

When she performed the song for me to record, she began by arpeggiating a chord on her guitar, making sure that her instrument was in the standard guitar tuning. She repeated the gesture one more time before establishing a consistent rhythm six-eight meter for two measures. Lijon sang softly with a steadfast conviction. Her voice cracked slightly on the first word, and as she continued to sing and strum the guitar, she encountered moments of hoarseness and vocal instability. Lijon would push through these moments of grainy timbre, which would result in a soft vocal waver. These dynamics shaped the song, which to my ear sounds reminiscent of a lullaby. Melodic transcriptions of the song belie the internal rhythms as "sentient elements," transformed as timbre and fortitude to endure outside the limits of acoustical vibrations. The refrain dates endurance as survival.

> CH: Ilo Ṃaaj juon raan in 'fifty-four
> Juon mejatoto enana
> Eḷap jorrān ear walok
> Iar ilbōk im ruj kōn aō jañ
> Iar jab loe ṃaan kōn dānnin
> kōmjaalal.

> On the day of March 1 of 'fifty-four
> A bad atmosphere
> There were big problems
> I was startled and woke up crying
> I couldn't see clearly (look forward)
> because of my tears.

As Lijon continued, the song's texture layered a continuum of silences that spans the spectrum of voice (voiced language that represents the silences caused by the bomb) and voicelessness (the literal moments that Lijon's voice "failed" her or, I should say, the literal moments that the failures of modern justice [as a regime of silence] were formalized by Lijon in her singing voice as acoustical breakage, or roughness). When Lijon's voice lowered and sounded a grainy, rough vocal timbre, she worked through her spirit, the breath and throat muscles, to transform this timbre into a sweet, airy, almost ephemeral tone. Her vocal remediation shares with us a communicative struggle at the physiological level. It reminds us of the durative physical labor of individuals and their communities that fight to sing and share songs as matters of systemic connections and refusals of being reduced to tears, without voice in colonial complacency. Her vocal struggle is decolonial dissonance, which resonates a refusal of resilience to close an injurious system. Rather, by layering the song as a continued composition, she continued the fight within the system she relied on to survive. Her vitality, her spirited *bōro*, in voice resounds the work that goes into sustaining a voice and voices "worth" hearing and, by extension, memories and lives "worth" caring for and remembering. She is the lineage for which she cared, and she protected her voice when her throat was operated on: "I made sure to ask the doctors about it, though, to make sure they did a good job."

After she repeated the chorus twice, she sang the second part of the song. Lijon told me she wrote this part "a long, long time ago while I was living on Ebeye."[35] The second part of the song does not contain the radiation language that became part of public culture in the early 1980s, the first generation of radiation songs. Taking the entire song, *"Juon Jotenin"* is part of the second generation of political protest songs; they are musical petitions that demand the "changed circumstances" and extant nuclear issues are heard in response to the negotiations of Compact II and the Changed Circumstance Petition that was still under review in the US Congress.[36] It topographically maps the continuation of the Rongelapese nuclear exile through an activation of sensory memory wherein the present activates past knowledge in service of energizing present communal action. Consistently incongruous internal rhythms of the performance develop its internal logic of generative decay, following the logic of radiation. This second-generation radiation song thus conveys the double knowledge of the break, the good atmosphere and bad atmosphere, which is articulated to the singer's home routed through the injured throat. This knowledge is conveyed through an experience of narration, or the sharing of experience, in the second half of the song, which is sung as a whole verse entirely in first-person narrative mode in which Marshallese place-naming practices and other communicative forms are embedded. The temporal prior is used in the service of the present becoming, at the textual level, to provide material as fragmented narrative. The fragmented narrative employed in the first half of the song is delivered in first-person narrative mode, but the informative mode of articulation interrupts (fractures) the narration, decaying the narrative and the sharing of experience, perhaps intimating the break in the throat as the fractured community, itself split and being removed from the land. The information (data) that marks the tests is part of the nuclear-centered language:

(II) Juon jotenin iar kiki
im ettonake ijo jiku im
aō lamoren
Eo rej ṇa etan Jelaen Aelōñ,
juon āne emake iaan
ilo kar ettōñak eo aō,

iba wōt ij jijet iarin
aelōñ eo
Im lale aer dedoorlok aḷ,
juon mejatoto eo eṃṃan
Ij roñ iññurñur
ṇo ko
iaar ilbōk im ruj kōn aō
jañ,
ak ikar jab loe ṃaan
kōn dānnin kōmjaalal.

(II) One night I was sleeping
on the porch of my place,
of my homeland
They call it Jelaen Island,
it's a very isolated place
On my porch,
I was sitting on the lagoon side of
the island,
and I saw a sunset,
a good atmosphere
I heard the murmuring of the
waves
I was startled and I woke up
crying,
but I couldn't see clearly (lookforward)
because of my tears.

These are the sensible elements that participate in the grammar of radiation (decay). The fragmented first-person narration as narrative decay, or a muting of the subject in the service of information production, is made audible by both the nuclear-centered language and the poetic device of constructed onomatopoeia. Through her vocal performance Lijon fashions onomatopoeic accounts of restricted data: restriction of sound as data. Lijon abbreviates the year "1954" to "'fifty-four" and sings the words in English. She takes the United States and abbreviates it as "US," as opposed to the Marshallese word for the country: *Amedika*. These moves are therefore political at the sensible level where restricted data are the shared material that forms an affective alliance between Lijon, as the good politician, the vocal representative of her community, and the RMI as intermediary voice in relation to the United States as (governmental) representative of Americans.

The chorus is repeated, and the restricted data are marked again by dating. Both data and dates are part of the restricted histories and the sensory memories that the Rongelapese cannot *share* in total because their bodies and lands are irradiated; they are severed. The shared space of the song, the affective alliance, is created with the intelligible words and sentiments surrounding the bomb and the Americanized site of detonation. The labor of the negative, or the labor of making radiation sound, in which Lijon attaches feelings and movements (including pains of loss and suffering) to discourse, is ultimately unknowable to the non-Rongelapese listener, for although the non-Rongelapese (or non-Marshallese) listener "knows" the bomb through mediated means, such as the radio and the television, she knows them through the poisoned atmosphere of her living lands and her body, as well as her family's experiences, which I discuss in the next chapter. The onomatopoeic or felt soundings of distanced waves caused by the bomb denote the restricted Indigenous knowledge contextualized and territorialized by the United States. It is the memory of isolation that connects the prior to present becoming that Lijon seeks to alter through her activistic song. The motif of crying is amplified, musically, through the intimation of the production of tears that causes the throat to seize up. The song's form demarcates a space where this throat-based injury can resonate through vocal production(e.g., as arrest).

Equivocality can also be heard herein. When we consider the word *isolation*, there is an ambivalence written into it. For the Rongelapese, isolation from being at the center of World War II was positive, and they were afforded the space to listen to the fighting over the radio.[37] Because the war did not devastate her land, Lijon was able to learn navigation and its attendant *roro, al, ikid*, and *bwebwenato* at the traditional navigation school (that was later destroyed by Rongelapese fleeing from Bravo's radiation). The self-determined Rongelapese were isolated from imperial violence, such that the place of her knowledge and her place of knowing (itself sentient) was protected. Now it is isolated from her and her family. The movements she must feel from it come from her embodied knowledges in sounds and in the space to dream, which is overtaken by nightmares, creating further stress and pressure. This separation is detrimental, for neither she (and her family) nor her lands can care for one another. Such breaks are part of the extant and always changing (as does time and knowledge) circumstances; life moves and with it those persons in isolation from their living lands.

These sentient elements, like the internal rhythms of the song, sustain and reveal important mechanisms of survivance marked by the unvoiced voiced political speech of a radiation language that makes the insensible atollscape sensible as part of the nuclear colony.

BŌRŌ WŌT JUON AND IPPĀN DOON: SOUNDING SITES OF RESISTANCE

Every two years WUTMI, the country's umbrella women's collective, holds a General Assembly. The assembly brings together mainly Pacific but also some global organizations focused on women's health and empowerment with respect to their diverse cultures. At the 2008 WUTMI General Assembly, Iju in Eañ engaged in a public performance that drew from Indigenous expression.[38] They performed a collection of songs that drew from customary and colonial harmonic arrangements. In addition to the upbeat Yamaha electronic keyboard and vocal numbers that included jubilant dances, Iju in Eañ shared two chants and the accompanying dances and percussion.

Indigenous movements articulate ways of feeling ancestral land to move through the world, like navigational practices, and shaping land by consubstantial listening. There are customary stories about women and the *aje* drum, which is an important mechanism to sound out Indigenous vitality. In the *jebwa*, a story-song-dance protected by the *iroij*, a handsome male spirit seduces the women by dancing. The women become distracted by this handsome spirit, and they are unable to maintain rhythmic cohesion in their drumming. When the women's drumming falls into dysrhythmia, the "community begins to fall apart," and the iroij gets angry, sends the men after the spirit, and eventually tricks and kills him.[39] Although the story is often read as one about chiefly power and masculinity, I read it about femininity and the female voice in terms of bōrō wōt juon: all one throat/heart (one throat only). Women's Indigenous sounding practices that communicate with the ancestral spirits (humans, land, etc.) keep the community together. Marshallese Indigenous instruments carry with them other relations to power and action by way of sounding, listening, and feeling. Moreover, Indigenous instruments and voices are not dependent on fixed notions of what constitutes a characteristically "female" or "male" voice or sound as taught by the missionaries to Marshallese in an aesthetic education that was dependent on the separation of the senses, genders, and ancestral worlds and the rerouting of Marshallese voices in prescribed harmony. The aje drum is thus an important symbol and tool of women's customary power. Playing the aje drum contributes to alter/native women's health, which is all health for her voice is all voice, the ultimate voice of the lineage. Although some encyclopedic entries relegate women's drumming to "the past" ("women no longer play drums"), this section shows how, at least within the Rongelapese community, the drum, as an element of public culture and performance, did not go away.[40]

The image in figure 2.2 is from Conard's 1992 report, "Fallout: The Experiences of a Medical Team in the Care of a Marshallese Population Accidentally Exposed to Fallout Radiation."[41] The report stresses that the subjects made "lifelong friendships," then talks about the rampant illness, and toward the end mentions a woman by name who had a "brain tumor" that was "successfully removed." She and her four children all had thyroid tumors removed. Conard said one daughter suffered injury. Not twenty years after the report was published, I watched as the Rongelapese community mourned the loss of that woman and her son in the same week. Nuclear incorporation makes reports and spectacles of lives and entertainment out of the connective energies of communities. Note the women in line, drumming, which is labeled as "entertainment." And the children continue to learn about American culture in their staging as part of the society of the spectacle. The women's drumming animates the resounding atoll umbilicals, which are crisscrossed over by the cable umbilicals through which entertainment is pumped into the archipelago.

As I mentioned, these silences and the deaf ears on which they have fallen have a lineage at least as far back as the American Protestant missionaries, who used shame to actively discourage expressive culture in favor of teaching God's divine silence and hymnody in an aesthetic education aimed at redirecting the moral compass through aural conversion that set up harmony as an ideal.[42] Rerouting moral power through sounding Marshallese bodies and lands, Lijon offered a customary stick dance, the *jiku*, which foretold the coming of the Gospel. The women would tap their jiku sticks, percussively interlocking with one another and interweaving their patterns. In the late nineteenth and early twentieth centuries, explorers and ethnographers noted a handful of Indigenous dances that involve spears, sticks, or women's use of a drum.[43] Krämer and Nevermann observed a "staff round dance performed by men with dance staffs or dance spears. The men trip in one line, waving staffs and spears, and turn around themselves from time to time. Often several lines of men weave in and

Children enjoying a Laurel and Hardy movie.

Marshallese entertaining the medical team at the party.

2.2 Staged images of children and women from Robert A. Conard's report.

out as in the round dance."⁴⁴ The jiku dance persists today, albeit with all Rongelapese women performers.⁴⁵

The roro accompanying the jiku was never translated for me, but there are some discernible place-names and directions. When I spoke with Lijon about the navigation dance, she told me that the word *jiku* really referred to "Gospel sticks." She said the dance and chant were very old and that most people do not know it these days. The dance is meaningful because it was a prediction of the Gospel just before it came to the Marshall Islands. The song predicted that there would be "a message from heaven."⁴⁶ A skilled navigator, Lijon told me about the roads from Rongerik to Ebon at the bottom of the ocean floor, which is what the missionaries followed to get from Rongerik (where they stopped first, but the people on Rongerik did not want them there) to Ebon. Lijon chants a line, and this prompts the others to respond in unison. Perhaps the prediction of the Gospel was possible because of the atollscape epistemology.

Lijon also told me about a chant, a schooner song. This song is not sung anymore because people don't travel back and forth from Ailnginae to Rongelap to get food (only a few Rongelapese who participate in economic-development projects live on Rongelap). The women and children would sit in the middle of the boat squeezed together and unable to move, surrounding the food. There would be three strong men directing the boat and catching other sea animals, such as turtles. The waves would be huge all around them, stretching way up over the boat, and to amass strength the men and women would sing a song of strength. Lijon was a small child when this was happening.

MEMORIAL DAY/NUCLEAR VICTIMS' AND SURVIVORS' REMEMBRANCE DAY

In 1994 during the Clinton administration, the Marshall Islands government received documents pertaining to Project 4.1 that had recently been declassified. These documents speak to the human radiation experiments carried out on Marshallese citizens immediately after Bravo, when they were subjects under the Trust Territory of the Pacific Islands (TTPI). However, many of the documents were redacted, so there were blank spaces. Project 4.1 was only partially declassified. The RMI and the populations that were most directly affected, such as the Four Atoll communities and the Rongelapese, were once again shown that they had been lied to and manipulated in their homelands and in US courts. The documents gave the Four Atolls and the RMI government the material basis to paint, along with their oral testimonies that they fought to have the NCT consider, a coherent picture of "changed circumstances" for which they sought remediation.

The Rongelapese women have remained active in contributing to nuclear restagings at nuclear remembrance events. Since 1998, the Rongelapese women have shared their stories and songs with members beyond their community. Often the ceremonies will last all day, and the Rongelapese women have consistently performed songs directly pertaining to the nuclear issues in addition to sharing individual testimony from members of the community. Direct presentation of nuclear damages and indirect requests contribute to a nuanced politics of indigeneity. The women perform on Indigenous instruments—their voices—compromised by violence, weakened by fear of the uncertain, and threatened by loss. They resound the precarity of Western structures aimed at global ideals, which have created distance between men and women, children and elders, and Marshallese and their ancestral lands. These Americanized ideals, like that of harmony, become unreachable without a healthy throat.

On the momentum of this partial declassification, in 1998 the inaugural Nuclear Victims and Survivors' Remembrance Day (hereafter NVSRD) was initiated by ERUB, the NCT, and the RMI government, which wanted to have a space to educate people outside the immediate Section 177 communities about nuclear information from the declassified documents. Anthropologist Holly Barker, a former Peace Corps member, was helping the RMI government secure evidence to submit for the Changed Circumstances Petition (CCP). She also used her research to teach a course at the College of the Marshall Islands (CMI), which became the CMI Nuclear Institute. Barker led the students' "nuclear club" in the creation of a database to hold the newly released documents and in educational efforts to raise awareness.

Anthropologist Julianne Walsh was tasked with being the host coordinator and received help from a Marshallese woman, Biram Stege, "the emcee and last minute co-organizer." The committee invited Youth to Youth in Health, a Majuro-based group founded by a Marshallese woman, Darlene Keju, who was married to *Marshall Islands Journal* founder and American expat Giff Johnson. They also invited the US ambassador, who declined to attend. Walsh recalls how the NVSRD began with a prayer and then the national anthem. After welcoming words from the Council of Iroij, Rongelapese sang a song called "177," which Walsh said was "the most moving part by far. . . . In the context of numerous representations including photos, students' drawings, documentary broadcasts, and radio coverage about the testing and its consequences, the expression of the Rongelapese almost disappear. . . . Marginalized by the assumption that they can care for themselves since they have compensation money, their needs are often dismissed, their claims ignored."[47]

The NVSRD created a space in which Marshallese aimed to use their means of being heard, but it remains limited because of the aural orientations of auditors. Just prior to the US Congress's rejection of the CCP, the RMI held a substantial fiftieth-anniversary Bravo commemorative ceremony with a geographically diverse audience of diplomatic officials, antinuclear activists, Japanese *hibakusha* (survivors of the atom bombs that fell on Japan), and other supportive parties. The mayor of Rongelap, James Matayoshi, spoke passionately through what can be considered the rhetoric of liberal democracy. "Bravo is not over," he explained in a speech contoured by descriptions of the ongoing military activities on Kwajalein Atoll and the mistreatment of the Marshallese and the "democratic alliances" of the nations. He then listed the amount the United States spends on its continental cleanup, affirming that the "truth" can come out about the "Marshallese story" and that "Americans need to hear it." However, Americanized auditors are attuned to the suffering of the individualized, divided, and bounded human rather than hearing the partible voices that are directly working on them. Americanized auditors also assume a static voice and static notions of space and time (as moving forward) rather than understanding the historicized voices of the liberal democratic genre, the singers' harmonies that followed, and regenerative possibilities that inhered in listening. Without the historicization of the mediated genres through which voices connect to ears and the accountability of auditors, Americanized audiences cannot and do not hear. In what follows I briefly discuss the Rongelapese performances at the fiftieth anniversary and suggest that with the rejection of the CCP, Rongelapese women's performances began to evince the decay that was mapped onto them by denying them the space to be heard and thus the room to move, especially following their NCT testimony in 2001, after which they felt like they had "won."[48]

The 2004 commemoration also included a performance of approximately twenty-five Rongelapese, mostly elderly women who donned maroon or black shirts that read, in bold white, "Project 4.1," visually restaging their ongoing role in the only partially declassified program (see figure 2.3). A man dressed in black stood in the back behind an electronic keyboard: the only musical accompaniment to the vocal performances. The three-

2.3 Rongelapese women perform "177" at Nuclear Victims and Survivors' Remembrance Day, 2004. Photo courtesy of Mission Pacific Archive.

song set began with the Rongelapese anthem, "*Iakwe Anij*" ("Love to God/ Hello God"), in the style of an *al in kamōlo* (welcoming/party song), which refers to the Marshallese understanding of the gathering or space to cool off (*kamōlo* means "to make cool"). Cooling off and winding down enable an openness in togetherness, unlike the alert-based culture that creates hypervigilant, protective, and guarded individuals. Marshallese parties, as a time of reconnection, are meant to enable moving in bōro wōt juon. The anthem, as al in kamōlo, plays with the aporia of hospitality, as discussed by Derrida, where the host becomes hostage.[49] The song opens by extending thanks to God (*Anij*) for granting them the time and space for ippān doon. The acoustic index of the Rongelapese corporeal copresence (ippān doon) and the presence of the audience to whom they sing creates the performative dynamic of their anthem as an anthem of displacement.

The women sing, "*Iakwe, iakwe* from the [group] Iju in Eañ / We sing to you to bring you peace and the spirit of happiness." Thus far, the lines of "*Iakwe Anij*" have suggested a togetherness, a wholeness; however, the song sounds itself as a product of nuclear modernity's sensorial fragmentation epitomized by removal from one's ancestral land, which necessitated the cultivated of an anthem (as representative of an atoll) in the first place:

PRECARIOUS HARMONIES

"We stay on Majuro and while it is almost like our island, it is not, and we stay here and think about our island / We came from our islands—but our hearts stay there, and our minds wander back there / We recall its environment, the immense beauty of its surroundings and wholeness." Taking the second line as a matter of the Marshallese burō, we can read this in terms of their song (the work of the throat) that brings them back to their homeland through singing al in keememej. As an al in keememej, the anthem also works to vocally remediate the erasure of Rongelap, bringing its beauty rather than its devastation back into collective memory.

The second song, "1954," composed by Tarines Abon ("the Rongelapese Elvis") for the 2004 Nuclear Remembrance event, marks pivotal detonation that irrevocably changed Rongelapese lives. Dates and terms that are associated with fracturing processes and fragmentation are often highlighted in songs as American imports. Prior to the performance, Abacca gestured to ippān doon and announced that all the islands, not merely the Four Atolls selected by the United States as worthy of compensation, were gravely altered by the bomb. She urged the Marshallese-speaking audience to *"emukat ñan justice"* (move toward justice). Further, she explicitly acknowledged the two populations of Likiep Atoll and Ailuk Atoll, which had received fallout from Bravo but were not evacuated by the US military. The song affectively conveys the constant *mal de débarquement*: of being adrift from land, a nuclear exile subject to US policies and provisions. The semantic sound posts (navigational sound marks) are two English words—*Four Atolls*—and the Marshallese word ERUB, meaning damaged and defined by the United States.[50] The break is embodied by the RMI nation with the political exclusion of the other radiation-damaged atolls, such as Likiep and Ailuk, which have sustained political denials manifested as embodied nuclear silences of a collective amnesia (see chapter 1).

There are many ways to hear the musical form of "1954." It can be heard as the affective break, the ERUB rupture of the bomb. Western musical conventions locate it as AABA with a 3/4 meter, marked by the bass of the electronic keyboard alternating from F♯2 to C♯3 on the downbeat of each measure in the A section.[51] The ostinato creates a stable or unceasing rocking motion. The formal frictions produce the rhythmic movements. Women's voices prevail, and enthusiastic shouts and claps punctuate the softly rolling contours of verses: "On March 1, 1954, four atolls were destroyed by the bomb with radiation // God is kind and loving. Move our atolls from the huge problems today // Sail ahead on the Oceanside and face the world today, like platforms of beautiful roses on the ocean // Four atolls (×11) // It's broken."

The lyrics specify that the destruction of their atolls has to do with the nuclear bomb because of its radioactive debris. The line that follows thanks God, and it draws on the Rongelapese anthem, "*Iakwe Anij*," for protecting their community in spite of the nuclear damages. The women dance with each other in enthusiastic waltzes, and their iteration and reiteration of the reductive term *Four Atolls* performs the reductive measures of the United States' numbering, categorizing, and ultimately obliterating land and people. "Four" remains whole, concrete, on the downbeat, and watching the women, wearing the 4.1 shirts—there is an affective connection between the introductory number "4"—we almost hear "point one" as the silent harmony to "a-tolls," and with the stark rhythmic delineation in 3/4, the swaying feeling like one is out at sea remains, while the atolls are audibly broken apart: "a-tolls." The twelfth word of the chorus is the only Marshallese word in the chorus, and its syllabic distancing is not emphasized.

As the song unfolds, its affective form takes on new remedial dimensions through the senses and the figure of the rose, the beautiful gift. The Rongelapese sing their cultural experiences of feeling momentum to face these international problems sailing on the oceanside, which would be facing outside of one's atoll, "like platforms of beautiful roses on the ocean." Debased and staged as test subjects, dismissed in courts, Rongelapese remind one another and themselves of their strong platform and their beauty, thus restaging themselves against their fragmented representations as data and images in the nuclear archive. Roses, which are beautiful manifestation of deep roots in the land, beautify the air, as do the Rongelapese voices. In contrast to the bad atmosphere and a world out of balance (symbolized earlier by Shirley's anecdote "too many funerals and not enough flowers"), the Rongelapese sing a good atmosphere, the living roses, back into being—purifying the air and asking others to help in their endeavor as they advance social justice ("*emukat ñan* justice"). Roses are symbolic of gifts to the chief after a typhoon (disaster), and the Rongelapese singing is a giving of time and an appeal to the chiefs and government, an invitation to hear radiation sounding through the political break and try to mend it through that break, where precarious voices sound strength. The oceanside is where the international begins; it is where currents bring people together. The Rongelapese women's *ainikien* (vocal currents) create the beautiful platform, as a gift/appeal, to do precisely this. The roses, which are worn as a *wut* on the head, which is the highest part of the body, also show that they are giving their most precious gifts—their songs—at this meeting of international participants. They are the reason the community is listening.

Prior to the final song, the Rongelapese waited in relative silence as Abacca briefly introduced the performance: "The final song is called 177." All of her words were in Marshallese except "177," which was spoken in English.[52] The title of the song refers to the section of the COFA that outlines compensation for problems associated with the nuclear testing program, and much like the previous song, "1954," created continuity with the opening song, "*Iakwe Anij*." The musical material of this performance of "177" intimates a Marshallese connection to 1950s America from the outset. This musical scaffolding is the generative labor of the negative that acoustically restages American-Marshallese historical alliances (Atomic Age diplomacy) affectively, as foundational and inextricable to the consequent issues that are presented lyrically. Recalling the sound-scape of the displaced Rongelapese on Kwajalein Atoll, the unmistakable sonic reminiscence to a 1950s American country song à la Conway Twitty is uncanny. The musical material also resounds the silences of an erased, irradiated nuclear working class: the American GIs who shared their love of country music with Marshallese who were in the military and stationed at Bikini and Enewetak for the tests and also the Rongelapese women singing the song, laboring for answers under the political clause of Section 177. The song redistributes the insensible connectedness of radiogenic communities not across ethnicity or gender but rather as the making of those laborers who accumulated resources for American empire.

American country music was played through a Japanese Yamaha keyboard—through their words, which they sing without compromise for the international guests. The unintelligibility of the Marshallese language to American listeners mirrors the initial unintelligibility of the nuclear language the Rongelapese had to learn. The first verse is repeated twice: "All these thoughts of mine I give to you / These are the experiences I see in these days that don't belong to us."[53] The song laments the unwanted inheritance. The Rongelapese reject their present-day experiences resulting from the nuclear legacy as not being their own.

During the chorus we begin to hear a marked tension between the unassimilable, silent, and silencing mechanisms that impose upon the lives of the women and the unintelligibility and silence of a nonexistent "peace of mind." The lyrical delivery communicates the existence of present degenerative silences and future conditional silences. The intervallic movement between these temporally significant silences shapes the feeling of time *and* space between what is and what could be. Of note is the line that rises from Ab4 to Eb5, "Oh, ñe ij pād ilo aō radiation." The syllabic delivery of the words in melodic ascent preceding the climax (Eb5) of "radiation" stands in contrast to the descending melismatic ornamentation on "radiation" that returns to the tonic.

Through almost identical melodic contours and an emphatic, heightened delivery, with voices strained on the melodic climax, *jojolāār* echoes insensible "radiation." *Jojolāār* is the suffering of being abandoned and lost: a stranger to oneself and one's surroundings. It speaks of not being in one's home and the unintelligibility of feeling estranged from oneself, signifying what David Morris terms the "irreducible otherness of suffering."[54] Similarly, what is not yet "home" but what *is* home, "a peaceful place," exists in the world of appeals, and here the women draw from perhaps their lifetime of Christian musical education and end with a plagal cadence.

The final words of the chorus, "*Nomba en 177*," underscore Rongelapese feelings of powerlessness. In addition to the silencing of their voices, they feel dehumanized by being identified as part of a number. This reflects back to the dialectical interplay between the materiality of sound and silence, to Project 4.1 and radiation. The temporal markings and the tonal structure signify the conclusion of the verse on the word "177." As part of the nuclear-centered language, 177 is a political classification that both alienates and identifies Rongelapese. The nuclear experiences "don't belong to [the Rongelapese]" alone: they are connected to other radiation communities and those responsible for their situation. Even if it is unwanted, this assumed political identity is fractured by its participation under a number and secures the maintenance of a silent remainder of all those who are not included and can benefit from being labeled "177" (e.g., nuclear compensation).

In the final verse the declarative sentiment of the song fades into questioning ambivalences: "When will I be released from my sufferings that I still now do not understand?" Here the "irreducible otherness of suffering" becomes twofold: neither the Americans nor the Marshallese can understand this suffering. The suffering, or the silence of suffering, becomes a constitutive othering.[55] It separates the Marshallese from a present they feel is not theirs, yet it reaffirms what is only theirs: the suffering caused by the nuclear legacy and the responsibility to share their voices to evince experiences of what most of the world stills deems as "unthinkable."

The final question, which is repeated, "Would you guide me and give me strength?," is an indirect request that transfers the dominant role and control from the questioner to the respondent. The Rongelapese relinquish power to the respondent, to the Other (here, God, the United States, or both) through aesthetics of indirect questioning, or re-silencing of the self. The questions that invest in a higher power reflect on the journey from "Iakwe Anij" and "1954." "Iakwe Anij" opens by thanking God and parlays the gratitude into a reminder of the debt or the gift. Appeals to Anij make an appearance in the second verse of "1954" only after the date of 1954, the bomb, and radiation are mentioned. By the third song, "177," the United States and God are affectively aligned in the ending gesture, but God is never directly mentioned. As more time passes, we hear the silence of unanswered questions hanging as negative space at the end of the lines. These structural silences, which are resonances of the foundational nuclear silences, prompt more sound that will inevitably reveal and conceal the public secret of past destruction, current classifications, and the future silences resonating from the bomb. The appeal is one that shares how Rongelapese are included in Section 177, which means they are a nuclear-affected community, but as a political entity and social community the Rongelapese are excluded from receiving answers from the United States about how extant nuclear issues have affected further means of redress. The musical petitions are the enactment of the public secret of this fragmentation and the labor done to maintain their representative distance.

"THESE ARE MY QUESTIONS FOR YOU NOW (STILL)"

Five years later, during the March 1, 2009, NVSRD, fifteen Rongelapese—all women—stood in front of memorial wreaths and paintings depicting the Bikinian exodus with a song composed entirely of questions. They faced the audience and sang *"Kajjitok in aō ñan kwe kiiō"* ("These Are My Questions for You Now/Still"), the song I heard at Shirley's house in 2008 and the one most frequently performed by the Rongelapese women. Lijon has watched as members of her community are "visited by doctors, issued a clean bill of health, and then wind up in the emergency room two weeks later."[56] Lijon told me that the impetus behind the song's composition was in line with that of "177": the continued unresponsiveness of the United States. The DOE's unresponsiveness was buttressed by the RMI's political representation. At that time, representatives from the DOE visited the RMI to meet with the government. The Rongelapese women asked to attend the meeting, but their request was denied. Therefore, together with the Utrikese women, they met the DOE at the airport and later threw a party (*kāmolo*) for the DOE. Two days before the party, Lijon decided to write "*Kajjitok in aō ñan kwe kiiō*" and use the party, a space of entertainment, to voice serious concerns in the song. With this subversive move the Rongelapese and Utrikese women turned a party into an affective (and effective) extension of court hearings and other, more-official hearing spaces. Lijon penned lyrics of both testimony and appeal, sharing a compilation of questions that continue to circulate among the Rongelapese community.

Lijon composed on the guitar, if she could find one, or on the keyboard, and she demonstrated her own "country western" style that she learned from Americans on the military base and in school. For her, "*Kajjitok in aō ñan kwe kiiō*" shares a responsibility to give voice to what she hears as still-present voices, claims, and appeals, even if Americans register the voices of those that have passed as the absolute silence, or voicelessness, of the dead. Lijon offers her take on vocally remediating the ongoing suffering that exceeds a human life by citing those who passed away and did not have the opportunity to share their suffering or receive answers from the United States. The song also helps her to educate the younger generation on the difficulties they are facing and may encounter: "I wrote the song because of the questions that would come to my mind and also the minds of my sisters, some who have passed away. . . . One time my little sister came to me and asked the same question, and when she asked this, I said in my heart that I will compose a song concerning these questions, because she asked the same questions [that] my older sisters, who are dead, would often ask."[57]

"*Kajjitok*" is a sonic history that is woven from these questions and the questions in motions that have been prepared, shared, and filed in US and RMI governmental archives. The sonic history activates the heart (throat) to continue this sharing when the courts and other legal spaces for hearing write them out. Figure 2.4 is an excerpt from the "Statement of Senator Anjain on Behalf of the Rongelap Atoll Local Government before the Subcommittee on the Insular Affairs and the Committee on Interior and Insular Affairs" in Washington, D.C., on November 16, 1989, in which he describes how the Rongelapese people have asked "fundamental questions . . . over and over again," only to have the DOE refuse to answer.

The English words for doctor (*takta*), aspirin, calcium, thyroid (*tyroit*), kidney, and problem are used and transformed by the Marshallese language in "*Kajjitok in aō ñan kwe kiiō.*" Within the overarching aestheticization of a state of continually imposed silence, the threading of borrowed

IS RONGELAP ATOLL SAFE?

The contemporary story of Rongelap begins with fundamental questions asked by the Rongelap people, over and over again:

- IS RONGELAP ATOLL SAFE?
- ARE THE RONGELAP PEOPLE HEALTHY?
- IS RONGELAP ATOLL SAFE TO RESETTLE?

We ask these questions of the Department of Energy.

We ask them of the DOE doctors.

We ask them of the DOE environmental specialists.

Most of all, *the Rongelap people ask these questions of one another.*

No matter how many times we ask the questions, answers are not forthcoming. The questions are reasonable. DOE's refusal to respond is not.

The Rongelap people moved into exile in 1985 because of the overwhelming belief that we were not safe at Rongelap and that the people, and especially the children, were at risk.

Since that time, we have attempted to find out if the environment at Rongelap Atoll -- the soils, land, birds, fish, and foods -- is safe and if our atoll is habitable. We have not been successful.

The Department of Energy will not answer our questions. They refuse. The Compact -- the law -- provides for an independent process to obtain this information. That is what we want.

EXPERTS DECLARE RONGELAP ATOLL CONTAMINATED

The Rongelap Council, in 1987, at the recommendation of the RepMar Government contracted with one of the nation's leading radiation cleanup companies, Holmes and Narver, of Albuquerque, NM to prepare a plan for the rehabilitation and resettlement of Rongelap Atoll. Holmes and Narver is one of the prime contractors to the Departments of Energy and Defense with three decades experience in the Marshall Islands.

2.4 Transcript of hearing. "Is Rongelap Atoll Safe?" (excerpt), 1989.

and modified words that signify what was detrimentally imported (doctors, problems, medicines) into the lyrics recalls the inclusion and exclusion of the Rongelapese from the ownership of nuclear knowledge. These words amid the other Marshallese words convey the affective alliance that predicates strategic trust, which "is the sign of something ultimately unknowable."[58] The unknowable is twofold: the women's pain and the unanswered questions (the answers to these questions are not known by the Rongelapese, and it is unclear if they are known by the American doctors and scientists), and the incommensurability of cultures with deep, meaningful legacies of articulation and corporeal attachments that exist outside aesthetic, affective alliances.

Lijon was not present for Iju in Eañ's performance of the song at Nuclear Remembrance Day in 2009, but she recounted a story about the preparations for the event. Lijon explained that she wanted the elderly women to come up with a skit that would convey their disabilities to outsiders. She said that she proposed getting props for the women, such as wheelchairs and canes, and have them hobble out in an exaggerated way. After she explained her unrealized vision, she laughed softly and said that the "other ladies" did not want to do the skit because they felt no need to accentuate their disabilities, which were to many observers already painfully obvious.

During their 2009 performance of "*Kajjitok in aō ñan kwe kiiō*," the Rongelapese women arranged their nuclear remediation through an aural mediation of their sensorial impairments through their throats in the relational space of the International Convention Center, which had been built, indirectly, on the grounds of the research done on and professionalism afforded by their bodies. Center stage, again, life had not changed much for the women, except that they had used nearly every means of voicing their injuries possible for Americanized auditors who still refused to hear. Rather than meaning or spectacle, the women broke with harmony and made felt the sustained acoustical roughness of this international relationship. At three minutes into the song, the women stopped singing. Some in the audience, believing the song was over, began clapping as the conductor, Betty, turned to the audience and exclaimed, "Ah, *tyroit!*" as she thrust her head upward and pointed to her throat, to the location of the thyroid scar (see figure 2.5). She shook her head.

Betty had pointed to us, the audience, earlier in the performance. She had used gestures to show us the parts of the body that the women were naming, like *ni* for "teeth." These are the women's body parts that have been extracted and used in biomedical research. Their voicelessness can be read

2.5 "Ah, *tyroit*." Performing the insensible.

in the context of these biomedical extractions that are linked to geopolitical erasures through which nuclear-enforced global harmony was procured. As such, the singers' voicelessness can be heard in terms of voice-based extractions from global harmony—beyond the interrelated juridical, metaphorical, and actual voicelessness of suffering—and in terms of the precarious system in which we are all implicated. I believe that our equivocal clapping let Betty know that the audience didn't know how to hear, for we interpreted incorrectly, perhaps in the same ways that data have been incorrectly interpreted and instrumentalized. The petition that demands declassification through music proves another reason why "data sovereignty," the repatriation of that which has been stolen from Marshallese and used as data, is necessary for sovereignty. Betty returned the audience to the breached throats of the women in her capacity as conductor, silencing the audience to listen otherwise. As Abacca explained, you do not clap for a musical petition.

This skit is a direct critique of US nuclear biopolitics and the secrecy system. As the women reassert their vocal abilities, they ask questions with answers that exist beyond the disabled voices that work within, and at the same time challenge, the confines of the song as a series of notes in harmonic organization. If "the sound of the voice is the sound of social life," as theorized by Aaron Fox, then the sound of social death, or the unmaking of bōro wōt juon, can be heard in the defamiliarized voicelessness or acoustical roughness of the voiceless singing group in the midst of a song, for it was as if the song kept moving silently on while the women's voices had been left behind.[59] This vocal technique also created an acoustical roughness that, as with Betty's gesture, intimated the thyroid damage, which has pushed women's voices down or lowered them. The gendering of being pushed down echoes Lemeyo's sentiment of that which Marshallese men have begun to do, showing the international spread of radiation as the destabilization of women in ways often not associated with radioactivity. Yet it is important to recall that this song was composed because the women were not allowed at the meeting of the two sovereign representatives—at the time both men—such that they and their sisters were rendered voiceless because their voices were incarcerated or barred from the DOE meeting.

Harmony mitigates violences that it effaces. The decolonial dissonances in this performance were layered in ways that recall the historical lack of consent that persists in keeping the women from the answers and information they seek: "The ability to be a sacrificial self, in other words, was always structured by the ability to consent, itself dependent [on] one's embodied 'location in the material world.' Possession of an intentional, free self, a prerequisite for self-sacrifice, was a quality defined only in relation to bodies said to be lacking intention and freedom."[60] Similarly, the ability to consent depended on the ability to have a voice, which depended on the (1) self-possessed speaker who (2) depoliticized listening through truth claims that were produced through the (3) modern, individuated five senses. And this was entangled with citizen-subject status and gender. The doctors who defined themselves in relation to the Rongelapese did so predicated upon the self-possessed and progress-driven mind-set of scientific virtue and the powerful concept of the "gift of voice" as gift of humanity. Within democracies the question of informed consent—where equals can ask questions and debate the merits of such projects—and the ability to enter freely into contracts as equals was upheld following World War II, but this has not been the case in the Marshall Islands with respect to declassification, through which the women's voices are routed in their acoustical roughness. To deny declassification is to deny self-determination. This is heard in the injured throats and undemocratic impositions through which voices are restrained, held back. The scars mark this fissure and the failure of returns—of Indigenous knowledge in the archipelago and in the archive.

There is the trace of the failing, the falling, the precariousness we made possible by listening in. We have not only listened in to them, but also we listen in to the future of their children and their children's children. As the

Rongelapese women empty out their responsibility to bear the burden of global harmony at their communicative expense, they strategically sing this future as their presence, which is a presence in which they must deal with their incorporation as "part of this whole nuclear craziness [and they make heard] their bottom line. . . . 'We care about our children's future.' Because they know they are contaminated. They know that they'll be dying out soon. They are dying now—slowly."[61] Thus, the aftermath, the acoustical remains, are the ultimate returns to Death on Earth, to the DOE in the silent spaces that are political voids, without spirit or soul. In the ethical space of address the Rongelapese women communicate the time for redress is "now" and "still" (*kiiō*).

FUTURE SILENCES: WHAT IS NOT BEING SAID

Jodikdik ñan Jodikdik ilo Ejmour (Youth to Youth in Health) performed a poignant musical skit at Nuclear Remembrance Day 2009 titled *"Emukat Eo Aō"* ("My Moving"). Markers of loss pervade this present-day "reenactment" of the Rongelapese story and the Bikinian story. The skit conveys the ongoing devastation wrought by nuclear weaponry on the generational level. On stage left, a sign reading "RMI" is held up to indicate that the dejected, downcast children are located in the Republic of the Marshall Islands—no longer a US trust territory. In the middle of the stage stands one lone doctor. Although he is Marshallese, it is unclear if he is pretending to be American or if he is one of the Marshallese health aides trained by American doctors. The lone figure beckons to the children from the RMI side of the stage, returning our attention to the isolation of the individual and the medical atomization of the body. Stage right is occupied by a handful of children happily playing catch with a basketball.

The sign "USA" is held up. Each child who is examined by the doctor never makes it to the USA; s/he is sent back, completely forlorn, to the RMI side. The individuals on the RMI side cover their faces with their hands, blinding themselves to the reality of being trapped in a place where illnesses abound. The lyrics align the nuclear testing program with loss of health and culture. They are repeated to a slow keyboard accompaniment: "I am moving from the place where I grew up, from my roots. I am moving from my culture and the life on my homeland. Still, dangerous sicknesses emerge from the nuclear testing . . . and we live, but suffer from day to day." Clues to, and missed cures for, the problems presented lyrically are in what we cannot hear; they are in what is not being said.

A Marshallese man role-plays the "doctor." He stands in between healthy, happy children in the United States and dejected children in the RMI. He encounters young girls and boys in a line, examines them, and then sends them back to the RMI without saying a word. Let's take a closer look at *how* the doctor is listening. Rather than speak to the children, he listens with a stethoscope (a medical instrument). And he listens to their *hearts*. Even more commonly, he quickly takes their pulse from the inside of their wrists. This instrumental mediation hears their hearts as barometer of health. Western culture locates the heart as the center of the soul, and science (or medicine) positions it as the center of our livelihood. With respect to music, when we think about the Western heart beyond the conceptual location of the emotional register, the heart rate, beats per minute, is used with respect to tempo in music.

In the National Cancer Institute's 2008–2009 Annual Report, *Reducing Environmental Cancer Risk: What We Can Do Now*, the authors stated that "of special concern, the U.S. has not met its obligation to provide for ongoing health needs of the people of the Republic of the Marshall Islands resulting from radiation exposures they received during U.S. nuclear weapons testing in the Pacific from 1946–1958."[62] The latter statement is powerful, but it does not expose the enormity of what "health needs" are to the Marshallese. The disjuncture in what the United States considers "health" and what Rongelapese have needed for their health creates a silent excess of "illness" unthinkable to the United States. *Jodikdik ñan Jodikdik ilo Ejmour* provides music and a silent skit that demonstrates while sicknesses abound and these medical needs must be addressed, Americans (the West) keep listening in the wrong places for answers. This mode of nuclear listening is not so much that Westerners listen in the "wrong" place for answers (nor is "wrong" a moral judgment on Western science or health care) but that such an aurality is part of colonial exploitation in developmental dependencies. I want to ask that we think through "dependency" and collaboration at the level of the sensible and at the level of radiation as a collaborative discursive production. Songs are petitions that enable us to hear how radiation, as a collaboration, sounds these historical dependencies through the labor of the negative. The labor of the negative is a discursive chain that articulates freedom to loss to silence to radiation, back to loss to freedom, which is complicated by the fact that Marshallese and American values and terms of freedom are contested from the outset. By singing, meaningful speech concerning radiation is a matter of voice (that which connects, or "ties," the body and language) rendered through the throat.[63] The voice attached to radiation as restricted data, in its affective capacities, sonorizes an imprint of the body, irradiated and restricted, which is damaging. The revoiced voicings of a radiation grammar and expressive language, sent forth from the irradiated communal body, share radiation and, consequently, the irradiated body previously withheld from the shared space as a collective concern and experience of *partial* declassification.

CHAPTER THREE

MORIBA

"EVERYTHING IS IN GOD'S HANDS"

On a Sunday morning in 1946, just after church services, US Navy Commodore Ben H. Wyatt, the military governor of the Marshall Islands, arrived by seaplane on Bikini Atoll. A number of Wyatt's staff and the paramount chief of the Marshall Islands, Iroijlaplap Jeimata Kabua, accompanied the commodore. Having already received Iroijlaplap Kabua's permission to relocate the Bikinians, Commodore Wyatt's task to remove the 167 inhabitants of Bikini Atoll was partially complete. The work that remained was twofold: convince Bikinian leader Juda and his people to move off their atoll for an unspecified period of time and capture film footage of the transaction so the production team could make the encounter appear like a seamless transaction between the paternal United States and the agreeable, if not grateful, Native population.

Wyatt called Chief Juda the "king" of the Bikinians, and he appealed to (now) King Juda on Christian grounds with a quick homily and an elocution likening the "Bikinians to the children of Israel whom the Lord saved from their enemy and led unto the Promised Land. He told them of the bomb that men in America made and the destruction it had wrought upon the enemy."[1] Wyatt asked Juda if the Bikinians would leave their atoll for a while during the US atomic weapons experiments. According to Wyatt, Juda agreed proudly at first to participate for "the benefit of all mankind," although the terms of the agreement are inconsistent and not documented. Wyatt waited while Juda conferred with Bikinian community leaders over the course of a few days. Most did not want to leave, but they felt grateful that Americans had ended the war. Moreover, they knew that a definitive "no" would be useless at best because the United States was such a powerful nation, as evidenced by its material wealth and military might. The *aḷaps* were offered different islands to which they could be relocated, and they chose Rongerik, given that they believed they would be away from their homeland for only a short time. They also chose Rongerik because it was not under the jurisdiction of Iroijlaplap Kabua, openly defying his wishes for the Bikinians to move to an island under his customary control.[2] The Bikinians believed that he had not come to their rescue during World War II. Why should they be beholden to him, especially when the US government had chosen their atoll to test this powerful device?

As the countdown to the Bikinian departure neared day zero, the American military was clamoring to document all aspects of the nuclear exile preparations. Hollywood, for the first and only time, stopped filming because of the massive atomic efforts, and directors treated Bikini Atoll like it was an extension of the global film capital, arranging Bikinians and staging their final moments with their ancestral homeland. Bikinian lawyer Jonathan Weisgall describes the Bikinians' confusion when American film crews instructed them to repeat everything multiple times. They even had the Bikinians do a "retake" of their final church service, which they repeated twice for the cameramen. Weisgall quotes elder Kilon Bauno: "We were very confused. I couldn't understand why they had to do everything so many times."[3]

On Wednesday, March 6, the Bikinians decorated the graves of their ancestors to say goodbye and offered prayers as a preface to the reenactment of the initial February 10 meeting between Wyatt and Juda. The Bikinians' relocation was even delayed by one day so that the crew could get the right footage of the transaction.[4] This US restaging of the "historic scene" where Wyatt and Juda first talked was done for the "benefit of Navy sound cameramen" (see figure 3.1). The original caption reads, "When the proposal was made, Chief Juda responded that the Bikinians were very proud to be part of the undertaking, and would move elsewhere."

While Wyatt had the Bikinian men sit patiently as his crew filmed dozens of takes for the US media, he regaled them with promises that the United States would lead the Bikinians "to the 'land of salvation,' much as God had for the Jews." At the commodore's request, James Milne, the Tarawa-born translator, explained to Juda that the powerful weaponry was "for the good of mankind and to end all world wars."[5] Wyatt had Juda stand and give an answer on whether he and his people would be willing to relocate to Rongerik. Juda stood and said, "*Emṃan. Men otemjej rej ilo bein Anij*"

CHAPTER THREE

3.1 Staging removal "for the benefit of Navy sound cameramen." Photo published in *National Geographic*, July 1946.

("It's good. Everything is in God's hands"). Wyatt then responded, "Well, you [James] tell them and King Juda that everything being in God's hands, it cannot be other than good."[6]

The US media circulated the diplomatic exchange as an amenable transaction. The US Navy film crew recorded interactions that didn't make the cut, which I situate as the germinal political performance of the Bikinian nation, which coheres in response to RMI autonomy and the COFA in the mid-1980s. Wyatt assumed that Juda, after taking some space from the commodore to speak with his family and the political leaders, would accept dislocation with a show of pride that was already written into the US removal story line.[7] During the consequential moment, when Wyatt asked whether Bikinians were ready to leave "for the good of mankind," Juda responded with "*Men otemjej rej ilo bein Anij*" ("Everything is in God's hands"), disrupting the prescribed narrative. Unsatisfied, Wyatt asked a second time. Juda plainly affirmed what he said before: "Everything is in God's hands." The commodore tried dozens more times to take full directorial control, to script and choreograph Bikinian gratitude and subservience to the United States in line with the postwar liberation myth. Juda never swayed from his position. Frustrated by the repetition, Wyatt stopped filming and walked off set.

"*Men otemjej rej ilo bein Anij*" (abbreviated by the Bikinians as MORIBA) is an "equivocal" phrase, and it marks the contested historical moment of uneasy transference (what many Bikinians consider forcible evacuation).[8] The archival outtakes complicate American Atomic Age diplomacy's positioning of the US government and Bikinians. They evince how the American myth of liberation is dependent on mediatized (revisionist) histories and how American history is made through the filter of the myth of liberation, sharing the significance of breaking with the frameworks and filters through which history is universalized. Equivocal statements that are necessarily ambiguous afford the many voices that make up the sentiments, as those that precede into and from the moment of utterance, to assume multidirectional possibility through partial recuperation and selective aesthetic negation. To the film editors, what becomes Juda's vocal currency (repetition) was noise (unwanted sound) to be cut from the media portrayal of the event. Those assumed to be and who would increasingly become more-vulnerable segments of the atoll population—women, children, and elders—were grouped together and aligned with the private, distinct from the public space in which this diplomatic act was staged, for it was staged over the living lands.

From the archival excesses, Bikinians ritually stage a sociality comprising many socialities in need of remediation. For "the good of mankind" remains a promise—a peace—unfulfilled, so multiple ways of being in harmony remain broken. The weakened moral grounds on which America stands (broken promises) are met with Bikinians' constant iteration of MORIBA, which exists as Bikinian collective memory but might also compel Americans, and the RMI echoes of the nation-state, to revisit their moral and, in turn, military inheritance. The repurposing of staged repetition as microtemporal re-fusals, or the rejections of one progression, enables MORIBA to be remediated. As a detour, MORIBA belongs to an unsettled present-past futurity that reaches beyond Bikinians' projected erasure "as natives." Drawing on Juda's equivocal statement, which Wyatt could not argue with because of the shared language of morality, Bikinians' detours to MORIBA become detours to their ancestral spirits and their Indigenous worldviews, movements, and embodied throats from which their embodied voices resonate the connections that are forcibly spaced through radioactive dispossession. In what follows I explore the constitution of the Bikinian nation in the mid-1980s during the RMI COFA signing through contemporary constellations that retain Indigenous harmonies through displaced fragments and broken soundings.

Today, MORIBA is the Bikinian motto. It marks a moment when Americans were on Bikinian land and, without the right to be there, were subject to Juda's practical deliberation. It announces a time before Bravo and before nuclear testing began, when Bikinians were on their atoll, providing an opening through which soundings (as returns, as detours) are possible. MORIBA also signifies Bikinians' unique struggles and relationships with the US government that have developed since 1946 and their difficulties with the RMI government. As well, it marks Bikinians' insubordination: they openly defied the paramount chief, which was unheard of. MORIBA symbolizes Bikinians' mobilities in transpacific diaspora: potential, promised, and positioned to structurally reify the impasse that is felt and lived away from their homeland. Bikinians have worked to develop their national media, public image, and political voices in ways that will help make sense of these mobilities within the context of their broader struggles and intergenerational investments.

As Andrea Smith explains, "Whereas nation-states are governed through domination and coercion, indigenous sovereignty and nationhood is predicated on interrelatedness and responsibility."[9] For the Bikinian nation formed in the mid-1980s in self-determination to protest the COFA, MORIBA might be read within "an 'industry of forgiveness' that utilized a Judeo-Christian formula to produce an institutionalized language of reconciliation."[10] Yet forgiveness as a moral concept is articulated to intentional forgetting, a culture of collective amnesia in this respect, what Lisa Lowe studies as the "politics of remembering and forgetting," which is generated through disciplinary formations in archives that are structured through violences effaced by legal means, such as the COFA.[11] The songs in this chapter share how Bikinians have developed their testimonial voice or political voice through the fissured throat in ways that maintain US accountability and also share the lineage of militarized violence that has displaced them from their spirited lands and their "iakwe" (referring to love, a pathway, and love as a pathway). Memories of this love enable them to return to the currents through which they can enter the lagoon, which I explore in the next chapter. To understand the importance of the cry break or the sounds of the breached throat, it is crucial to understand this chapter in terms of the tear (watery formation)-as-tear (rip) to the oceanic waves, such that wave-pattern navigation to and through the spirits (ancestors) is possible. Although the gendered nation thus sounds feminine loss, I stress that is important to reposition this loss within the frame of the cameramen and American Atomic Age diplomacy, for Bikinians need to survive in exile, which, as chapter 1 and this chapter share, has been filled with patronizing Americans who have withheld food and monies while promising church beams for hearing Americanized harmony.

Bikinians negotiate musical systems of meaning—overlaying harmonic systems—to perform a national sentiment of loss, which aims to transfer the affective force of music as moral pressure from which Bikinians might secure compensation for nuclear damages. In doing so, they create their nation as distinct. Bikinians take seriously the notion and power of the sovereign (namely, the RMI and the United States), and the performative reconstitution of a "nation" predicated on a nuclear ethics of reciprocity (e.g., land for protection, money) works to reconstruct a "mythico-history."[12] The gendered performative reconstitution of a "nation" predicated on a nuclear ethics of reciprocity (land for protection, money) affords Bikinians moral authority and thus authorial rights of claims to their land on moral grounds, which can be read in terms of the political performances through which Bikinians endeavor vocational empowerment even in the absence of the state's "monopoly on violence" or the use of physical force.[13] The "mythico-history" that detours through MORIBA does so through equivocality and strength, legitimizing Bikinians' many voices that preceded and proceeded from the MORIBA utterance as right to moral authority over their land, the protection of which is part of gender complementarity. The delegitimization of Bikinian voice through its contemporary displacement (silence of the formal human, the patriarchy, the voice-over) demands a detour of frozen voice to the many voices that were severed in the making of American Atomic Age diplomacy.

The staged fragmentation of (non)human Bikinians "for the cameramen" was disrupted by Juda's defiant MORIBA, which was a re-fusal of the Christian moral ideology; by protecting Bikini or not relinquishing it lightly, Juda *rejects* the thorough erasure of Indigenous relations and matrilineality through the *re-pairing* of biblical words from exclusively having to do with "one world" and "one humanity" to being constituted by equivocality ("many" voices/*bwijen*) of Bikinians and Americans. As the investment of the *bwijen* (many, umbilical) into a poetics of the bomb (something deeply having to do with US military culture), MORIBA can work to strengthen the atoll umbilicals when it is placed in context with Indigenous movements that resound "gendered loss" and "ancestral loss" *relationally* to the many (bwijen) possibilities of historical movement rather than the "one world or none" binary. These many movements become Bikinians' navigational means or vocal currency to prove that they offered the Americans other options that were not taken; the fixity of the cameramen did not necessarily need to lead to the seemingly permanent separation of the Bikinian body politic, yet it has violence and force that have been privileged over moral reciprocity or the cultivation of a new sociality that values Bikinians. In other words, the United States systemically privileges the silent violences—the actions of silencing through boundary making—in the original promise or contract rather than the terms of the agreement (MORIBA). I now turn to the structure of radioactive colonization in which the modernizing movements of decay, as *emakūt* ("moving" as culture loss/loss of the senses and sensibilities), must be thought of in terms of "politics as vocation" or "vocal currency."

Nuclear silencing is endemic to the capitalist-democratic liberal economy where the decay of voices resounds the dispossession of many material lives and onto-cosmologies into the accumulation of the one (voice, state, superpower, universal) while the promise of liberation, freedom, and equality is retained. American Atomic Age diplomacy thrived off the tension between capitalist ideology and liberal, representative democracy. The universalizing superpower projected fixed accumulation by erasing the material means of producing global inequity, which are the means of vocational empowerment or claims to democracy and the public sphere that enable power over the modern state laws of securization and protection, from border patrolling to internal incarceration. It would do us well to remember that European colonization was justified by the Enlightenment sciences, which were based on an onto-cosmology (patriarchal relations that order the spheres, domination of nature as culture via manipulation of earthly "nature" to project its "laws"), such that what we consider "voice" or "vocation" that inheres in the nation-state politics and policing as protective or security has been, from the start, a project of "biological determinism" of the "body" ("nature, women, racialized, harmonized") and the "head." As shown on the illustrated title page of Hobbes's *Leviathan*, the bodies that constitute the body politic are attuned to the "head of state" (e.g., the spectral white man's head reflected on US currency). When it comes to matters of the modern, territorial state, attunement through "resonance" or vibration relies on a closeness that amplifies sharing in the apposite. It is counterproductive to "universal justice" as a promise of modern law because it amplifies the failures or wrongs of universalist notions of "rationality" as people from social groups that have been divided (rationalized into groups, seemingly fixed identities) based on state-sponsored, capitalist-driven scientific fictions that "voice-cross" into new socialities that don't and can't conform to the state, such that they stand together and against the state's democratization of silences (boundary-making means) as science co-opted by the democratic state to legitimize its institutions as universal.

Thus, when Andrew Dobson defines *sensory democracy* in terms of "apophatic listening," I understand it to refer less to listening and more to the ability to hear, to vibe or resonate *with* life and beings, to make sense with one another in ways that are not determined by one auditor with one sensibility or perceptual reality.[14] In this way what comes into sensible being is the negation of individualism or a disidentification with identity politics as voice in democracy and recuperates the democratic impulse through sensorial interconnectedness or feeling the ways in which voices cross and systems (dis)entangle, however nuanced. By detouring the contemporary injustices wrought by radioactive colonization that disproportionately affects minoritized groups or, according to Attali, "dissonance" in harmonic universalism, there is potentiality to refuse its easy, taken-for-granted, projected (telic) resolution.[15] Heard in terms of advancing sensory democracy, dissonant refusals are voice-based modes of critique that challenge hegemonic categorical individuation and divisive fixedness. These refusals are ways of contemplating the fixity of idealized identities (sounds articulated to people) related to human classifications, such as racialized identities (via geo-phenotypic filters) and colonial identities (via expropriation of land for profit), that have been constitutive in what can be considered the harmonic inclusion-exclusion "boundary silences" of the state. Such boundary silences not only affirm identities (identity assemblages) in particular hierarchical formations, they bolster foundational historical erasures to promulgate fixity through moralized (legitimized) violences that appreciate as "protection" of the state through modern law and the juridico-political archive of the West. In this respect, harmonic boundary silences corroborate a particular way of hearing (listening and voicing) that is tethered to modern democracy in terms of the representative principal, or head, of the state system. Voice-based refusals (such as Marshallese Indigenous refusals) of hegemonic democracy emphasize organizing practices through differently networked sensibilities.

"RADIATION," A PETITION

I met Valentina on Ejit Island while I was renting a room on the land that had once been the site of Rongelapese nuclear exile and that was now the site of Bikinian nuclear exile. Since 1979, the year of Marshallese constitutional independence, (a few) families opted to move to the island, which is about the size of a football field, to be close to the seat of power of the new Marshallese government and that of the US government. We made time for an interview, during which she sang a number of "removal songs" while her son Jackerik and his daughter were present. I was surprised when she suggested that I return a few weeks later so she could sing "Radiation" again, for the musical petition was one that was recorded and played on the radio (see chapter 1). Perhaps this was the point, I realized, for when I played the song for other Marshallese, they would explain that Valentina was, through vocal technique, singing like a man to "bring out the meaning" of the song. Valentina explained the reasoning behind the lyrics: "There is no cure (medicine) for radiation," meaning "the only cure for radiation is more radiation," in which she refers to the many aggressive radiation treatments that those with cancer underwent, the rates of which were not detected in the Marshall Islands prior to US nuclear weapons testing and that have yet to be recognized as being caused by radiation and its aftereffects. Particularly in this context, Western medicine does not make sense, nor do the sensibilities through which Western medicine has been produced and administered make sense. Although there is no immediate cure, singing is one way to create community and mobilize solidarity in the creation of new political subjectivities and communities of sense.

The song's form can be analyzed in a number of ways: AB, AA'A", verse-chorus in three parts, three sections with a call and response. The song can also be read as a layered tripartite appeal or petition with three main sections (I, II, III) within which are three parts rendered in five lines. "Radiation" is the preliminary statement. The first two lines are a statement; they begin with a plaintive "O" ("Woe") followed by explanation of the lament. There is a statement of facts, and the emotional tenor of the hearing is set. These two lines are followed by three questions, each of them presenting her "summary of argument" as she clearly expressed in Marshallese and English during the first interview: "What things will solve the problems that her community endures?" Implied in this question is the connective silence that it is incumbent upon Americans to respond in kind by doing that work, which would be the ethical/right of interdependent action rather than maintaining some structure of "dependency." Finally, each section closes with the justification of the overall argument. Such rhetoric speaks to the role of the moralized voice that aims to combat the political legislation of violence through the creation of an ethical bond as legal right (to land, to recompense).

As the promissory note that hangs in this and other removal songs, MORIBA is part of the motivation, but so too is Bikini, not only as the homeland but also as a way of relating sensibly to the world. "Radiation" shares in melodic form why, through a series of provocations, the singer is *būromōj*. She tries to return, but because of radiation she is denied community in her "home sweet home." The musical form also becomes a place wherein sonic histories become ordered through markers of displacement, increasingly refusing the hierarchical order of harmony through detours from home that should be home, such as a deceptive cadence and off-kilter melodies. Singing becomes a way to exercise these throat-based memories, to reinvigorate the singer and resist the deadened perceptual habituation to life in diaspora via detours to "home sweet home" that is performed in melodic flow relative to the word *radiation* and the line "I am *jojolāār* on an island that is not mine," which stress displacement as well as the reason (radiation) and the result of displacement (jojolāār).

Radiation

I'm *būromōj* about my island
The place where I was young and I grew up
What things will make my throat (heart) peaceful?
So I can stop thinking about it
My island is my "home sweet home"
Oh, I'm *būromōj* about my island
So much radiation has appeared (on the Geiger)
What things will solve these problems
Because there is no cure (medication)
cure to get rid of radiation
Oh, I am *jojolāār* on an island that is not mine
There is a great deal of suffering that is appearing
What things will help get rid of this suffering?
Because I am one
Who has no place [*bōnbōnin*] in these islands

Throughout this journey the singer makes a detour to the grounded sensibilities of an intimated chant that resounds "on an atoll that is not mine," which is an antiphonal invitation that remains without response, further intimating the distance that radiation has created. Displaced, her "throat" is restless. She wails/sings because she is not at peace. In pursuit of a "cure" she must make sound, both in defamiliarized nonsense and the melodic wailing of the contours of "radiation" that are in her "home sweet home," where she is not (and therefore not herself). Connecting loss of mother/ matriline, hunger/loss of fullness, and malnutrition (radiogenic ailment/ depression) to displacement, jojolāār is "used as an analogy for landless people who have been evicted from their land." Adding the component of suffering, a man from Enewetak in exile told Tobin, "To be moved away from one's home atoll to another is a little like dying."[16] The word *jojolāār* refers to a chick without its mother and means that the singer lacks guidance (mother, feminine voice from her land) and is left without her senses: her mind (stomach) is empty and her throat desensitized because she cannot feed herself; she has no agency within this milieu. The term speaks to Bikinians' political positioning through displaced indigeneity as "third-class citizens," according to a councilman, and their positional (dis)identification with violence and morality (military and missionaries) as political legitimacy via Americans. Bikinians refer to themselves as "America's children," so the name in the context of the song might recall less a pejorative moniker than critical commentary on the US refusal to care for (or feed, as this chapter details) Bikinians, stripping them of commensality on multiple levels.

Modernity's political performatives cohere through iterations of pain and suffering, which creates the sense of pain as a possible effective political alliance.[17] The presence of radiation *in the bodies* of Bikinians (and in Bikini), one that would remain there indefinitely, became first a stigma. Later, when compensation for nuclear damages was awarded and the Bikinians had more money than the other atoll communities, their fragmentation from their atoll was desirable. But at the root of the money was the uncertainty and upheaval caused by radiation and dislocation. For any hope of healing, new communities of sense and modes of belonging need to be redrawn. A detailed reorientation of emotions and language to articulate such an orientation is required as is the thorough reorientation to concepts of porousness, immunity, and protection. Gendered relations are a powerful way in which the Bikinian community resounds its "voice-crossing" to the US systems of communication and remediation.

In both recordings of the song, Valentina sings in an alto register and is within what, in Western soprano, alto, tenor, bass (SATB) logic "sounds" conventionally feminine.[18] There is a part in which Valentina intimates a chant in which she pushes the bottom limits of her range, but I later found out that her singing style "like a man" was caused by a more restrained, "less" throat-based, dynamic approach that intimated a political stance, a diplomatic veneer to the song. Sharlynn, a Marshallese woman living in

Arkansas who had married a Bikinian, listened to the recording over the phone and without skipping a beat said, "I know that song. It's a Bikinian song. She is singing like a man to imitate all the elder men—those leaders who were men, such as King Juda. The leaders would compose the songs, not the women. Most of our history is not written; it is passed down by our voices and movements."[19] Here she refers to the political leaders, and, as such, Valentina's relational voice is male. Although the radio version normalizes the male vococentrism of the modern voice, Valentina's song defamiliarizes the male voice with respect to timbre, register, and gendered optics. As a mother, Valentina sings in a male voice because in her displacement, it is the disembodied male voice that has been normalized as the protective "political medium (representation of citizenship)" in the national envoicement of men. In the Bikinian nation, Valentina envoices this masculine national envoicement in ways similar to how she resounds onomatopoeia of the voices of machines and other moving bodies.[20]

When listening to this song, however, Sharlynn reflected: "There is no movement. She is sitting by herself, and because there is no movement, the voice must convey the meaning.[21] She is not with us. She looks to the past and the future, but not now. Where can she survive? She is lost without her land, and it is like she is crying. This situation is *beyond slavery*."[22] Sharlynn points to the myth of voicing as freedom or overcoming, particularly when the voice is attached to the nation, as this song is through the representative voice as genre of the political leaders. The exhaustion of the voice in secular modernity comes from the notion of the human and particularly the male figure as that which has agency above all else. The male voice is the genre through which Valentina, a respected song leader, must make her testimony, questions, evidence, and appeals heard given the limits of secular modernity and the social imaginary that positions her as an agent, albeit an agent who is compromised as an Indigenous woman, which is juxtaposed with the freedoms of Marshallese women in their customary positions of empowerment. Away from her land, "beyond slavery" or in her post-liberation space of contemporary liberalism—liberated as individual voice of self-mastery heard as detached from all but the body that sings it—she labors with her voice to be heard within society, with the authority and respect that Marshallese women are due but that are now afforded only to men and masculine gestures of protection, such as the cultivation of the nation.

"Radiation" is an example of the forcible immobility of being bound by violence as vocation. Valentina's voice is trapped in a gendered register, regardless of sonority, within which she sings counter-dispositive motions (appeals) against the "full and final settlement of all claims arising from the nuclear testing program."[23] To hear themselves as critically present—as witness and plaintiff, as representative and politician, and as Christian subject in exile—Bikinians reinvent their voices through a repertoire of songs that inscribe the juridical, political, and ethical coordinates of their nuclear experiences in performances that are both exceptional and structure their daily lives. Bikinians continue to develop the themes of their nation to connect with others, and they approach this through the cultural figure of the *lōrrọ* (flying women, wailing in grief) with a consubstantial *būromōj* (grounded man, speaking nonsense), both of which connect the body politic through the unintelligible voice to throat to stomach to inability to be nourished. They draw their motto and national symbolism from the restaging of an already staged encounter, vocally remediating the terms of loss while manifesting the spirited unrest in moments of rest and rejuvenation through remedial vocality. Being decisive as an individual voice depends on a particular certainty or desire of an end, such that in cases outside of a goal-driven settlement, starting from the end point would afford a telos or narrative consistency. Focusing on the structures of feeling and on senses of becoming ancestral (spiritual unrest as endurance and outreach) demands an entanglement of thinking, listening, and voicing together as sharing sounds and circulating rules and roles, taste (gustatory) as tear-wet/tear-rip, touch as sharing feeling, and smell as hearing (atmospheric closeness), where harmony can be sung sweetly (as in aural or smell or taste).

THE BIKINIAN NATION

The Bikinian nation is led by the Kili/Bikini/Ejit (KBE) local government, which has offices in Majuro Atoll and, as of 2016, in Springdale, Arkansas. In 1985, after voting an overwhelming 80 percent against the COFA, the Bikinians decided it would be politically efficacious to define their own national identity to stand apart from the RMI. The Bikinian community leaders, all men, worked together on the design of the nation. They worked with American men, particularly Jack Niedenthal, the Bikinian liaison to the US government from 1987 to 2016. The nation draws on Bikinians' cultural history, tied to Marshallese customs and American geopolitical culture, including but not limited to the nuclear disasters that poisoned their ancestral homeland and Bikinians who returned (1972) to Bikini Atoll

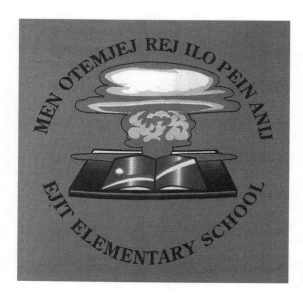

3.2 Ejit Elementary School uniform logo.

before being evacuated (1978) for a second time. The nation pushes back against its denied access to the US sovereign through political interference (the RMI). Bikinians' national productions include Bikini Day (March 7, day of removal), a flag, a motto, and an anthem.

The motto, when visually depicted, usually appears as the acronym "MORIBA." MORIBA functions to mark American exports and, through their incorporation, repurpose them. On Ejit Island, the letters grace everything from T-shirts with the Nike swoosh to refrigerator magnets to the backboard of a basketball hoop. The school uniform for Ejit children (grades K–5) is one of the most stunning visual representations of the Christian and nuclear biopolitical confluence, and MORIBA (spelled out) is elevated in the design, emphasizing its importance (see figure 3.2). The uniform is a bright-orange shirt with a fiery mushroom cloud extending upward from an open book draped in the RMI flag, which rests on a podium tabletop. Over the mushroom cloud is a halo that separates a white cloud, trumping the size of the mushroom cloud. The top semicircle of words reads "Men Otemjej Rej Ilo Pein Anij," and the bottom semicircle reads "Ejit Elementary School."

The back wall of the inside of the school has the symbols of the two atoll chains that form the republic (the RMI) in red and white (keeping with the American color symbolism), conflating the two countries. A black rectangle with the words "MEN OTEMJEJ REL ILO BEIN ANIJ" and another

3.3 Bikini Atoll flag. Illustration courtesy of Jack Niedenthal.

representation of the mushroom cloud coming out of a book are on this wall. The hallways, which I discuss in the next chapter, show pathways to Bikinian-Marshallese culture rather than this Bikinian-American culture. There is one visual representation of the islet that reads "Ejit Island, Almost Heaven," referring to the current impasse, singing out between Bikini Atoll and the United States. The flag also represents the outstanding promises and debts that Bikinians believe accrue interest over time (see figure 3.3).

The Bikinian flag was adopted in 1987, shortly after the United States recognized the RMI as a politically independent nation. The twenty-three white stars represent the islands of Bikini Atoll. The three black stars in the upper right corner symbolize the three islands vaporized by the Bravo thermonuclear test. The two black stars on the lower right side stand for Ejit Island and Kili Island. The words "Men Otemjej Rej Ilo Bein Anij" are etched into the flag. The close resemblance to the US flag acknowledges an outstanding obligation that the Bikinians maintain and locates national development as part of American postwar "permanent alliance" projects. As such, everything is not simply in God's hands. The marked American flag marks the "generalized reciprocity" that thoroughly enmeshed Bikinians with the United States.[24]

These diplomatic fragments are recollections and re-fusals of the Bikinian diasporic legacy via American Atomic Age diplomacy. For the Bikinian community, they work hard to keep the MORIBA memories alive. A number of songs have the theme and/or title of MORIBA. Glen Peters, originally from Arno and who married a half-Rongelapese, half-Bikinian woman, wrote the theme song "MORIBA" in 2003 for the Ejit baseball team of the same name.[25] The team had planned to travel to Hawaii, but because of "financial reasons" their trip was suspended indefinitely. Peters told me that his inspiration for writing the song was the initial relocation of the Bikinians as connected to life on Ejit Island today. His compositional inclination was to express the movement of the Bikinians from their homeland and the back and forth, the uneasy and uncertain feelings of daily life on Ejit. While I was on Ejit, "MORIBA" was performed almost every week at a community event or after church service. Sometimes it was performed twice in one day. Once it was performed a cappella in three-part harmony in the church, and three hours later it was performed during a meal at the community center (which is about twenty steps from the church) on an electric Yamaha keyboard with programmed music that simulated a slide guitar reminiscent of a country song. Specifically, I recall the triple meter of the second rendition, with the keyboard timbre as it transformed the song from its earlier "sacred" sound performed in the church to the more "secular" country sound when it was performed in the community center. Bikinians, and Marshallese in general, adapted American working-class sensibilities during the trust territory period, and Marshallese still have an affinity for country-western music and baseball/softball, which are coded with a masculinity shared by troops and through American media but are performed and played by all.[26]

The motto is also considered by some Bikinians with whom I spoke to be akin to a untranslatable *jabokonnan*, a Marshallese proverb that means "end" or "edge" "of talking," in the literal sense.[27] MORIBA cannot be translated as "Everything is in God's hands" in the way that it is often explained for its allying affect, because, like any ṃwilaḷ (deep) word, MORIBA is part of the meta-sense that is memory. It is the memory of the Bikinian and US nuclear encounter as it manifests in the diasporic situation in the present. As Councilman Hinton Johnson explained, "Even though the words *men otemjej rej ilo bein Anij* are not explicitly said in the national anthem, when you talk about MORIBA, you always imagine the national anthem. So we always sing the anthem and then say the words, and then we pray for the words. This is how the MORIBA always goes with the anthem."[28] It is significant that Bikinians pray on the words, for this is the political economy in diaspora where investments are in words on paper and in the air.

CHAPTER THREE

THE ANTHEM

National anthems exemplify the "imagination" or the ideas, aims, and ideals that are representative of a coherent community. "*I jab pād mol, aet I jab*" sounds a politics of loss, of mourning, as defining the national imaginary in a dissonance with the (concept of the heavenly gift) of Bikini as full. The Bikinians' adoption of their anthem was a political statement. It is sung for foreign guests and when the community has a large celebration. It is not sung at *kemems* (first-year birthday parties), for example. For large events (New Year's Day, Liberation Day, Bikini Day), the anthem always opens the ceremony and sets the tone. It never closes a ceremony. Deacon Johnny Johnson, a Bikinian elder and councilman, was one of my main Bikinian mentors. He explained that it must be sung prior to the event to set the keynote. He brought up the Fourth of July and said that Bikinians will sing it for Americans because they want to "make an impact" and share the "feeling" of their "hospitality and kindness," which translates to the performative moral reciprocity of their atoll having been taken for the *good* of mankind.

Kessibuki's composition "*I jab pād mol*" ("No Longer Can I Stay, It's True") was written in 1946 while he was in exile on Rongerik Atoll.[29] Stricken with grief, the community leader was nauseated and beside himself, crying uncontrollably. He recalls leaning up against a rock, and out of nowhere, the song—words and melody—just flowed from him. The song begins with the statement of a fact ("No longer can I stay, it's true"). Lore cannot stay on his atoll because he was removed so the United States could test nuclear weapons. Because of this, he cannot stay in "peace and harmony." The last verse shows his spirit drifting away and becomes "caught in a current of an immense power," and only then will he "find tranquility."

No Longer Can I Stay, It's True

I. No longer can I stay, it's true
I cannot stay in peace and harmony
On my sleeping mat and pillow because of
my atoll and the full environment there
II. The thought is overwhelming,
Rendering me helpless and in great despair
III. My spirit leaves, drifting around and far away
Where it becomes caught in a current of immense power
And only then do I find tranquility

In 1991 Kessibuki, who died in 1994, shared his recollections of composing the anthem in an interview with Jack Niedenthal, who documented Bikinian elders' oral histories and translated the song. Niedenthal's translation of the anthem, which stems from his impressions of conversations with Kessibuki, is used by Bikinians to make the song intelligible to English speakers and has been made available to Bikinians and non-Bikinians alike. This anthemic translation is afforded by Kessibuki's reminiscence, which might be considered along the lines of a restaging of the Bikinians' nuclear exile, for they were portrayed in the American—and global—media as actively enjoying (and even appreciating) their lives on Rongerik, even though they were literally starving.

When thinking about this song in terms of the modern political agency of the secular citizen subject, the voice dialogues the three privileged senses in secular modernity: the eye (sight), the ear (hearing), the hand (touch/taking). The voice connects the imperial gaze to territorialization via sounding text that touches or tethers through promises, promissory notes, and singing in harmony, reminding Americans of their breached promises. Taking Indigenous sensibilities via the throat, voices thus forge direction and relational paths. Depathologizing the individual voice can create new pathways and routes for community building in the struggle for solidarity in health and healing that exceed citizenship as the normalized mode of belonging. Listening to the Bikinian anthem by way of the voice articulated to the land and person through the throat and the stomach shares how the strong currents become a type of noise (see chapter 4), which is related to nausea, for Bikinians feel their promises have been breached: "It is no coincidence that the word [noise] has its etymological roots in the Latin *nausea* . . . noise is frequently the name we give to the element of disruption or dissonance in both sound and the social: a failure properly to harmonize, the breach of peace, a kind of sickness."[30]

Extending and expanding upon a politics of the voice, the throat is the material from which (dis)connection is possible, yet it also shares spiritual unrest (būromōj) as anguish and distress. Bikinians feel that singing literally connects them with Americans and allows them to maintain Indigenous self-determination by employing their voice in intelligible musical forms, resisting while expressing depression and unintelligibility, and preserving vocal traditions that animate cross-generational sociality and education, while pointing to the conundrum that their Indigenous grounds and prospects of sociality and education have been compromised. Bikinians' (in)equality and (un)democratic voicings were described by Councilman Johnson:

The [Bikinian] national anthem and those songs written by the elders and the songs from this generation with the word MORIBA speak to the circumstances of [us] Bikinians. And another thing I would like to share with you is, like I said before, according to what we know from our custom, the Marshallese custom, especially the Bikinian custom, I would say, people who are lonely or have lost something, you can tell those people in the Marshall Islands because they always sing songs.

It is like people who get divorced and the husband feels sorry [about] the [loss of his] wife. He keeps singing songs all the time; every time when you see him, he always shares those songs with you. So, for us, it is like that—losing Bikini really makes us keep singing and singing and singing. It is like people who divorce from each other, so they feel sorry.

In our custom, we always sing songs. So this is what you see—what you will find with the Bikinian community; they always sing songs, or [in other words]—they are always keeping their memories of their homeland—so that is why they always keep singing songs.

Johnson references important Marshallese understandings of the function of singing, both in terms of activating memories of Bikini (homeland) and political engagement, both of which depend on the voice as a question of the community in distress. Here he alludes to an important figure in the Marshall Islands, the lōrrọ. The lōrrọ has a counterpart, the male būromōj, both of whom suffer from the grief caused by the loss of their male or female counterpart, respectively.[31] Today, the figures are representative of the nuclear exiles away from their land who, in societal upheaval, can be lōrrọ and būromōj. The lōrrọ appeared around the Japanese period on what was both the German and Japanese administrative base of Jaluit Atoll.

Not coincidentally, this period was a time of upheaval in which communities were displaced for war fortifications. Marshallese women also had Japanese partners who would leave, or the women would be taken from the Marshall Islands. Chapter 1 points out that "*Ioon*" was rumored to be (in part) about Laabo's inability to reach her Japanese pilot boyfriend in the midst of war. The relational voice emerges from the broken heart, or throat, following a departed partner in flight (*kalok*). Lōrrọ are "real" women, my interlocutors stressed. Some explained that they took flight through their voices as materialized souls because the soul escapes or leaps from its seat in the throat. The disruption of customary symbolic weight distribution, such as relative height, is telling because women, who are customarily in charge of land-based activities and are "heavy" (*dedo*), become so light that they fly and can sit on a pandanus leaf, wailing. The soulless body is on the beach, facing the ocean and sobbing, perhaps at the edge of where the departed love connects through the waves. Even though one of the women's characteristic mobilities is the freedom to fly like a bird, this flight and melodic wailing is deemed uncontrollable.

Similarly, men are customarily in charge of the surrounding waters and skies, which are gendered male (the dry lands and sky are gendered female for the guidance and stability); men are mobile in their political capacity to articulate the guidance that is given by the women's direction. However, the būromōj becomes blind and sedentary. He eats feces (lacks nourishment) and speaks *kajin bwebwe* (crazy talk). He is directionless and nonsensical. Both figures are removed from the collective, and both incessant vocalizations are, on some level, nonsense or noise (nausea). In their soul loss they cry out to the community for help in their own disentangling capacities. The Bikinians, away from their land, sing themselves a consubstantial community with the traits of the lōrrọ and būromōj in number of intricately composed songs. The voices of the lōrrọ and būromōj, the melodic wailing and the nonsensical noisiness, materialize in ways that become sensible and sensical when heard within the overarching structures of musical harmony, such that non-Marshallese hear their appeals as musical outreach or performance-based activism. In this respect it is crucial to hear the severed throat and split voice in terms of the individuated political voice, which resounds the disembodied male subject of normative schizophonia (on record), produced through being forcibly removed, set above the waves, and needing to talk about it (pray on it).

Rather than recognizing the songs only in terms of diplomacy, the lōrrọ can be perceived in terms of "spiritual unrest" or "soul loss."[32] According to Erdland, "the Marshallese Soul" as quoted in *Traditional Medicine in the Marshall Islands* sees the lōrrọ as the soul taken flight: "The soul is considered a limpid being deeply hidden in the interior. . . . But it does not represent the absolute principle of life, because it can be separated without causing it to disintegrate, on the other hand it can be united with the body without having a reviving influence. The first case we have when women fly out of distress . . . according to the natives the flying being is nothing else than the soul."[33] He then explained that this accounts for the lightness of the flying woman (lōrrọ), who sits on a pandanus leaf (because she is so light). Erdland also writes that there are a number of stories in which the spirits carry off the soul. (Spirits have come to be called "supernatural beings" by anthropologists and "timons" [demons] by missionaries, but Marshallese understood them to be "real human beings.") There are different accounts of the lōrrọ. Most Marshallese say she is a human woman or a spirit (like a fairy) "with outstretched body, flowing hair, and arms folded over the back. She glides slowly through the air in this position and is clearly recognizable as a human being."[34] Marshallese say that she becomes so light that she flies around, and she flies to uninhabited parts of atolls "where there are heavy strands of trees. There, she alights on pandanus or palm leaves, without sliding down" from the very edge and continues to sing and sing. While the lōrrọ is singing her melodic elegy, the woman in mourning is crying on the shore, her physical body distanced from her spirited body: "In order to bring her to herself again, a witch doctor gives her a medicine, made of the juices of herbs and beetles, that makes her vomit. The 'throat' is thereby cleared of anguish, and the woman no longer feels sad. At that moment, the astral figure vanishes, as does the ability to fly."[35] Once the throat is cleared of anguish, of what is poisoning her or blocking the throat, the woman becomes "heavy" or grounded.

In both "The Marshallese Soul" and "Mental Sickness" in *Traditional Medicine*, the lōrrọ is mentioned as having to do with soul loss:

> According to the Marshallese, emotions, and this includes sadness and fear, are related with the throat, and the throat actually "is" what in the western concept is ascribed to the heart. To be afraid is called būromōj and means the throat is restrained [there are many definitions for this word]. Thus many Marshallese will refer to matters of the heart by pointing to the throat. For the concept of lōrrọ, flying women, the throat is responsible. [August] Erdland, with his keen interest in the Marshallese perception of the world, regretted never to have seen a lōrrọ. . . . "Unfortunately I have not been able to see a flying woman myself. I also disputed with the natives a woman's ability to fly. They pitied me because of my disbelief and thought the white man would not be able to understand deeply felt love. Then they cited the names of many women, who had been seen flying and would not budge from their view."[36]

More frequently than not, the archetypes for what can be seen or heard, felt or thought, have been via the sense as sensibilities of the modern Westerner (the "white man"), such that his sense (universalized mind) and sensibilities (particular body and mind) are congruent and therefore his reality *makes sense*. Here, Erdland's position disabled his perceptual stability, such that he was never able to see a lōrrọ. The flying woman is but one manifestation; it is through her melodic wail that she summons attention from the community to help her clear her throat with Marshallese medicine. The administration of this medicine (*uno in majel*) is meant to help her vomit to relieve the anxiety from her throat, given that she is būromōj and her throat is "restrained" or "deadened"; in the case of radiogenic attacks on the throat from thyroid, lymphatic, and nodule surgeries/removals without remedial aftercare, the definition of būromōj as "cut throat, means to be very sad" takes on a layered, pernicious meaning. Similarly, part of the remedial, healing process is the community's intervention in which they forcibly "ground" her and make her vomit to alleviate the tense throat.[37] The administration of Marshallese medicine, such as plants from the atolls, effectively causes *disgust* that provokes *nausea* and the regurgitation of the contents of the lōrrǫ's stomach back through the esophagus and the throat to beyond the (now grounded) body.

Disgust is an emotional response akin to aversion or repulsion to something that is toxic, poisonous, or spoiled. Grief and lament might persist for days, weeks, months, or even years, whereas disgust is often more acute and ephemeral. When it comes to the splitting up with a romantic partner, nostalgia and self-blame can perpetuate grief, which can cause isolation and further ailments. Rather than lamenting the loss of a partner, disgust with the situation might help clear the stomach (the mind in Marshallese body perception), and doing so through the retrograde pathway avoids further absorption through the intestines, such that the toxins are cleared from the mind and body and the former lōrrǫ can think clearly and assess the situation with her community. For Bikinians in nuclear exile, the onset of disgust might be politically efficacious. Instead of being consumed by grief, disgust creates the impetus to clear one's stomach and mind of toxins, allowing the person to be more open to participating in the community and engaged in what can be read as sensory democracy, through which the import of the cosmological system inheres in place-based values that are routed through sensibilities.

Attention to the lōrrǫ/būromōj redirects participatory belonging and potentiality from the schema of modern progress and linear (democratic) inclusion model, in which a private citizen uses voice to be included in public-sphere decision making to the relational, interlocking voice that "shakes the spirit." The mother/son, gender, intergenerational, (non)human voices are ideally complementary through their movements that are part of the harmonic composition of Bikini Atoll's "fullness," which Bikinians would often lament as something to which they no longer had access. The private/public divide has been mapped unequally onto gendered subjects and the concept of voice whereby the male "head of the house" would be the vocal representative for his family in the public sphere while the woman tended to the private or domestic matters and would not concern herself with politics. This dynamic is incommensurable with Marshallese feminine political authority that arises from values of gendered complementarity; it is incommensurable with the notion of the silent, passive, and senseless or spiritless land.

Rather than treat Kessibuki's composition in terms of a voicing in the liberal democratic model of participation as inclusion into an Americanized structure that requires particular rigors of voicing to be heard in the first place as an individual self, an agentive subject, the lōrrọ figure shares "soul loss" as a particular disabled voice as (non)human gendered dissonance, where anguish and pain recall two specific aspects. One, gender is not applied customarily to humans alone such that the human and nonhuman binary needs reappraisal in intersections of compulsory disability and compulsory voice in foundations of the nation-state (via the Bikinian nation). Two, the model of linear progress from private to public enabled by the gaining or honing or using of voice to make harmony (agreement, MORIBA), which assumes a moralized move to the inclusive *good* (for mankind), must also be reviewed if ontologically societal belonging was never in question but a performative realization based upon cosmological values and rules—rules that established hierarchies, roles, and responsibilities based on systems of cultural reproduction—created such distress and pain. Taking the anthemic grief as disability aesthetics read through the de-pathologized or de-individualized voice, the voice that cannot be voiceless, approaches accessibility from the terrapolitical, which is the communal Indigenous body politic, and the biopolitical, which is the individual (liberal) body politic or the sovereign and subject.[38]

Poetics of Lōrrọ (from Kessibuki's Compositional Narration)

1. Nausea: weak and sick stomach, intelligence and strength fading
    — lōrrọ in need of vomiting, clearing "mind"
2. Coconut tree: sustenance, sprouting, and regeneration (metaphor)
    — lōrrọ, away from her land, sits on tree leaves
3. Images/memories rush into his mind about Bikini (fragments of remembrance, crack in the painful surface)
    — formation of base on which to build

4. Composing in the cracks of despair a new world, a hope, a vision (a "dream")
    — "in my soul" (burō), process of rerouting nausea to clarity (process of lōrro)
    — Bikini, repetition (×4), ongoing—still there, like a roro (endurance)
    — Helps him put together, connect, Bikini through the multisensorial recollections (memory of the senses)
        — White beaches with long walks and sand in toes (spatial)
        — Lush jungles with childhood adventures (temporal returns)
        — Taste—delicious fish (taste, strength, self-sufficiency, lagoon)
        — Touch—tombstones of elders (touch, protection, love, intimacy, ancestral connection)
        — Sailing in canoe across lagoon with fresh tuna—movement and fullness
        — Talk with family, here refers to *jitdam kapeel*, connecting knowledge
5. Reduced to tears: reflective moment of pause, būromōj
    —"crumbling" and "crying"
    —"losing my mind?"
6. Constructs powerful song: flows from depths of being, words from unknown source (ṃwilaḷ)
    —song of lōrro composed from the feeling of būromōj

POETICS OF SPIRITUAL UNREST

Kessibuki's narrative (as told to Niedenthal) can be read, according to Johnson's assessment, in terms of a poetics of the lōrro, whose grief from a separation makes her "take flight" (kalok).[39] He goes from walking on the beach with sand in his toes to "talking story quietly" (*bwebwenato*) and putting his head together with the heads of the elders, symbolizing knowledge transmission (jitdam kapeel) from toe (youth) to head (leader). The dreams Kessibuki had—the memories—were activated at the moment of the "cry break," from which the depths of his knowledge and the memory of the senses returns in words, which are the knowledge of the ancestors. This cry break will come to be of great importance intergenerationally to recall the ancestors such as Kessibuki and their journey, and it might also be drawn from an affective alliance with working-class Americans, given the importance of the cry break in country music as a technique that denotes or intimates crying, for Bikinians and Marshallese more generally have a appreciation for country music as being from the heart (throat) and having to do with loss of land and/or love.[40]

The vocal lament recalled the strong current in Bikini, and, Kessibuki said, it emanated from a deep collective *depression*.[41] This vocal currency materializes from the embodied movements of the homeland through which the song form *cleared his nausea* (noise) or his mind once he shared it or materialized his memories through voice, as a direction home to and through the current. Singing can be considered a vocal remediation of the body politic; the voice that connects in excess of the page redraws the very shape of the community in ways that alleviate the sociality of depression. This is not to say that the depression is *cured*, however. The Bikinians keep sharing this emotional song, which is not only like a strong current but *is a strong current* that gathers feelings, people, and provides the opportunity for critical contemplation and thus deliberate direction and political participation. The Bikinian anthem is part of sensory democracy insofar as it helps navigate the multimodal currents of the body politic, providing direction from feelings rather than letting them consume or set a person adrift. "Bikini is like a relative to us," Kessibuki lamented. Bikini is therefore more than a part of the body politic that needs re-pairing; Bikini is the familial, familiar body with which Bikinians shared a depth of love that nonnatives might not be able to perceive (but can respect). The compositional narrative is retold as a parable of perseverance, thus providing the "relational" focus of the Indigenous nation and its ability to be responsible by holding the United States responsible for disrupting its ability to compose societal cohesiveness via *iakwe* (relational pathways, atoll umbilicals, love), invested and sedimented over generations.

The soul moves through the throat from the stomach (intellect) and the gall(bladder) with the wind or breath: "While the throat is considered the seat of the emotions, the stomach is looked upon as the 'brain' while the gall is the center of life."[42] There are many different terms for throat, more than most body parts. There is also the expression for the onset of feelings, which happens when wind or breath moves through a person, spiriting or inspiring them (*bun*). The throat is part of this process of moving the wind through and activating the brain and gall, which aids in digestion. Food is a central part of the consubstantial culture and collective spirit. To be hungry, to lack sustenance, to feel nauseous, or to taste (take in) that which is spoiled, sour, or artificial are aligned figuratively and literally with spiritual unrest and separation from the community, and result in situational materializations of voicelessness.

THE CRY BREAK (DETOUR)

The figure of the lōrṛo is used by contemporary artists, such as Kili Excess, who were once the popular youth group from Kili Island and whose members, now older, have switched their band name to the MORIBA Band. The figures of spiritual unrest tie both names together, for Kili Excess and the MORIBA Band are spaces in which to organize records of the Bikinian journey across the KBE diaspora. The performative aspects of the songs, lectures, and stories that enable "cry breaks" or productive moments of harmonic decay that resist modernity's unrelenting forward motion are cultural modes of historical resistance to further erasure: the clean slate, what Mayor Alson Kelen in 2008 at our first meeting voiced in his concern about younger Kili Islanders who are trapped by a "metaphorical black screen." The black screen/clean slate, which is akin to living "in a dark room" and trying to imagine outside of the box, or outside of the room, he said, is akin to imagining the throat as "void" in some respects. And all the voided throat can do to be meaningful, recalling Steven Connor's statement, is become "something" as meaningful speech.[43] Kelen spoke to the ways in which Bikinian youths engage in a "labor of the negative." "[They talk about] the *lack of freedom* on Kili Island . . . because they can't talk about Bikini," he explained, "They are trying to imagine something they have never sensed."[44] He said of the all-male youth group Kili Excess, "I think bands like Kili Excess help people to understand these issues," he said with resolve. "Every time there is a youth gathering or church gathering and every time they write the songs, a lot of them are about Bikini. We are Bikinian—we live on the rock [Kili], so the story continues within the music within the culture because now [Kili] is part of the culture."

Kili Excess's "I'm Sitting on Green Leaves" opens with the lyrics "I am sitting on green leaves like a lōrṛo," homesick and dreaming about Bikini.[45] Within the song there are interplays that speak to Bikinian mobilities. The words *green leaves*, I was told, refer to money, and compared to one's land, money is light.[46] Money (*ṃani*) holds a contested place in Marshallese society in which the word even reflects broken Marshallese culture (*ṃani* is *ṃanit* [Marshallese culture/ways of being] without the "t"). Money is light, like the lōrṛo, and is part of the kalok, the taking flight of the soul without Bikini Atoll as a grounded sensibility. The song remediates aspects of the Bikinian anthem as intergenerational journey. "You are sleeping on a mat that is not yours" is a response to Kessibuki's anguished "No longer can I stay it's true, I cannot stay in peace and harmony on my sleeping mat and pillow. . . ."

Women weave the mats from the land, and here the line also speaks to the dispossession of the feminine voice, doubly so, and references the inability to be in "peace and harmony." Thus, the community is in perpetual unrest, only partially able to sleep and to dream, and partially able to be Bikinian in the sense of interlocking voices, which remain split as the lōrrọ recalls.

Of note are the lines that refer to the aḷap (landowner) not being on his or her *wāto* (land plot), which is the Indigenous form of belonging and inheritance, often matrilineal, rather than the political entity of the atoll municipality. The final verse explains that the situation is "beyond understanding"; it is senseless. The aesthetic negation (that which negates the sensorial and intelligible possibility of the song) throws into relief the orientation of the singer as lōrrọ. From the outset to the end of the song, the singer who wishes to return to the grounded sensibilities of the atoll sings in musical outreach "I know you'll do all you can" but remains sitting on green leaves, like a lōrrọ, nauseous or "homesick" for his atoll. This sickness is real and materializes in the voice itself, for we would not hear it in this way unless there was a broken system and relational problem in which singing in memory of the now intergenerational lōrrọ persisted. When reflecting on racial capitalism and indigenous dispossession, the work that Bikinians continue to do to appeal to be heard in their injustice of not being heard as a matter of the COFA must be taken as part and parcel of the soul loss. The voices of the musicians are only part of the cries of the lōrrọ; they are the melodic contours of the intelligible part through which the testimonial or appellate voice can be heard, as the male political voice: disembodied and light, sitting on green leaves, in flight.

The motif of "crying" emerges in many interlocutors' accounts of the performance of the anthem; this is the breakthrough of the būromōj. The anthem, as a song, structures the cry break that enables them, as Bikinians, to "touch" and therefore vibe, or resonate, with these non-modern-day-human Bikinians who are equal to and more than (reductions to) modern-day-humans, such as Bikinian spirits, ancestors, non-Marshallese, US/Americans, and non-Bikinian Marshallese. The musical bookends give amplification to the cry-break material, which sounds like a choked-up throat, and they direct all eyes, ears, and throat hearts toward the singers. Tears flow from the audience, showcasing their vocal currency through multiple harmonies and therefore socio-natures. Moreover, Bikinians can connect with the equivocal meaning of MORIBA and the "many" voices of the ancestors (*bwij*), thereby remediating the fictions upheld by US cable umbilicals through which a "dusty" past is strategically presented as an anesthetized record.[47]

A highly ranked Bikinian political official uses a stark, nearly minimalist conveyance of what might otherwise be, in Hollywood, shown with blaring soundtrack in "exilic" grandeur:

> Our anthem is sung on Bikini Day and other days, and whenever anyone asks to have it sung. It is a song that was written by an elder, Lore. It was written on Rongerik . . . the first land of relocation for the people of Bikini when they were starving. They had no food. This period of time was filled with many hardships, and some people died because of hunger. They had no water, and it was hard for them. One day he couldn't take it, and he decided he would compose a song, and he did. Now it's the "national anthem." You can go on the website and see the lyrics and translation.[48]

Bikini Day sets apart Bikinian collective memory from that of the nation state's holiday (holy day), NVSRD. What strikes me is to think about the relative "fullness" that Bikinians would talk about and the realization of the near starvation, which is how US American trust territory anthropologist Leonard Mason was able to appeal to the US government to remove Bikinians from Rongerik and place them momentarily in Kwajalein, then Kili, then Bikini, then Kili and Ejit. How many steps and how much energy are wasted in denying Bikinians communication, movement, connection, resonance with US Americans in ways that might enable them to demand that they are heard on and in their terms? Breaking Bikinian resonance and community—Bikinian harmony—is also told here. Their means of eating and eating together, being commensal community (sensorial, eating, sharing immunity), were torn from them.

The song, the official explained, "expresses dissatisfaction." This political sentiment evinces dissonance, rather than consent, of the governed—with US representations of Bikinians when the anthem was written (voiced over by the United States) and today (voiced over by the RMI and then by the United States). The official paraphrased Kessibuki: "I am not happy with what I am going through now, especially when I think about my islands." He shifted back to explanation: "It is a very emotional song for people, and even people who don't understand the song when they listen to it. Maybe it is the rhythm, the tune of the song. But when you sing, especially the old people, when they sing the song and they hear the tune, and they see the facial language, you can see every time they sing it that it is not just a song to sing; it is a song that comes from the heart—a song that tells their story."[49]

Breaking with harmony in the Bikinian anthem, I believe, materializes as a break with "peace" as/and "the flow" literally and physically, such that

Bikinians can connect affectively from their national political medium "MORIBA" (as Bikinians) in ways that do not make Bikinian an "other" to anyone. These performances are part of the emergence of new codes from lack (negation), such as the statement "no longer" and sentiment "no peace, no justice," that are imbued with the equivocality of voicelessness. This equivocality of voicelessness becomes a connective force that is tied to respect and subverts the prospects of listeners' adjudicative overdetermination whereby listening becomes akin to "giving voice." Adults and children are offered the Bikinian anthem as a space wherein crying is socially acceptable and promotes social bonding with Bikinians, non-Bikinians, and the ancestors. Bikinian children perform the pain of the elders through their own catharsis and contribute to the mode of lōrrọ as mode of tuneful recuperative loss. In this sense the break is a detour from the "just here" and "just now" space of the singers and audience. And as a detour from the "modern" harmonious moment, yet within the context of a harmonious, melodious song that shares pain, suffering, and long, the song is also "modern." The cry break, as Indigenous detour via disidentification (with non-Bikinian, nonnative audiences), becomes a way to subvert harmonic rhythm in ways that underscore Bikinians' "temporal multiplicity."[50] Through an audible detour from "universal harmony" that would sound some quality via temporal synchronicity to be judged, Bikinians commune with their absent-present and present-absent homelands and the intervening spirits that move through them, resisting the imaginary that they can be reduced to one time, one space, or one set of possibilities as "Bikinian."

Dissatisfaction becomes disidentification, which affords Bikinians self-determination through markers that have been used to define them as erased, their voices vaporized, and their bodies nameless laborers, save "King Juda" as a diplomatic relic "in the past." The recuperation of MORIBA by the Bikinian nation becomes an exercise in onto-cosmopoetic cosmopolitics or "a politics of harmony" that is addressed through different and similar notions of being and their relations that I discuss more specifically in the next chapter, when I write on "noise" not as unwanted sound but necessary to "clear" radioactivity from their Indigenous worlds (the best they can). The noisiness of the cry break clears some of the anesthetizing dust, perhaps, of the US nuclear spectacle through a subversion of what can actually be framed and shared and what is actually felt. And what is felt, the official explained, is the impress of time through the ancestors and, and *as*, the duration of the song in nuclear diaspora. Thus, this performance of displaced indigeneity is that which demands the "flow" to be heard not only in the harmonies but also in the breaks, as movement, perhaps a movement for justice: "Every time they sing it, because we have been singing it for *so* long—every time we sing it, we feel the presence of our ancestors next to us and we think about the hardships that they went through. We listen to it, and everything just comes back and hits us individually as we sing." This detour, which enables youths to sing into feeling and thus know that they can be empowered as a community to call upon their ancestors, even in the diaspora, to communicate or *resonate* with them in ways that shift the sensibilities of the spirit via movements (temporalities) that can be understood as a remedial, recuperative, and rejuvenating *rest* insofar as the ancestral spirits become through the young: "I think . . . the younger kids don't understand the full extent about Bikini, but with the anthem in particular, I think the spirit is still there because every time we sing the song you can even see it in the young people's eyes . . . tears."[51] Music is remedial education in this capacity; as a feeling, it becomes through the individual as sensory democracy.

The "affective alliance" thus needs to be troubled at the site of the liberal democratic voice, for this song is not about communal participation in total, but it is the split stage—the dividing line—that shares the freedom and lack of freedom *to sense* community (spirit) via voice. Crying enables MORIBA, as the motto, to become the multisensorial "memory of the senses," and with it the meta-sense of living with the word MORIBA can make sense. The projected commensality shifts from Bikinians starving together to being "in" the hands of God to the "sour taste" of the elders that the youths can taste through their tears, as means of feeling the current, as lightness, on their faces, to paraphrase Pastor Percy Benjamin of Ejit Island. He explained: "They left with broken hearts, and every time they share this story about leaving Bikini—oh, people cried out loud, and nowadays, people imagine, people felt, even taste how sour things were for the ancestors and how strong the leader, King Juda, was when he said 'everything is in God's hands.'" Juxtaposing the "sour taste" with "strength," Pastor Benjamin concluded his thought through a mode of identification that resounds displaced indigeneity as moral connection: "And this word is really strong, MORIBA. People from Bikini are really living with this word."[52]

(Dis)identification with Bikini works through songs and national productions that affirm a sense of loss as togetherness and diasporic strength. Without the experience of life, the land, and the senses in this way, it is difficult to imagine the land, so one must first feel the loss as something remarkable. C. Nadia Seremetakis speaks to the way in which things, foods that have disappeared and tastes forgotten, are digested as words. With the experience of *būromōj*, the throat is deadened. People with deadened throats are unable to produce the words that people can digest. Men, those who have a political obligation to speak on behalf of the community, are silenced and cannot provide for their family. Women, who are the vocal cheerleaders (shake the spirit) for the men with whom they consult on political decisions, cannot express their needs. What consequence might this have had in the RMI's abilities to espouse the claims of its citizens? The palate is deadened; what one tastes is neither the synthetic processed food from the USDA nor the *moña in majel* (Marshallese indigenous foods) from Bikini. The taste of tears, as history embedded in the materiality of its presence, brings forth memories of isolation in exile. These memories "remind" the population of its lack of agency for connection, and this is manifested presently as well in the inability for speech. The reminders, within the taking economy, demand movement in the form of connection, and this prompts the song to continue to be sung. The efficacy of the song is therefore in both the silence (dead throats) and sourness that connects the community, which produces and is a production of feeling the spirits through the song and anthem.

Social bonding, as feelings of love and togetherness, is afforded through acoustical crying and the production of tears. In this musical process, spiritual feelings and testimonial records coalesce into memories that can be voiced, documented, and shared. Singing therefore enabled Bikinians to keep their memories of their homeland alive through generations while being able to talk about their issues in an emotional or "throat-felt" way. Whereas Bikinians are remembering or keeping the memories of their homeland alive, as the feeling of the spiritual ancestors and in connection with Americans (as part of their affective and geopolitical history), they must also defamiliarize the harmonic contours of the song (e.g., through the collective cry break) in order to escape the confines of the modern limits on their citizenship and space of belonging that keeps them from testifying and makes their political voices (and their ancestors' political voices) impossibilities.

CURRENTS OF REMEMBRANCE

Some Bikinians refer to "*Ñe ij keememej tok aelōñ eo aō*" ("When I Remember My Atoll") as their "second anthem." Bikinians often performed the song for me when I asked about their "emakūt (movement/relocation)."[53] A Marshallese pastor penned the song while stationed on Kili Island in support of the exiled Bikinians. The composition onomatopoeically works to animate Bikinian collective memory in ways that materialize interlocking movements as the guidance afforded by the lineage and land. As they sing, Bikinians recollect feelings of guidance by the spirits or ancestors and the currents. The second anthem thus encourages an embodiment of the sensorial and epistemological values realized through wave-pattern navigation (e.g., sonic, oceanic). Here, the song positions emakūt—the felt motion and emotion—as a dynamic complex of exilic struggle and Indigenous survival. By echoing an incomplete MORIBA, "Ñe ij keememej tok" channels Kessibuki's determination to remember and echoes the leaders' call to "talk about it."

The melodic line reaches its climax on the word *strong* ("God is strong, leads us and protects us"). This is followed by the repetition of *"men otemjej rej ilo bein."* Interestingly, the line translates to "everything they are in the hands," which is a reference to MORIBA. The melody from the first verse is used for the second verse: "We thank our iroij and our elders, for they sacrificed so much for us to be here today and overcame life's strongest currents." The contemplative and reflective mood of the penultimate line is articulated with voices that gently ornament one another's movements like ripples, like *jipikra* (waves that encounter each other and transform each other's movement), on the words *jukae, ribukae, jelatae*, which are the three "zones of distinctive wave patterns that indicate relative distance toward land" (first zone, second zone, third zone).[54]

These wave patterns, or reflected navigational swells, are caused by "current streams [that] form choppy waves in an otherwise normal sea state irrespective of tidal movements and equatorial current streams." The three current zones enable the navigators to know how far they are from their "home atoll" and how close they are to the destination atoll. The first zone is ten to fifteen nautical miles from the home atoll, the second zone is midway between the two, and the third zone is ten to fifteen miles out from the destination atoll. Anthropologist Joseph Genz points out that this conceptualization of the currents acts as markers along the *dilep* (navigational backbone formed in between the atoll chains) and also "reinforce[s] the *kōkḷaḷ* and *kameto* in extending the range at which land can be detected" in addition to gauging the distance.[55]

The disrupted current patterns are important for way finding, and they are another example of decolonial dissonance, which marks distance and direction. Upon return, the current zones reflect the voyage, so the first current zone will always be called "jukae" and so forth (see figure 3.4). And the last line of the song, *"jukae, ribukae, jelatae,"* is the only other line to be

CHAPTER THREE

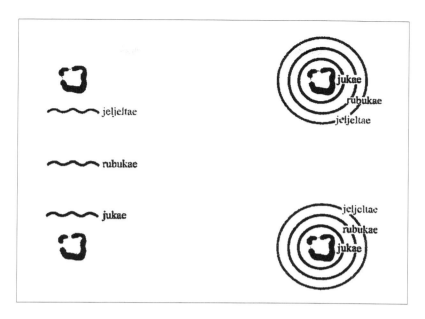

3.4 Conceptualizations of *jukae*, *ribukae*, and *jelatae* currents. Illustration courtesy of Joseph Genz, "Marshallese Navigation and Voyaging."

repeated (aside from "*men otemjej rej ilo bein*"). This gives the feeling of ongoing movement, but it might also be suggestive of a return to Bikini. Motifs of navigation and spiritual transformations are in the song text as well. The nuanced sensorial perceptions of the musical gestures offer the rhythmic modulations of feeling the transformations across the choppy currents to and from the atolls. The motion is smooth at first as the choir sings about the initial swell of the currents near the islands. With an additional repetition of the final line, the difficulty in overcoming the currents is audible. The lyrics that depict the currents farthest away from the atoll rhythmically convey increasing movement. The final lyrical gesture of the song is often executed with a decrescendo on a reverent plagal cadence that fades to silence.

VAPORIZED VOICES

The anthems provide directional guidance, and in this respect they are modalities of processual, relational voicing in the definition that voice is like a current insofar as it guides listening through the sharing of sounds.

Briefly, I want to introduce how the United States, in addition to threat-based radioactive envoicement, created the vaporization of voices both as disembodied male figure qua the written word and other schizophonic record-based echoes *as well as* the literal vaporization of lands through which voices are shared. Aerokojlol, Bokonijien, and Nam are the three islets that were vaporized by Bravo, leaving a mile-wide crater when irradiated coral, vegetation, and water were sucked into the atmosphere and shortly thereafter rained down onto the Marshall Islands, poisoning those in its path. Before March 1, 1954, however, Nam had a different distinction. It was part of a roro (reductively translated "chant") for "all the islands that combine to make Bikini," Johnson explained. The chant materialized from collective memory when the community, including Bikini, was mobilized in the construction of the canoes and the large trees with lumber they would get from Nam. Johnson, who was away from Bikini at the time, did not recall the chant himself, but he did stress that women were involved in the recitation and material production of the canoe as well as its launch, which meant knowledge of how to get the materials, assess and adjust to the tides, and push the trees from Nam to Bikini, "twenty-some miles away [on] really open ocean," all of which were on record in the oration. He continued: "They call [the island] Nam. And they push [the lumber] all the way to Bikini. So during the days and nights, the chant goes on . . . we pass it on to each other, but [these days] people don't consider them as important as the songs. I don't know why, but only a few people know the chants. But the songs, most of the people in the community know." Johnson would often distinguish the role of women from the political milieu of the male-oriented liberal democratic space in which KBE operated. He encouraged me to speak with women on Kili about older songs and chants because Ejit was more oriented toward political outreach.[56]

Communications systems are feedback loops, and when part is vaporized, be it an islet or the activity within the head/knowledge base, other parts atrophy. Johnson's comment thus refers to the deterioration of Bikinian communications systems, and the fact that he was speaking with me about songs that were not widely shared or commonly sung, especially those from the old women that he had heard growing up that now lived on Kili, speaks to the vitality and strength of people to recall their means of activation and form new connections that make meaningful sense. This process takes time and support, which is not what the Bikinians believe has been returned to them. For example, an Associated Press reporter who visited Kili just two months after Bravo characterized the island as the "land of the hungry people," whose only food at times was coconuts and copra.[57] Juda, the Bikinian magistrate, explained how the Americans had said, "We can never forget you. You gave up [your] atoll so America[ns] can go ahead of everyone in [the] world. The Americans gave me a new name. They called me King Juda. They said anything [I] need, come to Kwajalein and they will give to me." Juda died of cancer on Kili Island in 1968.

In 1968 Bikini Atoll appeared on the front page of the *New York Times*. President Lyndon B. Johnson explained that cleanup was underway and that in less than a year, Bikinians would safely be back on their atoll.[58] In 1972 three families moved back to Bikini, and a new generation was introduced to the reality of Bikini. In 1978 the Atomic Energy Commission first found unacceptable levels of radiation at Bikini Atoll, and the people who had moved to Bikini were becoming ill. The Bikinians petitioned the US government to leave, but an exhaustive study wasn't done until 1979. It was at this moment that many vowed to make sure they would go back, but only when the atoll was restored to its precontaminated state. This is not yet possible. Some of the most striking images of Bikini were those that contrasted the fullness of life and in particular the foods—all around— that nourish the soul (in the stomach) and thus the voice through the throat (seat of soul). The vocal attrition, which might sound to some as of Bikinians needing voice or help or handouts, actually comes from being starved by being denied of their foodstuffs in addition to their homeland. Memories through song can help, as Juda's son, Senator Tomaki Juda, recalled, can give people strength in times of depletion, such as Kessibuki's composition was done in lieu of food and spiritual sustenance to *"make him alive*, or to *make him strong*, to make him to try to *remember what was good* for the Bikinians in the midst of being forced to leave, which was *not good for them*."[59] The link of the lack of food with hardship is something that is woven into the teachings to give voice, as loss, to Bikinian youths as a memory of spiritual unrest, of hunger and being hungry.

Bikinian leaders teach stories of hardship to their youths by citing the Bikinian anthem as an educational tool, along with published materials drawn from American scholars and the media. Bikinian elder Bourn Johnson quoted the anthem multiple times during one such lecture to the Ejit community:

> [They can eat] only pandanus (*bob*) but the hard, the bad kind. On the trees only *nin* (tiny, tiny fruits). So the babies and the mothers, they are really, *really* crying a lot because they are *hungry*. They cannot look for food. So during this time, Lore, Lore is the one who composed "*Ijab pād mol, aet ijab*

pād"—that song. He saw the ladies and the babies . . . the women, they are really crying and they don't know to do at that time. So he went to the lagoon side, and when he sat on the big rock, the song comes to his mind—like, it just comes *"ijab pād mol, aet ijab pād"* . . . , and then when he is done, he went back to the camp and sang it to the men: *"Ijab pād mol, aet ijab pād."*

Drawing from American media and published materials, he delivered an account of life on Rongerik, his agitation increased and underscored in his repetitive use of the negative. Later, when I asked him to tell me about the lecture, he restaged it: "They cannot eat fish; they cannot swim on the beach because of mosquitoes," he explained. "They are allergic because of the poisoning of the fish. And, no, no, *no, no,* no coconuts. No more breadfruit. No more pandanus."[60] His explanation of the Bikinian anthem shows how it also marks a formative transformation in gendered roles when the men had to take care of the women and children within the context of scarcity, which had not occurred on Bikini Atoll, unlike other parts of the Marshall Islands during World War II.

Instead of the chant that brings Bikini together as fullness, the MOR-IBA national repertoire mobilizes the community to give it representative voice (testimony) and collective history (memory). The chant is positioned as bringing all the islands of Bikini Atoll together based on an entire system that was organized and self-sufficient, where everyone worked in the community (emphasized are women and men) to launch a canoe, which is symbolic of "the people" and their navigation or movement, and, through patterned rhythmic recitation over the course of days, would recall place-names that would "reveal" how to treat those places with respect to the connecting sea (tides, currents, animals), atmosphere (animals, winds), and land (all that is there). From this knowledge, they would know where to collect materials, which materials to collect (e.g., which trees or wood was best to use for specific parts of the canoe), and so forth. The negation of this knowledge becomes all the voices that leapt from Kessibuki's mouth, which can be read as the vaporized voices of the fragmented or (fully) unheard roro (chant). Bikinians would move through the land, needing at times to increase their emotional intensities, and thus they would employ roro. Singing affords another kind of harmonizing and bringing of spirits together; it is another communication pattern within another sociality. Here, through cry breaks and tears, Bikinians pause to feel and respect the ancestral spirits as well as to bring Americans close, such that Bikinians do not forget their spirited selves and Americans do not forget them either.

UNFINISHED CONCLUSION

Bikinians take in songs and materials written by others that speak to their experiences, as we have seen, and they use them as affective allying material to keep gathering more people until they no longer are lōrrǫ. However, songs of lōrrǫ aren't trying to teach Americans how to find deep love as some programmatic lesson. These are not "entertainment" packages. Bikinians believe that singing connects them with Americans, as does the departure from their land that was used in moralized destruction of the land and their emplaced identity. The moralization of displacement is akin to salvation or "suffering for science," particularly around nuclear weapons testing. The certain *feeling* that Bikinians attribute their anthemic gesture to is a bundle of dynamics that speaks to the relationality of the anthem, which is educational to Americans and to Bikinians. Aaron Fox writes that "feeling is a concept . . . that mediates between cognitive and embodied domains of cultural experience." This definition can also stand for "the throat" as resonant means of reasoning when time is afforded, which it has been since the anthem was first composed. Layered with research and lectures, Bikinians' and Americans' "feelings" that link the "subdomains of words and embodiment" are mediated through common and different histories and common and distinct socio-natures that "comprise an overarching and conceptually distinct third dimension" of the breach (difference) within harmony (in common) or/and of harmony smoothing the ontological breach.[61]

What is coded as morality, kindness, and love can also be read in terms of common histories through which morality and state-sponsored violence as political legitimacy are put into play and mapped through musicality that coheres the social domain. Bikinians' "love," "kindness," and "hospitality," as concepts, return us to the mediated space of their "friendliness" singing "You Are My Sunshine" to Commodore Wyatt. These essentialized traits of Bikinians—of their nation—are historically produced emotional connections that come to and through Bikinians and Americans when Bikinians sing their anthem. Sara Ahmed, following Marx, argues that "emotions accumulate over time as a form of affective value," which are then attached to objects wherein "feelings become fetishes . . . only through an erasure of the history of their production and circulation."[62] Love, kindness, and hospitality are the emotional orientations to the objects that constitute the Bikinian national sonic history through which violence and the vaporization of voices have, on the one hand, become constitutive of listening. Such listening is connected to love, lust, and the fetishized fragment that can be commodified, neutralized, and objectified—owned and possessed—which is necessary in this history of nuclear dispersals and radiogenic ruination for survival in the immediate present.

MORIBA marks this intensity, which, on the other hand, can be extended as part of the Pacific historicity of *longue durée*. Perhaps we can call "deep time" the love that is lost on "the white man," making it a historical love bound in the sonic event or listening, rather than the "apophatic listening" of sensory democracy that is an openness to hear and to be guided. For this is the type of love that seems necessary when beginning to reflect, not to mention sense, the appearance and audibility of the lōrrọ. Ahmed writes that "one could even think of love as a form of waiting. . . . To wait is to extend one's investment and the longer one waits the more one is invested, that is, the more time, labour and energy has been expended. *The failure of return extends one's investment.* If love functions as the promise of return, then the extension of investment through the failure of return works to maintain the ideal through its deferral into the future."[63] There are, of course, issues with the prefabrication of empathy, as a nineteenth-century concept of universal in-feeling as being in-common, which Ahmed points out, as well as the tendency for proprietary feelings, feelings that individuate us while making us feel connected in a supposed empathy where one person imagines they can feel something *for* someone else or on that person's behalf. This is where the time of investment as engendering resonance becomes so important. Like the unfolding of radiation, resonance takes time to hear and feel as hearing when it is produced together. The problem with the lōrrọ and the Bikinian anthem performed for Americanized subjects is thus a problem of the violence articulated to moralized political legitimacy that manifests in the voice guided by nuclear listening. Bikinians are listened to, particularly when they sing in the Marshallese language, as "othered," having been exoticized and linked to nuclear erasure in US media, not to mention connected by name to the hypersexualized bikini bathing suit. More about their name as part of fetishized violence (the bikini swimsuit, the atom bomb) is known than their Indigenous sensibilities. Without the ability to collectivize and work together in long-term fashion, the song becomes another story to feel good about telling or knowing to tell, like disaster tourism and nuclear listening to extract a story.

It is here that I want to briefly mention how I first heard the anthem from Deacon Johnny Johnson, for it speaks to his impact on my work and on this chapter in particular. After Johnson sang the song with his closed eyes, he opened his eyes and looked directly at me: "I think the song needs a conclusion. I want to write one. What do you think? Can you help me finish our anthem?"[64] His eyes lit up while he emphatically expressed his vision for a global Bikinian anthem. Citing the song "We Are the World" as his template, Johnson shared the prospective lyrics that would voice the ongoing trials and tribulations of his people as a global concern. There is much to be said about the problematic role of humanitarian aid and "the gift of voice," and "We Are the World" is no exception. However, I read Johnson's attempts as more rhetorical, especially because he mentioned how, given my role in academia, perhaps I could help by working on a fellowship for a Bikinian student to attend college. The conclusion is beyond listening to the anthem, beyond marketing the tears of youth that are racialized, classed, gendered, and written off as voiceless until they are heard otherwise. I hear the conclusion of the anthem in the rewriting of the system from which it was born, which is no simple task. The rewriting of the system comes with instrumental breaks, fissures, and detours to alternative sites of communality, collectivity, and sociality. They breach harmoniousness mediated from above and demand the noisiness of being and becoming to comingle between us as thoughtful, sensible, reasonable, and historically shaped beings. Johnson's invitation, along with my other experiences in the Marshall Islands, prompted outreach of my own within and beyond the limits of the academy with Bikinians and non-Bikinian Marshallese and non-Marshallese persons. For now, I want to turn to the noisiness of Bikini or the spirited noise of Bikinians' vocational remediations of their atoll and work with Rongelapese, which is a familial connection fissured, but not fully broken, by the US nuclear weapons testing program.

UWAAÑAÑ (SPIRITED NOISE)

No man is an island, entire of itself; every man is a piece of the continent, a part of the main . . . any man's death diminishes me, because I am involved in mankind, and therefore never send to know for whom the bell tolls; it tolls for thee . . . this bell, that tells me of his affliction, digs out and applies that gold to me: if by this consideration of another's danger I take mine own into contemplation, and so secure myself, by making my recourse to my God, who is our only security.
—JOHN DONNE, "Meditation XVII" (1623)

....

12.24.09 (2 PM)

Christmas Eve. Kili Island (RMI)

"You want to know what life is like here? That's what it's like." Simon pointed over to the aluminum dinghy caught on the reef, being tossed about and pummeled by the ocean waves. People and their belongings were flung about like toys, the former struggling against the clout of the currents, the latter giving in. The hot sun illuminated the assembly line of men unloading the three-month allocation courtesy of the USDA and the 177 agreement. We just stood there in shock. People were risking their lives for packaged ramen noodles, and I could hear nothing more than a rustling of concerned voices muffled by the wind and waves.

WAVES AND DEFENSES: PROTECTED LISTENING AND APPEALS

A church bell tolls on Christmas Day, 2009, between 9:00 and 10:00 AM. I step outside of a cinder-block house on Kili Island into a wash of dazzling sunlight illuminating dark-green leaves that lilt from pandanus trees and mingle with the broader yet equally as vibrant leaves from palm trees. Just five degrees north of the equator, the sun boldly illuminates the landscape of Kili Island. Waves crash, roar, and shimmer as the wind whirs over the Pacific expanse. My attention to the physical environment is overtaken by the sound of the church bell, a suspended rusted oxygen cylinder that produces timbral similarities to a bass octave almglocken. The noise expands throughout the auditory space weighted by thick, salt-tinged air. The range of the bell's resonance pushes the limits of the 0.36 square miles of land that hosts 1,200 exiled Bikinians.[1] The sound acquiesces to the choppy, whitecap-tipped waves of the Pacific Ocean, where it fades into the rumble of the choppy sea.

The bell tolls more frequently. The pressure of the sound, its weight, and its ephemeral quality compel my movement toward its source. I walk across the grass on dirt roads past a baseball field, an elementary school, and a town hall. Summoned by the bell, the displaced Bikinians, who now refer to themselves as ri-Kili (Kili people), emerge from their cinder-block houses and walk across the unpaved roads lined with telephone poles toward the Protestant church, which was built on the most elevated part of the island. I walk into the church and turn my tape recorder on, capturing the last moments of the bell's deep yet fleeting chime. Women, dressed in floral print muumuus, sit on the right side of the church. They fan themselves and their young children. Men, wearing dress shirts and slacks, sit on the left side. Dotting the middle row of pews, a few men and women wait for the commencement of the ceremony. I donned a red dress given to me for the occasion by Shirley, the Rongelapese woman who had been a consistent mentor.

The resonant bell hums its sonic decay, and the fading volume reveals noises from the external environment. Dogs amble into the vicinity in search of shade. Under a steeple with three crosses, we sit closely together in front of three flags: the Christian flag, the RMI flag, and the Bikini Atoll flag. There is no wind in the church; the flags hang listless. The affective force of the bell—its acoustic overload—reorients our bodies to the church,

4.1 Greeting sign on Kili Island.

the place safe from external movements of the wind and waves. The silent or unsaid nuclear context pervades the space "inside" (the core or nucleus) sanctioned by Christian and nuclear biopolitics. We wait for the *rikaki* (preacher and teacher) to set the musical key, the keynote. And with the Word, from inside the church, voices push the air and form its contours with religious songs and rhetorical echoes of MORIBA.

This chapter chronicles the role of "spirited noise," which is opened through the tear or cry break (see chapter 3) in Bikinian vocational reempowerment through various means, such as education, religion, and navigation, which are treated as protective in diaspora. As Jacques Attali wrote, "The only possible challenge to repetitive power takes the route of a breach in social repetition and the control of noisemaking."[2] US Americans via the missionaries have aimed to control the noise of Marshallese. Beginning and ending with *Kūrijmōj*, the Marshallese Christmas celebration of Jebro and Christ, two chiefly (*iroij*) figures, I share instances of how Bikinians remediate the sounds of the bomb or the power of L'Etao (trickster) through their chiefly lineage, which repositions Bikinian self-determination as a matter of the unrecognized sovereign. And it is the lack of recognition of their sovereignty that has denied them a direct voice in US adjudicative hearings. Bikinians trace their own chiefly lineage and modes of protection through their atoll or national god, Wōdjapto, who is also called a reef god, recalling the importance of the nourishing lagoon to combat the nausea that is linked with the noisiness of the Bikinians in diaspora (the *lōrrǫ* and *būromōj*), who sing songs to keep the memories of Bikini alive. Linking with the previous chapter, I show how gendered forms of protection and interconnected movements, such as navigation, reconnect Bikinians to their atollscape and to Rongelapese.

US neocolonial violence and militarization are shot through Bikinians' very pursuits for justice, their removal from the waves and testimonial voices, and their determination to return to and navigate the oceanic space rather than being reduced to the figure of a tear, a voice, a man, a woman, a "person." The aesthetics of the "manly" spirit or the Bikinian warrior figure, which is also the son and the sovereign (chief) in self-determination, that navigates the currents and the waves, the flow and the fight (while carrying his mother, as Bikini), are part of the politics of militarized performance through which noisiness is reclaimed by and through bodies in motion that uphold promises breached by US nuclear militarism.[3] Through these performances, Bikinian leaders narrate their diasporic masculinity in terms of these protective figures, which are also vociferous figures.[4] However, like the lōrrǫ, the vociferousness cannot and has not been heard by US Americans, who had assumed the atoll to be empty so that they could conduct nuclear tests, and Marshallese who reject Bikinian spirited self-determination. Bikinians refuse to be unheard and resist being devalued as or overwhelmed by (historical) noise, and they locate their spirited noisiness in the heart of Bikini Atoll's protective lagoon, which, I argue, resonates through Bikinians into the capital and in their transpacific diaspora. Bikinian men locate their "manly spirits" in church services, the collective singing of religious songs, in ritualized religious ceremonies, in navigational formations, and other ways that activate the "spirit of sharing," imbuing these spaces with *belief* in ethical and political possibilities, or what might better be understood as real terms of equity (moral reciprocity).[5] These songs are nuclear restagings that show how their protection and perseverance rest on material ties to Bikinian translations of moral affectations that allied them with the Americans (and the missionaries). Bikinians maintain their strategic moral trust in order to continue to appeal on moral principles—extending the scope of MORIBA—using a collection of these affectations through which Americans continue to try and indoctrinate them into a telos that refuses their existence as Bikinians. Affective alliance relies on both structured, intelligible sounds and manly voices but also *uwaañañ* (the nonlexical vociferousness of nonhuman spirits). I spoke with Bikinian men about their lineage in a universalized patriarchal culture with respect to dependencies, and this chapter shares some of their practical critiques surrounding extant dependencies and ways in which vocational empowerment can prepare them in case the United States "leaves." Their singing activates memories of a self-determined, spirited lineage in diasporic formation; these performative searches, musical outreach, and reclamations of occupied spaces, such as their lagoon, are part of their larger decolonial struggles.

RECLAIMING THE LAGOON

Bikini Atoll continues to be present in the global imagination. The lagoon of Bikini Atoll means different things to different people. Even Bikinian children, who watch the trials and tribulations of SpongeBob SquarePants play out in his "home" locale, "Bikini Bottom," might have a different understanding of the aquascape. Through stories, songs, and discussions of Bikinian masculinity, I offer insight into the importance of Bikinians' discursive-material reclamations of their protective lagoon, which has been claimed by popular culture, UNESCO, dive programs (and the wealthy who can afford them), American media, and warships with unexploded ordnance. I trace forms of protections, from the Bikinian lagoon through Christianity, to consider how Bikinians' dissensual sounding (here: deep diving and making audible) of their lagoon contributes to critiques of postwar historicization that grapple with remembering and forgetting what some call "monstrous" pasts that resonate as noise—antiphonal masculine chants, the roar of Godzilla, the explosion of the bomb (both nuclear and that of the Word of the Gospel light), and the booming practices of Marshallese celebrations.

The front page of the December 11, 2009, edition of the *Marshall Islands Journal* pictured an aluminum motorboat plated with palm fronds that was full of Marshallese men in grass skirts holding paddles and sticks. Termed "Gospel warriors" by the editor, the caption read, "Protestant Church members spiced up this year's Gospel Day celebrations by organizing a lagoon 'parade' around Majuro Atoll that attracted numerous boats and plenty of attention from the shore."[6] (See figure 4.2.) As indicated by the media attention, the public reception, and buzz around Majuro for weeks afterward, the lagoon parade was an exceptional event, even for the festive celebrations that occur throughout the holiday season in the RMI. Prior to the parade itself, which was held after Sunday church services, the event was advertised throughout the day on the radio station V7AB. By the time the boats were circling the lagoon, people from across Majuro Atoll were already waiting to see the spectacle and reap the benefits of those spreading

4.2 "Gospel warriors," front page of the *Marshall Islands Journal*, December 11, 2009.

the word of the Gospel in 2009: the Bikinian community from Ejit Island, holding the MORIBA sign high.

Gospel Day is an RMI national holiday that celebrates the coming of the Gospel to Ebon Atoll in 1857. It began after World War II, when Marshallese embraced the return of (Christian) Americans. It is important not to conflate the two: Christians and Americans, particularly in the discerning Marshallese culture that has adapted Christianity, most often Protestantism. Both American missionaries and American military position themselves as liberators who helped rid the Marshall Islands of warfare, first chiefly warfare and then Japanese warfare. Yet as has been evident throughout this book, warfare persists in the RMI. Not only has conflict moved into the courts, but nuclear warfare also exists at the cellular level in the reproduction of radiogenic disease in (non)human bodies and the severance of those bodies. The myth of imperial salvation that brought "peace and democracy" thus plays out as war, perhaps; it becomes a day that can be celebrated for the coming of the Gospel—the bomb and the Bible—or, as an elderly interlocutor explained, it can be a "day of mourning" for the coming of the Bible and the bomb that have literally made light of Indigenous grounded sensibilities. He was not the only one to share this sentiment with me. For others, to be sure, the festivities were about being together and making something in the image of their identifiable MORIBA brand. Many of the youths on Ejit worked hard on the signs and costumes, and the island seemed abuzz with enthusiasm when the Gospel Day parade was announced on V7AB.

Gospel Day also marks the return of Christian culture as a means of subversive affective alliance on both sides. In the Marshall Islands the enthusiastic embrace and revitalization of Christianity may have also been facilitated by the complex relationship that Marshallese had with Japanese. Prior to the war, they felt the Japanese treated them relatively well, and during the war, many felt scorned and suffered brutal treatment.[7] Some Marshallese recall helping both Japanese and Americans during the war, and they felt torn, especially those with close relationships to Japanese individuals. Americans strategically used Christian culture to align with Marshallese (see chapter 1), and it is worth noting that Marshallese also strategically used Christian culture, as well as the teachings and skills acquired, to relate to Americans and other colonial governance.[8] Prior to the end of World War II, Marshallese Christianity was a modest practice that included community worship, which included singing hymns and reading Bible passages. Following World War II, Marshallese Christian celebrations incorporated the message of the Gospel and the American message of (disposable) materialism, both of which participate in "moral narratives of modernity."[9] Bikinians paved the way for this new celebration style based in conspicuous consumption, due to receiving cash payments from the United States. Other Marshallese see Bikinians as "exceptionally religious," which is thought to be a result of the nuclear testing. To the Bikinians removed from their land, American infrastructural protections of church, school, government, and media became even more necessary.

The all-male "Gospel warriors" occupied the most spectacular role. Those pictured are wearing palm-frond headdresses and skirts that look nothing like the everyday attire of the men, who wear basketball shorts, T-shirts, flip-flops (zoris), and the like. They accentuated their manliness by drawing on the depths of their vocal registers to perform heaving chants. The Gospel warriors mode of "playing heathen" can be taken as a complex metaphor for the public secret, what is known but cannot be articulated:

1. Political: The Bikinians have been treated like present-day heathens, third-class citizens in their own country and by the United States.

CHAPTER FOUR

2. Gendered: Men get to play war in public, or they get to be staged in the political position of playing war for the cameras. Women do not have the freedom to play "heathen" on this stage, at least in a way that can be captured by the eye or ear. They do not don female warrior garb, nor do they chant battle songs.
3. Nuclear colonial: The presence of the warring Americans (US military) who follow the Americans in the moral MORIBA boat intimates that the real heathens they are playing are actually the American nuclear colonizer contingent in the savage destruction of their atoll.

"The narrative of 'savagery' that the colonizer constructs, reveals, then, a complicity in which the masquerade of terror unveils the mask of the 'savage' as the face of the colonizer," Gareth Griffiths writes.[10] Maybe this savage face isn't a face of the colonizer at all but the colonial processes of harmonization through which Marshallese voices have been led in ways that have created the exclusive stagings for the male political voice (see chapter 3). Perhaps it is the making of the "key" or the "keynote" through which Native dispossession resounds itself insensible as Western facade, as disenchantment.

"JAB KE RORO!" (DISENCHANTMENT)

Preparations for Gospel Day would often require all-night practices. The *ri-pālle* (American) teachers would often complain during this season about how loud the Gospel Day practices were and that they kept Marshallese children from doing well in school because they would either not come to school or would be overtired. For those of us who lived near the practices, there was no denying that they were loud and noisy. Yamaha accompaniments became fuzzed out and distorted when they were blared through speakers at the maxed-out volume, while songfest groups sang even louder to compensate for any additional noise, projecting their voices. The adults had jobs, the children went to school, and it was dangerously hot for the elders (at eighty-eight degrees and humid). The concern over Marshallese worship as "noise," which came with the missionaries who first brought the Gospel in the mid-nineteenth century, became an international issue as Marshallese moved to places such as Springdale, Arkansas. The Springdale mayor said that although he appreciated the church-based activities, there were too many complaints about the noise, and, he said, the city has noise ordinances to solve these things.[11]

UWAAÑAÑ (SPIRITED NOISE)

Resonances of missionary and colonial practices, logics, and systems that worked to excise Marshallese spirited communications can be heard in the archival records of the US nuclear program and more quotidian exchanges. The phrase *jab ke roro* translates to "stop chattering," and it is used colloquially in schools by teachers to get children to stop talking. Given that roro are the incantations of the spirit, those that animate the spirit and the word *roro* can be translated to the endurance of humans (*ro* is the plural of human, and repetition shares durative ongoing), perhaps the call to "stop chattering" recalls a more deeply entangled lineage of disenchantment and *rikaki* musical key making to phase out the spirited noise of the ancestors. Noise can be read as a blockage in the system, a coded form of communication, or something that impedes understanding and needs to be resolved. In the previous chapter, King Juda's resistant equivocation was deemed noise or off-script with respect to Commodore Wyatt's interests. I extend the premise of Bikinians' complex equivocality through refusals of noise as spirited means of sensory democracy that contest the limited forms of moral, democratic engagement proffered by US Americans and American missionaries. While Marshallese worship practices both in ceremonial performances and quotidian reverence held for the ancestral land were denigrated throughout the atolls, the Bikinians' militarized detachment from their ancestral land and means of customary worship via US moralized, religious justifications shows the continuation of spiritual debasement and with it the treatment of Bikinians as unwanted presence with their cares, contributions, and concerns dismissed as noise. In fact, the Bikinians have been treated as unwanted sounds within various hearing spaces: their homeland, the Kwajalein military base, US courts, and the RMI. With each mediation came the rationale to remove Bikinians from where they were living at the time.

Harmony, or the proper organization of voices and proper placement of sounds (notes), excises noisiness. In the geopolitical and social senses, this reflects the proper organization of communities, the placement of bodies, across scales, and their sounds—all of which lend to questions concerning the politics of noise when it comes to belonging, citizenship, assimilation, and the means of relating in the continual process of community formation, cohesion, and affirmation: communication. Returning to the complicated genealogy of moralized or proper communication (human to human and human to spirit) from the mid-nineteenth century missionization of the atolls onwards, the church and the school were both spaces that architecturally bounded human voices from the noises of nonhumans (breaking land and human complementarity) and positioned male and female subjects in different places (breaking with Indigenous gender complementarity). In some contemporary, Westernized school classrooms in the Marshall Islands, while I was in the RMI, the Marshallese language was prohibited from being spoken, and children, especially in elementary classes, would be admonished to "jab ke roro" if they were speaking in Marshallese (or any language besides English) or if they were talking among themselves without permission of the teacher.

Although the phrase takes shape in colloquial usage, it can be read in terms of its ties to control of the senses that are animated through transcorporeal attachments, for example, via spoken language and the rhythmic movements of breath that create communicative, cultural continuity. The phrase, more literally, translates to "stop making roro." Roro are the Indigenous incantations that Marshallese explain are part of the spectrum of what animates their spirits—from the ritualistic navigational orations to the mnemonic means of bringing an atoll together (for it to make sense in various contexts) to accompaniments to everyday tasks that afforded the maintenance of their society. There is an important temporal component to roro that is heard in the word itself. Roro can be translated to the "endurance of humans" (or souls) because "ro" is the plural of humans (souls) and when some word is repeated in the Marshallese language, it speaks to duration or that something continues or is ongoing. The ongoing human souls or durative spiritedness afforded by roro might be explained, in part, through the sensible filters that animate Indigenous interconnected epistemologies. Roro inspire humans through the sense-making practices whereby the production of sounds shapes the orator by animating particular relations through knowledges that reconnect her to her place and her place to itself in ways that might not have been previously sensed. Moreover, roro shapes bodies in time through its temporal realization. Such practices can be understood in terms of "enchantment" or movements of the spirit and inspiration (inspired shifts in perceptual realities) through incantation.

"Jab ke roro" can thus be read in line with other vocal controls that stem from white supremacist, colonial mentalities surrounding Indigenous noisiness, such as how missionaries debased Marshallese roro and called it "chant" (a reductive term positioned in telic relation with and as the basic predecessor to the supposedly more developed tonal harmony, thus assigning primitive chant with primitive societies that needed Western education). In this way, the phrase recalls a deeply entangled lineage of *disenchantment* that is related to the ultimate detachments and upheavals experienced by Bikinians removed from their lands. Such disenchantment can be read in the *rikaki* musical key making that harmonically aimed to phase out the spirited noise of the ancestors. As this chapter shares, although a musical key might seem to set the sound-stage of a song, Bikinians refuse (and re-fuse) voice to equivocality by infusing spirited noise and roro into their cultural momentum, as well as sharing the quiet testimony of tears that mark ancestral knowledges of oceanic rhythms.

LISTENING FOR SPIRITS TO NAVIGATE THE IMPOSSIBLE

Church provides a space wherein the Bikinian communities perform rituals of hope, commitments to faith, and play with dynamic expressivity. Church activities, both in church and in preparation, structure much of the community's time. Church services often last an hour or an hour and a half, but songfests and gatherings will continue throughout the day well into the night. Singing and listening in church are ritualized practices, but they also prove (because they are) authenticity as religious and moral in the effect of doing them. Although the concept of authenticity, particularly with respect to Indigenous persons, is complex, Bikinians must learn how to voice sincerity and authenticity within their claims to courts and to other auditors.

On Ejit, Sunday church services begin between 10:30 and 11:00 AM. Men sit on the left side, and women sit on the right side. Children are free to sit wherever they wish, and they often end up switching locations throughout the service. After the community is assembled or while the community is assembling, the pastor begins with a call to worship, a reading of a psalm. The structure follows: a hymn (*al*), the Lord's Prayer, a unison reading, another hymn, greetings and announcements, another hymn, a short prayer, a responsive reading, another hymn, "the message" (or sermon), the offering accompanied by a hymn, the closing hymn, and a closing prayer. A deacon from the Ejit community chooses the songs for the service, and certain hymns from the *Bōk in Al kab Tun Ko nan Ri Aelōñ in Marshall* (*The Book of Songs with Tunes for the Marshallese People*) were consistently sung in the weekly repertoire. Songs with text that narrates movement, perseverance, and the celebration of community are the most common. "Standing on the Promises" (no. 323), "Onward and Upward" (267), and "What a Gathering" (287) were often sung along with songs from the *Bōk in Al* that specifically seem to address issues caused by the nuclear testing and the Bikinians' relationship with the United States, such as "Pilot" (203) and "Jerusalem, My Home" (179). And these songs were always performed with an immense rigor and volume.

"Standing on the Promises" and "Onward and Upward" both, through melodic and harmonic rhythm, make space for the women to vocally soar above the men (most audibly in the choruses). The rhythmic movement of the lower male voices in contrast to the sustained duration of the higher pitches sung by the women's voices creates an affective dynamism, resounding the not-yet-there realization of the promises. They are striving together, and the vocalizations labor in rhythmic fashion similar to the customary men's work chants to "move" heavy things (both words in the political realm and, for example, rocks for building and bringing canoes to the reef shore). These songs provide the affect of soaring, and the act of flying is framed as both an attribute of a "healthy" woman (when it is her choice) and a lōrrọ (when her loss is so overwhelming). Here the women and men are in control of their vocalizations. The "soaring" in both songs brings the women "closer" in tonal range to the alto voice in melodic descent. This is prior to the ascending melodic line when they become melodically synchronized with the other three voices. The "freedom" of the women's voices is often realized with light ornamentations, such as wide, uneven tremolo.

The pastor on Ejit Island, Percy Benjamin, who was born and raised in Kwajalein and later lived in Hawaii, is married to a Bikinian woman from Kili Island. He is committed to helping the Bikinian population experience a sense of agency, protection, and freedom through feeling the spirit of God. The community is plagued with financial difficulties, encapsulated by a statement made by Senator Tomaki Juda, King Juda's son. Senator Juda lamented the "hardships" of Bikinians that have resulted from the transition from living off their land to subsisting on US food supplies and money.[12] The difficulties that Senator Juda lists concern life on Kili Island: the increase in imported food prices without an increase in payments to the Bikinians and the high price of travel—international and domestic fares on planes and ships. He also mentions that hospitalization in the United States can be prohibitively expensive, which poses problems because medical care in the Marshall Islands lacks the facilities, medications, and specialized resources available in the United States. The hardships stem, according to Benjamin, from the lack of educational and employment opportunities, which is endemic to the Marshall Islands. However, the Bikinians are in a nuclear diaspora, which adds stress and exhaustion to extant social conditions. It is not simply a matter of being displaced from their homeland, Benjamin explained, but also because they have been shuffled back and forth mentally and physically. For Senator Juda, musical worship in church is one important way that Bikinians have learned to deal with these hardships.

Benjamin explained his role in helping "young men" with the "impossible" by hosting a space where directed speaking and listening were accepted.[13] He emphasized "listening," which is how Bikinians use prayers. God is always listening for them, as spirits, and they are listening for God in the performative sense. Listening for God and the Bikinian spirit is a noisy endeavor, which is wanted sound. These are also the ritualized soundings and listenings that provide connections to the elders and ancestors, which is crucial without land. Singing, listening, and carrying the hymnal are the materials through which Bikinians become ancestral beings:

> They come and talk to me . . . they just want to talk—nothing really major—they just want to come and "talk story" with me. They say, "Thank you for the message; thank you for trying to get us together." Some young men in our church tell me that [they really appreciate] me for coming and helping out [with] something that they thought was *impossible* to be done on this island, but I told them that I know the spirit of God is in this island and within your families: "You have to *really listen*—try to feel where He is, or where the spirit is because it is there somewhere." And see, sometimes when we don't have food, we get food. I just try to make them feel good and feel happy and feel like they have to do something good. We start from now.[14]

Senator Juda finds that singing hymns every week, specifically by reading the printed words, adds weight to the belief that, in his father's own words, "everything is in God's hands" (MORIBA). The senator exuded a thorough sadness when he shared his feelings that the United States has disregarded its promises to return the Bikinians to their homeland. He told me that it was especially painful hearing his father talk about the dissolution of the moral-political relationship on the part of the United States. Neither his father nor Senator Juda could fathom how the United States could engage in other wars without fixing the situation in the RMI. The inability to understand motivations of people and their representative governments can result in a genuine frustration that, for the Bikinians, is often assuaged by their faith. The community must express this faith in order for the notion of faith to be empowering. Senator Juda named the two songs by which they felt particularly inspired (203: "Pilot" and 179: "Jerusalem, My Home"). By reading the biblical imagery of "Jerusalem" as a promise by God, and applying this message to the promises of the United States, the Bikinians actively remediate these songs as part of the nuclear repertoire, connecting them back to MORIBA as an offering to God in this moralized restaging of the ongoing nuclear relationship.

Taking "Pilot" as an example, we can see the oceanic motifs that become meaningful in other Bikinian songs, such as "*Ñe ij keememej tok aelōñ eo aō*" ("When I Remember My Atoll"), and as "*Konnan Kake*" ("Talk About It") (see chapter 3) reminds us, forced relocation (foam spraying in their faces en route to Rongerik) and compulsory dependency created conditions that left Bikinians' customary agency to hone their skills as navigators, which requires modes of perceiving not limited to the five modern senses. Reflecting on "*Ñe ij keememej tok aelōñ eo aō*," oceanic literacies that register the zones of currents between atolls, which produce choppy waves, are highly developed sensorial skills that come from a deep understanding of the currents. If somebody wanted to learn a navigational chant, s/he had to go through a rigorous regimen. Jack Tobin explains the process by which the navigational knowledge was sought for survival and how it "was a serious breach of etiquette to ask directly," which is a learned part of political participation: "The deep meaning (ṃwilaḷ) must be learned. Archaic or esoteric words or terms further tended to obscure the meaning of the chant to the uninitiated."[15]

"Pilot" can be read in the way of the chief who teaches the ways of the choppiness in modern life as Bikinians move from landmass to landmass, and also in terms of singing to appease the foreign chief spirit that they are requesting knowledge from so they do not die. They sing their struggles to the chief: they are on the "rock" (Kili) and "reef" (Ejit and Kili), and the impact of "storms" (such as Typhoon Alice, which wiped out their agricultural work in 1979). Like the Bikinian anthem and second anthem, the oceanic imagery works as part of the complex and intricately meaningful representational system of Marshallese sociality, which includes networked navigations (communication/transportation/mobility). However, it does not teach Bikinians the oceanic rhythms and sensorial modalities of wave-pattern navigation. This is because the church project, along with colonialism, emphasized incorporation through the division of the five moralized senses as a way to break with Indigenous animate lives.

DECOLONIZING VOCATION

As Katerina M. Teaiwa explains, "Despite the almost universal adoption of Christianity in the Pacific and amendments to clothing, choreography and the ways in which gender relations, for example, are displayed in the dance events, Pacific Island performance still maintains and actively invokes connections with the 'visible and invisible' environment."[16] Marshallese adaptations of Christianity are woven into the cultural dynamics, which are textured through choreographies, genderings, and fashions. Yet these textured elements are crucially connected to Marshallese cosmologies that maintain Indigenous grounded sensibilities through which vocational empowerment, as education, can emerge beyond the church and school, effectuating new ways of moving (not just in forcible exile) and registering Marshallese sensibilities.

Indigenous vocational empowerment as education extends beyond the ideological state apparatuses of the church, school, and government.[17] In "We Are the Land, the Land Is Us," Jibā Kabua emphasizes that education must belong to the Marshallese. The author closes with a call: "Education for survival is a call to duty for every Pacific person. Land, culture, and education are the only tools available for the Pacific family to brace itself against the powerful forces of globalization that now threaten the very survival of the average Pacific person."[18] In the Bikinian community, Mayor Alson Kelen recently drew on his chiefly lineage and political position to reinstate an Indigenous navigational school, which is meaningful for many reasons, not least because Bikinians participated in a navigational school with Rongelapese on Rongelap Atoll, the site of a shallow reef that was considered the ideal site to teach wave piloting. Bravo destroyed the possibility for its continuation. However, the skill of wave piloting was remembered by Korent Joel, who trained at Rongelap as a boy and passed this customary knowledge to Kelen. Along with an American, Denis Aleppo, Kelen began a navigational and canoe-building vocational school (mainly for lower-class/commoner nonelite youths from different atolls that were not exclusively Bikinian or nuclear affected) called *Waan Aelōñ in Majel* (Canoes of the Marshall Islands, or WAM). Lijon also shared her knowledge of the waves and the roro; she had been inspired as a girl by the story of Litermelu, who learned how to navigate through wave immersion.[19]

The school uses Marshallese materials and methods to build the outrigger canoes, but the student volunteers also develop other useful skills (such as educating youths in financial literacy). The hymnal songs, preserved by the elders, were coded ways to help Bikinians remember their connections, and Kelen remediates these connections through communal construction of canoes, which are the material motions of *ājmour* (health). Each part of the canoe is meaningful, and when youths build and sail the canoes, they learn these ṃwilaḷ words through an embodiment of the sounds as motions connected to the navigational motions. The shapes of the canoes re-

4.3 Mayor Alson Kelen as Wōdjapto in *Ainikien Jidjid ilo Bon* (The Sound of Crickets at Night), a film directed by Jack Niedenthal, 2012.

flect certain Marshallese movements that are part of an Indigenous musicality and the rhythms of Indigenous life. The canoe patterns that represent movements are drawn from parts of fish and sharks, and they are inscribed onto other surfaces to represent vitality and movement, such as the tattoo motifs.[20] These tattoos also share the clans and chiefly lineages. Women would pound the drums as chiefs were being tattooed to mitigate pain and weave the energetic power into the surface designs, which are deeper than the eye can see. Thus, the visual tattoos resonate womanly percussion, much as some of the canoe segments that are modeled after fish parts have stories. The tattoos worn by Kelen (see figure 4.3, a still image depicting Wōdjapto, the reef god, from a film, and illustrations in figure 4.4) represent sharks' teeth. The pattern also looks like the canoe sail, which resemble a shark's fin, and which tells the story of Loktanuur and Jebro. Kelen told me that "mothers are heavy," a reference to Loktanuur, a mother who carried the first sail in a bundle that enabled her youngest son, Jebro, to win a canoe race among his brothers, each of whom had refused to carry their mother in the race because of her heavy bundle. The crests of waves, the shark's teeth and fin, and the sail all afford movement through pathways that are supposedly "unforgiving" or "violent" to humans (sharks, ocean).

When considering Indigenous education within schools, we can look at the walls of Ejit Elementary, which are not only about MORIBA but also display reminders of Marshallese pathways and Wōdjapto, who is a "manly spirit" that resides at the bottom of the Bikini lagoon and protects them

UWAAÑAÑ (SPIRITED NOISE)

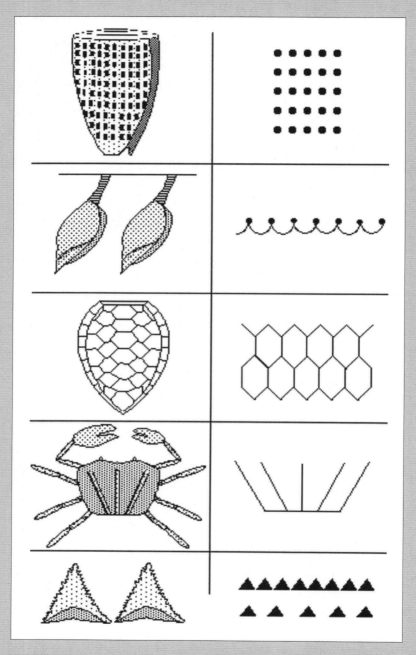

4.4 Marshallese tattoo motifs. Courtesy of Dirk Spennemann, Digital Micronesia.

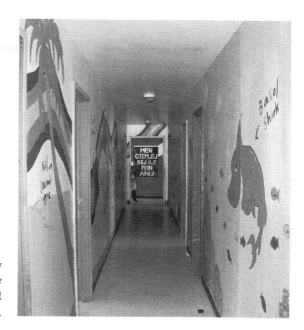

4.5 Ejit Elementary School hallway: *iakwe* (love), coconut (*ni*), and shark (*bako*).

(see figure 4.5). These reading practices, like the antiphonal chants, enable Bikinian children to read their historical worlds and perhaps displace some of the interference from others. These images show how the nation and its productions are engendered male. They also show how the face of Bikinian education is gendered male through the figure of Wōdjapto or MORIBA. As the stories, songs, and cosmological ties through the land animate the imagery, however, the gendered entanglements of voices emerge through the navigational process.

Navigational chants are performed in a low, monotonic, and metered delivery, with the navigator often lying in the boat or crouching low. Some Americans who have studied this delivery assume that it is about preserving secrecy. Although this is one interpretation, I would like to offer another that, to my mind, complements the preparatory animations and pedagogies: telling stories and chanting magic through the stick chart, which yield highly poeticized and interwoven literacies that cannot easily be learned even with vocal volume. The lower rumbling of rhythmic words performs the contrapuntal motions to the oceanic flows: "Singing can be thought of like surfing or skiing in this way. If I push too hard with the breath one way or another, I'll throw myself off balance and off pitch."[21] So as not to deplete oneself midway through a long journey where drifting means death, chanting in a low manner, nearest to the waves, lets the rhythmic sounds interact with the aquatic undulations, and it reduces the energy expended of the orator. The chant is not in the voice per se. It is in the inner ears and the diaphragm, connected/activated by the throat; voice is processual, and it collects and connects the body in motion.

Kelen's prize outrigger is called the *Jitdam Kapeel*, named after a proverb: "Seeking knowledge guarantees wisdom," which speaks to a m̧wilaļ (deep), intimate, intergenerational practice. Anthropologist Monica LaBriola provides insight into what m̧wilaļ "means" by way of *jitdam kapeel*, which is less about the "ability to memorize facts" and more about the process of learning "place in society in terms of their age and gender, and as well as their place in and the rank of their family, jowi [clan], and bwij [lineage, matrilineal kin, clan, race]," which is highly valued.[22] The outrigger canoe is an expression of communal efforts and the know-how to work together in the cultivation and navigation of the *wa* (vehicle).

Kelen's outrigger is an expression of this Indigenous vocational education; as a process, it is resistant to the data-driven and goal-based "learning outcomes" of standardized Western education that refuses to respect Marshallese for their culture, treating them as "just people" or blank slates (reminiscent of *terra nullius*). His comments were about curricular choices in Marshallese schools that privileged learning about US American places rather than reefs in front of the students; method was also an issue. Critical of investments without return to the community, Kelen mused that the institutional structure of the church was similar insofar as people give their money and time, and their efforts leave them without, say, food for their children. Here, the *rikaki*, or the preacher and teacher, are linked as the intermediaries for the church or state that has historically been in the service of a sovereign with headquarters in the Western world and not the Marshall Islands. With respect to these democratizing spaces of moral uplift and societal mobility, the material returns have historically gone elsewhere. That is why it is crucial for Kelen and other Bikinian leaders to invest vocational empowerment in the community through indigenous modes of interconnection that help youths from different atolls navigate modernization.

The Marshallese word for peace is *aenōm̧m̧an*, which has within it *ae* or currents (processes of gathering and circulating through different media) and *emman* ("good"), such that a poetic reading situates Marshallese notions of peace as good currents or that which flows. Karin A. Ingersoll develops the concept of "seascape epistemology" to reemplace Indigenous knowledge of oceanic connectivity and fluidity that cannot be occupied, dominated, and exploited:

> Oceanic literacy becomes a political and ethical act of taking back . . . history and identity through a rhythmic interaction with place: the swing of tides shuffling sand, the sharp tune of swells stacking upon each other at coastal points, the smooth sweep of clouds pulled down by the wind. Rhythms don't just represent the ocean; they constitute figurative layers. Merging the body with this rhythmic sea enables a reading of the seascapes' complex habits, as well as all the memories created and knowledges learned within this oceanic time and space but have been effaced by rigid colonial constructions of identity and place.[23]

A poetics of oceanic hope, of those "submerged mothers," pulses from their *bwijen* (umbilical cord) at sea through "*Luuji Bikini*" ("Losing Bikini"), (although the lyrics of the Kili Excess song discussed later might not suggest this at first read). Peterson Jibas said that it's about "hope" stemming from the Bikinians' "new campaign" that pushes back on the culture of loss proffered by journalists, scholars, and charitable foundations. He believes there are three key aspects of Marshallese—Bikinian—culture at the present time: government, church, and *mantin majeļ* (Marshallese custom, conduct) which were once part of the chiefly purview but have now been fractured. In order to maintain the chiefly ability to listen to and carry one's mother, these factions need to work together. Music is part of all of them, and because it is *manit* (culture), it can be used as a tool. "In Marshallese culture," he said, "your first mom is your mother [and her sisters], but your second mom is your island." Jibas explained that this is how his two mothers will not be lost because Marshallese culture can provide the conceptual direction for the other interlocking components. Both mothers (women and the feminine voices of nondominant nonhuman culture), he stressed, become stronger through their incorporation into the musical scaffolding that signifies not culture loss but directional movement to the bwij through the throat:

> You take the first verse and apply it to **Bikini**. "So, *jino* [mother], don't worry." So, "Bikini, don't worry, when I grow up, I'm going to become a leader—you know I'm going to try my best, so I don't want to lose Bikini." So that is what the meaning of the song is about. *Jino jab inepata*.
>
> You take that meaning of *jino*; there are two kinds of mothers. Your first mom is your **real mom**, and your second mom is your island, so you talk about your mom in the first verse, say, "Mom, don't worry—when I grow

up, I'm going to take care of you," and then the last verse says I don't want to lose Bikini.

So you apply the second meaning of your second mother or your first mom and put it on **Bikini Atoll**. So that is the meaning of the song.[24]

"*Luuji Bikini*" echoes and refuses the discourse of loss. Kili Excess draws on contemporary and customary tropes and words that signal and signify directional movements (*ean jen nan rak*, from north to south). There is a transformation of the word *mormor* (foam) to the off-homonym *murmur*, which means making "ancient" chants and "conquering" ("steering" or navigating). *Al in mur* are particular steering songs, which are actually ancient chants that would be sung as chiefs brought the atolls together for war. The male chief, with his knowledge of the chants, directions, and the tides (oceanic movements), would have the women accompany him to battle, drumming so they were audible to the atoll population. Interatoll warfare was noisy, and there was no such thing as an unalerted population. To change the tide through its songs, Kili Excess marks and performs a murmur, thus bringing Bikini Atoll together with the mother through the Jebro/warrior figure of the son, which is a chiefly figure and can intimate Juda and the line of Bikinian chiefs, which can be traced to a chief of the Ijjidik clan, Larkeloñ, whom Bikinians described as a powerful chief who came through Rongelap and conquered Bikini in a noisy war that displaced the previous Bikinians who would have left rather than remained as categorically conquered. The chiefly lineage shares their connection to Rongelapese, which, as some Bikinians encouraged, could also be traced to a "spirit of sharing."

SPIRIT OF SHARING

Kili Excess performed during the New Year's Day celebration, which extended the Gospel Day/Kūrijmōj season, on January 1, 2010. They began with "*I jab pād mol, aet*" ("No longer can I stay, it's true") and later sang "*Bikini, Jake Jebōl Eo*" ("Bikini, Spirit of Sharing"). I was familiar with the song from the many times it was performed on Ejit. Bikinians did not sing this song to Americans as a point of connection like the anthem. Rather, they sang it among themselves and to other Marshallese. *Jake Jebōl Eo* means "pass the arrowroot." Sharing largely stems from sharing food, and maintaining the collective palate is therefore central to the community's ethics.[25] Arrowroot is talked about as having disappeared with the bomb, yet there is scientific evidence to the contrary. Scholars believe that the arrowroot stopped being cultivated because people became afraid of the contaminated soil. Therefore, the title also houses in it a nuclear silence of the fear and uncertainty that has led to diminished resources, such as arrowroot, American scientific dismissals of Indigenous knowledge, and (failed) development programs centered in nonindigenous epistemologies, all of which have led to sustained dependencies.

Jibas explained how the historical song was about the pillars of the community and how Inben and Lañinbelin maintained the Bikinian culture; through their manly strength and knowledge, such as navigation and weather prediction, they taught everyone how to share. Mayor Kelen pointed out the rhythmic and translational dissonances, as well as the problems with translation, for the song mainly comprises chants:

> It's like a short phrase from every chant that if you know them you really . . . it makes you . . . [*contemplative silence*]. Bikinians are well-known for their sharing, so this is a phrase that describes the Bikinians. Jake jebōl eo—sharing of the richness—this song was like a chant kind of a song. Well, it's common to place the [music] and chant together. If you listen to the song, it doesn't really *floooow*. It's like the rhythm is almost level—it doesn't go like this [*makes a physical sweeping gesture to indicate rolling melodic contour*]; it's choppier [*referring to staccato and monotone/conjunct melodic delivery of the recitation*].[26]

The incantations form the verse material, the story, and are ṃwilaḷ. The tonal melody offers the chorus "Bikini, Bikini *aitab, tab in eṃṃan*," which is ṃwilaḷ because of its meaning. As Kelen clarified, *aitab tab in eṃṃan* refers to the process of getting men excited, "a lot of men up in arms." The repeated call of "Bikini," which denotes that it is ongoing, is to the men. "Yes, [the song] is derived from the chants," he reiterated. "It is a combination of sharing and waking up the manly spirit." "The spirit of sharing" also means "share the richness." Rather than men calling on their mothers, on the women, to "shake the spirit," it is Bikini that offers a call to arms so that men will "shake the spirit" and protect the atoll through their vociferousness. Jibas said this of the sung incantation:

> It's not like American music, but it is still in that range—you have to go down because the notes changed. [The chant] still has melody and rhythm to it. So it is a little different, but it is not like if you were to do it in a chant way. But then they will sing [the chant] [*vocal dynamics and enthusiasm seemingly*

increase], you know, behind the singer, like if I were to sing it [*begins to sing the chant as incanted melody*]—let's say you'd be singing it, I'd come up right behind you and do it in the chant way.²⁷

I played a version of the song I recorded on Ejit, and Jibas jumped in and began to chant, almost encircling the female singer's throaty melody with his slightly higher-pitched and rapid incantation. With the hymns, women and men move through a song in harmony and occasionally counterpoint, but when the chant is inserted in the song, there is room for vocal negotiation, and the way Jibas painted it, the element of spatial and temporal play as the partner sneaks up behind and starts excitedly chanting the antiphonic response, which is outside of a harmonic system. Stylized roro provides a space in which Marshallese elicit the fulfillment of their performative aurality and antiphonic vocality to awake and lift their spirits.

WŌDJAPTO

Wōdjapto is the Bikinian protective spirit. He is also called "a manly spirit." "Bikinians are strong, and they have wide feet because of the genealogy that follows the spirit Wōdjapto. They inherited it from the spirit," Deacon Johnny Johnson said as he expounded upon the importance of Wōdjapto. He continued that Bikinian men were "ugly like the spirit" with "big noses, big lips, and eyebrows [that are] not as good as everyone else." Johnson continued to explain that even if this is the case, women still want to be intimate with Bikinian men, and once they do, they stay with Bikinian men. The gendering of desire was now also patrilineal, from the "ugly" and "noisy" spirit. Wōdjapto, the reef god and medicine "man" spirit, is protected by Bikini Atoll, the gendered feminine land, which complicates all notions of gendering in Western society. As the lōrrọ disrupts the liberal democratic notion of voice or identity-based political participation, Wōdjapto traces Bikinian diasporic being to displace notions of rootedness (that Bikinians are not Bikinian without land) while maintaining the importance of the sensible dimensions and physical returns through which nourishment, care, investment, and love are part of appreciating the "manly" protective spirit.

The story of Wōdjapto provides insight into the importance of land to gendered imaginaries of protection. Wōdjapto is a strong, protective spirit, and he can use his powers for good or evil, depending on whether or not he is properly respected. Bikinians gave ritualistic offerings to Wōdjapto. When the Gospel first came to Bikini Atoll via a Marshallese man, Lainer, in the early twentieth century, the Bikinian elders were very distressed by the thought of another god, according to Jack Niedenthal's interview of Jamore Aitab, especially because they already had a preeminent protective and powerful god, Wōdjapto, but eventually they changed their beliefs.[28] The following reading acknowledges that Bikinians' beliefs did indeed change and considers the ongoing importance of Wōdjapto and the noisy spirit as an intersensorial practice of protection related to contesting Western fixed senses, which are related to the structures that foster them. Johnson takes great pride in Wōdjapto and his spirit of uwaañañ. He recounts the facts: Wōdjapto was the younger of two brothers who were massive and strong. Like Larkeloñ, whom Johnson described as a powerful chief who came from Rongelap and defeated his brother Lañinbit to conquer Bikini, and like Commodore Wyatt, they came from outside of Bikini:

> This legend is about *our* spirit, the spirit of the Bikini people. In fact, this spirit came from the northwestern part of the Pacific. We don't know exactly where, what place, but some Bikinians who know about the geography, they think that this spirit came from Pohnpei, Chuuk, Yap, or Palau—those areas. But nobody really knows exactly where this spirit came from. It is a story about this spirit. One time—[aside] this spirit is a man—him and his brother, older brother, they have an argument. . . . And because this younger brother, this spirit of the Bikini people, is called Wōdjapto . . . two brothers, these two spirits were big spirits, very huge. In fact, if they put up their hand, they can touch the cloud. And they, the distance between their step is one thousand miles. . . . [He] took off and came across the ocean to the Marshalls from the northwestern [direction], . . . and finally *he stopped at Bikini because Bikini was the center for all the spirits in the entire Marshall Islands.* . . . That's why they usually, if there are big events coming up, they—it has to be held on Bikini for all the spirits so they have to go and gather together on Bikini for the feast.[29]

Johnson positions Bikini as the center of the spirit world, and he does so in terms that retain their significance today. He distinguished the time period that Wōdjapto came to Bikini from the "good old days," which are considered when the missionaries first landed on Ebon Atoll in the southern Marshalls (1857) through the beginning of the nuclear testing program (1946). From the outset, the legend paints a different history of the Marshalls, and in particular Bikini Atoll, from the myth of isolation and the

American reasons for choosing the atoll. Here, Bikini Atoll is the center of the world, already exploding with the booming noise of spirits. He reiterated: "The Bikinians always say that Bikini is an island of uwaañañ. And that means when people are talking loudly and you don't understand the talking, it's called uwaañañ in our Marshallese language." Wōdjapto could sense that Bikini was the center for spirit gathering only from hearing the uwaañañ (howling, bellowing, hollering, crying loudly) or loud, unintelligible spirit noises. The Bikinian foundational spirit was, in fact, uwaañañ, and it called to Wōdjapto. But the uwaañañ is also relayed as the Bikinian spirit that is considered to be (by Bikinians) the spirit of sharing. Within the context of songs of lōrro, Bikinians keep singing; thus, they keep sharing their noisiness of the būromōj. Bikinians make noisy appeals (they persevere) just as the spirits of the land; they are spirits of the land.

Americans were perhaps drawn to Bikini not because it was isolated but because it was the center of uwaañañ, even if they couldn't make sense of it (literally and figuratively). Bikinians, with their spirit of sharing, entrusted Americans with their vitality for "the good of mankind." Americans injured Bikini to sound out their power across the radio airwaves. Then, based on a theory by Charles Darwin about the ancient volcanic character of an atoll—how the atoll could lead to the depths of the Earth—oceanographers, who did not have occasion before to have an entire atoll or two (Bikini and Enewetak), worked with the military and, along with other scientists, created a modern scientific understanding of how things "fit" called "ecosystem science," in which they classified matter and used knowledge produced by atomic energy scientists (who worked on and supported the thermonuclear bomb) to carbon-date materials they collected from the reefs.[30] Again, the yields from Bikini in terms of American profit have not made their ways back to Bikini(ans).

Kelen reflected on this disjuncture and considered the multiple epistemologies through which knowledge has been produced at and of Bikini Atoll. Decolonial dissonances emerge from conflicting knowledge. He remembers when an American teacher taught his class about sharks and said that it was impossible for a shark to stay put. "I knew otherwise," Kelen responded with a confident laughter in his eyes. Americans associate sharks with masculinity, aggression, power, and movement. Kelen knew of the shark that stayed around one part of the reef, indicating the location of Wōdjapto. The shark reveals where Wōdjapto is and disproves Americans, suggesting that their toxic colonialism that pollutes the sea, from noise to chemical, forces sharks to keep swimming to find their next meals and to get away from unsanitary conditions. Americans also normalize people in constant motion—here, poignantly, Bikinians, who have been in forced exile, running from starvation and contamination since the Americans came with the atomic bomb and moralized promises of "care." Kelen's recollection challenges Americans' naturalized "flows" of animals and peoples—those things in an ecosystem—to justify geopolitical toxic projects of "accumulation through dispossession."

"Wōdjapto . . . stayed on Bikini until today," Johnson said, "and if you go to Bikini, you will see a coral inside the lagoon of Bikini" marking where Wōdjapto remains in the depths of the lagoon. Bikinians continue to "wear" Wōdjapto for their protection.[31] Rather than revere Wōdjapto through distance, Bikinians perform a connective, tactile transubstantiation of the Wōdjapto mixture into their spirits. When Bikinians visit Bikini with a scientific team or group of tourists, a point is made to retrieve the mixture. The smell of the potion is, by all accounts, noxious, and Bikinians have personal testimonies of its effectiveness. Smell is a sense that contributes to desire. If someone smells bad, s/he is less desirable, so the noxious potion keeps people at a distance. Like various protective mediations through which Americans have kept their distance (coded "manly": the law, weapons, silence, loud noises/bombs), Bikinians use their Wōdjapto potion to keep them distant and differentiated from others. Most specifically, Johnson told me about using the mixture to protect himself from other Marshallese. Uwaañañ is an atmospheric sensibility that might also recall the ways in which Bikinians were used for money and stigmatized, necessitating such protections:

> People who believe in that spirit always go to that reef where Wōdjapto lives and take a coconut shell with them and collect the saltwater from that area. When they first go down, they have to cover the opening of the coconut shell and go down deep to where the coral is, uncover the hole of the coconut shell, and collect the saltwater. Once they finish it, they come ashore and put some coconut oil inside. You cannot go anywhere else and collect the saltwater, only in that area, in that place by the house of Wōdjapto.[32]

The Wōdjapto mixture comingles smells of the Earth (land and water) and the physical touch of the mixture that has been "prepared," which enables the absorption of Wōdjapto's power. Often, pre-"conversion" spirits or gods are characterized as healers or referred to in terms of their medicinal value, and the power of "medicinal value"—as communal health and well-being (holistically)—gets lost in translation.[33] By breathing in and wearing the Bikinian atollscape and the spirited center (Wōdjapto), Bikinians route the spirit (breath) through their throat and into their lungs, and they become grounded (like the lōrro that becomes heavy through *uno in majel*). Johnson told me the potion is only for Bikinians: "We don't give it to outsiders because [the potion is] ourselves—our life."[34]

Bikinians remediate and literally remix the fracturing and fragmenting of Bikini that they now must take in small doses, like "medicine" for health through their "manly" spirits and the lived journeys of uwaañañ. Another part of the story has to do with how Wōdjapto wins another fight with his older brother and gets the prize of "the queen of all the uwaañañ," according to Johnson. Naoki Sakai reminds us that "the domination of one group of men by another group of men is reinscribed in the domination of women by men. The domination of a woman by a man can always be interpreted according to the scheme of homosociality and reduced to an item of gift exchange, . . . [ceasing] to be an interactive personality . . . instead [she] would be a property . . . and owned."[35] Perhaps there is another reading where we take the concept of murmur, the conquest chant, which already includes women's percussive soundings on the drums. But this mode of complementarity has been severely compromised by nuclear testing and the Bikinian diaspora, which is registered in the "bad luck" of Bikinians off their atoll that can be remediated by the Wōdjapto mixture.

When Bikinians leave Wōdjapto, the protective spirit feels abandoned and becomes angry, vengeful because his spirits of uwaañañ are leaving too. As Randy, a Bikinian who lives on Ejit and leads the children's church song group, explained, "When we moved from Bikini Atoll to [Ejit Island], it was a really shiny day—really smooth on the ocean. Then we were told we had to get on the boat. The moment we got on the boat [to leave], [the water] became really rough. That's because there is a spirit [in the lagoon]. There is a power, an evil power, and they call that man Wōdjapto."[36] Here Wōdjapto becomes "evil" as opposed to the "healthy" protector. Spirits, when they are abandoned, whether it is a spirit at the bottom of the lagoon or a spirit that takes on human form, are vital because of being woven into life, not unraveled from its texture. Bikinians, when they were removed from Bikini Atoll, had no means to take care of Wōdjapto, who was therefore not properly cared for. Americans pulverized not only the coral reefs of Bikini but also staged the lagoon as a testing ground. The Bikinian lagoon is the "heart" or throat of Bikini. Sailing across its depths enabled Bikinians to bring the atoll together through the winds, waters, and solids (that were foods). They would never pollute the lagoon because that would be polluting their lives.

Randy believes radiation is the cause of his ailments he began to feel while he was living on Bikini Atoll in the 1970s, eating local foods.

There was another silencing of Wōdjapto that could have also upset the protective spirit, which was the political transition of Bikinians from Team Wōdjapto to Team MORIBA. Randy and Johnson told me about the basketball team called Wōdjapto. The theme song Randy shared, which has a melody slightly reminiscent of "take me out to the ballgame" but could easily be a sea chantey, was taught to Randy by "an old man" on Bikini. He says that the younger children on Ejit do not know this particular song and that if any Ejit people know the song, it's because they lived together on Bikini for that brief period of time.

Wōdjapto, the Lagoon of Bikini

Wōdjapto, the lagoon of Bikini
He lies in the reef from day to day
My life jacket (preserver)
always makes me remember him
and directs my thoughts toward
the atoll belonging to the people of Bikini.

Wōdjapto "makes" those who "wear" him (like a "life jacket") "remember him" as he "directs" thoughts toward Bikini, which is where uwaañañ is. The protection of touch and smell goes beyond pushing people away to giving Bikinians the space, the stasis, like the cry breaks in songs, to remember amid their hurried, over-politicized lives in modernity; the mixture works like the noise to pull Bikinians toward their homelands in which they have invested. Randy said that MORIBA also encourages Bikinians to find strength as a spiritual community in times of "bad luck" or misfortune in exile, which occur when Bikinians live in a place outside of their atoll, and he referred to the Wōdjapto spirit making the seas rough, such that resonances of uwaañañ might be considered in this "back luck" that is felt throughout the diaspora. MORIBA is collective memory of the nuclear promise through which Bikinians would be able to remediate Wōdjapto; Wōdjapto is collective memory of why the nuclear exploitation is so important to remember, given their contemporary struggles. Recalling the spirit of manliness through the spirit of sharing is crucial to vocational empowerment and not just interatoll warfare but also to remediating connections, as with Bikinians and Rongelapese in oceanic navigational schools that resonate the quiet noisiness of indigeneity (as that which disrupts Western supremacy) such that Marshallese grappling with "radiation" or the language of modernization and nuclearization can learn from those displaced who are remembering their embodied voices.

GOSPEL OF MORIBA

The stories of the manly spirit and the noisy spirit are crucial to framing the Bikinian religious productions wherein noise becomes a part of the church, bringing the resonances of Wōdjapto and uwaañañ into protective spaces wherein "bad luck" or struggles can find recourse in other ways. The first Gospel Day song that was performed occurred in the Ejit church during the dark of the night. Tak in al, a song group meaning "Sunrise," stood at the front of the church and faced the congregation. The group's song leader, Jakerik, played a slow, resonant audibly marked "tribal" (e.g., processed synth *djembe* drumbeat occurring at regular intervals, pan flute whistle timbre for the execution of the melody) instrumental piece on the Yamaha keyboard. Scholars have suggested that Marshallese cannot explain the "cognitive" discord between their claims to an idyllic/Edenic past and the often self-referenced "savage" past.[37] The split, or irony, is that Marshallese were presented as "savages" living in "Edenic" tropical islands but too indolent to "cultivate them." The savage and the idyllic are part of a negatively construed imaginary in the affective alliance. This complex construction becomes reproduced when alternative readings of the performances are not taken into account. Such alternative readings take into consideration Indigenous accounts of the production of colonial savagery (that places the United States in the position where it must take accountability for violence, manipulation, and the inability to properly care for and cultivate life on the atolls). The "tribal" aesthetic is a warrior aesthetic, be it the Jebro (son) figure or the defamiliarized space of L'Etao, the trickster wherein the *colonizer is the real savage* for poisoning their lives (yet possesses great strength).

Songs with a focus on Gospel Day or on the Gospel itself are part of the competitions and offerings to the pastor. The offered objects are foods (nourishment), mattresses (rest/recharge), and cleaning products and towels (renew/cleanse). Money is also part of the offerings. Monetary offerings convey one's dedication to the church during Gospel Day and at all other church services where the collection basket is passed around. In weekly performances following church and on special occasions, the collection plate is placed in front of a performing group, and members of the community form a circle around it. As they walk in a circular motion, they put a dollar in the collection plate. The circle becomes smaller as people spend their available contributions. One song that speaks to the "giving" component of the moral reciprocity on which the Bikinian kinship structure is currently based is a song originally from Kwajalein that was written for the iroij by Sunrise Lib. The song opens with lyrics explaining that the chiefs know about their lineage, they know how to sail, they know how to sing, but they forgot how to distribute properly (because of the introduction of money—the song "Spirit of Sharing" counters this sentiment). On Ejit the song was performed with lyrics that substituted the chief with the people on Ejit and accused them of "forgetting" how to contribute to the collection for God. The songs are often upbeat with lyrical content that frequently sings the praises of the Gospel and tells the story of the iroij on Ebon Atoll who told the islanders to not "destroy" the ship (*jab rup e*: "don't break it!"). The order to "not break" the boat allowed for the "explosion of light" (*rup meram*) to occur in the islands. The three words *jab rup e* are, in most of the songs, clearly articulated, and the form of the command makes the words memorable. It is a lesson that is applicable to other events beyond the coming of the Gospel.

Bikinians compete for attention, space, and ultimately place in the political capital by becoming Gospel, as with V7EMON ("good news"), by navigating waves and amplifying their voices.[38] MORIBA is an iteration of or the occasion of jab rup e, and it was staged by the US Americans as such. And like the staging of MORIBA—the initial encounter—Bikinian men are the visible leaders of the lagoon-based occupation: they are the "heathens" on the paddleboats, and they are the "savior chiefs" and "the helpful/moral outsider/foreigners" (e.g., Pastor Percy Benjamin; see chapter 3), and a couple of Americans were along for the ride. By remembering that MORIBA is Gospel (Bikini, 1946), broadcast over the airwaves and moving through the oceanic waves, Bikinians remediate nuclear history within Marshallese histories of break-based conversion, offering continuity within modern moralized narratives. However, the warrior aesthetic shares a particular masculinity that emerged from within these breaks that is distanced from the figure of the mother and the indigenous sail that captures the winds and waves.[39]

After a quick packaged lunch—donuts, hard-boiled eggs, hot dogs, Kool-Aid, and soda—the Ejit Youth fished out their Gospel Day signs, men went to retrieve the heavier components for the journey around the lagoon (the speakers, the keyboard, and plastic containers filled with various items such as fish and sodas), and women helped bring items out and oversaw the preparations. Young men whom I was accustomed to seeing in basketball shorts and T-shirts appeared in grass skirts with headbands. Youths put the final touches on the posters on which they had been working since church. Kelen was there, and he told me that he expected a good turnout because the event was announced on V7AB. This meant that throughout the Marshall Islands people would hear about the Bikinian Gospel Day parade.

The front page of the newspaper of record, the bilingual *Marshall Islands Journal*, did a feature story on Gospel Day with photos from the spectacle on page 28 (see figure 4.2). Pictured is the MORIBA boat, resting on a heavenly looking aquatic platform, with a caption that reads in English "Members of the Protestant Church in Majuro organized a spirited boat 'parade' for Gospel Day last Friday, circling the lagoon to promote their message about the gospel." The alignment of MORIBA as the sign from which to infer that this was the Bikinians' message is obvious to Marshallese readers, and it is not written in Marshallese. The Marshallese message beneath the caption specifies that the Gospel is acting in the present: "The Gospel of 2009" is "changing dark to light, scorn to love, and fighting to peace."

The MORIBA boat was the only boat equipped with an electronic sound system, a Yamaha keyboard and speakers, and the various containers of food, candy, and sodas. The MORIBA boat led the way, extending its six-hour long occupation of the Majuro lagoon with amplified song and the distribution of goods. Husband and wife Los and Sweetlina Regino led the musical performances (figure 4.6). As we passed groups of people, we, the women, would wave our fans from side to side (the men waved their hands or clapped on each beat) and sing songs welcoming the Gospel. Shouting and exclamations of enthusiasm were not uncommon during the sail. Los sang and played the keyboard, and he led us in song. Sweetlina would continue to sing with him on the off chance that the entire boat was not singing. The songs varied, but they were primarily religious-based songs with Gospel Day narratives. Los would rhythmically play chords to auto-accompaniment styles, such as country western, and insert commentary periodically. The music did not stop. That seemed to be crucial.

We first sailed across the lagoon to a community with women I recognized from spending time with the Rongelapese women. As we threw money, eggs, and Tupperware into the lagoon, the people who lined the interior of the atoll jumped into the water to retrieve the "gifts" of the Gospel. The other boats full of "pre-Christian Natives" circled around us mimicking pre-contact chants or calls. This consisted of masculine posturing

4.6 Playing the "portable organ" at Majuro lagoon.

or monosyllabic bursts on the beats of the keyboard music "huh-who-uh-who." As the men "chanted," they thrust their upper bodies outward and pushed the sticks or oars backward in the air, gesturing paddling. Some of the "lesser" boats had "recent converts" already on the boats, as could be seen from the "normally dressed Natives" on palm-frond-covered aluminum motorboats. Those boats, which had primarily younger women in them, displayed crosses, and some had the Youth Group MORIBA signs to show their faith. Some had balloons streaming from them that would eventually get flung into the lagoon. There was laughter from all parties, and the rest of the atoll played along. People of all ages dove into the lagoon, and when we neared the end of our journey and were out of things to throw, people started throwing cash and batteries and even the hats off their heads.

Bikinians have "located their identities within their very displacement, extracting meaning and power from the interstitial social location they [inhabit]," and because monetary compensation structures identify slippages by fixing identity, the "very ability to 'lose' one's identity and to move *through* categories [has been] for many a form of social freedom and even security."[40] By remaining within the framework of nuclear identity, Bikinians could afford to spread the word of the Gospel and help others hear

UWAAÑAÑ (SPIRITED NOISE)

the word of the Gospel via modern listening technologies, which include Bikinian voices in their performative roles as spreading the burst of light of the (nuclear) gospel, MORIBA. The spectacular performance enabled them to take on the roles of the American missionaries, the Ebon missionary, the pre-Christian heathen population, and Bikinians (e.g., navigators of tradition within modernity, modernity within tradition). MORIBA was the visible evidence of this exceptional identity, and this identity, albeit dynamic, encompassed their relationship to me and to other Americans.

Relationships are reconfigured during the Gospel Day/Kūrijmōj season, which is a time to role-play (as it has been historically); groups can act on certain tensions built into the customary power dynamics (social hierarchy) by temporarily "overturning" the power dynamics. This is also a time for appeals to higher powers. Spreading the Gospel in these ways connects with the elders who began this tradition after World War II. Moreover, it resonates uwaañañ through Majuro Atoll, announcing loudly that Bikinians, marked for detonation and death, are alive, vital, and present. And much like the elders, Bikinians are proving themselves flexible, transforming the Majuro lagoon into Team MORIBA, perhaps claiming this RMI capital and former US administrative center (and current claim of the Kabua chiefdom) in a symbolic remediation of their own toxic lagoon where Wōdjapto remains and from which Bikinians make his resonances felt. If we rethink "Gospel warriors" in the MORIBA context, in the context of male political voices, then Inben, Lañinbit, Larkeloñ, and Juda are voices detached from the spirited bodies that speak to them. Bikini Atoll becomes the manly spirit and space of conquest. But if we interpret the "Gospel warriors" as vocally remediating their lagoon and their reef god, Wōdjapto, where his silence is politically strategic, even though he is in all the animated voices (perhaps some are even wearing/breathing in the potion "on their skin" like shark teeth) and thus is the uwaañañ queen, Bikinians are listening back and playing with their soundings to hear the multisensorial hidden transcripts wherein ancestral depth is revitalization. They know that Juda was neither "savage" nor "savior" living in an "idyllic" or "empty" place. Rather, he was the youngest son in a line of iroij, remembering from the lessons learned through those who had taken care of his ancestral land, asking the Americans to "*jab rup e*" (don't break it) for the good of the world, according to Bikinian kind. In a sense Juda, like his male chiefly and spiritual lineages, functioned like the archetypical youngest son, Jebro, who met the weight of the world (mankind) not with deception or greed but with a moral statement that would be revealed in time.

CHAPTER FOUR

SONGFESTS

Songfest competitions are part of the Kūrijmōj season. They are known as *jepta* (jep-a-ta: "chapter" or song group based on location and affiliation). Every day of the week for at least three weeks prior to the first church event, everyone in the community practices at all hours of the day and night. Food is usually shared at the practices. One member of the jepta writes a song and brings it to the group. One person from the practicing song group is in charge of leading the practice. This entails performing on the keyboard and instructing members with song lyrics written in large letters on flattened cardboard boxes, a method of communication used at the end of World War II by the Americans to share messages/songs with the Marshallese. The cardboard is fastened to the wall for all to see, but the jepta members are often familiar with the songs or at least some of the melodies. Practices are intense and demanding if only for the amount of time one is sitting or standing, singing, in the same spot. However, the practices also allow people to come and go as needed. Children are always present. Everyone, regardless of age, hums or sings this repertoire of Gospel Day songs, depending on the jepta to which you belong.

At a songfest group competition in Arkansas in 2013 called "Battle of *Jepta* Concert," jepta were appraised on a number of parameters, which were articulated by Marshallese Consul General Carmen Chong Gum on a scorecard: timing (synchronicity and counterpoint), general appearance (outfits, jewelry, presentation), singing band (keyboard accompaniment and singers), march (entrance and exit), marching dance (militaristic dance based on the march), main dance (*piit*), chants (roro), two songs (stationary, a cappella, often dynamically projected), and the overall presentation (jepta) in its entirety.[41] The parameters, which are consistent with what I had seen in the Marshall Islands, show the interwoven and stylized components of the songfest, which, in part, come from Indigenous war-training exercises (competition over land), church singing, line dancing, and the energetic moments of roro. Some of the elements of the musical-dance performances often involve taunting and mocking, braggadocio, combative moves and gestures, and imposing your fragrance on members of the other jepta and the high-ranking members of the community (as well as guests).

The choreographies are synchronized with the songs, and some songs can also be about tying a knot (which has symbolic meaning) or the process of copra harvesting, with directions that share where the winds are best to let the husks dry. The jepta performances that included vocal dynamics and shouts, whistles, and other strong nonlinguistic bursts; double entendre; sexual innuendo; hip swivels; and the "taking" of people with the touching or covering in perfume often received the most enthusiastic response. Men and women form different lines or are in different groups. A leader with a whistle faces the two lines and makes sure that the physical movements align by shrill staccato blows into the whistle and shouted directions. The performance lines will interlock momentarily and switch positions in a rondo-style dance. The content and actions often depict various atoll practices through which *ippān doon* and *bōro wōt juon*—thus *ṃanit*—are maintained, like building a canoe. The Yamaha keyboard player provides accompaniment, with auto-metered beats that enable the group to stay in time and *piit* (beat) together. Despite its name, which sounds like the English word *beat*, Pastor Benjamin told me that piit has been going on "ever since before 1857, but back then, they used drums, not Yamahas."[42]

Randy told me about the Ejit songfest performance by his jepta chapter that I watched the night before. It was written by one of the older women living on Ejit: "[Our performance] last night was about a fight. This was not a real fight, it's just an analogy, but it was a fight between the east and the west. The fight was about who was the best at making up songs and dramas. The song is about who you are, what you do, and how you make the jepta, or how you work with the singing group." Like "*Bikini Jake Jebōl Eo*," the sharing within the jepta is not a given; it is revealed in their performative Indigenous futurities, wherein utopic hope reminds them of the not-yet and almost heaven. Randy finished: "The song is about your life; it [provides commentary on] your life. Wherever you go, you bring this [song], enjoy the [music], and the goods. So the song talks about your life to make it good."[43] Bikinians distinguish American individualistic competitiveness from their "play" competitive jepta. But the necessity of having real time (noisy practices) to re-create roro (spirited being), engage in play competition, and remember Bikinian vitality among sharing (as real) helps them stave off negative representations and stigmatization, and reminds them of their strength in excess of real violence and removals, which can still be used within battles in courtrooms and legislative houses where the warrior figure must emerge through particular articulations to protect inheritance.

CHAPTER FOUR

LIGHT AT THE END OF THE DARKNESS: THE MESSAGE, THE EXPLOSION, AND THE MONEY

I conclude with the Kūrijmōj explosion in the middle of the night on Kili. The explosion exemplifies Bikinian spirited sharing through a violent noisiness that can be read in terms of the nuclear project's resonances. Kūrijmōj is, as Laurence Carucci writes, an entire festive season that includes Christmas Day (for which it is named) in the middle of the span from late September or early October through mid-January. Kūrijmōj is a "series of continual and repetitive exchanges."[44] It is a time for giving-while-keeping love, kindness, and celebrating the figure of Christ, whom the Marshallese god-chief Jebro (known for caring for his mother, Lōktañūr) has been folded into as a benevolent leader through activities that maintain communal bonds. The principal reason for giving, as Carucci explains, is to be able to retain. Bikinians *must* keep their identity as Bikinians, they must keep their resources, because without land, what they have is money and an identity that speaks of a land. Their mythico-history is a protective mechanism that marks them, and thereby sustains them, as Bikinians and as the Bikinian nation.

The morning began with a toll of the makeshift bell and climaxed in the middle of the night with music and recitation based on passages from the Bible: the Gospels of John and Mark. The musical messages lead to the presentation of the "trees" (*wōjke*) from the two jepta on Kili Island, which explode. Men with cameras crowd around to videotape the words of the Gospel from John 3:16 that speak of God's sacrifice to the world. God gave his one and only son, and whoever believes in him shall have eternal life. The theme of sacrifice for the greater good of the world has obvious resonances with the community as does the explosive world secured safely inside the church. Bikinians were put in the position where without consultation or warning they were becoming Christian soldiers in a culture in which "suffering for science" was considered part of a salvation narrative, a moral narrative of modernity. And their suffering for the sciences (oceanography, ecology, radiography, radiology, sociology, anthropology, ethno-musicology, and so forth) exists within a discursive-material chain of those academics, nonprofits, and others that "give of themselves" to "help" bring stories to light.[45] History teaches lessons, and the Kili people give each other fair warning that the explosion is coming. While they sing, they plug their ears.

Harmony, Attali reminds us, made people believe in certain representations of moralized order.[46] Bikinians, for hours of singing and dancing, of performing faith, and remembering sacrifice, had played within and in excess of Western harmonic frameworks, orderings, and resolutions. The energetic exertion demanded a renewal, and Bikinians were ready for the explosions and the gifts that they bring (the excess of the explosion). Analogy would read that the Bikinians, Kili people included, are the sacrificed "son" of God, or "America's children" as Bikinians and other non-Bikinian Marshallese refer to them. These ceremonies renew feelings of moral kinship (*jouj*) through the activation of feelings of time deferred and thus indebtedness also by connecting intelligence (indigenous foods, those served to chiefs and foreigners) to knowledge (served on *enrā*, the plate woven from pandanus fronds), all activated by the Marshallese throat heart (singing in jouj).

The globe explodes and produces a moderate sound, but the sight is stunning. American dollar bills make up the core (nucleus) of this sacrificial world, which the people run to collect. However, their individual paper scraps with "heads of dead presidents" become a collection when it is returned to the world as they circle the globe (which they were first introduced to on Rongerik by Commodore Wyatt), but it is now their object to play with. The Bikinian women walk circles around the globe, and with each cycle they deposit more money than they received from the explosion. They continue to recite the praises of God throughout the act, symbolically connecting them to multiple dimensions of created worlds, some of which were afforded by their displacement.

Another box, larger than the first one, is brought in for the second explosion, and again the congregation members take their positions to wait. Exemplifying the performative antiphonal aurality, they chant "*Kwoj ba wot*" ("You say so") again and again. The reference is painted on the casing of the offering: the explosive object. The words are from Mark 14:2. This is the passage just prior to Jesus Christ's crucifixion, when Mark asks if Jesus is the king of the Jews. Jesus replies, "You say so." It is the power of the spoken word that resonates and transcends Mark's agency. Jesus's equivocal answer is powerful precisely because it is nonconfrontational, echoing MORIBA and all that comes with it. "*Kwoj ba wot*" expressively forces, or puts pressure, on the respondent rather than the usage of excessively forceful language. The corollary truth is later revealed by an absence of the corporeal (material) when Jesus ascends to Heaven, to his homeland and his inheritance. The words on the large box, "*lomor emoot lok*" (salvation is gone, has left), refer to the disappearance of Jesus from his tomb after his crucifixion. This absence marked by words signifies the "missing" reminder of the debt: the gift of life.

The Kili people use the space of the church and the time of "darkness" to remediate and correlate the nuclear and missionary encounter among those encounters that remain insensible (to me, at least). The Yamaha electric portable organ visually presents the musical keys that the keyboardist plays so that the others can "listen and learn" their sensible places. Cameramen surround the unexploded box, waiting to capture the verbal transaction and material transformation, much like American cameraman did on Bikini Atoll in 1946. What they both capture is the transformation of the Bikinian people and their capacity for self-transformation as actors on the global stage. And still the Kili people do not want to *hear* the explosion (the bomb). They plug their ears in extended anticipation, hinting at the anticipatory temporality introduced through their incorporation into "self-help" neoliberalism and ongoing militarism (that assumes ongoing potential of crisis, which is ongoing threat). They do not want to actually *experience* the traumatic event (again), but they do want to reap the privileges of its aftermath because they exist and often struggle to survive within the aftermath of the traumatic event.

The sound, in the form of the words "You say so," marks the traumatic (event-based, fixed) silences and silencings of cultural loss that Bikinians refuse to hear (the explosion that, on Kili, was not very loud). The Bikinians cannot see and will not hear those "sounds and sights" that denote the nuclear violence and mess (disorganization) that Americans made of their atoll. They refuse responsibility for devastating their land, but they can assume responsibility for their impact on global pop culture. There is no utopian function or moralistic motif that can be attached to the sound "boom." It has to be made, but this white noise had to remain silent to their ears because the production is about human agency; specifically, it is about the agency that the Bikinians inherited from their ancestral leaders' vociferous allegiances. The Bikinians have ontologically transformed themselves, placing them in the historical center where youths (Wōdjapto, the younger brother) and noisiness prevail in conquering/chanting/singing your way to Bikini, whatever your conception of Bikini Atoll is.

This explosion, like the first one, yields riches. The material is not vaporized into an empty core of paper money this time, but rather the paper money firmly attaches the sturdiness of the box to the sturdiness of the cross (to bear: the "heaviness" of the exceptional inheritance) to the lightness of the explosion and the seemingly abstract yet tangible lightness of the money. When the money reveals itself, the repetitive chant song continues for a few moments, and then Kili singers cease making noise. The pastor shares the cognate message from the Bible, and instead of receiving, it is time to continue giving. The collective voices reveal the movement affectively with a transformation of the sound-scape from the affective repetition (the recitative "*kwoj ba wot*") to rolling melodic contours and an accentuated tonal range to illuminate, through hymn, the story of the Gospel. Pastor Albin shifts from his lowest bass register to baritone as he leads the congregation from roro derivative to hymn. Roro and hymn contrast each other in response to the quintessential question asked by Mark to Jesus that redefined all of mankind: "Are you the King of the Jews?"

Kwoj ba wot also means "you thought" ("you were under the impression" or "you concluded"), and the choice of this passage is the repetition of the nuclear transaction with reflexive commentary. Anthropologist Webb Keane looks at authorship and agency in terms of the moral narrative of modernity as one where "self-awareness is a condition for freedom."[47] The reflexive commentary "you thought" layers multiple dimensions of agency on top of "you say so." "You thought" may be directed at the United States, which thought it could break its promises and lie to the Bikinians without repercussion; there are too many speculative possibilities such that the "indexical ambiguity" of the repetition is part of its affective force.[48]

Kūrijmōj performances that restage the explosion of light restage a break from the so-called past in a violently moral or morally violent way that protects some relationships over others. For example, the chief's injunction to not break the missionary boat, the *Morning Star*, and the Bikinians' performance of this pivotal moment align them with Americans and chiefly power, moral power. However, the affective alliance is one that resonates a debt, and this debt is to be found in the noisiness of their land, which turns the power structure of Bikinians' dependency on Americans to Americans' dependency on Bikinians, affirming the Marshallese notion of freedom, anemkwōj (interdependence).

The first sounds of an atomic explosion heard during "peacetime" came from Bikini Atoll, and the Americans benefited greatly from this taking of the land and collecting its richness. Bikinians' spirit of sharing asks, in moral reciprocity, to share the richness so they can develop the infrastructure they believe is best for their diasporic community. Here, Bikinians show themselves to be the givers of light (atomic bomb, morality) rather than the "takers" of financial resources from the US government as in development narratives and commonplace stereotypes about "developing nations," "wards," and international aid, which cast Indigenous people and people from the global South as lacking industriousness (lazy) and thus recasts them negatively as "heathens" and uncivilized, when civilization amounts to industry. Decolonial dissonance emerges as the struggle to hear these appeals or requests, like the chants in song, as necessary sound in fulfilling the promises made by Americans that they would support Bikinians (people with a unique and shared cultural repertoire) rather than neglect and incorporate Bikinians as emptied-out people waiting for someone to make the key for them. The Americans took much more than land; they took entire worlds and structures built, loved, cared for, and kept together by women and men. Uwaañañ is the expression of Indigenous vitality and co-gendered conflict resolution, where women sounded rhythms alongside their men.

The uwaañañ is not noise at all; rather, it is the audible, perceptible, and nonlexical structures that are related to the force behind the talking that does make sense in political arenas and intimate worlds of the "taken for granted." The fights of the men and manly spirits—brothers or chiefs—and their resolutions, which, at times meant the displacement of a population, are circulated in song and story to remind Bikinians how not to be nearly inaudible or completely silent. The prize, the queen of uwaañañ, is the hidden transcription of all Bikinian ājmour, but modern interpretations can easily render this story as a part of masculine domination and female transaction via her silence. So too the sound-symbolic world of a flexible Bikini becomes effeminized and read as penetrable in her fertility, as a surface of coconuts (according to the translation of the name, "pikinni"). Bikinians retain the maternal sensibilities of the Ijjirik clan and the sensibilities of spirited noisiness by speaking loudly about the strength of a big man, Wōdjapto. However, the valorization of the masculine is problematic because it promotes the silencing of the feminine voice in returns to the land that protects the lagoon and Wōdjapto, who protects it, the feminine voice through which Wōdjapto must resonate. Yet the voice that cannot be personified (or anthropomorphized as an animal, even, with a name) becomes, in its equivocality, voiceless or unheard through the figure of sound alone. Nuclear silences are the resonance of this voicelessness. By naming this sensibility, the maternal continues to inform men's political speech and creative dissent, but it is, like the lōrrọ, that which the "white man" (spectral) cannot hear: the antiphonal interplay of the copresence of women and their land-based lineage, which cannot be humanized or gendered in binary oppositional, public/private ways (yet must be to be claimed and redressed through the Fifth Amendment).

Part of the painful yet hopeful story of the Bikinians is this acknowledgment and the fortitude to resist the demise of their worlds in the face of "moral narratives of modernity" that seek to dematerialize and thus dematernalize them, rendering them an optics of the vanishing frontier through scientific journals, the media, and heritage-making sites.[49] Bikinians and Rongelapese move to their spirited sounds while the world continues to imagine and thus render them voiceless. I read uwaañañ as a re-fusal of the present past making of Marshallese indigenousness through the bomb. For this spirited noise provincializes the bomb and absorbs it, like the women who encircle the globe, for the white noise it is. Devastating and world changing, yes: this is how Bikinians and Rongelapese see the injurious and violent acts done to them. They are also much more than the reduction to a dehumanized humanity, a senseless or voiceless people for whom enlightenment came with the word on a boat. Bikinians know their interwoven inheritance: the spirit of sharing alongside Rongelapese, Marshallese, Ijjidik, Oceanic, Christian, American, and so forth, all of which persist through competitive strength, self-determination, and force of agency. Spirited noise is the force that puts moral pressure on the world to work with them to address and demand restitution from the United States as equitable remedy for the taking of Bikini. This means recognition of their lives as meaningful and the conditions to performatively make manifest these lives. The precondition for moral reciprocity is the space to be vociferous, which, as I showed previously, was shut down by the US Supreme Court. Therefore, Bikinians use the structures of noisiness, uwaañañ, to animate and send the gift of their voices (Gospel/MORIBA) to their outside moral kin, and they maintain public secrets (Wōdjapto) to affectively keep trust grounded and strategic.

CHAPTER FIVE

ANEMKWŌJ

After a year and a half in the Marshall Islands, one of the songs I heard performed most often was "*Bōk mejam*." Translated in English as "Take a look" or more literally "Bring your face," it was one of the few songs I heard sung across atoll populations at their parties, at larger events, and on the radio as recorded covers. At a Rongelapese women's picnic, Shirley and I were sitting together, unpacking food, and she was humming the song. I asked her about it, and she explained that the song was to welcome people (*al in karuwanene*). She motioned to her face and looked upward, and she described the title as facing those you are welcoming and looking, taking a look and bringing it all in, asking those you are welcoming to do the same. Performed, it appeals to its singer and asks of its auditor to share what is most precious by facing one another and turning to the land and recognizing that this is a Marshallese place through which "freedom" materialized for the world. The Marshallese word for freedom is *anemkwōj*, which translates to the ability to take liberties. Within its poetics a setting of interdependence is performed; the phonemes together interconnect "hers/his/its-and-you." "*Bōk mejam*" situates freedom through the grounded sensibilities of Kwajalein landowners, who, as intermediaries between the commoner class and the *iroij*, are tasked with protection and care. They stress that freedom is a coproduction.

Like rock 'n' roll and fast cars, Americans have particular sound symbols when it comes to hearing freedom that deafen other processes through which freedom manifests. The hypermasculinized, speed-driven war technologies that have been lauded as being the "sounds of freedom," epitomized by (sh-boom) the atomic bomb, have indiscriminately and categorically bound bodies to and through spatialized logics driven by forcible expediency toward death—as an afterlife, clean slate, *terra nullius*, or simply "no future." Carried by "missiles" and/as "missives," the resonant cadences to nuclear hymns, these "sounds of freedom" disrupt "places" into spatio-temporal grids from which "places" are made, whether it be pummeling Kwajalein waters with uranium-tipped missiles or disrupting sound-scapes of middle-class America (see figure 5.1).[1] Kwajalein Atoll exists in multiple scaled networks that resonate in the tapestry of sounds of freedom that, as songs, are formal means through which claims to freedom are politicized via the grounds of freedom that have been censored; in these songs, censorship is sonorized. The interrelatedness of the future that shapes the present-past can be heard in re-fusals of modern time through lapses in liberation of the not-voiceless workers, the not-voiceless landowners, and the not-voiceless lands that speak their movements in place-names shared across generations, still and now. This concluding chapter focuses on the continuing struggle to hear matrilineal futurities of the durative movements of (non)human feminine protectiveness, security, and strength as they are routed through the treatment of Kwajalein's militarized lands and lives. As Gregory Dvorak explains, "Kwajalein's turbulent twentieth-century history is one punctuated by a masculinist language, a grammar of male power and privilege . . . , which has been spelled out in the layering of colonial concrete on the land. The male coded narratives of imperial expansion, heroism, battle, liberation, and victory have left their marks, from land registration systems to the images of US missiles penetrating the 'virgin' lagoon on reentry."[2] Musical movements collect traces of the masculinist language in ways that work in tension with matrilineal memories. The violent force that is the mark of an event-based history is, like a percussive attack stripped of resonance, a sonorized effect in radioactive citizenship that becomes part of a composite termed the "sounds of freedom" in ways that efface the multiple movements that crisscross the militarized landscape offering multiple directions that face, confront, are complicit with, challenge, critique, celebrate, and detour from prescriptive US freedoms through Marshallese relational notions of freedom or the ability to take liberties.

"*Bōk mejam*" works on a temporal register that emphasizes how the future shapes the past present and the present past through context, frames, and filters in ways that unsettle modernity's nucleated past, present, and future. The imagination of freedom as externalized sounds to be listened to in pursuit of a future happiness or a present state is challenged by the situated processes of freedom in the relational negative that take shape throughout "*Bōk mejam*." The song's compositional narrative becomes

5.1 "Freedom has a new sound!" *National Geographic*, August, 1955.

a proverbial warning, itself an injunction to "take a look" and watch the (postwar) remedial processes as they unfold. Composed as a celebratory song in the postwar moment of (mythic) liberation, "Bōk mejam" becomes recontextualized amid the sail-in-style protests of US military occupations of Kwajalein and the treatment of the landowners, in which both women and men played a central role. By emphasizing singing and place naming in terms of the processual and interconnected energies that inflect protest, the situated story of "Bōk mejam," along with other homecoming songs, disrupts the conventional orders of protection and empowerment through militarized hierarchies, which echo in globalized radioactive citizenship and its resonant sounds of freedom.

Militarization relies on the state apparatus through which processes of harmonization or hegemonic social differentiation (e.g., gender, race, capital-based class, age, ability) and territorialization become coconstitutive and justified under "security" measures.[3] Processes of social differentiation and territorialization prefigure and come to justify militarization when "freedom" and security become synonymous with, or when freedom is administered by, the state, which happens through rights afforded to citizens as humans.[4] The concept of radioactive citizenship is helpful in disentangling the historical layers of territorial appropriation and erasure. By listening to the "grounds of freedom" as they become the "sounds of freedom," we can hear how bodies and labor become effaced in instances of globalized vocal currency that draw on the sounds of the military-industrial complex that cannot or do not directly recognize, acknowledge, or yield returns to the grounds of military occupation, even if hymn-style harmony and military sounds resonate the intertwining of American missionaries and military that pervades nuclear ideology. Decolonization studies, as a method of engaging globalizing music, demands place-based, situated accounts that take Indigenous perspectives on political alliances, such as the COFA, into account. Sonic histories that layer place naming and historical markers complicate US security definitions and musical measures that retain a militarized metrical association with rigor, strength, and coordination. Attention to the complex topographies of singers' narratives through their embodied throats, dis-emplaced from the lands, can become a productive detour from dominant sensibilities through which war is associated with victory; they can also affirm and challenge the particularities of the victor-victim binaries that are interrelated. For example, along with "Bōk mejam," there are songs that recall matrilineal place-names and locations of the 1983 Strategic Defense Initiative (SDI), also called "Star Wars."

Movements of massive expenditures in the arms race that included technology employed at Kwajalein, in missile detection sensors, and against Marshallese sensibilities via the throat in the instance of these songs demand reconsideration of contributions to "US victory" as the retention of the ability to globalize a moralized military via the cold war.

FROM THE SOUNDS TO THE GROUNDS OF FREEDOM

Perusing a copy of the *Territorial Survey of Oceanic Music* at the Marshall Islands Music and Arts Society in Uliga Village in Majuro, I found information about "*Bōk mejam*" that credited a Bikinian man with authorship.[5] The lyrics were included, and I noticed immediately that the bomb was a parenthetical part of the song ("shelter [from the bomb]"). When I read that the song was from Bikini Atoll, its popularity made sense. The Bikinians, as the most visible representatives of atomic diplomacy, were often recognized as the spokespersons for (or the "face" of) a country embroiled in nuclear issues, and they were often at the forefront of diplomatic contestations. I photocopied the page from the survey and asked some Bikinians if they were familiar with the song. Some people seemed slightly surprised to see the song credited as Bikinian, whereas some enthusiastically claimed it.[6] One of the people on Ejit who took issue with my letter-based claim was Pastor Percy Benjamin. Pastor Benjamin was from Ebeye Island in Kwajalein Atoll. In our formal interviews he described how throughout his childhood growing up on Ebeye he heard uranium-tipped missiles "whiz" overhead and crash into the lagoon. He eyed the paper and handed it back to me with the conviction that the song was from Kwajalein Atoll. "Maybe the Bikinians made it theirs too," he said. "Everybody sings it. Everywhere."[7]

Bōk mejam

(I) *Bōk mejam im reilām aluluje*
kāān tirooj ko rejul im nōr.
(II) *Ijo in jo kōmar roñ pellok kake*
joñan im dettan im aetokan in.
(III) *Amñe edik ke baj wombu eo in.*
Jikū jikū jikūn ami
anemkwōj.[8]

ANEMKWŌJ

Bōk mejam   Take a Look

(I) Take a look and watch the "tea rose" flowers
germinate and bloom from the tree trunk.
 (II) Here, this place was our temporary shelter,
about the size and length of it.
 (III) Although it's small, it is just for cover.
My place, my place, a place for you to have
freedom.

I met up with Kwajalein Senator Tony deBrum to discuss how my musical ethnography had been going over the year and a half that I had been in the Marshall Islands. I spent a number of evenings at deBrum's "kava club," where political talk and song circulated like the halved coconut shell cups of kava. From the first night we met, he seemed engaged with the project because it combined his lifelong investments in Marshallese decolonial processes and music. When I showed deBrum the paper that stated "*Bōk mejam*" was Bikinian, he looked bewildered. There were three songs on the photocopied page, and he asked, "Which one, this song?" He was pointing to "*Bōk mejam*." Before I could finish saying "Yes," deBrum interjected. "Yeah, wait." He quickly turned, looked behind him, and muttered an aside—"The *aḷap* is here"—and turned back quickly to me. "Give me two minutes here," he ordered. "A minute and a half."

DeBrum returned. "He's a Kwajalein aḷap," he explained. "After we talked about it . . . as far as I know, this song is a Kwajalein song." It is hard to convey just how baffled deBrum sounded. He was almost laughing in disbelief, but he didn't find the situation humorous. He continued: "[The song] may have been adapted to the Bikini people in the seventies, but it has always been my understanding that is was a Kwajalein song, and it was composed by a gentleman named Labaañ. And where does this sheet of paper come from?" I explained that I had photocopied a page in the *Territory Survey of Oceanic Music*, offering "I believe Alele [a national museum] had the recordings, but they lost them or misplaced them. . . ." Again, deBrum interrupted me: "I confess, I am totally floored by this reference being about the initial relocation of Bikini to Kili." He took a moment. "It's interesting. There are songs that people say [are] someone's, but it's actually someone else's, but I've always thought this one to be very clear where it was from . . . and here [*deBrum's voice became a bit deeper*], we have a classic example of a translation issue. . . ."

The "translation issue" resulted in part from literary or reading practices. This translation issue was not a literal word-to-word translation issue; the problem is that "writing is too often conceptualized as synonymous with the alphabetic script."[9] The translation had to do with the records of knowledge through which Western and Indigenous cultures circulate political legitimacy. Although both rely on the written word, matrilineal entitlements are a place-based knowledge of the archipelago, rather than exclusively of the written archive, where the vast grounds of lived experienced can become sounds of claimed dominion. Of course, as the previous chapter shows with the Bikinian story, wars and displacement are part of the unrecognized grounds of Bikinian life (and Marshallese life) before the US military, before World War II. However, the moralized promises of freedom, democracy, and equality through which US Americans forged affective alliances—the sounds of freedom as promises—have been created as part of an ongoing war and are part of the internalized tensions through which Marshallese have been denied agency and freedom through systematized sounds as projections of these concepts in the harmonization of globalized society. The future orientation from the present "just now" affective dimension that focuses on the political engagement alone through the division of the environment, women, children, elders, and so forth limits freedoms and directional resonances. This is an issue of transcribing "oral" histories, for the oral component that is heard is the disembodied voice rather than the processual socio-natural landscape robust with resonances, making intertextual, embodied, and multimodal "readings" beyond the archive so important.[10] And for deBrum, the words did just this: they conjured a hummed melody as place-based recollection that could not be relegated to the print alone. He took a moment and said, with the caveat that I could verify his statement, the word *wombu* is Japanese and means "homeland," but in the context of the Bikinian adaptation, it came out to mean "shelter [from the bomb]." Although deBrum conceded that the song might have taken on new meaning for Bikinians when they went to Kili, he believed that the line referred to a homecoming, a "returning to Kwajalein Island after hiding from all the bombings . . . [after] World War II. Returning to their islands . . . ," he repeated. DeBrum vocalized his interest in the claim to "*Bōk mejam*," which he and others had already expressed can be explained through meaningful, historical investment in not entirely dissimilar ways to investments in place (see the Bikinian story in chapter 4). In the current media-based, juridical culture, however, ownership is about whose name is on the paper—no matter who is doing the work "on the ground," as it were.

ANEMKWŌJ

After interpreting the song's lyrics, from the double entendre to the tea roses that grow on Kwajalein, deBrum had laid claim to the song's origin. He then encouraged me to pack my bags and accompany him, President Jurelang Zedakaia, and a host of other politicians and cultural authorities to Kwajalein Atoll for a Landowners Association meeting. He explained they could share with me their musical repertoire, composed of recollections of a "lifetime [of] involvement, directly or indirectly, with the US military."[11] Placed in context of their musical repertoire, deBrum assured me, it would be clear that a Kwajalein Atoll man wrote "*Bōk mejam*."

I journeyed to Kwajalein Atoll and stayed on Ebeye Island in April 2010 based on deBrum's suggestion, and I was able to better appreciate Kwajalein's central position in nuclear operations and as a location through which bodies, information, and music move, how lived embodiments of military occupation (grounds of freedom) become part of radioactive citizenship (sounds of freedom). Nuclear militarism of the many, which is a composite of affective sonorities, becomes circulated as individualized voices in musical harmony that humanizes the military as affective power. Globalized radioactive citizenship takes shape in musical or sound effects of missiles and bombs that, like censored words, retain violent power over life and its reproductive forces. The moment of violent power that reduces life, such as a bomb blast, can efface entire worlds yet can unwittingly become part of radioactive chains of appropriation, as with the example of "Sh-Boom," which may also depend on the auditor's positionality in recognizing violent impositions of force, such as various categorically policed persons. Ana María Ochoa Gautier has termed these circulations "acoustic assemblages," textured by various auralities in ways that emphasize a unintentional cooptation or spiritual appropriation.[12] My visit to Kwajalein Atoll was possible because of radioactive citizenship, including its systematized assemblages of violence and erasure. Unsettling radioactive citizenship requires ongoing decolonizing approaches, such as decolonial musical appreciation of land-based counternarratives that stem from grounded sensibilities through which Indigenous harmonies via place-based movements, recorded in singing-as-naming practices, resonate or project Indigenous futurities. These projections displace any notion or legal fiction of *terra nullius* and challenge globalizing media through interconnected fluidity, the feminine movements through all-gendered persons and places that have been categorically claimed and occupied by force and by law.[13]

Categorical disruption of musical form and content can unsettle the textual claims to lives, lands, and bodies. Following the editors of *Sensing*

Law, who call for scholars to "probe more deeply the complex ways in which the law, the senses, and property intersect," I am interested in how the sensorial entrainment of humans, in our protective capacities as "civil defenders," is mediated in song and what this can tell us about our attunements and attentions to the state and corporate culture, such as those that are meant to detect mediated adverts or missiles, and away from ourselves and each other's knowledges.[14] How does knowledge of the processual grounds of the "sounds of freedom"—be it in pill, fast food, or missile form—disrupt the managerial efficiency of mediated claims to legalized biopolitical controls? How might such modes of music study necessitate political detours as returns, reparations, and remediations? How might they demand attention to sensorial knowledges and interconnectedness that move beyond the primacy of the senses divided, particularly those that are highly valued (eye, ear, hand) in 1) the archive—as instruments of protection and security, and 2) the law (secular modernity) that manifests through voice and voice-based claims to legitimacy, necessitating the question of whose bodies have been silenced in the making of global defenses? Ultimately, the latter creates a racialized and gendered mind-body split, via the throat, in the making of vococentric subjects.[15]

I examine how "*Bōk mejam*," a welcoming song turned heated song claim, the musical form of *tabōḷ pile* (double play), and place naming counter a politics of erasure and contest intellectual property through limits of the mind-body split in terms of the Western notion of the body politic that propagate such erasures through divisive policies. Drawing upon the musico-poetics of wave-pattern navigation or Indigenous vocal currencies (matrilineal movements), I listen to how "homecoming songs" draw attention to returns to the lagoon and to Marshallese cosmologies that assert claims to the grounds of freedom. As Gregory Dvorak points out, "'Homecoming' is a proud narrative of Marshallese solidarity and dignity in the face of the kind of treatment Islanders endured in their encounters with Japanese and Americans. It is a direct reaction to both Japanese expansion and American 'liberation,' but at the same time it is also an affirmation of land, identity, and continuity. It is an avowal of perseverance in spite of extreme hardship, a celebration of survival."[16]

As with the Bikinian narrative, Dvorak recalls the centuries of land disputes and very serious consequences of land loss and demoralization.[17] Prior to colonization, Marshallese chiefs and persons who lost their lands would often be killed or incorporated into the winning chiefly clan as part of the *kajoor* population, the common persons (power class). Today, and

ANEMKWŌJ

specifically after German colonization, there are three tiers of society: *iroij* (chief, female chief is *leroij*), *aḷap* (landowner, intermediary), and *ri-jerbal* (worker). Everyone has land rights through their mother's side; Marshallese society is matrilineal. Women, led by eldest females with the highest rank, shared their voices to encourage men during battle, stop fights, and create peace. Today, their voices are still respected in these terms, and this is known as *leej man juri* ("When a woman speaks, the man must give way"). There is a strong association between *"leej man juri"* and "homecoming fights for land" because women who listen to and commune with the lands, often through drumming and vocalizations, had the final say on when to cease battle, as called out by the men. US strategy can thus be seen as categorical impositions on the inability to hear the matrilineage and the efficient co-optation of masculine alliances for power and profit.

Political legitimacy is found within the composite understandings of freedom that maintain an equivocal stance to such paper trails. Whereas the liberal notion of democracy is consent to be ruled and is based upon individual subjects tethered to the state through the ear and pen, eye and spectacle and vice versa, I argue that the word *freedom*, which features in this song, and its cognate *democracy* resound differently when taken outside the context of the law that upholds certain notions of this male-intellectual and female-bodied land and the security it affords. By approaching the terms of freedom and democracy (*anemkwōj* and *anemkwōj kien*, respectively) from these Marshallese terms, I explore how equivocality is embedded within the sensory terrain of democratic participation and decision making through the feminine voice that resounds protection and security in excess of the sensors that detect missiles at the Kwajalein military base. Here the method of sensorial democracy through a sonic politics of indigeneity positions Marshallese feminine voices as "prior" protections of the homelands, securing land and lineage not only for Marshallese but also for the world.[18]

Place naming cannot simply be written down as the word; it is an entire genealogy: "The name [of the land] speaks to the history, whose rights, and why those rights exist."[19] There is hope that taking to the airwaves afforded by the military installations will afford an intervention in ungrounded radioactive citizenship from the voices of those who know messages that Indigenous harmonies realized through wave-pattern navigation and matrilineal movements (*jitdam kapeel*). Homecoming songs require decolonial dissonances with the construct of "the voice" through harmonic breaks that detour the categorical separation of body/mind and nature/culture via relational place naming, which happens *over time*. This last chapter thus functions as a conclusion of sorts to review ways to rethink the sonic politics of displaced indigeneity via detours from militarized spaces that value the individual to the "many" atoll umbilicals (*bwijen*), lineage (*bwij*), and land (*bwidej*). In doing so I trace the remediations of war in songs not as unipolar "victory" but rather as processual togetherness, *ippān doon*, and a process where the people, the lands, and the flowers are important.

MATRIX AS CONTEXT

The name of Kwajalein Atoll defined in the *Marshallese-English Dictionary*:

Kuwajleen {qiwajleyen}. *cf*: <u>waj</u> "to you," <u>leen</u> "its fruit"; legend says that after a typhoon its only fruit was flowers which the people took to the chief as the only available tribute. —ABO ET AL., *Marshallese-English Dictionary*

As the songs share, the concept of the typhoon is related to battle, war, and political struggle. The chief, as the leader, was paid tribute through the communal efforts of the power base for whom he provided. The equitable distribution has not happened through US partitioning of resources, the landowners charge. What has led to the tensions, and where do we go?

Senator deBrum advised me to create a musical "matrix of listings," rather than a taxonomy, of Marshallese songs pertaining to the country's experiences with US militarism to show how songs took shape in different communities and transformed meaning and memory in the process. The matrix, deBrum suggested, would give the project direction, which came from the historical movements of people sharing the song.[20] A map showing the "movement of Marshallese from nuclear testing" makes clear how Kwajalein was center stage for the nuclear diaspora. If we think about "*Bōk mejam*" circulating with people who have experience with the US military and a continued rhetoric of freedom, we can see how, aside from Enewetak (although Enewetakese do work on Ebeye and live in Majuro), Kwajalein's musical culture brings the nuclear-affected atolls together in a specific type of radioactive citizenry, which migrates to Majuro with increasing development and national codification. The physical monuments of ongoing war—or culture of Americanized nuclear militarism—are daily reminders of the precarious harmonies of what Marshallese term "freedom," or anemkwōj.

It is the Kwajalein aḷap's responsibility to take care of the lands and peoples. Marshallese anthropologist Kristina Stege concluded, in a section on aḷap succession, that several interlocutors "referred to the saying, mejed kabilōk kōj or 'eyes that guide us,' to describe the traditional authority of a lineage head—commoner or chief—to tweak the rules of succession based on the perceived needs of the group at the time."[21] In this respect, "take a look" might refer to the "eyes that guide" in troubled times.

Kwajalein's population bears the brunt of militarization, and, as such, it is a highly masculinized space.[22] It served as the staging center for nuclear weapons testing, but its residents are not included in Section 177 of the COFA, the "nuclear-affected atolls." Additionally, there is new information that Kwajalein did receive radioactive fallout from Bravo and other less renowned (yet still classified) US nuclear detonations, such as the Operation Redwing (1956) and Operation Hardtack (1958) series (in total, 48.8 megatons), which created spikes in plutonium 239 and 240 counts in fish muscle in Kwajalein Atoll.[23] Declassified projects would undoubtedly bring new information that could help Kwajalein residents assess any latent radiogenic issues. Although the US nuclear testing program of the 1940s and 1950s has received more media attention, Kwajalein remains at the center of ongoing US military weapons testing projects in the Pacific that continue to affect the daily lives of Kwajalein people. The health effects of living so close to the missile launches and planned impact strikes with debris circulating through the air and sea, in addition to large-scale displacement, need to be addressed.

Reflecting on the contested terms of the written document that incorrectly asserted Bikinian authorship, when "*Bōk mejam*" is contextualized within the historical and globalized archipelagic atollscape of Kwajalein's name, it speaks of the gifts of the fruits or roses given to a chief after a typhoon. In its capaciousness, the name speaks to patterns of events that unfold in a musicality of beauty and freedom in homecoming songs archived in embodied musical movements, engendering a politics of harmony that is detoured through the force of reaching a tonic rather than remembering through *mwilaḷ* (deep/depth) processes of sensorial remembrance and place-naming practices. The Kwajalein landowners assert their legitimacy in protest of the US and RMI authorities and media portrayal of their lands. Songs such as "*Bōk mejam*" are petitions that, sung over time in different contexts, show how the relationship between the United States and the Marshallese on Kwajalein deteriorated in the postwar. "*Bōk mejam*" can be considered a welcoming song, a protest song, and even within the repertoire of battle songs that document Kwajalein people's persistence and self-determination to confront the US military and the RMI government when necessary. Although these battle songs often take on the tenor of the *ṃōṃaanan* (strong man), they include customary predictive tropes, centered in customary place naming and spirited communication, that emplace American military power within Marshallese ancestral matrilineage. Moreover, they push back on centuries of legal fictions predicated on the "excessive" value placed on the alphabetic written word and the scientific sovereign. Such practices debase the well-being of Marshallese by silencing Marshallese grounds and ultimate authority, the feminine voice, animated by sons fighting to protect her land (bwij).

A KWAJALEIN WELCOMING SONG

Our Continental Airlines flight left Majuro Atoll's international airport at 10:55 AM and arrived on Kwajalein Island, Kwajalein Atoll, approximately an hour later. The airport is on the military base, so we were not allowed to take pictures. I noted that there were some interesting aircraft, low to the ground, and the skyline of the island was filled with white globe-like structures, which are radars. After disembarking the plane, we were led into a room where a black dog sniffed all of our pieces of luggage. People staying on Kwajalein Island had to get special permission, and those of us who were headed to Ebeye had to get permits to remain on Kwajalein while passing through. The other *ri-pālle* (American) in our party of dignitaries had grown up on Kwajalein, and as we were driven through the island, she pointed out a number of landmarks, including the Marshallese Cultural Center, which she said is not frequently visited, the nondenominational church, the outdoor movie theater, the coconut trees without coconuts (the US government does not want to get sued if a coconut falls and hits someone on the head), and the old Macy's department store. The streets were nicely paved; the lawns were manicured. Our "special bus" (because of the elite company) was allowed to go to the "snack bar," where there was a Burger King and Subway, famed to all of the expats on Majuro. Then we made our way to the dock for a private boat to take us to Ebeye.

When we arrived at Ebeye, I was surprised by how calm things felt (compared to Majuro). Juxtaposed with Kwajalein Island, some of the sections were dilapidated, such as the northern section, which had "temporary" houses that are now permanent and shared portable toilets for those in residences without plumbing. There were sidewalks; the hospital appeared clean. Taxi trucks, called "love cars," drove along the circular road. The sun baked the concrete pavement, and the heat was intensified by the dust and lack of palm trees caused by overcrowding. Children swam in a lagoon where sewage was visibly being pumped into the water, creating a lingering stench on parts of the atoll.[24]

The meeting with the alaps began with an opening devotional song (*al in jar*), number 119: "I Am So Glad That Our Father in Heaven," followed by a prayer. The three Kwajalein senators, Tony deBrum, Michael Kabua, and Jeban Riklon, sat in the head of the large oval-like configuration. The meeting was recorded by V7AB, and we went through general introductions; Senator deBrum introduced me to the group. The RMI Historical Preservation Office/Internal Affairs (HPO/IA), led by Josepha Maddison, presented on the "protection of Kwajalein." Marshallese protection of the atoll, she stressed, was important because the US Army at Kwajalein Atoll wanted to continue to build. Moreover, she noted the "relics" that reflect Kwajalein's unique contributions to the world could be useful in promoting tourism and generating income, especially if the United States decided to withdraw from its missile base. Maddison emphasized that the relics are important for remembrance; they "help paint the picture of the past." The presentation stressed that although this is Marshallese land, the United States considers the island of Roi Namur a national historic landmark because of intense fighting that took place there during World War II. The United States focuses more on wartime sites than on traditional Marshallese archaeological finds, according to Maddison, and cultural, environmental, and protection regulation standards under the COFA are not as strict as similar laws in the United States.[25]

It seemed a pertinent aside when Maddison noted that a relic from the *Prinz Eugen*, a German cruiser that sank off Kwajalein and belongs to the RMI, had been sold on eBay. Customarily, Marshallese land is not for sale, but this has changed with the cash economy, alap rent collectors, and American proprietary profiteering. Marshallese societal organization was through customary land. The statutory land-tenure system was introduced during the German colonial period. Legal framings of Indigenous "ownership," even when the term conflicts with customary values, have proved difficult given that such ownership is often bound with an "individual" corporation or person and notions of "individual profit." This goes for all other protections of properties and claims to ownership, such as intellectual property, for which the RMI has no law.[26]

After the HPO/IA presentation concluded, Senator deBrum asked the aḷaps to sing a welcoming song (*al in karuwanene*). The song they sang was "*Bōk mejam*," and they made sure to note that it was for me. The a cappella chorus performed a slow, laborious progression interrupted by melismatic bursts and swelling volume levels. This performance was a particularly dynamic rendition of the tune with which I had become familiar, but the song made more sense to me after hearing the context in which it was sung in the meeting, which focused on the still-present discussions of US–RMI cultural recognition, ownership, and claims to the "relics" of World War II. The United States has intellectual property laws, which register the authorial rights of music to the composer. Textual misattribution of authorship must be challenged differently in the Marshall Islands; it must be routed through grounded sensibilities. "*Bōk mejam*" and the interactions that played out in our meeting on Kwajalein land were part of the story of Kwajalein Atoll as a meeting place for Marshallese and Americans, which brings claims to ownership and protection along with the decolonial dissonance of returning or remediating Marshallese sounds (voices, place-names, claims) to the fore.

The song threads multiple voices as languages (Japanese, Marshallese, and English) through the grounds of Kwajalein. It begins with the words "Take a look and watch the 'tea rose' flowers germinate and bloom from the tree trunk." The aḷaps' vocal styling included a dynamic melisma that occurs on the words "*kāān tirooj ko*" ("the tea rose flowers"). "*Bōk mejam*" asks of the listener to "take a look," but it is literally a command to "bring your face," as mentioned earlier. The welcoming song addresses us outsiders—Americans and other Marshallese who came to Kwajalein because of their own displacement or to work on Ebeye Island, for example—and asks us to recognize and respect the surroundings, which are always growing and regenerating when given the opportunity to thrive.

Brought to the Marshall Islands by the Germans in the colonial period, the hibiscus "tea rose" grows in Kwajalein Atoll, though not exclusively, and has become a powerful symbol of the natural landscape and in Marshallese cultural productions. This hope of reconciliation is symbolized by the "tea rose" beginning to bloom. During World War II, Japanese intentionally chopped down trees and placed "their trunks aimed skyward in hopes that Americans would count them as artillery."[27] Still, after the war, what is in the Marshallese terra-social wombu is life and beauty, the strength of roots that yield routes and peaceful interconnections, symbolized by the tea rose.[28] As beautiful and precious extensions of the land, flowers (*wut*) are associated with women and become powerful metaphors for matrilineal power, kinship, and cultural formations that have an ancestral depth and surface expression. These deep cultural formations refute the grounds of *terra nullius*, *aqua nullius*, and *res nullius* on which Pacific and here Marshallese lands and bodies have been "taken" throughout the centuries.

The prominence of the tea rose, according to deBrum, provides further evidence that the song was composed by Labaañ, a man from Kwajalein:

> The other argument I would advance for this song being from Kwajalein and not from the Bikini to Kili relocation is that the *tirooj*, the tea rose—the flower is a plant that is normally used to delineate *wātos*, land flats, land plots, and Kili had absolutely no tea roses because it was a single island, and there were no working plots on it . . . but the resurgence of the song as a patriotic song for the Kwajalein people in the eighties had to do with the occupation and their protests, and it is sung in almost every Kwajalein public gathering. Everyone. Both in the religious context and in the political context.[29]

The first verse was sung twice, and the second time, which follows the emotive thrust ("watch the tea rose flowers"), the aḷaps' voices collectively lilt with a timbral softening accompanying the decrescendo and a melodic descent toward the last word, *nōr* (germinate), that rests on the tonic. The second verse was sung one time with a rolling contour, varied by a sustained/lengthened rhythmic duration on prepositions and conjunctions; for example, *in* (of) *im* (and) *kake* (about). The lyrical content connects verses two and three, and three realizes the affective import of verse two: the emotional connection or the alliances made with the Japanese that were severed by war.[30] The promise of participation in the great Japanese empire had been shot down along with the warplanes, but the Marshallese were relieved that the brutal war had come to its end, and they welcomed the Americans, who gave them candy, gum, cigarettes, music, and movies (see chapter 1). The tokens of American "friendship" (kindness, generosity) were an extension of the Marshallese-American moral history of "friendship" that ceased warring between great powers (e.g., the missionaries and their work with the Marshallese and the Germans to quell interatoll chiefly warfare). The gifts were also a show of American strength and part of affective imperialism that had, at its base, the moral tenor of salvation ("for the good of mankind").

A transitional measure of silence connected the third and fourth lines of the final verse. As with the first verse, the final line was repeated twice, seeming to act as a partial mirror of the first line of the final verse. Both iterations of the line "*Jikū jikū jikūn ami anemkwōj*" were almost identical in contour and volume. The rhythm can be broken down into three parts: "my place, my place," "your place" (plural), and "for your freedom/liberty," creating three distinct realities, places, or spaces. First: Marshallese. The repetition of "my place" prioritizes that the land is Marshallese. The second space is the middle intervention with the words *jikūn ami*. In addition to the Marshallese meanings of the word, *ami* is also a Japanese term for "military boots or lace-up boots, primarily an Imperial Japanese Army term."[31] And the final word of the song, *anemkwōj*, the Marshallese word for freedom, softly flattens on the tonic.

"*Bōk mejam*," one of the most popular songs from the transitional period from Japanese to American occupation following World War II, was initially composed as a party song (*al in kamolo*), celebrating the cessation of the war and American victory. In 1944 US troops defeated the Japanese and expelled them from the archipelago, atoll by atoll, in brutal battles that often started with aerial bombardment, sometimes lasting for weeks and obliterating the landscape before ending in hand-to-hand combat. The battle over Kwajalein Island alone resulted in the deaths of roughly five thousand Japanese defenders, two hundred Americans, and an unknown number of Marshallese. When US Admiral Nimitz surveyed Kwajalein, he noted the "battle-scarred islands" where "fires were still burning."[32] American naval officers documented the desecration of the atoll, but they were more concerned with harnessing Marshallese labor to clean up the war damage, including seeing to mass burials, and to rebuild the military infrastructure than with helping the islanders return to their livelihoods. US military personnel worked with the *iroijlaplap* and other men because they viewed women in a subordinate status to men and saw to it that Marshallese men disseminated military policy.[33]

Kwajalein residents were soon joined by other islanders displaced from the violence of World War II and sent to the Kwajalein Labor Camp on the large island. Marshallese laborers, termed "husky natives" in the American news reports, lived in tents on the labor camps and sifted through the debris, pushing it into the Pacific currents.[34] The displaced Kwajalein residents had imagined themselves returning to their island, but they too were pushed aside for US military developments.[35] The United States renamed their lands, giving them male names "like Buster, Carlos, and Carlson" over what was "matrilineally-inherited land that had previously been understood in female terms."[36] The place-name changes were just one of the many violent erasures that exposed the "reciprocal relationship . . . between the processes of militarization and masculinization" that afforded the United States its colonial-imperial power in the Marshall Islands.[37]

Throughout the remainder of the war and the nuclear weapons testing program, Kwajalein Atoll played a central role as a refueling and support base. Kwajalein became the temporary home of the Bikinians, Rongelapese, and Utrikese, where the "nuclear-affected" populations were sequestered to their own tent camps and became the uninformed participants of Project 4.1 nuclear experiments. In 1958 President Eisenhower declared a nuclear testing moratorium, but the radiation lingered, absorbed by Marshallese bodies and environments. Additionally, radiation exposure at Kwajalein continued. Known today as the location of the Ronald Reagan Ballistic Missile Test Site, Kwajalein was selected as the target base for the US intercontinental ballistic missile program partly because of its 900-square-mile lagoon, the largest in the world.[38] Kwajalein would ultimately become a central component of US cold war and post–cold war missile defense.

The US military removed Marshallese who were working on Kwajalein and others who had been relocated there to the island of Ebeye, a seventy-eight-acre island three miles north of Kwajalein. Ebeye is the Americanized name of *Ebjā* (due to a misprinting on a map). The name, Ebjā, holds much cultural value, like most place-names in the Marshalls do, and it gives important information on the properties of the land in its matrilineal terms. This contrasts with American notions of taking land (or writing songs) as property and becoming author: giving it their name to reflect their image. Rather, by sounding m̗wilal̗ (depth) via/as ancestrally given place-names, Marshallese learn how to treat and respect the land. For example, Ebjā comes from a Marshallese *jabokonaan* (proverb): *"Ebjā bwe en ja"* ("Ebeye-bound, you'll *jā*—experience the windward toppling of the outrigger's sail and mast onto the canoe").[39] In navigational recitation, saying (or silently recalling) the place-name helped point to their direction. In the case of Ebjā, the name warned canoes that they should avoid nearing or making landfall on Ebeye. People give more-scientific (weather and current-based) justifications to the name, but customary legend held that there was a spirit that acted on the canoes, deterring them from approaching the islet. Both tell a similar story of why the land was taboo and at the time of the Japanese did not have many people besides the chief's commoner wives and offspring. One contemporary understanding of the Ebjā proverb is to live cautiously, which is meaningful for Ebeye's residents because they live very close to militarized technogenic risks and the biopolitical risks from underdevelopment.[40] Nuclear silences resound from the unheeded warnings of the ancestors.

As the population of Ebeye grew in the 1950s, the United States, as trust territory administrator, was frequently admonished for neglect of the people and lands it oversaw. A 1961 UN Visiting Mission's report sharply criticized US administration for "poor transportation . . . failure to adequately compensate for land taken for military purposes; poor living conditions at the American missile range . . . ; inadequate US economic development; inadequate education programs; and almost non-existent medical care."[41] Given the growing decolonization movement throughout the developing world in the 1950s and 1960s and the US government's self-imposed characterization as defender of freedom and democracy, the report was a political embarrassment to President Kennedy's administration, which sent Harvard economist Anthony Solomon to investigate conditions on Ebeye. The Solomon Report (1963) advised Kennedy to build up the health and education sectors, which entailed making English the official medium of instruction in Marshallese schools and suggested that "patriotic songs and rituals" be performed in class.[42] As a result, funds from the Department of the Interior were used to build new elementary classrooms, and American teachers were brought over with US textbooks, reflecting the emphasis placed on teaching and learning English.[43] The United States appropriated more money for trust territory expenditures to meet these new objectives, from $16 million in 1962 to $50 million by 1970.[44] Not surprisingly, conditions on Ebeye continued to worsen as basic infrastructure needs were ignored.

In 1963 a polio epidemic swept the island, paralyzing 190 residents who had not received a vaccine that had been available to the US public for nearly a decade. In 1964, when the military changed the target area, more Marshallese from nearby islands (called the Mid-Corridor area) were evicted from their homelands, now designated part of the impact zone, and forced to relocate on Ebeye. Unlike those before them who had received no compensation, islanders relocated in 1964 received housing and were paid a monthly stipend, however meager. By 1966, Ebeye hosted a population of 6,500, including those who came from other atolls and across this region of the Pacific seeking sought-after US jobs that offered higher pay. With no running water or plumbing, overcrowding turned the island into a toxic slum littered with refuse and human waste, while Kwajalein offered American service personnel and their families manicured lawns, baseball fields, and a movie theater.[45] Marshallese who made the daily ferry ride to Kwajalein from Ebeye to perform menial labor on the base were not allowed to purchase products in Kwajalein stores that were sold at reduced prices, nor were their children allowed to attend schools on Kwajalein.[46]

Frustrated with conditions on Ebeye and US inaction, in 1969 a group of disgruntled Kwajalein landowners sailed back to their homes to protest a scheduled missile test. Despite US objections, the Marshallese remained on their islands and stalled missile testing. In 1970 the US military acquiesced and agreed to pay the Mid-Corridor islanders a lump sum of $420,000 per year.[47] A decade later the US government signed a new lease agreement with the Kwajalein landowners for $9.9 million and agreed to make improvements on Ebeye, including an overhaul of the sewage system. Yet by 1982, the improvements had still not begun. When, after fourteen years of negotiations, the Compact of Free Association was negotiated between US and Marshallese officials in May 1982, it stipulated a fifty-year lease for the Kwajalein base but did not address human rights issues, specifically on Ebeye, that Kwajalein landowners had been requesting for years. Outraged, the landowners staged Operation Homecoming. In mid-June about forty landowners and their families, mostly from the Kwajalein Atoll Corporation (the landowners' association), camped out on a beach on Kwajalein Island in protest; within two and a half weeks, their ranks had risen to eight hundred.[48] Protestors also conducted "sail-ins," where small crafts circled the lagoon and their occupants shouted using bullhorns. There were clashes with base security forces, traditional leaders were arrested, and even Marshallese who worked on the base were harassed at checkpoints.[49]

During these protests, *"Bōk mejam"* regained popularity. With ultimately more than a thousand participants, it was the largest sail-in protest to have occurred since the protests began in 1969. Some of the islands that were reoccupied were directly within the missile zone, but the US Army refused to stop testing. American news briefs referred to the protesters as "militant islanders." Three months into the protest, the United States informed the protesters that it would not negotiate while the demonstrations were in effect, but the landowners stayed on their islands. The decision to remain emplaced on their land expedited the ongoing COFA negotiations. A month later, the two governments settled on terms that would reduce the lease of Kwajalein from fifty to thirty years and provide an additional $10 million for the infrastructural development of Ebeye.

During the sail-in protests, "*Bōk mejam*" was sung repeatedly, and it took on an anthem-like quality, becoming instrumental in sustaining momentum. DeBrum recounted:

> And every day when they would sing this song, they would [reinforce the] double entendre with the [word] *ami*.[50] So *jiku, jiku, jikun ami, anemkwōj*. My place, my place, but also the army's place to do so as they please. *Anemkwōj* is a great word in Marshallese. *Anemkwōj* we use to mean freedom and liberty, but it also can mean "to take advantage of," "to take possession of something [that is] not yours," or "to take liberties with property or with human beings or . . . taking liberties with things that do not belong to you."[51]

He referenced the US Army and the proclamations of "liberty" at the end of World War II, the myth of American liberation that has perpetuated political and economic dependencies: "But in this song . . . the connotation is not good because it was originally supposed to say, 'Welcome to my humble abode; what is mine is yours.'" DeBrum repeated over and again how "in this context" the army is doing "what it pleases." Much like the value of the word *anemkwōj* depended on the situation that it described, the song's meaning depended on the context in which it was sung. In other words, freedom is neither a universal nor a proclamation of a state of being. Rather, it is processual and relational; freedom is not something that can be bestowed. "*Bōk mejam*" pushes back on US liberation narratives (that Marshallese were "liberated"), which support notions of freedom as a matter of sovereign-meted emancipation. "*Bōk mejam*" is thus an acoustical restaging of the postwar liberation myth that the United States brought harmony through military force. When "freedom" is sung in Marshallese terms, the resonance of the word *anemkwōj* reclaims Indigenous agency by giving freedom a Marshallese heritage (here, Kwajalein heritage) by being rooted in and routed through the ancestral land ("my place . . . for you to have freedom"). An extension of the US myth of liberation, or the "gift of freedom," is the "gift of voice to the voiceless." Affirmations of "my place" can be read as affirmations of identity, entitlements, and voice that manifest in performances through equivocal embodiments of a history of struggle and survivance but also a history in which "the gift" following the war has been, like the name of Kwajalein explains, one in which the workers paid tribute to the United States for its help in World War II, thus giving the United States the gift of a place in which to broadcast its voice through nuclear military and radar developments.

ANEMKWŌJ

BATTLE SONGS (LANDOWNERS)

After a long day of meetings on Ebeye, I met the aḷaps at "Mon la Mike" (Mike's Club, literally Irooj Michael Kabua's club), a modest nightclub with an inside dance floor, bar, and raised stage where speeches are held and DJs play.[52] We spoke in a mix of Marshallese, English, gestures, and laughter to alleviate tension when discussing these fraught issues and the potential for mistranslations. The aḷaps shared with me a repertoire of war songs, or battle songs, and the discussion of "Bōk mejam" was included in this meeting. One Kwajalein aḷap (KA) often led the conversations, but all the aḷaps jumped in and spoke about their personal experiences, for most of them had been present for all the protests, occupations, and demonstrations, including Operation Homecoming, for which the United States called a "press blackout," which necessitated that Micronesian Congress Representative Ataji Balos fly to Honolulu to speak with reporters about the situation. They also spoke of the RMI's use of eminent domain (a concept borrowed from the United States) to take Kwajalein for "public use" or national security in the COFA.[53]

Songs are part of a distribution of the sensible that moves globally, like currents, but cannot be reduced to the universal. For the reduction of one place from its Marshallese Indigenous name will erase a history not only of Marshallese people but of matrilineal strength and protections, of Jined ilo Kobo and the atoll umbilicals, which are part of larger Indigenous movements for place-based recognition and equality. The "Indigenous voice" as genre can sound male and imply hegemonic masculinity to be intelligible, much like Marshallese music can sound like Western tonal harmony to be intelligible, yet the divots and markers recall nonhegemonic difference that evokes the multiple ontologies of a world that cannot be reduced to the universal—to "one world or none."[54] The provincialization of Western music history dictates a sustained critique of musicality as voice via male-directed events, compositions, and constitutions, through which progress (or style) is forged. I thought that the one female aḷap present marked the reality of the US political system, which refused to hear "her voice" (both matrilineal and nonhegemonic feminine) as mattering (materializing in protections, security, and value).

KA framed our gathering, explaining that Marshallese have "war songs from the Japanese times to American times."[55] As if this was a cue, Katnar Rantak, an aḷap from Ujae Atoll, began singing over KA. The aḷaps followed Rantak's lead, entering around a half to one and a half measures after he had begun, and this was typical of the performance style. They provided the bass and tenor harmonies, often in two parts. At times Rantak would sustain a syllable, and the aḷaps' vocal registers would drop as they created a chugging feel through subdivided rhythms, which sounded like a form of incantation. Rantak's support also enabled him to soar vocally and accentuate Marshallese sounds, such as the "r" trill. One of the aḷaps translated Rantak's words as he spoke to me, and he said that Rantak composed this "war song" during the "strike of the nuclear testing [1979/1982] in Kwajalein [because] the military moved people from all their islands and said that people were not allowed to go to the testing sites."[56] Here he is referring to the uranium-tipped missiles used in testing, thus connecting the material—enriched uranium—to the nuclear weapons, which is often overlooked in nuclear histories of the Marshall Islands (and elsewhere), contributing to the breadth of nuclear silences. The aḷap finished, "So they made a strike against the Army," and Rantak burst into the song "*Koj lum bok at*" ("We Don't Want to Stand Back"), which begins with a gesture of collective confrontation and resistance:

We don't want to stand back
We want to face it.
There's a huge problem that's befallen us,
and we are involved.
Because of our government,
we must face this difficulty.
The [RMI] government is pushing aside
the Kwajalein people,
who are searching for what is right and true.
Imata, where is our place, the place to which your friends and people are accustomed? Anjua, where is our place, the place to which your friends and people are accustomed?
I don't want to stand back, I want to face it.

Rantak explained the lyrics with an emphatic directedness: "The song was about the [workers'] strike—the strike of all the people in Kwajalein. All of them. The military didn't like that the Kwajalein people were occupying the islands." The other aḷap took over: "The US military, at the time, they were shooting missiles into Kwajalein. *At Kwajalein*. And the [Marshall Islands] government, they also gave the people a hard time when they tried to go to their islands, when they tried to occupy peacefully in the lagoon. So, all the people from Kwajalein, they went to the islands and stayed there." More than one thousand Marshallese took to the lagoons and lands to occupy their lands, and most of the participants were women.[57]

ANEMKWŌJ

Another aḷap explained that "it was during the demonstration. The landowners did not get what they wanted under the Compact of Free Association."[58] Prior to the 1982 Operation Homecoming Protests, in 1979 more than five hundred Kwajalein landowners set sail into Kwajalein lagoon and defied the threat of oncoming missiles.[59] Imata Kabua, the leader of the landowners' association, was clubbed during the protests. As another aḷap said, "The RMI government along with the US government used eminent domain. The police force came from Majuro and hit the people with sticks, put them in jails, banned everyone from the Mid-Corridor."[60]

The song speaks of deeper historical conflicts that began during the German colonial period and the power base or working-class solidarity that resists through moralized expression in solidarity with the American missionaries. There are two men who are referenced in the song, "Imata" (Kabua) and "Anjua" (Loeak). The great-great-grandfathers of these men (who were parallel cousins and therefore brothers) were the two major Ralik iroij and were thus front and center in the colonial politicization of the Marshalls, which also set a precedent for future foreign relations and shifted the power structure.[61] As customary battle increasingly adapted colonial weapons, women's participation was diminished. Moreover, hierarchical power was also fixed through the German and missionaries' banning of interatoll warfare, which had included women and expanded (incorporated or excised) lineages. Women's vocal currency became submerged, and the individualized, bounded atoll became the basis of colonial, political, and national voice-based identity, which is in tension with multiple land-based relations (bwij).

The German Protectorate came into effect, ratified by Germany and "King Kabua" or "Kabua the Great" in 1885. Germany named Kabua "king" (or paramount chief) around this time, which froze the power hierarchy in the Marshalls. His political opponent, or other contender for paramount chief, was Anjua Loeak, who remained a high chief, albeit not paramount. Today, land claims that were contested on the battlefield have moved to the courtroom, as Dvorak notes.[62] The case of Loeak's ascent to power was seen by some as swayed by the Western court system that judged in favor of Loeak based on skin color and bloodline (father), even though there are nuances in Marshallese culture that Western law could not register. As such, the song is perhaps a remediation of the court case, where claims to vocal authority and feminine choice (or freedom to fly like a flock of birds) become diminished under imperial war. Singing was also a means for women and girls to engage in diplomacy and democracy, by way of the missionaries, who worked with the power base.

Colonial relations established politics as patriarchal diplomacy. Moreover, Dvorak explains how anthropologist Julianne Walsh locates a shift from Kwajalein's matrilineal to patrilineal relations through this contest that "eventually resulted in [Kabua] being named 'King' by Germany in the treaty of 1885 [and] ultimately validated a shift to the patriline in Kwajalein Atoll."[63] He then explains that locals actually attributed the transformation "prior to the colonial administration, as the irooj of the Kapin-meto (northwestern atolls) ceased to produce female heirs."[64] Ultimately, like Dvorak, I find that regardless of the exact event or shift, colonial administrations from Germany through the United States have emphasized patriarchal succession and political authority; moreover, they have created masculine tropes in the Marshall Islands about which Dvorak writes, such as the US "Patriot" figure and the trickster L'Etao figure, along with the "Dankichi" figure, which is now remote. The absence of political female figures and voices beyond Marshallese attention to customary embodiments of gender complementarity is of interest here in globalizing hegemonic femininities beyond the (breakdown of the) soprano voice and the retention of recourse to cold war politics during which the (ongoing) women's liberation movements have taken shape.

As the aḷaps spoke to one another in hushed tones, I heard the words "*Ioon, ioon miadi kan*" a few times. The aḷap who was leading the conversation said, "and there are lots more war songs, during the war from Japanese times until American time, your time." Everyone chuckled at the mention of international politics mediated through lived, embodied existences subtended by civic privileges through which dissonances and consonances that resonated between us became all but buried in the bounded mire of nations, sides, wars, and times. Some performers explained that Leroij Laabo was the mother of Anjua Loeak. Here I wonder if the persistence of the song also resounds a counter-history to justify or contest the ascent of Loeak's rise to power through the Westernized court system and patrilineal "bloodline." If the memory of Laabo is one of predictive strength and genius, then the ways that her son has taken responsibility to look after his people and support women's reempowerment, which he does through funding the women's organizations WUTMI and BAWAJ (the latter name taken from the names of islands Bouj, Airok, Woja, Aenkan, and Jeh in Ailinglaplap), might share a belief in his political legitimacy per the moral of the Loktanuur legend in which the son who respects (carries the weight of) the mother wins the title of chief.[65] Or perhaps this song, which also traces the Marshallese, English, and Japanese languages and therefore means of becoming entangled in projected global futurities, is a

ANEMKWŌJ

memory of Laabo's disease and containment in ways that complicate this political legitimacy.

Ultimately, I cannot answer that question, but it brings up larger issues of geopolitical power and legitimacy to govern. Whereas military might and the law have been the means of modern political legitimacy, "*Ioon*" records how battles that determined geopolitical control overwhelmed the atoll-scape with structures and weapons of war—missiles, radars, missile sensors (watchtowers)—that did not, proverbially, carry the weight of women. To the contrary, women, their life-giving practices and life-sustaining knowledges, and their voices were increasingly ignored and positionally lowered to what can be intimated as voicelessness. The equivocal song—as in many languages, an ambivalent section in which Laabo wants to escape by taking flight or being in a position of power, and that she is in between death and life (see chapter 1)—shares militarization in the Marshall Islands and is sensed viscerally and poetically by Marshallese women, *in predictive capacity*, as constitutive of radioactive citizenship in which Laabo gives voice to the bombs, missiles, and other modern voices of war, including the disembodied male voice as testimony to violence and suffering. Because it is her predictive voice, however, what listeners are hearing is not the disembodied male voice but rather the impressions of an Indigenous woman who knew how to hear, record, and protect matrilineal movements, knowing ultimately that these conditions would persist. "*Ioon*" resounds a warning that will be heard in other feminine vocational spaces.

The next song they shared, "*Gallon ioon deck*" ("Gallon on deck"), was described as a "typhoon song" that recounted men sailing out on large canoes and through rough seas, encountering and conquering all the largest problems together.[66] This song is about the boat breaking through the waves and the men bringing the boat back to land together, which recalls the breaks in harmony or that which is oppressive and seemingly insurmountable through teamwork and navigation. After a typhoon at Kwajalein, all that was left, as the name explains, were flowers, which would be brought to the chief as tribute. The budding of the flowers, which were used to demarcate wāto delineations or land plots, shares the regenerative possibility of life following devastation, which connected the song to "*Bōk mejam*."

"*Bōk mejam*," which archives the "meaning" of Kwajalein through the flowers (as a symbol of the regenerative wāto or land tenure through which societal organization is afforded) as freedom, was then performed. Prior to this performance, KA firmly stated that a Kwajalein man composed the song, *not* a Bikinian or a Rongelapese. In fact, no Bikinian had ever wholeheartedly claimed the song, and nobody from Rongelap claimed it. The miscommunication in the book had, because of the notion of textual fidelity or "word as law," become inadvertently reproduced through different forms of media, including through my embodied American voice. This was radioactive citizenship in global capacity, working through our interaction. By returning to the song through which the *wāto* is symbolized through the *tirooj*, which also intimates peace, the aḷap explained how "the song originated as a leisure song for parties, birthdays, and marriages." The female aḷap laughed, at which KA repeated "for marriage time." I'm not sure whether this insinuated a double entendre, but she would actively make side remarks and chuckle, playing interference with the aḷap's recollection.

When the discussion turned to the switch from the postwar celebration to the use of the song for protest, the aḷap's speech became very emotionally inflected and labored, as if each word was difficult to let go of or communicate. "Because," he struggled, "[there are] a lot of words that have big meanings, and it makes you cry [and] makes you remember. Compose your mind to your intestines. And because, especially for me, for my own interpretation because Americans took my land by force and not by law, yeah. Americans took my island by force, nuclear, like the atomic bomb, not by law. The US didn't have a law at that time." The United States did not have an agreement with the landowners at the time, so it used eminent domain, as the aḷaps previously attested.

Crucially, the song presents a structure for words to unfold as ancestral collective memory and, with this m̧wilaḷ, changing circumstances to become felt over the course of performance. These are the changing circumstances of political and social histories between the different people and parties that passed through the islands and engaged in various encounters, from marriage to war, and they are also the experiential changing circumstances of the aḷap's cultural body when the m̧wilaḷ words give him pause to make him remember. And he is able to remember because that pause momentarily offered a rerouting of his corporeal system; he composed his mind (knowledge) to his intestines (intelligence), thus activating the bwij-bwijen connectedness through the burō and distanced himself from other distractions.

The aḷap centered the import of the meaning of the words as that which allows him "time to remember back." The time and space that he is afforded to remember back is the moment of crying, as indicated in the grammar of his speech. The momentary pause is the crack in the surface of modernity's recuperation of the Kwajalein song that made it available to be claimed by all, much as his land was claimed for all (mankind). The cry break, as *kōkḷaḷ*, energized the depth in the aḷap's being via the integration of the senses composed through song. Like the recitation of place-names, Marshallese collective memory does not recompose the past, but it composes a Marshallese ancestral present, which is crucial under the US military's erasure of a Marshallese ancestral future.

All the memories flooded back and became overwhelming; he became "*būromōj*," saddened and choked up:

> So this song really has a sad meaning for us—for individuals. When you sing, you cry. (*female aḷap chuckles lightly*) (*KA, defiantly*) Yeah, you cry. You cry because the words in the song, they have meaning that give you time to remember back. At that time [of composition], your ancestors were having a good time, but because of the nuclear, they dropped the bombs in some of the islands and ruined all of the islands, and in Kwajalein with the missiles. The military took Kwajalein and took missiles and sent the missiles from California and Florida to Kwajalein, and they move all the people from the individual islands in Kwajalein Atoll.

(sounded as)

Be cause, a lot of words that h ave BIG MEAN ing and it MAKE YOU CRY MAKE YOU REMEMBER compose your mind to your intestines And because especially for me for my own interpretation because *American* took my land (x) by force (xx) and (x) not by (x) law

(The *x* indicates a percussive noise made by the aḷap hitting the table for emphasis.)

Periodic disruptions, such as "*Bōk mejam*," in a larger complex of temporal overlays speak to the need for these moments of stillness where people can listen to themselves and each other's mishearings. The printed word is often violently incorrect, and communication is never easy in these respects. The work that "*Bōk mejam*" does has a double structure, as noted, and structural excess at that. The first structural mode is the one of the surface waves, wind, and other markers that help one navigate and bring things together. The deeper structure is the currents in constant motion that can be connected to directional movement instead of drifting, the pursuit of justice and inclusion of the grounds of freedom as a subversion of militarized metrics lived in daily routines of the global working class.

The song, as surface, tells a story of freedom betrayed. The currents are the Marshallese roots in the land that blossom into tea roses through routes. The gift is the song, like the stem that grows, that connects the flower (head/wut/gift) to the unseen germination (stomach/intestinal region/below the bwijen). The song can resound freedom when people feel free because freedom is relational. Americans' version of freedom, as individual strength as voice via militarization as the erasure of the body, has impeded Marshallese interconnectedness from being realized in the postwar in ways that leaders have imagined to be equitable. This is shared in the creation of new forms of sonorous sociality through the predominantly male voices and Americanized systems of harmony, which have historically, systemically discriminated against matrilineal empowerment and nonhegemonic political strength. KA's singing remembers this and becomes generative freedom within the song space. Self-determination is a collective process that draws on ancestral knowledge, making antiphonal choirs outside the range of the ear attached to the voice of modernity, yet it was the instance of us being together for the aḷaps to sing the song in the durational detour that was my trip to Kwajalein's Ebeye Island.

This dialogue, in its gesture toward an ethical relation, began as a heated statement, a claim, and an indictment against two groups for the wrongful ascription (not use) of the song to the Bikinians or Rongelapese.[67] Its land-based history is one of persistence and struggle, not only in the face of war but also in the face of force, of affective and military manipulations. The song began as a party song because of the excitement felt by Kwajalein residents after the United States defeated the Japanese, and today it remains a song of hospitality and a cautionary song, a predictive warning about the fact that what can be trusted takes time, such as the roses germinating and blooming.[68] The definition of freedom changes over the course of the song's performance. Marshallese protestors emphasized the word *ami* (*your souls, yours* plural), which is indexically ambiguous, to refer to the US Army during Operation Homecoming. The word is transformed in the song insofar as the host of freedom emplaced becomes hostage via their hospitality and their freedom is displaced.[69] The song resounds an affective decolonial dissonance as a pull between freedoms: freedom as individual, rights, not in kind/the production of difference addressed to an "other" that needs to "take a look," and anemkwōj, or freedom as relational, debt, the production of kindness. However, that "other" can be the Marshallese singers addressing the United States or their self-address as warning, displaced. The tenor of the song—its affective dissonance within the parameters of decolonization—was created systematically; it did not arise from the genesis of the song but was already contained within the historical spacing of war, victory, and victimhood.[70] "*Bōk mejam*" exemplifies how anemkwōj realizes the sounds of freedom as the grounds of freedom as part of a neocolonial production that has been dependent on the United States, the RMI, Marshallese, and US Americans as victors, victims, subjects, agents, and allies singing in precarious harmonies. The tides can turn, it seems, from celebration to survival in an instant. Similarly, freedom is performative, and it cannot be bestowed. The song, directed at the United States, could also be its own detour to the processual roses and sites of subversion that refuse certain alliance formations as necessary for political survival and life in general.

The emotional discussion of *"Bōk mejam"* preceded one about the ultimate voice of authority, the mother, composed by Rantak. Disrupting hegemonic ideals of Anglo-American-as-globalized masculinity, the song is about a "real man" (*of aelōñ kein ad*) who is "competitive" and takes on "whatever comes," including "typhoons." Again, the foundation of the man's strength is in the lyrics: "Mother, don't stand back because it is time to compete. Mother, give encouragement, mother. Your son is really heated. Real man, he's a real man because she finished *anjin berane*." Before a fight or competition, a mother will come to her son and do "anjin berane," which means to cast a spell so the son is revved up and not afraid. The mother backs her son as inspiration; she "shakes the spirit" with roro or her durative movements that resound in voice and matrilineal connection. And it is this connection that created a song cycle, reflecting the first song in which the men refused to "stand back," perhaps because they were fighting on behalf of their mothers in the first and second sense of lineage and land who moved their spirits with roro, words, winds, and waves as well as the embodied throat and sail to harness and navigate through movements. The figure of the mother was thus sustained through World War II's *"Ioon"* and its aftermath, *"Bōk mejam,"* as resonances of contemporary militarization or COFA harmonization that engenders nuclear silences as the excision of Kwajalein and Ebeye workers from the nuclear narrative and resources.

TABŌḶ PILE: VOCAL REMEDIATION AND DURATIVE ALLIANCES

The aḷaps' war songs situated political legitimacy in the sounds of Marshallese attached to the symbols rooted in and routed through the atollscape in ways that maintained customary values to homecoming through wave-pattern navigation or the created markers, such as the aḷaps' cry break, that

5.2 Eddie Enos, far right, at Mon la Mike with Katnar Rantak, center foreground.

enabled returns to the spirits in experiences of force not resigned to feeling only the force of the US takings. Eddie Enos (see figure 5.2), a famous Marshallese musician respected in the larger diaspora for his commentary about everyday life and commitments to upholding Marshallese culture, was present during many of the talks and performances at Mon la Mike, but it wasn't until the day our party was set to return to Majuro Atoll that I was able to sit down with him outside his house on Ebeye. Enos and I decided the best thing to do would be for him to perform a set of songs that most articulated the conditions of life on Ebeye and Kwajalein. When I met up with him, he was sitting outside by the lagoon; a number of children approached as Enos took out his readily available Yamaha PSR 2100 keyboard to share a song set about life.

One after another, with snippets of commentary, Enos played six songs reminiscent of the history and (therefore) life on Kwajalein. All the songs except for "*Bōk mejam*" and "The Kwajalein/Ebeye (hymn) anthem" had upbeat tempos, and they were conducive to dancing. Enos explained that he often performs the four upbeat songs at Mon la Mike. The songs he performed for me in order were "*Mour ilo ad ioon Kūwajleen*" ("Life on Kwajalein"), "*Yokwe Radar Song*" ("Greetings Radar Song"), "*Yok yokwe*" ("Greetings to You"), "*Bōk mejam*" ("Take a Look"), "*Elōñ ro rej dike doon kōn men ṇe mani*" ("Some People Hate Each Other Because of Money"), and "The Kwajalein/Ebeye (hymn) anthem."

ANEMKWŌJ

The song "*Elōñ ro rej dike doon kōn men ṇe mani*" stresses a reading of expropriative radioactive citizenship driven by the cash economy. From within the song, Marshallese genealogies and literacies grow from having "love" and "knowledge" of one's land and lineage. The song regenerates through place naming and creating double knowledges of places through the form of *tabōḷ pile* (double play), which resounds Marshallese endurance in the manner of a contemporary roro. Written by Tokran Kuli of Sunrise Lib, whose music was frequently played in Majuro, the song was familiar to me. But Enos's version was performed as a combination of two different songs, which were attached seamlessly through the Marshallese compositional technique called *tabōḷ pile*.

Enos's practice of historical storytelling should be understood as vocal historical remediations, restagings of the Marshallese heritage of the US military's might. The tabōḷ pile lyrically and affectively offers a "[source] of cultural continuity and evidence of active and formative political action," and, I would add, durative alliances.[71] We can think of the tabōḷ pile technique, more aptly, as a Marshallese form guiding the events that unfolded spatial and temporal interventions into and through the present linear time. The tabōḷ pile is a technique where the performer extends the length of the song by combining the lyrics of two different songs sequentially and conforming the lyrics into the same tune. One of the songs seamlessly transitions the other song, and it is a mechanism used to keep people dancing at clubs. The tactic is also of educational value. Enos would tell the children who had gathered around him to clap, and they listened, clapping on the second and fourth beat of the song, which is in strict quadruple meter. Part of learning the rules of the system, even if it is the military system of disciplinarity, is staying in time. Once you learn how to stay in time as part of a sensible system, the logic goes, you break those rules to bend the system to your needs, creating decolonial dissonance and resistance to fixed fate. The music was also upbeat, and the song was driven by two complementary rhythmic ostinatos. First, the keyboard rhythm begins with rapid sixteenth notes, followed by two eighth notes and a quarter note. Second, the children's syncopated claps continued throughout the song. During the naming of the places, the harmonic rhythm of the song speeds up, carving out a distinct acoustical space.

The two songs, when combined within the musical form of the tabōḷ pile, are often used as lyrical resources to contribute to or reinforce the meaning of the other song by recontextualizing or adding to the narrative (see table 5.1). And, as Enos explained, this was the case with his performance of "*Elōñ ro rej dike doon,*" which he played that evening at Mon la Mike. The first song, "*Elōñ ro rej dike doon*" (sections A and B), is credited to the Sunrise Band (Lib), and Kuli would tour with Enos to various places across the world (e.g., Majuro, Ponphei, Palau, and Hawaii), where they would perform the song. The song is an example of Kuli's commentary on the negative impact of a cash economy. The second song is a compilation of place-names and locations in Kwajalein Atoll. As Enos explained, "[The song] is about all the stories from the places listed. The story of *Būkien-Kālōñ* is at the airport terminal in Kwajalein. Star Wars is in Meck, where the Americans test their missiles. [It is] the missile range."

Each section is related with the tabōḷ pile form, and they are also connected conceptually and through the poetic devices of repetition (continuation). During the performance, sections C and D were repeated in order. Sections A and B are related through "honesty" and "sociality" ("I'm being honest with you"). Sections B and C relate "honesty" to having a place in the land with the first-person pronoun *Ña* ("I am" being from/of somewhere: here "Kwajalein"). Sections C and D are related through the place-name itself, and therefore having a place in the land ("Kwajalein") reveals itself in section D to the knowledge of the land as invested in place-names. This knowledge is the knowledge that connects the ancestral names with the American names, doubling voice as doubling knowledge. The continuation of conceptual linkage through lyrical repetition is disrupted by the introduction of linguistic difference ("Star Wars"), and we are referred back to the material in C ("*Na juon laddik*"), and this introductory material begins Section E, which concludes the song, noting the "fleet of canoes, planes, or warships, which is at *Enmaat*."

All of the lyrics are *returns* and *detours* that reroute from modernizing dispiriting; they are animated by the voice sent from the throat; they are homecomings. They list places that have value to both the United States and the Marshallese. For example, Enos mentions Ruot (Marshallese name for Roi), which was renamed Roi and is part of Roi-Namur, which now has several radar systems on it. Pikeej (Bigej) is north of Ebeye, and some landowners have proposed developing it for their uses. Enmat is *mo* (taboo) because it is the birthplace of the iroij and the chiefly lineage. However, no one can go there because it is in the Mid-Corridor, where active missile tests are conducted. Ane-buoj is the islet where US forces launched their invasion of Kwajalein Atoll during World War II. The *Prinz Eugen*, which was used in the Bikini Atoll test, rests in the islet's lagoon area. And Meck is the launch site for antiballistic missile testing.

TABLE 5.1 *Elōñ ro rej dike doon kōn men ṇe e mani* (Some People Hate Each Other Because of Money)

Section	Text Line	Marshallese	English Translation
A	A1	Elōñ ro rej dike doon kōn men ṇe e mani	There are people who hate each other because of money
	A2	Elōñ ro rej dike doon kōn men ṇe wāto	There are people who hate each other because of land
	A3	Ak ṇe ña, ij lukkuun mool ñan kwe	But me, I'm being very honest with you,
	A4	ij lukkuun mool ñan kwe, ñan kwe	I'm being very honest with you, with you.
B	B1	Ejjeḷọk aō mani, ejjeḷọk aō PhD	I don't have money, I don't have my PhD
	B2	ak ñe iọkwe, ekadik eḷap ippa	But I have a wealth of love within me.
	B3	Ña ij mool (kabōk!) nan kwe.	I'm being honest (clap!) with you.
T1		(I tabōḷ pile ke? Eṃṃan.)	(I'll do a "double play," okay? Good.)
C	C1	Ña juon ḷaddik in Kūwajleen,	I'm a boy from Kwajalein
	C2	jo jikū iar dik im rūttoḷọk ie	Here is my place where I was young and grew up
	C3	Ej jikū im aō jolōt	It's my place and my inheritance,
	C4	ej jikū im aō ḷāmoran ñan in deo	it's my place and my heritage forever
	C5	eṃṃan inaaj mej lok ie	it's best that I die there

Section	Text Line	Marshallese	English Translation
T2		ooo,ooo,ooo,ooo	ooo,ooo,ooo,ooo
D	D1	Būkien-kālōñ, epād i-Kūwajleen	Cape "jump off," it's located in Kwajalein.
	D2	Būkien lo-Akadik epād i-Pikeej	Cape "Akadik," it's located in Pikeej
	D3	Būkien Kōmḷaar, epād I-Ruot	Cape "Kōmlaar," it's located in Ruot
	D4	Ak Star War, eñṇe i-Meck	But Star Wars, it's right there in Meck
	D5	Ak Star War, eñṇe i-Meck, i-Meck	But Star Wars, it's right there in Meck.
C'	C'1	Ña juon ḷaddik in Enmaat	I'm a boy from Enmaat
	C'2	jo jikū iar dik im rūttoḷọk ie	Here is my place where I was young and grew up
	C'3	Ej jikū im aō jolōt	It's my place and my inheritance
	C'4	ej jikū im aō ḷāmoran ñan in deo	it's my place and my heritage forever
	C'5	eṃṃan inaaj mej lok ie	it's best that I die there

TABLE 5.1 (*continued*)

Section	Text Line	Marshallese	English Translation
E	E1	Ña, ña ij juon ḷaddik in Enmaat	I, I'm a boy from Enmaat
	E2	im ña ij jaab "K-Smart."	and I'm not "K-Smart" (I don't brag)
	E3	"Yo' baby, you betta' believe."	"Yo' baby, you betta' believe."
	E4	Inej wa epād Enmaat	A fleet of [canoes, planes, or warships] is at Enmaat.
	E5	Būkien Likajeer, epād i-Āne Buoj	Cape of Likajeer is located on Āne Buoj,
	E6	Būkien-Kālōñ, epād i-Kūwajleen	Cape of Kālōñ is located in Kwajalein
	E7	Kwōj disco iia?	Where do you go dancing?
	E8	Ekwe, imon lo-Mike, ekwe, imon lo-Mike	Well, Mike's Club, well, Mike's Club.
	E9	eññe i-Ebje	It's right there on Ebeye
	E10	Kwōj disco iia?	Where do you go dancing?
	E11	Ekwe imon lo-Mike, ekwe imon lo-Mike	Well, Mike's Club, well, Mike's Club.
	E12	epād imon Wiwi.	It's at Wiwi's house.

NOTE: "Wiwi's house" refers to, I was told, the place where the best part of the turtle (a traditional delicacy) is prepared.

Place naming is part of Marshallese harmony—a mythology that cosmologically positions people central to global power relations through predictive functions, reminding them of the routes they have paved and the roots they maintain through these global networks. The musical form and borrowed melody that emerges in the chorus, which is reminiscent of the Beatles song "Come Together, Right Now, Over Me," is an Indigenous sounding: a "coming together" and a call "to be free" with a response that is perhaps open and intimates the ability to take liberties and work together. This call and response, literally "double play," allows the songs to come together and keep coming together through *iakwe*, the pathway that animates the singer. There is a vocal remediation of modern feelings of "hate" into real "love" in the singer through Indigenous soundings *as proof* not of expertise or even authenticity but of the m̧wilaḷ knowledge of ancestral land and the wave patterns that pull and push and that cannot be captured in figures of sound or image that become circulated globally or data that are studied. Decolonial dissonances thus resound in the need to maintain sovereignty over the grounds from which things are taken and sold on eBay or used in experiments.

When I returned to Majuro Atoll, I spoke with Alfred Capelle, a coauthor of the MED, to learn more about the place-naming practices:

> These are the capes. *Būkien-Kālōn̄*, that is the cape. *Būkien* means "cape," where the reef extends out into the ocean right at the eastern end of the airfield on Kwajalein.
>
> As the plane goes and lifts off, right over there, they call that Būkien-Kālōn̄. And it is interesting because *kālōn̄* means "to fly up." It is like when the birds fly up—kālōn̄—so they knew, our ancestors knew there was going to be an airfield there because the plane comes here and lifts up. Būkien-Kālōn̄—"Cape of Flying Up"?

Capelle continued to explain the stories of the place-names and their significance for the Marshallese people, and I asked him why these names would be listed in a contemporary dance song. He responded:

> They say that Kwajalein is important because people are always, from all over, they use Kwajalein for research, for military, and then people from other islands come in, so they are all coming to reap the benefits from Kwajalein as a military base. They get jobs, and [other] good things that they get from Kwajalein, and they said that historically, traditionally, Kwajalein is important because of Būkien-lo-Akadik and Būkien-Kālōn̄.

It is not only the people who come to the base that get the benefits but also, to varying degrees, people in the other constructed centers, and many of those people have never been to, seen, or heard the Marshallese Būkien-lo-Akadik and Būkien-Kālōñ.

Capelle also recounted the "predictive" function of the name of *Būkien Likajeer*, which means "Cape Ms. Turn-Around." This cape, he reminded me, is where the Continental airplane banks west prior to its initial descent into the Kwajalein airfield. "Būkien Kōmḷaar," Capelle noted, "it is the one in Roi-Namur, and that is where [the Americans] have these powerful radars that goes around in space to look for spaceships and missiles when they come. So you see it is in the song also: *kōmḷaar* means 'to scrape the sky.' These names are not recently made up."[72] So these customary names had again predicted the actions of both the Marshallese and the Americans. These place-names were most likely in *"al im bwebwenato"* (talking story songs) that helped connect their different functions for various aspects of communal life and navigation, making connections through directionally based incantations. Recall that in chapter 1 the Rongelapese boys' song had similar naming practices of "Ms." with locations to learn positions, functions, and formal names, giving these places and the people/spirits that inhabit them characteristics. Men who had since passed away communicated the stories of the place-names to Capelle when he was resources manager at the Alele Museum and Library in Majuro: "The older men, who are dead already, would say, 'You know, it's interesting and amazing how our ancestors foresaw all this—everything that was going to happen to Kwajalein, that Americans would come and build all of these things, bring all the people and build all these radars, [the] airfield, and then the planes would come and fly and show us what they mean.'"

Protected and transferred in the musical form of a "double play," we can understand the inheritance of the land continuing and pushing back, not in direct masculine warfare-speak to the military's erasure of their place naming but through educational means of song. Place-names and the poetics of place naming in diaspora, for Marshallese, are ṃwilaḷ: deep and meaningful words that can remind communities of stories and habitable places—not only for them but also for their loved ones. Place-names share societal relations and investments—care, love, and labor—over generations on lands that change in surface detail but continue as Marshallese (aelōñ kein). The "high-context" function of ṃwilaḷ is not that it is "nonsense" but rather that it is deeply coded and flexible to predict and reveal through humans mediating its sounds, which are articulated to the archipelagic atollscape.

Capelle has worked hard to protect Marshallese place-names because they give direction and warning to Marshallese not afforded by the US security state voice-overs. Some 1989 correspondence between Capelle and Major Frank Moore III, US Army military liaison officer, shows an example of this:

> We sincerely appreciate the Army's concern and interest in helping us preserve and perpetuate Marshallese culture and language. When I met Col. Philip Harris in the Chief Secretary's Office, he asked if Oscar and I could suggest a Marshallese name for the new housing area on the north end of Kuwajleen Island. This past week I happened to be on Epjā (Ebeye) and had a chance to discuss the subject with Alap Atidrik Maie of Kuwajleen. Consequently, we would like to suggest the name LIBARWATO.
>
> LIBARWATO is the cultural name for a relatively large rock which was once situated on the lagoon shore near the north end of Kuwajleen, in the vicinity of the new housing area. Briefly, the story behind the rock was that once upon a time a lady called LIBARWATO turned into a rock. Being amicable and friendly she helped her fellow islanders in times of difficulty. When she died she continued to help by forewarning them of invaders and impending disasters such as typhoons, tidal waves, etc. Her forewarnings always came true. Whenever deep and resounding rumbling sounds emanate from the rock of LIBARWATO the islanders would know what it means and take the necessary precautions.[73]

Libarwāto (Ms. Coral Rock Land Parcel, also Ms. Land Parcel Again) was a matron deity. She carried a drum, and if danger approached, she would begin to drum, rhythmically beating her warning for those ordained to hear her call. At more than one meter tall, Libarwāto, the coral head, stood proudly on the reef in her role as "one of the 'island support posts.'"[74] She stayed on the north end of Kwajalein, the lagoon side. She had been a woman once. While she was alive, she helped her people when they faced struggles. When she passed, she turned into the beach rock pillar, and she continued to help her community by audibly rumbling. This was unlike the rumblings of bombings and dynamite blasting that upended the reef and sea floor when Americans, working with Hawaiians and Marshallese, mined for materials to enlarge Kwajalein Island and Meck Island.[75] In doing so, they also destroyed many cultural formations, such as trees and coral heads, including Libarwāto, which can translate loosely to "Ms. Again wāto (land tract). The place-names are suggestive of movement and transformation: flying, turning, scraping the sky, and, in the case of "Libarwāto," the ability to sense movements in the environment and warn others through sonorous transmission in excess of the SDI missile system's sensors. Libarwāto's demise is another example of the militarized violence against Indigenous populations through their maternal landscapes. However, by protesting the nuclear silence of American voice-overs, she can be heard and remembered, activated by Marshallese voices, such as Capelle, who closes his message to Moore with the following:

> As the activities on Kuwajleen are similar in a number of ways to what once upon a time happened there, we feel the name LIBARWATO is appropriate for that housing area instead of "Silver City." While LIBARWATO herself had achieved it, the residents of Kuwajleen are engaged in trying out a defensive system that can protect lives from either natural or man-made disasters. No one then should be surprised when one of these days the deep and rumbling sounds of LIBARWATO are once again heard across the water and sky.[76]

The resonance of the feminine voice, across the water (waves) and sky (winds), guides and directs Marshallese sons and daughters in musico-poetic homecomings. Overlaid with musical tonal harmony, there is friction through the double voicing that emerges from the split throat, which resounds radiation as decay and regeneration, precisely through the endurance of the wāto or land tenure through which women have customarily been empowered. Yet in their displacements, women and men, atoll groups, and landowners have been tasked with new pressures of protection that are linked with and must be distinct from the militarized and political violences that impress upon and depress them, making them lọrrọ and būromōj. They perform in musical harmony to archive testimonials and break through harmonies to reveal protections in excess of the confines of the universal liberalisms of the West.

These breakthroughs are not overcomings but detours to alternative sites of knowledge and security that maintain Marshallese sensibilities, which are precious and meaningful in organizing the political body and body politic according to cosmological values of the relational mother-son-land movements. For these musical movements, which promote ājmour (weaving life) through voice as matters of health and healing, are crucial to remembering how radiation sounds against nuclear silences or how Marshallese interconnected futurities cannot be contained by the limits of the West and Marshallese voices cannot be contained by musical histories, even though both are produced as intelligible through these constraints. Listening beyond the intelligible voice, as fixed identity, to textural voice(lessness) demands collective movements that refuse prescriptions. Displaced and unsettled, we are forced to consider the possibilities of thinking political movements beyond the human, beyond the "one world" model that has been given through Western, voice-based democracy. Representative liberal democracy has the potential to objectify and exclude from movements that become systematized, meaning that we are always responsible for our participatory actions, our attunements, and our relations.

When it comes to the hegemonic histories of nuclearization afforded by "one world or none" projections, radiation sounds the effaced grounds of Marshallese matrilineal sensibilities and empowerment as freedom. Silenced and censored in periods of civic unrest and social reform protest—the civil rights movement, women's liberation movements, LGBTQ movements, disability rights and ongoing labor movements, musical protest from folk to punk to rap, the Nuclear Free Pacific movement, and Indigenous movements—the Marshall Islands, and particularly COFA minorities (ERUB, Kwajalein), have been in so many ways fragmented from these globalizing movements through nuclear silences. It is the hope of this book that by respecting Marshallese music as the ongoing collection of political and social potentiality rooted in and routed through Marshallese grounded sensibilities and harmonic literacies, the ultimate authority of the feminine voice in complementary relation to the masculine voice can resound in concert with all-gender voices in our unique intersections and movements and without the threat of being "one world or none." Radiation has been a weapon of imperial sensibilities, promoting the notion that sociocategories which mediate our being, such as gender, can be detached from race, ethnicity, class, (dis)ability, religion, and other modes of bounding through which oppression (and privilege) making occurs (harmonization). This book refuses such a notion and detours to find recourse in alternative sensibilities that transit in (non)hegemonic intersectionality, which amplifies a politics/poetics of negation or, in the context of nuclear politics, voicelessness or detours via breaks as well as the recuperation of voice in sharing harmonic potentialities.

ANEMKWŌJ

NOTES

INTRODUCTION

1   Rijen Michael (Utrikese man), interview with author, February 27, 2009.
2   Yostimi Compaj (Utrikese man), interview with author, March 10, 2010.
3   As a point of reference, Connecticut is just over 5,500 square miles. See Rowberry, "Castle Bravo"; and Kunkle and Ristvet, "Castle Bravo."
4   Molly (Rongelapese woman), interview with author, March 20, 2010. Name changed at interlocutor's request.
5   Compaj interview.
6   Aruko Bobo, interview by Holly M. Barker, August 27, 1994, in Johnston and Barker, *Consequential Damages of Nuclear War*, 99.
7   Three of Bikini Atoll's islands were vaporized by the nuclear testing: Bokonijien, Aerokojlol, and Nam. When I refer to Rongelap as land that is uninhabitable, the atolls of Ailingnae and Rongerik are included. I follow Johnston and Barker and stress that in this book, "'the people of Rongelap,' or 'Rongelapese,' refers to those people exiled from Rongelap, Rongerik, and Ailinginae atolls" (*Consequential Damages of Nuclear War*, 43).
8   Castle Bravo was one thousand times more powerful than the first atomic tests in 1946, and it came as a shock to many that the Rongelapese had not been evacuated before the unprecedented test. The three islands vaporized at Bikini Atoll were turned into the "fallout" that covered Rongelap and other atolls in the Marshall Islands. It was then that the term *fallout* was introduced into our lexicon.
9   Molly interview.
10 Adult intake of radiation solely from the Bravo event was estimated at approximately 300–375 roentgens (whole-body dose), 10,000–20,000 rads (thyroid), and 20–300 rem (internal doses other than thyroid). Compare with the "current known health effects of ionizing radiation" that places lethal doses at 400 rem ("can kill 50 percent of exposed population"). Information from Johnston and Barker, *Consequential Damages*, 97; see Appendix V for tables and statistics pertaining to the tests and changes in dose limits because of the tests.
11 Johnston and Barker, *Consequential Damages* 12. The authors quote "excerpts from John Anjain," in "The Fallout on Rongelap Atoll and Its Social, Medical and Environmental Effects."
12 See Barker, *Bravo for the Marshallese*, for details about Project 4.1.

13   Keyes recalled this story in a 1994 CNN interview. See Aquila, "Sh'Boom," 106–18.
14   "Sh-Boom" by The Chords, last modified 2019, www.songfacts.com/facts/the-chords/sh-boom.
15   The Marshall Islands are in a region known (pejoratively) as Micronesia.
16   Johnson, "Rongelap Return Could Happen in Near Future." At the time of this writing the mayor of Rongelap was negotiating to lease parts of Rongelop to the People's Republic of China because efforts to encourage Rongelapese to return to their homeland have mostly failed.
17   For a more thorough discussion of the "distribution of the sensible" and the political work of an aesthetics that creates a dissensus making the part that has no part audible, see Rancière, *Disagreement*; *Dissensus*; and *The Future of the Image*.
18   See Rancière, *Disagreement*; *Dissensus*; and *The Future of the Image*.
19   See Amundson and Zeman, eds., *Atomic Culture*; Jacobs, *The Dragon's Tail*; Halliwell, *American Culture in the 1950s*; Grossman, *Neither Dead nor Red*; Weisgall, *Operation Crossroads*; and Winkler, *Life Under a Cloud*. See also Hanlon, *Remaking Micronesia*; and Friedman, *Creating an American Lake*.
20   Deleuze, *Francis Bacon*, 74.
21   Desjarlais, *Body and Emotion*; Seremetakis, ed., *The Senses Still*; Taussig, *Defacement*. Also see Gusterson, *Nuclear Rites*.
22   Harmony has been used as a means for European and US imperial powers to arrange the world. Referencing Foucault's *The Order of Things*, Christopher Hight argues that harmony "can be read as integral to the story of racial representation." Following Attali's work in *Noise*, he writes that harmony "is based on proportional ratios between units' places on a single axis of variation (pitch), an organic unity of these increments in both pitch and time, and a rich mathematics of their combinations in whole units. This harmonic system," Hight contends, "contributed to the conceptual organization of the colonial" (14). See also Bloechl, *Native American Song at the Frontiers of Early Modern Music*; Baker, *Imposing Harmony*; and Irving, *Colonial Counterpoint*.
23   Igarashi, *Bodies of Memory*, citing Lummis, "Genshitekina nikkō no nakadeno hinatabokko," 34.
24   Teaiwa, "Microwomen," 126.
25   Teaiwa, "Solidarity and Fluidarity."
26   Hartman, *Scenes of Subjection*.
27   Fortun, *Advocacy after Bhopal*.
28   See Fordham, *Building the Cold War Consensus*; and Manning, *John le Carré and the Cold War*.
29   Manning, *John le Carré and the Cold War*, 17.
30   Lee, "From GI Sweethearts to Lock and Lollers."
31   Ragan, *One World or None*.
32   United Nations, *Charter of the United Nations*. Italics mine.

33 O'Brien, *The Pacific Muse*.
34 See Rameau, *Treatise on Harmony*.
35 Ellingson, "Transcription."
36 Kunreuther, *Voicing Subjects*, 15, citing Taylor, "Speaking Shadows," 8.
37 Ochoa Gautier, *Aurality*, 17.
38 Ludueña, *La Comunidad de los Espectros*, as cited in Ochoa Gautier, *Aurality*, 18.
39 Grossberg, *Bringing It All Back Home*, 370.
40 Chakrabarty, *Provincializing Europe*, as cited in Bloechl, *Native American Song*, xvi.
41 See Bloechl, *Native American Song*, xvi.
42 Lowe, *The Intimacies of Four Continents*, 3–4.
43 Keever, *News Zero*.
44 See Johnston and Barker, *Consequential Damages*.
45 Walsh, "Imagining the Marshalls," 358.
46 Baxi, "Voices of Suffering and the Future of Human Rights," 135.
47 There are no nuclear powers in the global South. The global North maintains a nuclear hegemony and extracts resources from the global South.
48 See Rudiak-Gould, "The Fallen Palm."
49 DeLoughrey, "The Myth of Isolates," 171.
50 Rancière, *The Politics of Aesthetics*, 12.
51 Steingo, *Kwaito's Promise*, 9.
52 See Rubinson, *Redefining Science*.
53 Davis, *Stages of Emergency*; Masco, *The Theater of Operations*.
54 Hales, "The Atomic Sublime."
55 Edmond, *Representing the South Pacific*, 7.
56 Keane, *Christian Moderns*, 6.
57 Oakes, *The Imaginary War*, 38–39.
58 Masco, "Engineering the Future as Nuclear Ruins," 257. Masco cites the Panel on the Human Effects of Nuclear Weapons Development, *Human Effects of Nuclear Weapons Development*, 9.
59 Schumpeter, *Capitalism, Socialism, and Democracy*.
60 Seremetakis, ed., *The Senses Still*.
61 Herzig, *Suffering for Science*, 36.
62 Brinkema, "Critique of Silence."
63 Brinkema, *The Forms of the Affects*, 93.
64 Howes and Classen, *Ways of Sensing*, 12, 106.
65 See Wolfe, "Settler Colonialism and the Elimination of the Native" *and Settler Colonialism and the Transformation of Anthropology*. I use the term *social project*, borrowing from Elizabeth Povinelli, to describe the "specific arrangements that extend beyond simple human sociality or human beings" (*Economies of Abandonment*, 7). Povinelli cites her intellectual predecessors who have termed a similar arrangement or configuration that aims to or puts forth alternative ways of being, doing, living, connecting, and so on as "counterpublics" (Michael

Warner), "new social imaginaries" (Charles Taylor), "subaltern counterpublics" (Nancy Frazer), and "heterotopias" (Michel Foucault).

66 Kauanui, "A Structure, Not an Event."
67 Cavarero, *For More Than One Voice*; Weidman, *Singing the Classical, Voicing the Modern*. Even the idea of an ecology was shaped by the nuclear testing and the removal of humans from their lands at Bikini Atoll and Enwetak Atoll. See DeLoughrey, "The Myth of Isolates."
68 Stoler, *Imperial Debris*.
69 Ranciére, *Dissensus*, 38, 139.
70 Here I draw on the scholarship from anthropology of the senses, such as Seremetais, *The Senses Still*; and Desjarlais, *Sensory Biographies*. See also Taussig, *Defacement*; Classen and Howes, "The Museum as Sensescape"; and Geurts, *Culture and the Senses*.
71 See Eidsheim, *The Race of Sound*.
72 Hau'ofa, "Epilogue," 466.
73 See works of J. Kēhaulani Kauanui, including *Hawaiian Blood* and *Paradoxes of Hawaiian Sovereignty*.
74 See Jetnil-Kijiner, "Iep Jaltok." For quoted portion, see Rancière, *Dissensus*, 54.
75 Kirsch, "Lost Worlds," 171.
76 Seremetakis, ed., *The Senses Still*, 12.
77 Stras, "The Organ of the Soul," 173.
78 Geurts, *Culture and the Senses*, 5.
79 See Lippit, *Atomic Light*; Cartwright, *Screening the Body*; Kochhar-Lindgren, *Hearing Difference*; and Nixon, *Slow Violence and the Environmentalism of the Poor*.
80 Stone, Kowata, and Joash, eds. *Jabōnkōnnaan in Ṃajeḷ*, 39.
81 Seremetakis, ed., *The Senses Still*, 7.
82 Ceraso, *Sounding Composition*, 40.
83 Ceraso, "(Re)Educating the Senses," 112, which cites Bialostosky *How to Play a Poem*.
84 Erdland and Neuse, *The Marshall Islanders*, 1914.
85 Rifkin, *Beyond Settler Time*.
86 Muñoz, *Disidentifications*, 97.
87 McArthur, "Narrative, Cosmos, and Nation," 58–59.
88 McArthur, "Narrative, Cosmos, and Nation," 58–59.
89 McArthur, "Narrative, Cosmos, and Nation," 58–59.
90 Abo et al., Marshallese English Dictionary.
91 It is my aim to challenge, rather than adhere to, any fixed notions of gender. With respect to issues of gender and sexuality within the Marshallese community, see Schwartz, "'The Young Ladies Are Here.'"
92 See Denning, "Introduction: In Search of a Metaphor"; Jolly, "Becoming a 'New' Museum? Contesting Oceanic Visions at Musée du Quai Branly"; and Dvorak, "Seeds from Afar, Flowers from the Reef."
93 Rachel Lee, personal communication, August 30, 2017.

94 Ochoa Gautier, *Aurality*, 12.
95 Harjo, *How We Became Human*, xxvi.
96 Columbia law professor Micheal Gerrard, an advisor to the RMI in international environmental law cases, has done much to inform the public of the dangers on Enewetak at Runit Dome. See Marshallese Educational Initiative's "Michael Gerrard on Runit Dome and Our Shared Nuclear Legacy," https://vimeo.com/108142666. See also Okney, "Legacies and Perils from the Perspective of the Republic of the Marshall Islands Nuclear Claims Tribunal," in *The Oceans in the Nuclear Age*.
97 DeLoughrey, "The Myth of Isolates."
98 Wilfred Kendall, advisory meeting, Majuro, March 3, 1999, in Johnston and Barker, *Consequential Damages*, 63.
99 Coulthard, *Red Skin, White Masks*, 13.
100 Ingersoll, *Waves of Knowing*.
101 Maddison, "Oral Histories of the Marshallese Diaspora."
102 Rachel Lee, personal communication, August 30, 2017.
103 Massumi, *Politics of Affect*. See also Grossberg, *Bringing It All Back Home*.
104 Seremetakis, *Sensing the Everyday*, 164. Also see Buck-Morss, *The Dialectics of Seeing*.
105 El Dessouky, "Activating Voice, Body, and Place," 256.
106 Dobson, *Listening for Democracy*.
107 Blok, "War of the Whales"; Latour, "Whose Cosmos, Which Cosmopolitics?"
108 Grande, *Red Pedagogy*, 7.
109 Crenshaw, "Demarginalizing the Intersection of Race and Sex," 1989.
110 Dolmage, *Academic Ableism*.

CHAPTER 1. RADIOACTIVE CITIZENSHIP

1 Bob Gordon, "Bikini Atoll Residents Denied Compensation for Nuclear Tests," *Digital Journal*, April 7, 2010, www.digitaljournal.com/article/290200#ixzz4MGOKJR38.
2 Petryna, *Life Exposed*, xxv.
3 Kiste, *The Bikinians*, 3; Topping, "Review of U.S. Language Policy in the TTPI," 116; Kupferman, *Disassembling and Decolonizing Schools in the Pacific*, 114.
4 "Pacific Isles Aided By 2 New Statutes," *New York Times*, August 25, 1964.
5 Kupferman, *Disassembling and Decolonizing Schools in the Pacific*.
6 Braun, "Imagining Un-Imagined Communities," 145–6.
7 Kunreuther, *Voicing Subjects*, 11.
8 Antari Elbon, interview with author, September 10, 2009.
9 Jorelik Tibon, interview with author, October 5, 2009.
10 Jorelik Tibon, conversation with author, April 2009.
11 See Foucault, *Discipline and Punish*.

12   Tibon interview.
13   Australian Broadcasting Company, "State of Media Report & Communication Report, 2013." Although the report states that WUTMI ran two radio shows at the time of its publication, WUTMI member Daisy Momotaro disputes this. Shared personal communication, Momotaro and Winona Kisino, April 11, 2019.
14   For an extensive analysis of *"Ioon, ioon miadi kan,"* see Schwartz, "Between Death and Life."
15   Kwajalein Senator Tony deBrum, email correspondence with author, 2011.
16   Taafaki, Fowler, and Thaman, *Traditional Medicine of the Marshall Islands*, 13–14.
17   Chion, *The Voice in Cinema*.
18   Dvorak, "'The Martial Islands.'"
19   AAFR also played other shows, such as jazz and classical music, but given that country music seemed to be most important to my interlocutors, I focused on that genre. More information can be found in the *Old Time Radio Catalog*.
20   *Old Time Radio Catalog*; "Marshall Islands Natives Permitted Self Government," *Times Herald* (Olean, NY), September 30, 1944, 1.
21   "Marshalls Rule by Navy Is a Test," *New York Times*, February 6, 1944, 24; Trumbull, "Yaws Conquered in the Marshalls, U.S. Doctors Rid Natives of Most Prevalent Disease—Self-Government Restored," *New York Times*, October 1, 1944, 32.
22   "Our New Military Wards, the Marshalls," 334.
23   Weisgall, *Operation Crossroads*, 104–15.
24   Reed, "Operation Crossroads," 32.
25   Weisgall, *Operation Crossroads*, 115.
26   *Radio Bikini*, directed by Robert Stone (1988; New York City: IFC Films, 1998), DVD.
27   For example, handicrafts, which were popular souvenirs for troops. See Trumbull, "Yaws Conquered in the Marshalls." Straw bags (Kili bags) also became a major product. See "Return to Bikini Sought," *Honolulu Star Bulletin*, March 5, 1968, 14.
28   From the *Majuro Times*, "Radio Marshalls," *Honolulu Star-Advertiser*, December 9, 1953, 4. The ceremony was held on October 12.
29   Lacey, *Listening Publics*.
30   Coulthard, *Red Skin, White Masks*.
31   The name of the interlocutor has been changed at her request.
32   "The Atom," 23.
33   "Petition from the Marshallese People Concerning the Pacific Islands," April 20, 1954, as circulated to the UN Trusteeship Council T/PET.10/28, May 6, 1954. See Hacker, *Elements of Controversy*, 357.
34   A. M. Rosenthal, "Marshall Islanders Protest to U.N. on Nuclear Tests," *New York Times*, May 15, 1954. Italics mine.
35   Document 936, telegram from Deputy United States Representative at the United Nations (Wadsworth) to the Department of State, New York, May 3,

36   1954, *Foreign Relations of the United States, 1952–1954*, vol. III, *United Nations Affairs*, US Department of State, Office of the Historian, accessed February 18, 2017, https://history.state.gov/historicaldocuments/frus1952-54v03/d936.
36   Johnston and Barker, *Consequential Damages of Nuclear War*, 107.
37   Tony deBrum, interview with author, March 4, 2010. The nursery rhyme or song "*Kōṃṃan Baaṃ*" is transcribed here in part. During the interview it was shared in segments with commentary. DeBrum explained that he was fishing with his grandfather when Bravo occurred and has since described it as if a fishbowl were placed over the horizon and someone poured blood over it.
38   Advisory Committee on Human Radiation Experiments (ACHRE), *Final Report*, 371.
39   DeBrum interview.
40   Petryna, *Life Exposed*, xvii–xviii.
41   Much of the evidence on which the RMI based its claim had been reclassified by the Defense Department in the late 1990s and by the Bush administration following the attacks of September 11, 2001. Congressional committees continued to review the CCP in 2005, but the original ruling was not overturned.
42   See the text and history of the bill at GovTrack: www.govtrack.us/congress/bills/110/s1756.
43   See Stauffer, *Ethical Loneliness*.
44   Yostimi Compaj, interview with author, March 10, 2010.
45   "Claimants exhibit C–1, pp. 21–22." From Nuclear Claims Tribunal, *Memorandum of Decision and Order* (Majuro, Republic of the Marshall Islands, April 17, 2001), accessed Feb. 18, 2011, www.nuclearclaimstribunal.com/rongelapfin.htm.
46   For the ways in which the atomic bombings on Hiroshima and Nagasaki affected women, see Todeschini, "The Bomb's Womb?"
47   This is the reverse of auscultation, a foundational practice for sonic modernity. See Sterne, *The Audible Past*.
48   Molly (Rongelapese woman), interview with author, March 20, 2010.
49   Email correspondence with deBrum.
50   ACHRE, *Final Report*, 370.
51   Anderson, *Colonial Pathologies*, 5, which cites Kramer, "Making Concessions," 96.
52   Ostherr, *Cinematic Prophylaxis*, 14; Ahuja, *Biosecurities*, 203.
53   Nelson, *National Manhood*, 135.
54   For lyrics, see Barker, *Bravo for the Marshallese*, 93.
55   Barker, 93.
56   Maier and Paraskevas, *Fallout*.
57   Maier and Paraskevas, *Fallout*.
58   Walsh, "Imagining the Marshalls," 243.
59   Cooke, *In Mortal Hands*, 168.
60   Sakai, "On Romantic Love and Military Violence," 217.
61   In "Petition from Jeton Anjain, Senator of Rongelap Atoll, Marshall Islands, Concerning the Trust Territory of the Pacific Islands," UN Trusteeship Council

62   (54th Session, 1987), United Nations Digital Library, https://digitallibrary.un.org/record/134199?ln=en.
62   Rongelap Atoll Local Government, "Statement of Senator Jeton Anjain on Behalf of the Rongelap Atoll Local Government before the Subcommittee on Insular and International Affairs Committee on Interior and Insular Affairs," DOE Legislative Affairs Library, Washington, DC, November 16, 1989.
63   See Barker, *Bravo for the Marshallese*. The song is said to have been written by either Laelang or Ronnie Joel (Bikinian man) and his song group.
64   "Checklist for Drafting a Trial Brief (Modeled after a Brief Writing Checklist Prepared by Professor Janet Calvo, CUNY School of Law)," City University of New York, School of Law, accessed August 11, 2017, www.law.cuny.edu/legal-writing/students/court-brief/court-brief-3.html.
65   A 1977 survey found that the Bikinians' internal dose of radiation "had risen dramatically. . . . As one scientist put it, the coconut palms were 'sopping up' radioactive cesium 137 and strontium 90 at a much greater rate than anyone predicted." Jerry Reacher, "Bikini Islanders Lose Again to Radiation," *Los Angeles Times*, July 23, 1978. See also "Cloud of Controversy over Bikini," *Honolulu Star-Advertiser*, April 3, 1978, 17. King Juda died of cancer while on Kili Island in 1968. See Reacher, "Bikini Islanders Lose Again to Radiation."
66   Statement attributed to Ataji Balos, a Bikinian spokesperson, in Reacher, "Bikini Islanders Lose Again."
67   White, "Juda vs. the United States," 665.
68   Asad, *Formations of the Secular*.
69   Masco, "Engineering the Future as Nuclear Ruins," 252.
70   Walsh, "Imagining the Marshalls," 234.
71   Elbōn, "The Heartbeat of the Marshall Islands," 144–45.
72   Kupferman, "Republic of the Marshall Islands since 1990," 77.
73   Debie Singh, Report, Piango National Liaison Unit (NLU), Information & Communications Needs Assessment, June–October 2008 (Suva, Fiji: Pacific Islands Association of Non-Government Organizations [PIANGO], 2008), 22. Kilma was also adamant about not belonging to a side.
74   Fred Pedro, interview and conversations during tour of V7EMON, January 2010.
75   Fred Pedro, conversation with author via Skype/telephone, May 25, 2012.
76   Giff Johnson, "Kwajalein Landowners Agree to Extend U.S. Missile Base," *Variety*, May 9, 2011, published online by DMZ Hawai'i, www.dmzhawaii.org/dmz-legacy-site-two/?p=8811.

CHAPTER 2. PRECARIOUS HARMONIES

Epigraph: Abacca Anjain-Maddison (Rongelapese woman), interview with author, October 28, 2008. This statement originates from my interview with Abacca, but it is representative of a host of interviews I conducted with

Rongelapese who would discuss the songs as "happy" and "sad" for the same reasons as provided above.

1 The first phase is the *ilomej* (in-death or at-death), which approximates a wake. The second phase is the *kallib* (the actual burial), and the third phase is the *añak* (the "feast that normally [takes] place after the burial"). During the añak, mourners will sleep at the deceased's house with the family members, creating the space for a silent experience of *ippān doon* (togetherness). Silence is a sign of support, of respect. Funerals were some of the only times I saw outward bursts of weeping.
2 Public Advocate, email message to author, October 26, 2008.
3 Lijon has since passed away. She had asked that I refer to her as Lijon Mac-Donald. "Lijon Eknilang" and "Lijon MacDonald" refer to the same person, and I occasionally refer to her simply as Lijon.
4 I follow Clifford Geertz in defining *culture* as "an historically transmitted pattern of meanings embodied in symbols, a system of inherited conceptions expressed in symbolic forms by means of which men communicate, perpetuate, and develop their knowledge about and attitudes towards life." See Geertz, *The Interpretation of Cultures*, 89.
5 See Esposito, *Bios*, 2008.
6 Advisory Committee on Human Radiation Experiments (ACHRE), *Final Report*, 377.
7 Johnston and Barker, *Consequential Damages of Nuclear War*, 151.
8 Quoted in Johnston and Barker, 151.
9 For more information on the risks posed to men and women from exposure to radiation, see Makhijani, Smith, and Thorne, *Science for Democratic Action*.
10 For more information on permanent hoarseness and the other risks involved in thyroid surgery, see "Thyroid Surgery," www.thyroid.org/patients/brochures/ThyroidSurgery.pdf.
11 Stras, "The Organ of the Soul," 174.
12 Robbins and Adams, *Radiation Effects in the Marshall Islands*, 16.
13 Dr. Ryan Branski at NYU Langone Center helped inform me about the physiological basis for the impact of thyroid operations on the voice.
14 ACHRE, *Final Report*, 371.
15 ACHRE, 371, footnotes 153, 154.
16 Norio Kebenli, quoted in Johnston and Barker, *Consequential Damages of Nuclear War*, 170.
17 Almira Matayoshi, quoted in Johnston and Barker, 170.
18 Ellen Boaz, quoted in Johnston and Barker, 170.
19 Lijon MacDonald, conversation with author, October 2009.
20 Cognard-Black, "'I Said Nothing,'" 42.
21 Quoted in Alcalay, "Utrik Atoll," 27.

22   "Radiation and Your Health," www.cdc.gov/nceh/radiation/emergencies/breastfeeding.htm.
23   According to a May 2005 Congressional Research Service Office report, the United States paid the Bikinians more than $136 million for compensation for nuclear damages between 1964 and 2005. This figure does not include costs of cleanup or the billions of dollars spent on the nuclear or scientific tests themselves. See "Republic of the Marshall Islands Changed Circumstances Petition to Congress, May 16, 2005."
24   See Kleinman, *The Illness Narratives*.
25   Kleinman, *The Illness Narratives*.
26   Robie, "Operation Exodus."
27   "Rongelapese Angered by U.S. Remarks," *Marshall Islands Journal*, May 10, 1985, 3.
28   A third verse of the song is barely audible. I cannot translate it, and I was never able to get this verse translated. I can hear that it is about their elders on the atoll and their homeland and inheritance, which is important in terms of preservation.
29   Rongelap was the site of a regional navigational school, where a shallow reef made for an ideal location for wave-piloting training and which ceased to operate after the Bravo detonation. See chapter 4 of this book and Genz, *Breaking the Shell*.
30   Eknilang and Matayoshi, "Rongelap Survivors," 123.
31   Eknilang and Matayoshi, "Rongelap Survivors," 127.
32   Lijon MacDonald, interview with author, November 2009.
33   Seremetakis, ed., *The Senses Still*, 9.
34   MacDonald interview.
35   From our other conversations, I believe that Lijon lived in Ebeye in the 1970s.
36   Compact II marks shifts in the discourse of loss and political involvement. See chapter 3.
37   See Keever, *News Zero*.
38   Today, men have replaced women on drums in performances for tourists. However, the WUTMI gathering is an example of a public space where women can play drums and chant. Traditionally, drum playing was solely under women's purview, although this is now uncommon across Micronesia and the Pacific in general.
39   Dvorak, "'The Martial Islands,'" 67.
40   Lawson Burke, "Marshall Islands." For an image of an aje drum, see Schwartz, "Between Death and Life," 30.
41   See "Fallout."
42   As Krämer and Nevermann note, "The women Liman and Lidjera and the spirit Leo on Rongerik were the first to sing and dance at the same time. . . . With the singing of [the song they included in the text], the dance was invented. Now the priest has precedence in the singing." See Krämer and Nevermann, *Ralik-Ratak*, 398.

43   MacDonald interview. Nineteenth-century and early twentieth-century ethnographers who recorded the dances included Krämer and Nevermann, Erwin Steinbach, Otto Finsch, and Franz Hernsheim.
44   Krämer and Nevermann, *Ralik-Ratak*, 306.
45   The performance of the *jiku* by women was also noted by Burke and Smith in *The Garland Encyclopedia of World Music: Australia and the Pacific Islands*, 750.
46   Lijon MacDonald, interview with author, September 25, 2009.
47   Walsh, "Imagining the Marshalls," 412, 413–14.
48   Johnston and Barker, *Consequential Damages of Nuclear War*, 235.
49   Derrida and Dufourmantelle, *Of Hospitality*.
50   The acronym ERUB is also the name of a Marshallese women's antinuclear organization. See ERUB Survivors at http://erubsurvivors.weebly.com/index.html.
51   "B" works up from C♯2 to G♯2 (via F♯), then C♯3.
52   Video footage from the Mission Pacific Archive in Majuro, obtained by author in April 2010.
53   I use my own transcriptions and translations of "177" along with the transcription and translation found in Barker's *Bravo for the Marshallese*, 95.
54   Morris, "About Suffering," 29.
55   Morris, "About Suffering," 29.
56   Lijon MacDonald, formal interview with author, 2009.
57   Lijon MacDonald, informal discussion with author, October 27, 2009.
58   Morris, "Voice, Genre, and Moral Community," 27.
59   Fox, *Real Country*, 317.
60   Herzig, *Suffering for Science*, 11.
61   Darlene Keju-Johnson on the Rongelapese viewpoint of action for the benefit of the future, such as moves and establishing programs, quoted in Ishtar, *Daughters of the Pacific*, 36.
62   "Reducing Environmental Cancer Risk: What We Can Do Now," ix.
63   "The voice ties language to the body, but the nature of this tie is paradoxical: *the voice does not belong to either.* It is not part of linguistics . . . but it is not part of the body either—not only does it detach itself from the body and leave it behind, it does not fit the body either, it cannot be 'disacousmatized.' It floats . . . it is a bodily missile which has detached from its source, emancipated itself, yet remains corporeal." See Dolar, *A Voice and Nothing More*, 72–73.

CHAPTER 3. MORIBA

1   Kiste, *The Bikinians*, 27.
2   Weisgall, *Operation Crossroads*, 110–11; Don Whitehead, "King of Bikini Is Not Pleased at A-bomb Test," *New York Times*, February 27, 1946. The article describes Jeimata Kabwa [sic], identified as "King of Bikini Atoll," as unhappy

because the Bikinians, whom the article describes as having "no great affection for Jeimata," were relocating to Rongerik, an atoll not under his jurisdiction.
3. Weisgall, *Operation Crossroads*, 112.
4. Weisgall, *Operation Crossroads*, 112.
5. Friedman, *Creating an American Lake*, 122. James Milne moved to Ebon when he was eleven years old and was educated by the Japanese government. He spoke Gilbertese, Marshallese, English, and Japanese fluently according to Tobin, *Stories from the Marshall Islands*, 375.
6. Quoted from film footage presented in *Radio Bikini*.
7. There was mistranslation from the outset as well, given the lack of literal conceptual cognates between languages. However, I'm interested in the repetition and the refusal to change answers.
8. Jack Niedenthal termed the phrase "equivocal" in his public speech to World Teach volunteers, Marshall Islands Resort Hotel, Majuro, summer 2008.
9. Smith, *Unsettling Ourselves*, 159.
10. In *Cold War Ruins*, Yoneyama cites Derrida's attention to how these agreements perpetuate such an industry.
11. Lowe, *The Intimacies of the Four Continents*.
12. I borrow the term *mythico-history* from Malkki, *Purity and Exile*, to denote the moral hierarchy as justified via Bikinians' cosmological understanding of their relationship with the United States and with other Marshallese groups. This is also related to the nuclear testing and the Protestant missionary work.
13. See Max Weber's theory about the state establishing a monopoly on violence by claiming a legitimate use of force in *Politics as Vocation*.
14. Dobson, *Listening for Democracy*.
15. Attali, *Noise*.
16. See Tobin, *Stories of the Marshall Islands*, 332.
17. Asad, *Formations of the Secular*.
18. She sang in the contralto vocal range (E3–F5).
19. Sharlynn Lang, interview with the author, October 28, 2014.
20. Asad, *Formations of the Secular*, 5.
21. See Mahmood, *Politics of Piety*; and Asad, *Formations of the Secular*.
22. Lang interview.
23. Quoted from the "Report Evaluating the Request of the Government of the Republic of the Marshall Islands Presented to the Congress of the United States of America regarding Circumstances Arising from U.S. Nuclear Testing in the Marshall Islands pursuant to Article IX of the Nuclear Claims Settlement Approved by Congress in Public Law 99–239," November 2004, US Department of State Archive, https://2001-2009.state.gov/p/eap/rls/rpt/40422.htm.
24. Jackson, *The Politics of Storytelling*, 42–43. Jackson cites Marshall Sahlins's notions of reciprocity from his 1966 symposium presentation, published in "Notes on the Original Affluent Society."

25 Peters, since deceased, and his wife lived on Ejit at the time of the interview.
26 According to Cusic, baseball and country music have been inextricably linked in their trajectories from the working class to all-around American respectability. See Cusic, *Baseball and Country Music*.
27 Jetñil-Kijiner, "Iep Jaltok," 51, which also references Joash, Kowata, and Stone's *Jabonkonnaan in Majel*.
28 Councilman Hinton Johnson, interview with author, November 26, 2009.
29 Based on Niedenthal's translation in *For the Good of Mankind*.
30 Parker, *Acoustic Jurisprudence*, 161, which cites Hydaralli, "What Is Noise? An Inquiry into Its Formal Properties," 226; Serres, *Genesis*, 13, 20.
31 Hinton Johnson, interview with author, November 2009.
32 The figure of the būromōj is even less discussed, although the metaphor is often referenced.
33 August Erdland, quoted by Petrosian-Husa, "Illness and Treatment in the Marshall Islands" in *Traditional Medicine of the Marshall Islands*, 24.
34 Erdland, *The Marshall Islanders*.
35 Erdland, *The Marshall Islanders*.
36 Taafaki, Fowler, and Thaman, *Traditional Medicine*, 27–28.
37 Tafaaki, Fowler, and Thaman, *Traditional Medicine*, 39.
38 See Brigg, "Biopolitics Meets Terrapolitics."
39 Johnson interview.
40 Bikinians, and more generally Marshallese, are fans of country music, and I borrow the term *cry break* from the technique of the same name that is common in American country music, which intimates crying. See Fox, *Real Country*.
41 Lore Kessibuki, quoted by Niedenthal, *For the Good of Mankind*, 184–85.
42 Petrosian-Husa, "Illness and Treatment in the Marshall Islands" in *Traditional Medicine of the Marshall Islands*, quotes Erdland, 24.
43 Connor, *Beyond Words*, 120.
44 Alson Kelen, interview with author, May 2010.
45 Kili Excess, "Ij jijet Ioon Bolok Maroro," *Kili Excess Live from Kili Island*, date unknown.
46 Councilman Hinton Johnson, interview with author, May 18, 2010.
47 Stoller, "'Conscious Ain't Consciousness,'" 117.
48 Bikini political officer, interview with author, Uliga Village, Majuro Atoll, May 9, 2010.
49 Bikini political officer interview.
50 Rifkin, *Beyond Settler Time*, ix.
51 Bikini political official, interview with author, Uliga Village, Majuro Atoll, May 9, 2010.
52 Percy Benjamin, interview with author, November 2009.
53 Differing accounts credit the song's composition to either Enjen Lalmo around 1985 or Calvin Buñlik around 2004, or possibly both in extended collaboration.

54 Genz, "Marshallese Navigation and Voyaging," 164.
55 Genz, "Marshallese Navigation and Voyaging," 164, 165.
56 Johnson interview.
57 William J. Waugh, "The Hungry and Bewildered: Bikinians Gave up Homes for Sake of Atom Weapons," *Honolulu Star-Bulletin*, July 14, 1954.
58 Niedenthal refers to the *New York Times* (June 1968) in "Bikini History."
59 Senator Tomaki Juda, personal interview with author, Long Island, Majuro Atoll, 2010.
60 Bourn Johnson interview with the author, Kili Island, December 28, 2009.
61 Fox, *Real Country*, 155.
62 Ahmed, *Cultural Politics of Emotion*, 11.
63 Ahmed, *Cultural Politics of Emotion*, 131. Emphasis in original.
64 Johnny Johnson, interview with author, 2009.

CHAPTER 4. *UWAAÑAÑ* (SPIRITED NOISE)

1   Niedenthal, "Bikinian Demographics," http://bikiniatoll.com.
2   Attali, *Noise*, 132.
3   Meintjes, *Dust of the Zulu*.
4   Carabí and Armengol, eds., *Alternative Masculinities for a Changing World*.
5   Radstone and Schwarz, *Memory*, 4.
6   "Gospel Warriors," *Marshall Islands Journal*, December 11, 2009.
7   Robbins, in *Becoming Sinners*, draws from his work with the Urapmin of Papua New Guinea to consider marginalization and humiliation as two felt experiences that lead groups and individuals to embrace alternative structures as their own, such as Christianity, which de-marginalizes by connecting groups to global value systems.
8   In Pacific anthropology, there have been numerous debates on why Christianity has been adopted and, in terms I prefer, adapted with such conviction. The debates are summed up in various literatures and pertinently, with respect to gendered violence. See, for example, Robbins, *Becoming Sinners*; and Keane, *Christian Moderns*.
9   Keane, *Christian Moderns*, 12.
10 Griffiths, "The Myth of Authenticity: Representation," in *De-Scribing Empire*, 72.
11 Springdale Mayor Doug Sprouse, interview with author, June 4, 2013. As of this writing, approximately fifteen thousand Marshallese reside in the midwestern United States, and Springdale, in the northwest corner of the landlocked state of Arkansas, is the epicenter.
12 Senator Tomaki Juda, interview with author, December 3, 2009.
13 Pastor Percy Benjamin, interview with author, October 22, 2009.
14 Benjamin interview. The Marshallese use the term *bwebwenato* to mean "talk stories/story," and this meaning is the notion that when people "talk out"

some issue or past event, in culturally appropriate terms, the process functions to alleviate tension, etc. There are no psychologists, psychiatrists, or culture of "self-help" in the RMI. Here Benjamin is using "talk story" to mean talk about the Gospel/Bible lessons.
15 Tobin, *Stories from the Marshall Islands*, 386.
16 Teaiwa, "Saltwater Feet," 113–14.
17 See the work of Louis Althusser, including "Ideology and Ideological State Apparatuses."
18 Kabua, "We Are the Land, the Land Is Us," 190.
19 See Genz, "Without Precedent."
20 See "Tattooing in the Marshall Islands."
21 Gerson, "Singing Lessons."
22 LaBriola, "Iien Ippān Doon," 108.
23 Ingersoll, *Waves of Knowing*, 129.
24 Peterson Jibas, interview with the author, May 28, 2013, Springdale, Arkansas.
25 I take the term *collective palate* from informal conversations with Nicholas Kirby, who employs the concept to developing methods of sensorial directedness and refinement in barista training, 2010–2012.
26 Alson Kelen (former Bikinian mayor), in discussion with author, May 2010.
27 Peterson Jibas interview.
28 Jamore Aitab, interview with Jack Niedenthal.
29 Deacon Johnny Johnson, interview with author, September 7, 2009.
30 Geologists were among the various scientists who gleaned data from Bikini Atoll. In 1947 Bikini "boasts the deepest hole ever drilled by man on a Pacific atoll" as drillers "under the direction of the navy and the U.S. Geological Survey reached a depth of 1,346 feet," which surpassed the record depth by scientists from Britain and Australia by more than 1,000 feet. "Bikini Scene of Deep Test Hole by Geologists," *Honolulu Star-Advertiser*, August 7, 1947, 12. See also Bascom, *A Hole in the Bottom of the Sea*. For more information on ecosystem science, see DeLoughrey, "The Myth of Isolates."
31 Deacon Johnny Johnson interview.
32 Deacon Johnny Johnson interview.
33 The trend has been noted in scholarship on healers in Cambodia and Cameroon, for example. See Kent, *Medical Identities*.
34 Deacon Johnny Johnson, interview with author, September 7, 2010.
35 Sakai, "On Romantic Love and Military Violence," 207–8.
36 Randy, interview with author, November 16, 2009.
37 See Rudiak-Gould, "Being Marshallese and Christian."
38 Marshallese groups compete in similar ways, but they still know how to survive on their lands without being totally dependent on others who believe in notions of scarcity.
39 For more on the aesthetics of masculine militarized performance, see Meintjes, *Dust of the Zulu*.

40. Malkki, *Purity and Exile*, 16.
41. For more information about the "Battle of *Jepta* Concert," see Schwartz, "Marshallese Cultural Diplomacy in Arkansas."
42. Pastor Percy Benjamin, conversation with author, December 19, 2009.
43. Randy interview.
44. Carucci framed this reciprocity within Annette Weiner's theory that "all exchange is predicated on a universal paradox—how to keep-while-giving." See Carucci, *Nuclear Nativity*, 41; Weiner, *Inalienable Possessions*, 4.
45. Herzig, *Suffering for Science*.
46. Attali, *Noise*.
47. Keane, *Christian Moderns*, 53.
48. Tony deBrum told me that part of the power of these songs is that they can be used for both political and spiritual pursuits depending on the context. Interview with author, 2010.
49. See Byrd's *The Transit of Empire* for the ways in which the United States makes Native being "in the past" and denies ways of mourning, such as during Gospel Day, and for their metrical and gridded sonic inscription, conscription into the war for the "good of mankind" from which they have been excluded.

CHAPTER 5. ANEMKWŌJ

1. Derrida, "No Apocalypse, Not Now."
2. Dvorak, "'The Martial Islands,'" 68, citing Ferguson and Turnbull, *Oh, Say, Can You See?*
3. Runyan et al., eds., *Feminist (Im)Mobilities in Fortress(ing) North America*, 101–2.
4. See Lowe, *The Intimacies of Four Continents*.
5. The *Territorial Survey of Oceanic Music* was conducted in 1987 and published in 1989 by Mary E. Burke, a US American woman.
6. Younger generations of Bikinians, particularly those who had grown up on Kili, believed the song to be Bikinian and thought that the lyrics corresponded with flora on the island.
7. Pastor Percy Benjamin, interview with author, November 2009.
8. Burke, "Bōk mejam," in *Territorial Survey of Oceanic Music*.
9. Wieser, *Back to the Blanket*, 68.
10. See Ochoa Gautier, *Aurality*.
11. Senator Tony deBrum, personal correspondence, 2010.
12. Ochoa Gautier, *Aurality*, 22.
13. Teaiwa, "Solidarity and Fuidarity."
14. Hamilton et al., *Sensing Law*, 12.
15. Chion writes "that the presence of a human voice structures the sonic space that contains it." See *The Voice in Cinema*, 5.
16. Dvorak, "Seeds from Afar, Flowers from the Reef," 297; and *Coral and Concrete*.

17 See Dvorak, "'The Martial Islands'"; and "Seeds from Afar, Flowers from the Reef."
18 Cavarero, *For More Than One Voice*, 45.
19 Wilfred Kendall, advisory meeting, Majuro, March 3, 1999, quoted in Johnston and Barker, *Consequential Damages of Nuclear War*, 68.
20 Senator Tony deBrum, interview with author, March 4, 2010.
21 Stege, "'An Kōrā Aelōñ Kein' (These Islands Belong to the Women)," 12.
22 For more information on Kwajalein's masculinities, see Dvorak, "'The Martial Islands,'" 55–86.
23 Johnson, *Nuclear Past, Unclear Future*, 11, references April 9, 1975, letter from US Lawrence Livermore National Laboratory scientist V. E. Noshkin to William O. Forster.
24 Monica LaBriola argues in "Iien Ippān Doon" that the discourse around Ebeye as a slum or ghetto of the Pacific has done more damage than good, insofar as it psychologically affects the residents, further stripping them of the agency they have. LaBriola offers a much-needed counterpoint to the perspective of Glenn Alcalay, who so poignantly said that Ebeye was "made in America." In this dialogue, what comes across is that the ghettoization of the island is an American production, not that Ebeye is a ghetto. See LaBriola, "Iien Ippān Doon," 30–50; Alcalay interview in "Paradise Lost" and "Utrik Atoll."
25 As part of Operation Flintlock, US forces took both islands of Roi and Namur on February 2, 1944. Later that year, US Navy SeaBees filled in the area between the two islands and created what would be called Roi-Namur. See Chapin, "Breaking the Outer Ring: Marine Landings in the Marshall Islands."
26 According to the US Department of State, the RMI "is not a member of the World Trade Organization, the World Intellectual Property Organization (WIPO), or any other international agreement on intellectual property rights. There is inadequate protection for intellectual property, patents, copyrights, and trademarks. The only intellectual property-related legislation relates to locally produced music recordings, and it has never been enforced." See "2015 Investment Climate Statement—Marshall Islands."
27 Carucci, *Nuclear Nativity*, 8.
28 As World War II neared its close, the United States announced its symbol of peace, the "tea rose," on April 29, 1945 in Pasadena.
29 DeBrum interview with author.
30 The third verse is also sung only once. It sounds the other musical climax audible in the song on the lyrics, "*ke baj wombu eo in*." The clause means "it is just (or almost, nearly) cover." The word *wombu* is Japanese, and it means "womb," "birthplace," "homeland," and "field or cultivated land." Inserting this word in the middle of the song indicates that the temporary shelter is what nourished them and kept them safe. The Marshallese word for homeland is *ḷāṃoran*, so the Marshallese are expressing that they have become, through reproductive measures, in some capacity Japanese.

31 See Abo et al., *Marshallese-English Dictionary*.
32 Currie, *Kwajalein Atoll*, 74–75.
33 "Marshallese Natives Ready to Help Us: Show No Hostility as We Enter upon Program of Control," *New York Times*, February 10, 1944; "Marines Set Up Rule of Life in Marshalls," *New York Times*, February 15, 1944.
34 "Marshall Natives Ready to Help U.S.," *New York Times*, February 10, 1944, 4.
35 By 1951, the 550 Marshallese workers in the labor camps, who were still living on the island in makeshift residences, appeared to be part of that debris in the eyes of the US Navy, and they were removed to beautify Kwajalein Island. See Johnson, *Collision Course at Kwajalein*.
36 Dvorak, "Seeds from Afar, Flowers from the Reef," 83–84.
37 Camacho and Monnig, "Uncomfortable Fatigues," 159.
38 Hezel, *Strangers in Their Own Land*, 274–75; Johnson, "Collision Course at Kwajalein," 28.
39 "The Ebeye Story."
40 "The Ebeye Story."
41 Johnson, *Collision Course at Kwajalein*, 7.
42 Topping, "Review of U.S. Language Policy in the TTPI," 116. See also Kupferman, *Disassembling and Decolonizing Schools in the Pacific*, 114.
43 Chutaro and Heine, "A Double-Edged Sword."
44 Kiste, *The Bikinians*, 10.
45 Hezel, *Strangers in Their Own Land*, 325–27; Johnson, "Collision Course," 32.
46 In 1951 the US military had brought in Marshallese to clean up debris that were remnants from World War II and to build facilities for US Navy personnel on Kwajalein. These were the first workers relocated to the previously uninhabited island of Ebeye. See Johnson, "Collision Course," 32.
47 Hezel, *Strangers in Their Own Land*, 325–28.
48 According to a Honolulu spokesperson, the landowners opposed the US–RMI agreement for three reasons: "lack of provisions for improving the slumping economic conditions on Ebeye Island," "the granting of exclusive military rights in the Marshalls to the United States for an unlimited time, and a third involved concern over the continued use of the landowners' property in the development of nuclear weapons." See Robert Trumbull, "Marshall Island Landowners Protest U.S. Missile Base Pact," *New York Times*, June 21, 1982. The Kwajalein Atoll Corporation represented about five thousand landowners and was led by Chairman Ataji L. Balos and President Imata Kabua, who at the beginning of the occupation planned to lead protestors to the islands of Roi and Namur at the northern end of the atoll and fifty miles from Kwajalein Island.
49 Johnson, "Collision Course," 36–38; Hezel, *Strangers in Their Own Land*, 328.
50 The word *ami* means "yours" in Marshallese. I could not tell if Tony meant to say "word" or if he meant that the singers would "double entendre" the army.

Nouns can be turned into verbs. For example, *moña* is food, and when you want to say "I'm eating," you say, "*Ij moña.*"
51 DeBrum interview with author.
52 Irooj and Kwajalein Senator Michael Kabua is the younger brother of former president Imata Kabua. For more information of chiefly lineages and the ways in which foreigners view them, see Walsh, "Imagining the Marshalls."
53 Dvorak, "Seeds from Afar, Flowers from the Reef," 317. The United States has "strategic denial" over the RMI in the COFA.
54 See Clifford, *Returns*; and Tsing, *Friction*.
55 KA wished to remain anonymous.
56 Kwajalein aḷaps, conversation with the author, April 7, 2010.
57 See Dvorak, "Seeds from Afar, Flowers from the Reef"; and Horowitz's film, *Home on the Range*.
58 Kwajalein aḷaps conversation.
59 Johnson, *Collision Course at Kwajalein*, 28.
60 Kwajalein landowners, conversation with author, April 7, 2010. The aḷap, it is interesting to note, transitioned abruptly from the recent past to the present situation, where Marshallese are banned from the Kwajalein islands.
61 President Christopher Loeak was voted into office in 2011.
62 Dvorak, *Coral and Concrete*.
63 Dvorak, "'Martial Islands,'" 68, citing Walsh, "Imagining the Marshalls," 166–68.
64 Dvorak, 68.
65 Loeak and Maddison, "Women's Organizations," 90–92.
66 The song was composed in the 1970s by a man named Kuno from Ujae Atoll.
67 The wrongful ascription highlights the delicate way in which people exist and aim to express their struggles and communal bonds during massive social upheavals when they have recourse neither to rights nor to debt (the Bikinians, as I discuss in chapter 4, lay claims to debt with the United States, not the irooj).
68 Party songs (*al in kaṃōḷo*) specifically refer to songs for "Marshallese-style parties" (kaṃōḷo, literally "to make cool"). One specific genre of the al in kaṃōḷo is the welcoming song (*al in karuwanene*), the song to set the tone of the party. "*Bōk mejam*" is an al in karuwanene.
69 See Derrida and Dufourmantelle, *Of Hospitality*.
70 Affective dissonance has been studied alongside cognitive dissonance and in terms of colonialism has been seen to produce the sovereign (nation) as a "melancholic formation." See Khanna, "Post-palliative"; and Rudiak-Gould, "Being Marshallese and Christian."
71 Matsuda, "AHR Forum, the Pacific," 768.
72 Alfred Capelle, interview with author, May 2010.

73 Correspondence between Major Frank Moore III (US Army) and Alfred Capelle, July 22, 1989, accessed January 12, 2012, www.smdcen.us/pubdocs/files/usakafeis_lastpgs_f.pdf.
74 Dvorak, "Seed from Afar, Flowers from the Reef," 262; Carruci, *Nuclear Nativity*, 199–200.
75 Dvorak, "Seeds from Afar, Flowers from the Reef," 262; Dvorak's conversation with Jimmy Matsunaga, July 20, 2006.
76 Moore-Capelle correspondence.

Abo, Takaji, Byron W. Bender, Alfred Capelle, and Tony deBrum. *Marshallese-English Dictionary*. Honolulu: University of Hawai'i Press, 1977.
Advisory Committee on Human Radiation Experiments. *Final Report*. Washington, DC: US Government Printing Office, 1995.
Ahmed, Sara. *Cultural Politics of Emotion*. New York: Routledge, 2004.
Ahuja, Neel. *Bioinsecurities: Disease Interventions, Empire, and the Government of Species*. Durham, NC: Duke University Press, 2016.
Alcalay, Glenn. "Utrik Atoll: The Sociocultural Impact of Living in a Radioactive Environment (An Anthropological Assessment of the Consequential Damages from Bravo)." Utrik Atoll Local Government and the Office of the Public Advocate of the Nuclear Claims Tribunal, Majuro, RMI, 2004.
Althusser, Louis. "Ideology and Ideological State Apparatuses (Notes towards an Investigation)." In *Lenin and Philosophy and Other Essays*, translated by Ben Brewster. New York: Monthly Review Press, 1970. https://www.marxists.org/reference/archive/althusser/1970/ideology.htm.
Amundson, Michael A., and Scott C. Zeman, eds. *Atomic Culture: How We Learned to Stop Worrying and Love the Bomb*. Boulder: University Press of Colorado, 2004.
Anderson, Warwick. *Colonial Pathologies: American Tropical Medicine, Race, and Hygiene in the Philippines*. Durham, NC: Duke University Press, 2006.
Anjain, John. "The Fallout on Rongelap Atoll and Its Social, Medical and Environmental Effects." Edited and translated by Richard A. Sundt. Unpublished manuscript. Nuclear Claims Tribunal, Majuro, RMI, 1973.
Aquila, Richard. "Sh'Boom; or, How Early Rock & Roll Taught Us to Stop Worrying and Love the Bomb." In *The Writing on the Cloud: American Culture Confronts the Atomic Bomb*, edited by Alison M. Scott and Christopher D. Geist, 106–18. Lanham, MD: University Press of America, 1997.
Asad, Talal. *Formations of the Secular: Christianity, Islam, and Modernity*. Stanford, CA: Stanford University Press, 2003.
"The Atom." *Time*, March 22, 1954, 23.
Attali, Jacques. *Noise: The Political Economy of Music*. Translated by Brian Massumi. Minneapolis: University of Minnesota Press, 1985.
Australian Broadcasting Company. "State of Media Report & Communication Report, 2013: Republic of the Marshall Islands." www.abc.net.au/cm/lb/9268974/data/marshall-islands%3A-state-of-the-media-report-data.pdf.

Baker, Geoffrey. *Imposing Harmony: Music and Society in Colonial Cuzco.* Durham, NC: Duke University Press, 2008.

Bakhtin, Mikhail M. *The Dialogic Imagination: Four Essays.* Edited by Michael Holquist. Translated by Caryl Emersno and Michael Holquist. Austin: University of Texas Press, 1981.

Barker, Holly. *Bravo for the Marshallese.* Belmont, CA: Wadsworth, 2004.

Barker, Joanne. *Critically Sovereign: Indigenous Gender, Sexuality, and Feminist Studies.* Durham, NC: Duke University Press, 2017.

Bascom, Willard. *A Hole in the Bottom of the Sea: The Story of the Mohole Project.* New York: Doubleday, 1961.

Baxi, Upendra. "Voices of Suffering and the Future of Human Rights." *Transnational Law and Contemporary Problems* 8 (1998): 125–69.

Bialostosky, Don. *How to Play a Poem.* Pittsburgh: University of Pittsburgh Press, 2017.

Bloechl, Olivia A. *Native American Song at the Frontiers of Early Modern Music.* Cambridge: Cambridge University Press, 2008.

Blok, Anders. "War of the Whales: Post-sovereign Science and Agonistic Cosmopolitics in Japanese-Global Whaling Assemblages." *Science, Technology & Human Values* 35, no. 5 (November 2010). Accessed October 30, 2019. https://doi.org/10.1177/0162243910366133.

Brigg, Morgan. "Biopolitics Meets Terrapolitics: Political Ontologies and Governance in Settler-Colonial Australia." *Australian Journal of Political Science* 42, no. 3 (2007): 403–17. https://doi.org/10.1080/10361140701513554.

Brinkema, Eugenie. "Critique of Silence." *Differences* 22, nos. 2–3 (2011): 211–34.

Brinkema, Eugenie. *The Forms of the Affects.* Durham, NC: Duke University Press, 2014.

Buck-Morss, Susan. *The Dialectics of Seeing: Walter Benjamin and the Arcades Project.* Cambridge, MA: MIT Press, 1989.

Burke, Mary E., Jeben Butuna, Amram Enos, and Alfred Capelle. "Bōk mejam." *Alin Majel: Songs and Music of the Marshall Islands: Territorial Survey of Oceanic Music, Marshall Islands, June-October, 1988.* 1995. Alele Museum, Majuro, RMI.

Burke, Mary E. L., and Barbara B. Smith, "East Micronesia." In *The Garland Encyclopedia of World Music: Australia and the Pacific Islands*, edited by Adrienne I. Kaeppler and J. W. Love, 748–66. New York: Routledge, 1998.

Byrd, Jodi A. *The Transit of Empire: Indigenous Critiques of Colonialism.* Minneapolis: University of Minnesota Press, 2011.

Camacho, Keith L. and Laurel A. Monnig. "Uncomfortable Fatigues: Chamorro Soldiers, Gendered Identities, and the Question of Decolonization in Guam." In *Militarized Currents: Toward a Decolonized Future in Asia and the Pacific*, edited by Setsu Shigematsu and Keith L. Camacho, 147–80. Minneapolis: University of Minnesota Press, 2010,

Carabí, Àngels, and J. Armengol, eds. *Alternative Masculinities for a Changing World.* New York: Palgrave McMillan, 2014.

Cartwright, Lisa. *Screening the Body: Tracing Medicine's Visual Culture*. Minneapolis: University of Minnesota Press, 1995.

Carucci, Laurence M. *Nuclear Nativity: Rituals of Renewal and Empowerment in the Marshall Islands*. Dekalb: Northern Illinois University Press, 1997.

Cavarero, Adriana. *For More Than One Voice: Toward a Philosophy of Vocal Expression*. Stanford, CA: Stanford University Press, 2005.

Ceraso, Steph. "(Re)Educating the Senses: Multimodal Listening, Bodily Learning, and the Composition of Sonic Experiences." *College English* 77 (2014): 102–23.

Ceraso, Steph. *Sounding Composition: Multimodal Pedagogies for Embodied Listening*. Pittsburgh: University of Pittsburgh Press, 2018.

Chapin, John C. "Breaking the Outer Ring: Marine Landings in the Marshall Islands." Marines in World War II Commemorative Series. Marine Corps History and Museums Division. US National Park Service. www.nps.gov/parkhistory/online_books/npswapa/extcontent/usmc/pcn-190-003124-00/sec1.htm.

Chion, Michel. *The Voice in Cinema*. Edited and translated by Claudia Gorbman. New York: Columbia University Press, 1999.

Chutaro, Emi, and Hilda C. Heine. "A Double-Edged Sword: A Study of the Impacts of External Educational Aid to the Republic of Marshall Islands." Paper presented at the Rethinking Educational Aid in the Pacific Conference, Nadi, Fiji, October 20–22, 2003.

Classen, Constance, and David Howes. "The Museum as Sensescape: Western Sensibilities and Indigenous Artifacts." In *Sensible Objects: Colonialism, Museums, and Material Culture*, edited by Elizabeth Edwards, Chris Gosden, and Ruth Phillips, 199–222. Oxford: Berg, 2006.

Clifford, James. *Returns: Becoming Indigenous in the Twenty-First Century*. Cambridge, MA: Harvard University Press, 2013.

Cognard-Black, Jennifer. "'I Said Nothing:' The Rhetoric of Silence and Gayle Jones's 'Corregidora.'" *NWSA Journal* (Spring 2001): 40–60.

Connor, Steven. *Beyond Words: Sobs, Hums, Stutters and Other Vocalizations*. London: Reaktion, 2014.

Cooke, Stephanie. *In Mortal Hands: A Cautionary History of the Nuclear Age*. Collingwood, Australia: Black Inc. Books, 2009.

Coulthard, Glen S. *Red Skin, White Masks: Rejecting the Colonial Politics of Recognition*. Minneapolis: University of Minnesota Press, 2014.

Crenshaw, Kimberle. "Demarginalizing the Intersection of Race and Sex: A Black Feminist Critique of Antidiscrimination Doctrine, Feminist Theory and Antiracist Politics." University of Chicago Legal Forum issue 1, article 8 (1989): 139–67. https://chicagounbound.uchicago.edu/uclf/vol1989/iss1/8.

Currie, Ruth D. *Kwajalein Atoll, the Marshall Islands and American Policy in the Pacific*. Jefferson, NC: McFarland, 2016.

Cusic, Don. *Baseball and Country Music*. Madison: University of Wisconsin Press, 2003.

Davis, Tracy C. *Stages of Emergency: Cold War Nuclear Civil Defense*. Durham, NC: Duke University Press, 2007.

Deleuze, Gilles. *Francis Bacon: The Logic of Sensation*. Minneapolis: University of Minnesota Press, 2003.

DeLoughrey, Elizabeth. *Routes and Roots: Navigating Caribbean and Pacific Island Literatures*. Honolulu: University of Hawai'i Press, 2007.

DeLoughrey, Elizabeth M. "The Myth of Isolates: Ecosystem Ecologies in the Nuclear Pacific," edited by Godfrey Baldacchino and Erik Clark. *Cultural Geographies* 20, no. 2 (2012): 167–84.

Denning, Greg. "Introduction: In Search of a Metaphor." In *Through the Glass Darkly: Reflections of Personal Identity in Early America*, edited by Ronald Hoffman, Mechal Sobel, and Fredrika J. Teute, 1–8. Chapel Hill: University of North Carolina Press, 1997.

Derrida, Jacques. "No Apocalypse, Not Now (Full Speed Ahead, Seven Missiles, Seven Missives)." *Diacritics* 14, no. 2 (Summer 1984): 20–31.

Derrida, Jacques, and Anne Dufourmantelle. *Of Hospitality*. Translated by Rachel Bowlby. Cultural Memory in the Present. Stanford, CA: Stanford University Press, 2000.

Desjarlais, Robert R. *Body and Emotion: The Aesthetics of Illness and Healing in the Nepal Himalayas*. Philadelphia: University of Pennsylvania Press, 1992.

Desjarlais, Robert R. *Sensory Biographies: Lives and Deaths among Nepal's Yolmo Buddhists*. Berkeley: University of California Press, 1988.

Dobson, Andrew. *Listening for Democracy: Recognition, Representation, Reconciliation*. Oxford: Oxford University Press, 2014.

Dolar, Mladen. *A Voice and Nothing More*. Cambridge, MA: MIT Press, 2006.

Dolmage, Jay T. *Academic Ableism: Disability and Higher Education*. Ann Arbor: University of Michigan Press, 2017.

Donne, John. "Meditation XVII." *Devotions upon Emergent Occasions*. Luminarium .org. www.luminarium.org/sevenlit/donne/meditation17.php.

Dvorak, Gregory. *Coral and Concrete: Remembering Kwajalein Atoll between Japan, America, and the Marshall Islands*. Honolulu: University of Hawai'i Press, 2018.

Dvorak, Gregory. "'The Martial Islands': Making Marshallese Masculinities between American and Japanese Militarism." *Contemporary Pacific* 20, no. 1 (2008): 55–86.

Dvorak, Gregory. "Seeds from Afar, Flowers from the Reef: Re-membering the Coral and Concrete of Kwajalein Atoll." PhD diss., Australian National University, 2007.

"The Ebeye Story." Internet Archive. Accessed July 31, 2017. https://archive.org /stream/TheEbeyeStory/TheEbeyeStory_djvu.txt.

Edmond, Rod. *Representing the South Pacific: Colonial Discourse from Cook to Gauguin*. Cambridge: Cambridge University Press, 1997.

Eidsheim, Nina S. *The Race of Sound: Listening, Timbre, and Vocality in African American Music*. Durham, NC: Duke University Press, 2019.

Eknilang, Lijon, and James Matayoshi. "Rongelap Survivors." In *Life in the Republic of the Marshall Islands*, translated by Veronica C. Kiluwe, Maria Kabua Fowler, and Alson Kelen, edited by Anono Lieom Loeak, Veronia Kiluwe, and Linda Crowl, 123–32. Majuro, RMI: University of the South Pacific Centre, 2004.

El Dessouky, Dina. "Activating Voice, Body, and Place: Kanaka Maoli and Ma'ohi Writings for Koho'olawe and Moruroa." In *Postcolonial Ecologies: Literatures of the Environment*, edited by Elizabeth DeLoughrey and George B. Handley, 254–72. Oxford: Oxford University Press, 2011.

Elbōn, Antari. "The Heartbeat of the Marshall Islands: Radio Marshalls V7AB." In *Life in the Republic of the Marshall Islands*, translated by Veronica C. Kiluwe, Maria Kabua Fowler, and Alson Kelen, edited by Anono Lieom Loeak, Veronia Kiluwe, and Linda Crowl, 143–48. Majuro, RMI: University of the South Pacific Centre, 2004.

Ellingson, Ter. "Transcription." In *Ethnomusicology: An Introduction*, edited by Helen Myers, 110–52. New York: W.W. Norton, 1992.

Erdland, August, and Richard Neuse. *The Marshall Islanders: Life and Customs, Thought and Religion of a South Seas People*. New Haven, CT: HRAF, 2010 [1914].

Esposito, Roberto. *Bios: Biopolitics and Philosophy*, translated by Timothy Campbell. Minneapolis: University of Minnesota Press, 2008.

"Fallout: The Experiences of a Medical Team in the Care of a Marshallese Population Accidentally Exposed to Fallout Radiation." US Department of Energy, Brookhaven National Laboratory. September 1992. Accessed October 15, 2019. www.bnl.gov/stakeholder/docs/CAC/conard%20report%201992.pdf.

Ferguson, Kathy E., and Phyllis Turnbull. *Oh, Say, Can You See? The Semiotics of the Military in Hawai'i*. Minneapolis: University of Minnesota Press, 1999.

Fleming, Penelope, producer, and Bob Kerr, editor. *"Paradise Lost."* ABC News Primetime, New York, December 1990. YouTube video, 13:37. https://www.youtube.com/watch?v=pN3IP8bLJRI&t=643s.

Fordham, Benjamin. *Building the Cold War Consensus: The Political Economy of U.S. National Security Policy, 1949–1951*. Ann Arbor: University of Michigan Press, 1998.

Fortun, Kim. *Advocacy after Bhopal: Environmentalism, Disaster, New Global Orders*. Chicago: University of Chicago Press, 2001.

Foucault, Michel. *Discipline and Punish: The Birth of the Prison*. New York: Random House, 1977.

Foucault, Michel. *The History of Sexuality*. Translated by Robert Hurley. New York: Vintage, 1990.

Foucault, Michel. *The Order of Things: An Archeology of the Human Sciences*. New York: Vintage, 1994.

Fox, Aaron A. *Real Country: Music and Language in Working-Class Culture*. Durham, NC: Duke University Press, 2004.

Frazer, Nancy. "Rethinking the Public Sphere: A Contribution to the Critique of Actually Existing Democracy." *Social Text* 25/26 (1990): 56–80.

Friedman, Hal M. *Creating an American Lake: United States Imperialism and Strategic Security in the Pacific Basin, 1945–1947*. Westport, CT: Greenwood, 2001.

Geertz, Clifford. *The Interpretation of Cultures*. New York: Basic Books, 1973.

Genz, Joseph H. *Breaking the Shell: Voyaging from Nuclear Refugees to People of the Sea in the Marshall Islands*. Honolulu: University of Hawai'i Press, 2018.

Genz, Joseph H. "Marshallese Navigation and Voyaging: Re-learning and Reviving Indigenous Knowledge of the Ocean." PhD dissertation, University of Hawai'i, 2008.

Genz, Joseph H. "Without Precedent: Shifting Protocols in the Use of Rongelapese Navigational Knowledge." *Journal of the Polynesian Society* 126, no. 2 (2017): 209–32.

Geurts, Kathryn L. *Culture and the Senses: Bodily Ways of Knowing in an African Community*. Berkeley: University of California Press, 2002.

Grande, Sandra. *Red Pedagogy: Native American Social and Political Thought*. Oxford: Rowman & Littlefield, 2004.

Griffiths, Gareth. "The Myth of Authenticity: Representation, Discourse and Social Practice." In *De-Scribing Empire: Post-colonialism and Textuality*, edited by Chris Tiffin and Alan Lawson, 70–85. London: Routledge, 1994.

Grossberg, Lawrence. *Bringing It All Back Home: Essays on Cultural Studies*. Durham, NC: Duke University Press, 1997.

Grossman, Andrew D. *Neither Dead nor Red: Civil Defense and American Political Development during the Early Cold War*. London: Routledge, 2001.

Gusterson, Hugh. *Nuclear Rites: A Weapons Laboratory at the End of the Cold War*. Berkeley: University of California Press, 1998.

Hacker, Barton C. *Elements of Controversy: The Atomic Energy Commission and Radiation Safety in Nuclear Weapons Testing 1947–1974*. Berkeley: University of California Press, 1994.

Hales, Peter. "The Atomic Sublime." *American Studies* 32, no. 1 (1991): 5–31.

Halliwell, Martin. *American Culture in the 1950s*. Edinburgh: Edinburgh University Press, 2007.

Hamilton, Sheryl N., Diana Majury, Dawn Moore, Neil Sargent, and Christiane Wilke, eds. *Sensing Law*. New York: Routledge, 2017.

Hanlon, David L. *Remaking Micronesia: Discourses over Development in a Pacific Territory, 1944–1982*. Honolulu: University of Hawai'i Press, 1998.

Harjo, Joy. *How We Became Human: New and Selected Poems*. New York: W.W. Norton, 2004.

Hartman, Saidiya V. *Scenes of Subjection: Terror, Slavery, and Self-Making in Nineteenth-Century America*. New York: Oxford University Press, 1997.

Hau'ofa, Epeli. "Epilogue." In *Remembrance of Pacific Pasts: An Invitation to Remake History*, edited by Robert Borofsky, 453–72. Honolulu: University of Hawai'i Press, 2000.

Herzig, Rebecca M. *Suffering for Science: Reason and Sacrifice in Modern America*. Piscataway, NJ: Rutgers University Press, 2005.

Hezel, Francis X. *Strangers in Their Own Land: A Century of Colonial Rule in the Caroline and Marshall Islands*. Honolulu: University of Hawai'i Press, 1995.

Hight, Christopher. "Stereo Types: The Operation of Sound in the Production of Racial Identity." *Leonardo* 36, no. 1 (2003): 13–17.

Horowitz, Adam J., dir. *Home on the Range*. Equatorial Films, 1990. VHF, 58 min.

Hydaralli, Saeed. "What Is Noise? An Inquiry into Its Formal Properties." In *Reverberations: The Philosophy, Aesthetics, and Politics of Noise*, edited by Michael Goddard, Benjamin Halligan, and Paul Hegarty, 219–32. London: Continuum International Publishing Group, 2012.

Igarashi, Yoshikuni. *Bodies of Memory: Narratives of War in Postwar Japanese Culture, 1945–1970*. Princeton, NJ: Princeton University Press, 2000.

Ingersoll, Karin A. *Waves of Knowing: A Seascape Epistemology*. Durham, NC: Duke University Press, 2016.

Irving, D. R. M. *Colonial Counterpoint: Music in Early Modern Manila*. New York: Oxford University Press, 2010.

Ishtar, Zohl dé. *Daughters of the Pacific*. North Melbourne, Australia: Spinnex, 1994.

Jackson, Michael. *The Politics of Storytelling: Violence, Transgression, and Intersubjectivity*. Copenhagen: Museum Tusculanum, University of Copenhagen, 2006.

Jacobs, Robert. *The Dragon's Tail: Americans Face the Atomic Age*. Amherst: University of Massachusetts Press, 2010.

Jetñil-Kijiner, Kathy. "Iep Jaltok: A History of Marshallese Literature." Master's portfolio, University of Hawai'i, Manoa, 2014.

Joash, Bernice, Kinuko Kowata, and Donna Stone. *Jabonkonnaan in Majel: Wisdom from the Past: A Collection of Marshallese Proverbs, Wise Sayings and Beliefs*. Majuro, RMI: Alele Museum, Library & National Archives, 2000.

Johnson, Giff. *Collision Course at Kwajalein: Marshall Islanders in the Shadow of the Bomb*. Honolulu: Pacific Concerns Resource Center, 1984.

Johnson, Giff. *Nuclear Past, Unclear Future*. Majuro, RMI: Micronitor, 2009.

Johnson, Giff. "Rongelap Return Could Happen in Near Future." *Rimajol Online*. Last modified March 26, 2012. www.rimajol.com/forums/viewtopic.php?t=5219.

Johnston, Barbara R., and Holly M. Barker. *Consequential Damages of Nuclear War: The Rongelap Report*. Walnut Creek, CA: Left Coast, 2008.

Jolly, Margaret. "Becoming a 'New' Museum? Contesting Oceanic Visions at Musée du Quai Branly." *The Contemporary Pacific*. 23, no. 1 (Spring 2011): 108–39.

Kabua, Jibā. "We Are the Land, the Land Is Us." In *Life in the Republic of the Marshall Islands*, translated by Veronica C. Kiluwe, Maria Kabua Fowler, and Alson Kelen, edited by Anono Lieom Loeak, Veronia Kiluwe, and Linda Crowl, 180–91. Majuro, RMI: University of the South Pacific Centre, 2004.

Kauanui, J. Kēhaulani. "'A Structure, Not an Event': Settler Colonialism and Enduring Indigeneity." *Lateral* 5, no. 1 (2016). https://doi.org/10.25158/L5.1.7.

Kauanui, J. Kēhaulani. *Hawaiian Blood: Colonialism and the Politics of Sovereignty and Indigeneity*. Durham, NC: Duke University Press, 2008.

Kauanui, J. Kēhaulani. *Paradoxes of Hawaiian Sovereignty: Land, Sex, and the Colonial Politics of State Nationalism*. Durham, NC: Duke University Press, 2018.

Keane, Webb. *Christian Moderns: Freedom and Fetish in the Mission Encounter*. Berkeley: University of California Press, 2007.

Keever, Beverly A. D. *News Zero: The New York Times and the Bomb*. Monroe, ME: Common Courage, 2004.

Khanna, Ranjana. "Post-palliative: Coloniality's Affective Dissonance." *Postcolonial Text* 2, no. 1 (2006). Accessed August 20, 2017. www.postcolonial.org/index.php/pct/article/viewArticle/385/815.

Kirsch, Stuart. "Lost Worlds: Environmental Disaster, 'Culture Loss,' and the Law." *Current Anthropology* 42, no. 2 (April 2001): 167–98.

Kiste, Robert C. *The Bikinians: A Study in Forced Migration*. Menlo Park, CA: Cummings, 1974.

Kleinman, Arthur. *The Illness Narratives: Suffering, Healing, and the Human Condition*. New York: Basic Books, 1988.

Kochhar-Lindgren, Kanta. *Hearing Difference: The Third Ear in Experimental, Deaf, and Multicultural Theater*. Washington, DC: Gallaudet University Press, 2006.

Krämer, Augustin, and Hans Nevermann. *Ralik-Ratak (Marshall Islands)*. Hamburg: Friederichsen, De Gruyter, 1983.

Kramer, Paul. "Making Concessions: Race and Empire Revisited at the Philippine Exposition, St. Louis, 1901–1905." *Radical History Review* 73 (Winter 1999): 75–114.

Kunkle, Thomas, and Byron Ristvet. "Castle Bravo: Fifty Years of Legend and Lore, a Guide to Off-Site Radiation Exposures." Kirkland AFB, New Mexico, Defense Threat Reduction Information Analysis Center, January 2013.

Kunreuther, Laura. *Voicing Subjects: Public Intimacy and Mediation in Kathmandu*. Berkeley: University of California Press, 2014.

Kupferman, David W. *Disassembling and Decolonizing Schools in the Pacific: A Genealogy from Micronesia*. Contemporary Philosophies and Theories in Education 5. New York: Springer, 2013.

Kupferman, David W. "Republic of the Marshall Islands since 1990." *Journal of Pacific History* 46 (2011): 75–88.

LaBriola, Monica. "Iien Ippān Doon: This Time Together." In *Indigenous Encounters: Reflections on Relations between People in the Pacific*, edited by Katerina M. Teaiwa, 30–50. Honolulu: Center for Pacific Islands Studies, School of Hawaiian, Asian, and Pacific Studies, University of Hawai'i at Manoa, 2007.

Lacey, Kate. *Listening Publics: The Politics and Experience of Listening in the Media Age*. Cambridge: Polity, 2013.

Latour, Bruno. "Whose Cosmos, Which Cosmopolitics? Comments on the Peace of Terms of Ulrich Beck." *Common Knowledge* 10, no. 3 (Fall 2004): 450–62.

Lawson Burke, Mary E. "Marshall Islands." *The Garland Encyclopedia of World Music*. Vol. 9, *Australia and the Pacific Islands*, edited by Adrienne L. Kaeppler and J. W. Love. New York: Garland, 1998.

Lee, Yu Jung. "From GI Sweethearts to Lock and Lollers: The Kim Sisters' Performances in the Early Cold War United States, 1959–67." *Journal of Asian American Studies* 20, no. 3 (October 2017): 405–30.

Lippit, Akira M. *Atomic Light (Shadow Optics)*. Minneapolis: University of Minnesota Press, 2005.

Loeak, Anono L., and Marie Maddison. "Women's Organizations." In *Life in the Republic of the Marshall Islands*, translated by Veronica C. Kiluwe, Maria Kabua Fowler, and Alson Kelen, edited by Anono Lieom Loeak, Veronia Kiluwe, and Linda Crowl, 82–95. Majuro, RMI: University of the South Pacific Centre, 2004.

Lowe, Lisa. *The Intimacies of Four Continents*. Durham, NC: Duke University Press, 2015.

Ludueña Romandini, Fabián. *La Comunidad de los Espectros I: Antropotecnia*. Buenos Aires, Argentina: Miño y Dávila Editores, 2010.

Lummis, Douglas. "Genshitekina nikkō no nakadeno hinatabokko." Shisō no kagaku 17, no. 3 (June 1981): 16–20.

Maddison, Benetick K. "Oral Histories of the Marshallese Diaspora: Translation as Cultural Conversation." Paper presented at the annual meeting of the Pacific Coast Branch of the American Historical Association, Sacramento, CA, August 6–8, 2015.

Mahmood, Saba. *Politics of Piety: The Islamic Revival and the Feminist Subject*. Princeton, NJ: Princeton University Press, 2005.

Maier, Thomas, and John Paraskevas, dir. *Fallout: Brookhaven National Lab's Legacy in the Pacific*. New York: Newsday, 2009. www.youtube.com/watch?v=M54ZXHfvIbY.

Makhijani, Arjun, Brice Smith, and Michael C. Thorne. "Healthy from the Start: Building a Better Basis for Environmental Health Standards—Starting with Radiation." *Science for Democratic Action* 38, 14, no. 4 (February 2007). http://www.ieer.org/sdafiles/14.4.pdf.

Malkki, Liisa H. *Purity and Exile: Violence, Memory, and National Cosmology among Hutu Refugees in Tanzania*. Chicago: University of Chicago Press, 1995.

Manning, Toby. *John le Carré and the Cold War*. London: Bloomsbury, 2018.

Masco, Joseph. "Engineering the Future as Nuclear Ruins." In *Imperial Debris: On Ruins and Ruination*, edited by Ann L. Stoler, 252–86. Durham, NC: Duke University Press, 2013.

Masco, Joseph. *The Theater of Operations: National Security Affect from the Cold War to the War on Terror*. Durham, NC: Duke University Press, 2014.

Massumi, Brian. *Politics of Affect*. Cambridge: Polity Press, 2015.

Matsuda, Matt K. "AHR Forum, the Pacific." *American Historical Review* 111, no. 3 (June 2006): 758–80.

Maynard, Kent, ed. *Medical Identities: Healing, Well-Being and Personhood*. New York: Berghahn Books, 2007.

McArthur, Phillip H. "Narrative, Cosmos, and Nation: Intertextuality and Power in the Marshall Islands." *Journal of American Folklore* 117 (2004): 55–80.

Meintjes, Louise. *Dust of the Zulu: Ngoma Aesthetics after Apartheid*. Durham, NC: Duke University Press, 2017.

Morris, David B. "About Suffering: Voice, Genre, and Moral Community." *Daedalus* 125, no. 1 (1996): 25–45.

Muñoz, José E. *Disidentifications: Queers of Color and the Performance of Politics*. Minneapolis: University of Minneapolis Press, 1999.

Nelson, Dana D. *National Manhood: Capitalist Citizenship and the Imagined Fraternity of White Men*. Durham, NC: Duke University Press, 1998.

Niedenthal, Jack. "Bikini History." *Bikini Atoll Online*. www.bikiniatoll.com/history.html.

Niedenthal, Jack. "Bikinian Demographics." *Bikini Atoll Online*. http://bikiniatoll.com.

Niedenthal, Jack. *For the Good of Mankind: A History of the People of Bikini and Their Islands*. Majuro, RMI: Micronitor/Bravo, 2001.

Nixon, Rob. *Slow Violence and the Environmentalism of the Poor*. Cambridge, MA: Harvard University Press, 2013.

Oakes, Guy. *The Imaginary War: Civil Defense and American Cold War Culture*. New York: Oxford University Press, 1994.

O'Brien, Patty. *The Pacific Muse: Exotic Femininity and the Colonial Pacific*. Seattle: University of Washington Press, 2006.

Ochoa Gautier, Ana María. *Aurality: Listening and Knowledge in Nineteenth-Century Colombia*. Durham, NC: Duke University Press, 2014.

Okney, Philip A. "Legacies and Perils from the Perspective of the Republic of the Marshall Islands Nuclear Claims Tribunal." In *The Oceans in the Nuclear Age: Legacies and Risks*, edited by David D. Caron and Harry N. Scheiber, 49–67. Leiden, Netherlands: Brill, 2009.

Old Time Radio Catalog. Accessed July 22, 2017. www.otrcat.com/melody-roundup-p-1604.html.

Ostherr, Kirsten. *Cinematic Prophylaxis: Globalization and Contagion in the Discourse of World Health*. Durham, NC: Duke University Press, 2005.

"Our New Military Wards, the Marshalls." *National Geographic*, September 1945, 334.

Panel on the Human Effects of Nuclear Weapons Development. *Human Effects of Nuclear Weapons Development*. A Report to the President and the National Security Council. Washington, DC: Federal Civil Defense Administration, 1956.

Parker, James E. K. *Acoustic Jurisprudence: Listening to the Trial of Simon Bikindi*. Oxford: Oxford University Press, 2015.

Petryna, Adriana. *Life Exposed: Biological Citizens after Chernobyl*. Princeton, NJ: Princeton University Press, 2013.

Povinelli, Elizabeth A. *Economies of Abandonment: Social Belonging and Endurance in Late Liberalism*. Durham, NC: Duke University Press, 2011.

"Radiation and Your Health." US Centers for Disease Control and Prevention. Updated April 4, 2018. www.cdc.gov/nceh/radiation/emergencies/breastfeeding.htm.

Radstone, Susannah, and Bill Schwarz. *Memory: Histories, Theories, Debates*. New York: Fordham University Press, 2010.

Ragan, Philip, prod. *One World or None*. National Committee for Atomic Information, 1946. www.filmpreservation.org/preserved-films/screening-room/one-world-or-none-1946.

Rameau, Jean-Philippe. *Treatise on Harmony, Reduced to Its Natural Principles, Divided into Four Books*. 1772. Translated by Philip Gossett. Mineola, NY: Dover, 1971.

Rancière, Jacques. *Disagreement*. Translated by Julie Rose. Minneapolis: University of Minnesota Press, 1999.

Rancière, Jacques. *Dissensus: On Politics and Aesthetics*. Edited by Steven Corcoran. London: Continuum, 2010.

Rancière, Jacques. *The Future of the Image*. Translated by Gregory Elliott. London: Verso, 2007.

Rancière, Jacques. *The Politics of Aesthetics: The Distribution of the Sensible*. Translated by Gabriel Rockhill. London: Continuum, 2004.

"Reducing Environmental Cancer Risk: What We Can Do Now." US Department of Health and Human Services, National Institutes of Health, National Cancer Institute. April 2010.

Reed, Oliver. "Operation Crossroads." *Radio News*, September 1946, 32.

"Republic of the Marshall Islands Changed Circumstances Petition to Congress, May 16, 2005." CRS Report for Congress. Accessed September 1, 2017. https://fas.org/sgp/crs/row/RL32811.pdf.

Rifkin, Mark. *Beyond Settler Time: Temporal Sovereignty and Indigenous Self-Determination*. Durham, NC: Duke University Press, 2017.

Robbins, Jacob, and William H. Adams. *Radiation Effects in the Marshall Islands*. Edited by S. Nagasaki. Amsterdam: Excerpta Medica, 1989.

Robbins, Joel. *Becoming Sinners: Christianity and Moral Torment in a Papua New Guinea Society*. Berkeley: University of California Press, 2004.

Robie, David. "Operation Exodus." *Spasifik*. No date. Excerpt uploaded to www.academia.edu/14999943/Operation_Exodus.

Rowberry, Ariana. "Castle Bravo: The Largest U.S. Nuclear Explosion." *Brookings*, February 27, 2014. www.brookings.edu/blog/up-front/2014/02/27/castle-bravo-the-largest-u-s-nuclear-explosion.

Rubinson, Paul. *Redefining Science: Scientists, the National Security State, and Nuclear Weapons in Cold War America*. Amherst: University of Massachusetts Press, 2016.

Rudiak-Gould, Peter. "Being Marshallese and Christian: A Case of Multiple Contradictory Beliefs." *Culture and Religion* 11, no. 1 (March 2010). http://dx.doi.org/10.1080/14755610903528853.

Rudiak-Gould, Peter. "The Fallen Palm: Climate Change and Culture Change in the Marshall Islands." Master's thesis, Oxford University, 2009.

Runyan, Anne S., Amy Lind, Patricia McDermott, and Marianne H. Marchand, eds. *Feminist (Im)Mobilities in Fortress(ing) North America*. Oxford: Ashgate, 2013.

Sahlins, Marshall. "Notes on the Original Affluent Society." In *Man the Hunter: The First Intensive Survey of a Single, Crucial Stage of Human Development—Man's Once Universal Hunting Way of Life*, edited by Richard B. Lee and Irven DeVore, 85–89. Chicago: Aldine, 1968.

Sakai, Naoki. "On Romantic Love and Military Violence: Transpacific Imperialism and U.S.–Japan Complicity." In *Militarized Currents: Toward a Decolonized Future in Asia and the Pacific*, edited by Setsu Shigematsu and Keith L. Camacho, 205–21. Minneapolis: University of Minnesota Press, 2010.

Schumpeter, Joseph A. *Capitalism, Socialism, and Democracy*. 3rd ed. New York: HarperCollins, 2008.

Schwartz, Jessica A. "Between Death and Life." *Women and Music* 16 (2012): 23–56.

Schwartz, Jessica A. "Marshallese Cultural Diplomacy in Arkansas." *American Quarterly* 67, no. 3 (September 2015): 781–812.

Schwartz, Jessica A. "A 'Voice Sing': Rongelapese Musical Activism and the Production of Nuclear Knowledge." *Music & Politics* 6, no. 1 (Winter 2012): 1–21.

Schwartz, Jessica A. "'The Young Ladies Are Here': Marshallese Transgender Performance and Processes of Transformation." *Women and Music*, 19 (2015): 95–107.

Seremetakis, C. Nadia, ed. *The Senses Still*. Chicago: University of Chicago Press, 1994.

Seremetakis, C. Nadia. *Sensing the Everyday: Dialogues from Austerity Greece*. New York: Routledge, 2019.

Serres, Michel. *Genesis*. Translated by Geneviève James and James Nielson. Ann Arbor: The University of Michigan Press, 1995.

Smith, Andrea. "Indigenous Feminism Without Apology." In *Unsettling Ourselves: Reflections and Resources for Deconstructing Colonial Mentality, a Sourcebook Compiled by the Unsettling Minnesota Collective*, 2009. https://unsettlingminnesota.files.wordpress.com/2009/11/unsettling-minnesota-sourcebook1pointo.pdf.

Smith, Linda Tuhiwai. *Decolonizing Methodologies: Research and Indigenous Peoples*. London: Zed Books, 1999.

Stauffer, Jill. *Ethical Loneliness: The Injustice of Not Being Heard*. New York: Columbia University Press, 2015.

Stege, Kristina E. "'An Kōrā Aelōñ Kein' (These Islands Belong to the Women): A Study of Women and Land in the Republic of the Marshall Islands." In *Land and Women: The Matrilineal Factor: The Cases of the Republic of the Marshall Islands, Solomon Islands and Vanuatu*, edited by Elise Huffer, 1–34. Pacific Islands Forum Secretariat, 2008.

Steingo, Gavin. *Kwaito's Promise: Music and the Aesthetics of Freedom in South Africa*. Chicago: University of Chicago Press, 2016.

Sterne, Johnathan. *The Audible Past: Cultural Origins of Sound Reproduction*. Durham, NC: Duke University Press, 2003.

Stoler, Ana L. *Imperial Debris: On Ruins and Ruination.* Durham, NC: Duke University Press, 2013.

Stoller, Paul. "'Conscious' Ain't Consciousness: Entering the 'Museum of Sensory Absence.'" In *The Senses Still*, edited by C. Nadia Seremetakis, 109–23. Chicago: University of Chicago Press, 1994.

Stone, Robert, dir. *Radio Bikini.* 1988; New York City: IFC Films, 1998. DVD.

Stras, Laurie. "The Organ of the Soul: Voice, Damage, and Affect." In *Sounding Off: Theorizing Disability in Music*, edited by Neil Learner and Joseph N. Straus, 173–84. New York: Routledge, 2006.

Taafaki, Irene J., Maria K. Fowler, and Randolph R. Thaman. *Traditional Medicine of the Marshallese Islands: The Women, the Plants, the Treatments.* Suva, Fiji: IPS, University of the South Pacific, 2006.

"Tattooing in the Marshall Islands: The Tattoo Motifs." *Marshalls: Digital Micronesia*, http://marshall.csu.edu.au/Marshalls/html/tattoo/t-motifs-test.html.

Taussig, Michael. *Defacement: Public Secrecy and the Labor of the Negative.* Stanford, CA: Stanford University Press, 1999.

Taylor, Charles. *Modern Social Imaginaries.* Durham, NC: Duke University Press, 2004.

Taylor, Jessica. "Speaking Shadows: A History of the Voice in the Transition from the Silent to Sound Film in the United States." *Journal of Linguistic Anthropology* 19, no. 1 (2009): 1–20.

Teaiwa, Katerina M. "Saltwater Feet: The Flow of Dance in Oceania." In *Deep Blue: Critical Reflections on Nature, Religion, and Water*, edited by Sylvie Shaw and Andrew Francis, 107–25. London: Routledge, 2014.

Teaiwa, Teresia K. "Microwomen: U.S. Colonialism and Micronesian Women Activists." In *Pacific History: Papers from the 8th Pacific History Association Conference*, edited by D. H. Rubenstein, 125–41. Mangilao: University of Guam and Micronesian Area Research Center.

Teaiwa, Teresia K. "Solidarity and Fuidarity: Feminism as Product and Productive Force for Regionalism in the Pacific." Paper presented at the Gender, Globalization, and Militarism Conference, University of Hawai'i at Manoa, Honolulu, Hawai'i, February 4, 2005.

"Thyroid Surgery." American Thyroid Association. Modified 2012. www.thyroid.org/patients/brochures/ThyroidSurgery.pdf.

Tobin, Jack. *Stories from the Marshall Islands: Bwebwenato Jān Aelōñ Kein.* Honolulu: University of Hawai'i Press, 2002.

Todeschini, Maya. "The Bomb's Womb?" In *Remaking a World: Violence, Social Suffering, and Recovery*, edited by Veena Das, Arthur Kleinman, and Margaret Lock, 102–54. Berkeley: University of California Press, 2001.

Topping, Donald. "Review of U.S. Language Policy in the TTPI." In *History of the Trust Territory of the Pacific Islands: Proceedings of the Ninth Annual Pacific Islands Conference*, edited by Karen Knudsen, 105–32. Working Paper Series. Honolulu, Hawai'i: Pacific Islands Studies Program, Center for Asian and Pacific Studies, University of Hawai'i at Manoa, 1985.

Tsing, Anna L. *Friction: An Ethnography of Global Connection.* Princeton, NJ: Princeton University Press, 2005.

"2015 Investment Climate Statement—Marshall Islands." US Department of State, Bureau of Economic and Business Affairs. May 2015. www.state.gov/e/eb/rls/othr/ics/2015/241655.htm.

United Nations. *Charter of the United Nations.* Accessed October 19, 2019. www.un.org/en/sections/un-charter/chapter-i/index.html.

Unsettling Minnesota Collective, eds. *Unsettling Ourselves: Reflections and Resources for Deconstructing Colonial Mentality.* 2010. https://unsettlingminnesota.files.wordpress.com/2009/11/um_sourcebook_jan10_revision.pdf.

Walsh, Julianne. "Imagining the Marshalls: Chiefs, Tradition, and the State on the Fringes of U.S. Empire." PhD dissertation, University of Hawai'i, 2003.

Warner, Michael. *Publics and Counterpublics.* Brooklyn, NY: Zone, 2002.

Weber, Max. *Politics as Vocation.* Philadelphia: Fortress, 1965.

Weidman, Amanda. *Singing the Classical, Voicing the Modern: The Postcolonial Politics of Music in South India.* Durham, NC: Duke University Press, 2006.

Weiner, Annette B. *Inalienable Possessions: The Paradox of Keeping-While-Giving.* Berkeley: University of California Press, 1992.

Weisgall, Jonathan. *Operation Crossroads: The Atomic Tests at Bikini Atoll.* Annapolis, MD: Naval Institute Press, 1994.

White, James J. "Juda vs. the United States." *American University International Law Review* 4/3, no. 6 (1998): 665.

Wieser, Kimberly G. *Back to the Blanket: Recovered Rhetorics and Literacies in American Indian Studies.* Norman: University of Oklahoma Press, 2017.

Winkler, Allan. *Life under a Cloud: American Anxiety about the Atom.* New York: Oxford University Press, 1993.

Wolfe, Patrick. "Settler Colonialism and the Elimination of the Native." *Journal of Genocide Research* 8, no. 4 (December 2006): 387–409.

Wolfe, Patrick. *Settler Colonialism and the Transformation of Anthropology: The Politics and Poetics of an Ethnographic Event.* New York: Cassell, 1999.

Yoneyama, Lisa. *Cold War Ruins: Transpacific Critique of American Justice and Japanese War Crimes.* Durham, NC: Duke University Press, 2016.

INDEX

Abon, Tarines, 69, 118
ACHRE. *See* Advisory Committee on Human Radiation Experiments
acoustic assemblages, 218
Advisory Committee on Human Radiation Experiments (ACHRE), 88
Aelōñ Kein Ad Party, 79–80
aenōṃṃan, 188
Aerokojlil, 164
affective alliance, 13–14, 36, 56, 80, 109–10, 125, 154, 160, 166, 173, 176, 198, 217
affective break, 118
Ahmed, Sara, 167–68
Aillingnae Atoll, 104, 114
Ailuk, 2, 59–60, 118
ainikien, 36
Aitab, Jamore, 193
aje drum, 111–12
ājmour, 31, 34, 250
Aleppo, Denis, 184
al im bwebwenato, 248
al in kamōlo, 117, 225, 227, 239. *See also* "Bōk mejam" (song)
al in keememej, 105, 118
al in mur, 190
American Armed Forces Radio, 52–53
ami, 239
ane-buoj, 243
anemkwōj, 208, 211–12, 214, 220–21, 227, 231, 239
Anjain, John, 71, 76, 103
Anjain-Maddison, Abacca, 69, 83–85, 87, 102, 118
Anjua, 234
apophatic listening, 38
Aquila, Richard, 3

Arkansas, 143, 177, 203
arrowroot, 190–91
Associated Press, 164
atollscape epistemology, 36
atoll umbilicals, 34, 36, 112, 136, 221
Atomic Age diplomacy, 9, 52–57, 134–37
Atomic Energy Act, 22, 54–55
Atomic Energy Commission, 55, 73, 165
atomic scare film, 10
atomic sublime, 20
Attali, Jacques, 138, 172
authenticity, 180

"Bad Moon Rising" (song), 42
Balos, Ataji, 232
Barker, Holly, 58–60, 115
baseball, 146
Batkan Village, 89
"Battle of Jepta Concert," 203
Baxi, Upendra, 17
Beatles, the, 247
Benjamin, Percy, 160, 181–82, 204, 215
Benjamin, Walter, 27
Betty, 125–26
Bikinians: as "America's children," 141, 206; Bikinian youth, 156, 159–60, 165; Bikini Atoll as the center of the world, 193–94; Bikini Day and, 158; canoes and, 164, 166; church and, 180–82, 207; deterioration of Bikinian communication systems, 164; displacement of, 4, 54–55, 131, 161, 179, 181, 201; essentialized traits of, 167; flag of, 144–45; formation of the Bikinian nation, 135, 143–45; Gospel Day celebrations and, 174–76, 198–204; governance and, 143; how other

Bikinians (continued)
    Marshallese see, 176; on Kwajalein Atoll, 55; lagoon of Bikini Atoll, 174, 195–96, 202; manly spirit, Wōdjapto, 172–73, 185–87, 190–97, 209; moralization of displacement, 167–68, 205; moralized restaging of nuclear relationship, 136, 173, 182, 208–10; MORIBA and, 132–36, 144–46, 157, 159–60, 162, 197, 199, 202; move towards modernization and masculine character of United States, 56; national anthem of, 147–49, 155–56, 158–61, 165, 167–69; navigational school and, 184; opposition to COFA, 77, 135, 143; power of the sovereign and, 136; relocated to Kili Island, 55–56, 156, 164–65, 171; relocate to/ life on Ejit Island, 77, 138–39, 146, 181; relocate to Rongerik, 132, 166; resettle Bikini Island before they are again evacuated, 76–77, 165; restaging of the historic scene and, 53–54, 131–33; on Rongerik, 54–55, 148; second anthem of, 161–63, 183; self-determination and, 172–73, 205; sing with traits of the lōrro̧ and būromōj, 150; situation as beyond slavery, 142; spirited sharing through noisiness, 205, 209–10; as third class citizens, 141, 176, 178; using singing for political engagement and to activate memories of Bikini, 148–49, 161, 166; voice-crossing and, 141–43. See also "I jab pād mol, aet I jab"; Juda, King; Marshall Islands; mythico-history; "Ñe ij keememej tok aelōñ eo aō" (song); Wōdjapto
"Bikini Atoll" (song), 81
"Bikini Jake Jebōl Eo" (song), 190–92, 204
"Bikini Spirit of Sharing." See "Bikini Jake Jebōl Eo" (song)
Bingaman, Jeff, 62
bioethics, 88
biological citizenship, 44
biological determinism, 137
Bloch, Ernst, 27

Bloechl, Olivia, 14
Blok, Anders, 38
Bobo, Aruko, 2
Bōk in Al kab Tun Ko nan Ri Aelōn in Marshall, 180
"Bōk mejam" (song), 211–17, 219, 222, 225–27, 230–32, 236–40. *See also* al in kamōlo; bomb songs; Kwajalein
Bokonijien, 164
bomb songs, 3, 21, 27, 50–52, 59, 62–63. *See also* "Bōk mejam" (song); "Ioon, ioon miadi kan"; 'Kōm̧m̧an Baam̧' (nursery rhyme); radiation songs, Marshallese; singing; throat, the
Bond, Victor, 93–94
Book of Songs with Tunes for the Marshallese People, The, 180
bōro wot juōn, 30, 32, 94, 103, 111, 126. *See also* throat, the
boundary silences, 138
Braun, Sebastian F., 45
Bravo, 1–2, 18, 57, 98–99, 116, 164, 184, 222, 253n8. *See also* Marshall Islands; radiation
Bravo for the Marshallese (Barker), 69
breaks, 27–28, 46, 82, 91, 110, 118, 160. *See also* cry break; harmonic breaks
breastfeeding, 96
Būkien Likajeer, 248
būromōj, 143, 149–50, 152, 157, 238, 250. *See also* lōrro̧
bwij, 34, 221
bwijen, 34, 189, 221

cancer, 97, 139, 165. *See also* radiation; thyroid
canoes, 164, 166, 184–85, 188
Capelle, Alfred, 247–50
Cape Ms. Turn-Around, 248
capitalism, 137, 157
Carucci, Laurence, 205
cash economy, 242–43
"CCP." *See* "Compact II" (song)
censorship, 22, 211

INDEX

Chakrabarty, Dipesh, 14
Changed Circumstances Petition, 15–16, 42, 79, 108, 115. *See also* Compact of Free Association
chant. *See* roro
Christianity, 53, 79, 131, 136, 172, 174–76, 183. *See also* church; Gospel Day
church, 54, 171–72, 178, 180–82, 188, 198. *See also* Christianity
classification, 127, 130
COFA. *see* Compact of Free Association
Cognard-Black, Jennifer, 95
cold war, 9–10
collective memory, 105, 134, 158, 162, 164, 197, 237–38
College of the Marshall Islands Nuclear Institute, 115
colonialism, 6–8, 24, 32, 137. *See also* European colonization; United States
colonial savagery, 198
"Come Together, Right Now, Over Me," (Beatles, the), 247
communication, 178
communication systems, 164
"Compact II" (song), 41, 48
Compact of Free Association: Bikinians opposition to, 77, 135; COFA-based affective alliance, 37; COFA II, 16, 42, 79–80, 108; Kwajalein residents not included in Section 177 of, 222; Marshall Islands voice and votes constrained by, 16; US avoidance of accountability through, 15, 43–44; use of COFA funds, 78. *See also* Changed Circumstances Petition; Section 177; United States
Compaj, Yostimi, 1, 64
Conard, Robert A., 102, 112
Connor, Steven, 156
cosmology, 32–33
Coulthard, Glen, 36
country music, 120, 146, 154
courts, 234–35
creative destruction, 21
Credence Clearwater Revival, 42

Crew Cuts, 3
Cronkite, Eugene, 57, 67, 93–94
cry break, 154, 156–57, 159, 172, 237–38. *See also* breaks
crying, 157, 160
currency, 26, 137, 155
currents, 162–63, 183, 188, 238

dance, 112, 114
Darwin, Charles, 194
data sovereignty, 126
deBrum, Tony, 42, 51–52, 59–61, 216–17, 221, 226, 231
declassification, 114–15, 127
decolonial dissonance, 24, 127, 162, 194, 208, 220, 225, 239, 242, 247
decolonial musical appreciation, 218
decolonization, 44–45
Decolonizing Methodologies, research (Smith), 22
defamiliarization, 29
DeLoughrey, Elizabeth, 35
democracy, 14, 38, 46, 48, 116, 127, 137–38, 220, 251. *See also* liberalism; United States
Department of Energy, 4, 74, 85
Department of Homeland Security, 21
depression, 155
Derrida, Jacques, 117
desire, 192
Dessouky, Dina El, 37–38
developmental democracy, 14–15, 44
developmental dependencies, 129
diabetes, 65
dilep, 162
discontinuity, 27
disenchantment, 179
disgust, 152
disidentification, 31, 39, 159–60
dissensus, 25, 31, 174
dissonant refusals, 138
distribution of the sensible, 18
divide and rule principle, 7
Dobson, Andrew, 38, 138

domestic violence, 49–50, 79
Donne, John, 170
doo-wop, 2
double play. *See* tabōḷ pile
drum, 111–12, 185, 190, 249, 262n38
Dvorak, Gregory, 52, 212, 219, 235

Ebeye Island, 215, 218, 223, 228–30. *See also* Kwajalein
Ebjā, 228
Ebon Atoll, 175
ecosystem science, 194
Edmond, Rod, 20
Ed Sullivan Show, 3
education, 179, 184–85, 188, 229
Eisenhower, Dwight, 228
Ejit Elementary, 185
Ejit Island, 58, 77, 138, 144, 164, 180
Elbōn, 46
Elbōn, Antri, 46–47, 78
"Elōñ ro rej dike doon kōn men ṇe mani" (song), 241–43
emakūt, 47–48, 161–62
eminent domain, 232, 237
"Emukat Eo Aō" (skit), 128
English, 229
Enlightenment, 11, 137
Enmat, 243
Enos, Eddie, 241–43
equivocality, 34–35, 110, 159, 178, 220
Erdland, August, 150–51
erub, 26–27, 29, 118
"ERUB" (song), 82
erub epistemology, 29
erūp. *See* ERUB
ethical loneliness, 62
European colonization, 6–7, 11, 137–38, 219–20, 254n22. *See also* colonialism; Germans; nuclear colonialism

Federal Civil Defense Administration, 21. *See also* radio; radioactive citizenship
fetishization, 167–68
Fifth Amendment, 44, 77

flowers, 225–26, 236
fluidarity, 7
food, 67, 155, 158, 160–61, 165–66, 190–91
"Forever Marshall Islands" (anthem), 78
forgiveness, 135
Four Atolls, 118–19
Fox, Aaron, 126, 167
freedom. *See* anemkwōj

"Gallon ioon deck" (song), 236
"Gallon on deck" (song), 236
Gautier, Ana María Ochoa, 13, 34, 218
Geiger counter, 64–66, 71, 100–101
gender: gendered imaginaries of protection, 192–97; gendering of American vocational growth from nuclear experiments, 68–69; gendering of desire, 192; gendering of nuclear colonizing processes, 7; gendering of singing role assignments, 12, 95; Gospel Warriors and, 177; RMI and its productions are engendered male, 187; transformation of gender roles when men take care of family in context of scarcity, 166; voice as guidance in differently gendered spaces, 89; voice-crossing and, 141. *See also* matrilineal; women
Genz, Joseph, 162
Germans, 225, 234. *See also* European colonization
Geurts, Kathryn, 28
global harmony: certain representations of moralized order and, 205–6; as a metaphor for the organized modern system, 25; mitigates violences it effaces, 127; partitioning of the collective through, 13, 18; resistance to, 10–11, 38–39, 138, 251; US Atomic Age diplomacy promising, 9–10, 135. *See also* United States
Gospel, 112, 114, 193, 205–6
Gospel Day, 174–77, 198–204. *See also* Christianity; Marshall Islands
Gospel warriors, 174, 176
Graham, Bill, 103

INDEX

Greenpeace, 98
Griffiths, Gareth, 177

Hales, Peter, 20
Harjo, Joy, 35
harmonic breaks, 27–28, 91. *See also* breaks
harmonic universalism, 11
Hau'ofa, Epeli, 26
health, 31
heart, the, 88, 129
Herzig, Rebecca M., 22–23
Hobbes, Thomas, 137
Hollywood, 132
homecoming songs, 214, 219–20, 222. *See also* singing
homeland, 217
House, R. A., 60
humanitarian aid, 169
hymns, 11, 54, 180, 191–92, 208
hypervigilant ear. *See* nuclear listening

iakwe, 247
"Iakwe Anik" (song), 117, 119, 122
"I jab pād mol, aet I jab," 147–49, 155–56, 158–61, 165, 167–69. *See also* Bikinians
"Ij Iokwe Ļok Aelōñ Eo Aō, Ijo Iaar Ļotak Ie" (song), 78
Iju in Eañ, 89, 111, 125
"I love My Islands, Where I Was Born." *See* "Ij Iokwe Ļok Aelōñ Eo Aō, Ijo Iaar Ļotak Ie" (song)
"I'm Sitting on Green Leaves" (song), 156
Indigenous people: denial of personhood and rights for Indigenous people, 23–24; detour via disidentification of, 159; dispossession of, 157; education and, 184–85, 188; "Indigenous voice" as genre, 232; interconnected epistemologies and, 179; knowledge of oceanic connectivity and, 36, 189–90; land of, as central to Indigenous struggles for justice, 35–36; Marshallese values and, 25–26; militarized violence against maternal landscapes important to, 250;

nuclear silences and, 23; sounding and, 111, 247; sovereignty and, 135. *See also* Marshall Islands; MORIBA
individualism, 97, 116, 138, 239. *See also* United States
informed consent, 127
Ingersoll, Karin, 36, 188
interdependence, 208, 211
"Ioon, ioon miadi kan," 50–52, 149, 235–36, 240. *See also* bomb songs; war songs
iroij, 111
Island Rhythm, 81
isolation, 110, 194

jabokonnan, 146, 228
jab rup e, 199
Japan, 6, 51, 176
Jebro, 33, 185, 190, 202, 205
jebwa, 111
jepta, 203
"Jerusalem" (song), 182
Jesus, 206
Jibas, Peterson, 189, 191–92
jiku, 112, 114
"Jined ilo Kobo, Leej man juri!" (song), 49
Jitdam Kapeel, 188
Joel, Korent, 184
Johnson, Andrew, 45
Johnson, Bourn, 165–66
Johnson, Giff, 115
Johnson, Hinton, 146
Johnson, Johnny, 147–49, 158, 168–69, 192–97
Johnston, Barbara, 58–59
jojolāār, 121, 140–41
jowi, 34
Juda, King, 54, 131–33, 159, 165, 178, 202. *See also* Bikinians
Juda, Tomaki, 165, 181–82
"Juon jotiinin" (song), 105–8. *See also* radiation songs, Marshallese

K (name), 81
Kabua, Iroij Imata, 42, 45, 78–79, 131–32, 234
Kabua, Jibā, 184

"Kajjitok in Aō Nan Kew Kiio" (song), 4, 19, 85–87, 91, 122–23, 125
Kauanui, Kēhaulani J., 24
Keane, Webb, 208
Kebenli, Norio, 92
Keju, Darlene, 115
Kelen, Alson, 156, 184–85, 188, 191
Kendall, Wilfred, 35–36
Kennedy, John F., 45, 229
Kessibuki, Lore, 147–48, 153–55, 158
Keyes, Jimmy, 2
Kili Excess, 156, 189–90
Kili Island, 55–56, 164, 170–71, 205
Kilma, Alkinta, 42
kinaḷnaḷ, 63–64
King Juda. *See* Juda, King
Kirsch, Stuart, 27
"Koj lum bok at" (song), 233. *See also* war songs
'Kōṃṃan Baaṃ' (nursery rhyme), 59–63. *See also* bomb songs
Krämer, Augustin, 112
Kuli, Tokran, 242–43
Kunreuther, Laura, 46
Kūrijmōj, 172, 190, 203
Kwajalein: American Armed Forces Radio on, 53; Bikinians relocated to, 55; Bravo affected communities relocated to, 2; as center stage for nuclear diaspora, 221, 228; displacement of, 4; occupy the islands in opposition to missile testing, 233–34; ongoing US military weapons testing at, 222, 224, 228; Operation Homecoming, 230, 232, 239; relationship between United States and Kwajalein deteriorated in the postwar, 222, 227–30; shift to masculine space, 212, 222, 227–28, 235; in World War II, 227. *See also* "Bōk mejam" (song); Ebeye Island; Operation Homecoming
Kwajalein Atoll Cooperation, 80

Laabo, Leroij, 50–51, 149, 235–36
Labaañ, 216, 226

labor of the negative, 129, 156
Lacey, Kate, 56
Laelang, Walter, 76
Lainer, 193
land, 35–36, 57, 101, 111, 162, 192–94
Langinbelik, Rokko, 83
Lañinbit, 193
Larkelonñ, 193
law, the, 219
leej man juri, 220
Lemeyo, 89, 126
L'Etao, 33
Leviathan (Hobbes), 137
Libarwāto, 249
liberalism, 116, 137, 160, 251. *See also* democracy; modernity; United States
liberation myth, 134, 175, 226, 231
Lijenbwe, 33
Lijon, 85, 103–10, 112, 114, 122–23, 125
Likiep, 2, 59–61, 118
Limejokedad, 33
Listening Publics (Lacey), 56
Loeak, Anjua, 234–35
logic of elimination, 24
Lōktañūr, 33, 185
longue durée, 168
"LoRauut" (song), 69–70
lōrrọ, 143, 149–54, 156–57, 167–68, 181, 194, 250. *See also* būromōj
"Losing Bikini." *See* "Luuji Bikini" (song)
"Love to God/Hello God." *See* "Iakwe Anik" (song)
Lowe, Lisa, 14, 135
"Luuji Bikini" (song), 189–90

MacDonald, Lijon. *See* Lijon
Maddison, Josepha, 224
Majuro Atoll, 41, 89, 143
'Making Bombs.' *See* 'Kōṃṃan Baaṃ'
Mark 14:2, 206
Marshall Islands, 49–50; ability to be a free or independent nation, 16; adapt American working-class sensibilities, 146, 154; American and Marshallese postwar

positionality, 52–53, 226; American missionaries in, 11–12, 53, 95, 112, 172, 177; Americans' version of freedom impeded interconnectedness of, 239; Christian gender assignments take hold in, 12; Christianity in, 175–76, 183–84; constrained by COFA, 16; demands for United States to compensate, 15–16, 44, 49, 61–62; dependence on United States, 56, 67, 76, 139, 191; domestic violence in, 49; education in, 179, 184, 229; formation of the sovereign, 45–48; and how other Marshallese view Bikinians, 176; little value Americans have for lives of Marshallese, 64; Marshallese belief that United States intentionally exposed them to radiation for research, 67–68, 72; Marshallese concepts of historical space-time, 34; Marshallese cosmology, 32–33; Marshallese decolonial movement and radiation, 80; Marshallese indigenous values, 25–26; Marshallese petition the UN to ban US testing of nuclear weapons on the, 57–58; Marshallese population affected by Bravo but not relocated, 59–61, 118; Marshallese proverbs, 146, 228; Marshallese seen as a sacrifice for science, 22–23; Marshallese singers challenge division between public and private realms, 39–40; Marshallese songs challenge US American systems, 25, 40; Marshallese understanding of the throat, 28–30, 94, 155; mid-range atolls, 59–61; militarization of, 37, 48, 51, 221; money and, 156; racialized hierarchy between US scientists and Marshallese, 71, 103; radioactive citizenship in the, 43–44, 64; relationship between United States and, 4, 15, 32–33; singing as a point of connection between United States and, 11, 167; understandings of the function of singing on the, 149; US imaginations of Marshallese as savages, 22, 72, 104, 198; vaporized by Bravo, 164, 253n7–253n8; during World War II, 50. *See also* Bikinians; Bravo; Gospel Day; Indigenous people; place-names; radio

Marshall Islands Journal, 98, 103, 174, 200
Masco, Joseph, 20, 78
Mason, Leonard, 54, 158
Massumi, Brian, 37
Matayoshi, James, 116
materialism, 176
matrilineal: disenvoicing, 50–51, 56; kinship system as, 7; Marshallese emphasize listening to resonances of the, 25–26; place-names and, 214; son's movements afforded by his mother and, 33; US strategy as impositions on inability to hear the matrilineage, 220. *See also* gender; women
McArthur, Phillip, 33
Meck, 243
mediation, 74
medical ethnomusicology, 97
"Meditation XVII," 170
Mejato, 89, 99
memory, 105
memory song. *See* al in keememej
"Mental Sickness," 151
Mersenne, Marin, 11
Michael, Rijen, 1
Midkiff, Frank, 59
militarization, 37, 48, 51, 214, 221
Milne, James, 132
Minji, 96–97
missionaries, 11–12, 53, 95, 112, 172, 177
modernity, 27, 43, 49, 210. *See also* liberalism
modern liberalism, 14
Molly, 1, 66–68
money, 156, 176, 242–43
Mon la Mike, 232, 241
Moore, Frank III, 249–50
MORIBA, 132–36, 144–46, 157, 159–60, 162, 197, 199, 202

"MORIBA" (song), 146
MORIBA band, 156
Morris, David, 121
mother, the, 240, 250. *See also* women
"Mr. Urine." *See* "LoRautt" (song)
Muñoz, José, 31
musical petitions, 76, 85, 89, 108, 122, 126, 129, 139, 222
musical refusals, 29
musicopoetic homecomings, 29, 250
musico-poetics, 29
ṃwilaḷ, 34, 188, 191, 237, 248
mythico-history, 136, 205, 264n12. *See also* Bikinians

Nam, 164
national anthems, 147
National Cancer Institute, 129
National Geographic, 53
navigation, 162–63, 183, 187, 228, 238
navigational school, 101, 184
NBC, 70–71, 103
Neas, Maynard, 56
"Ñe ij keememej tok aelōñ eo aō" (song), 161–63, 183. *See also* Bikinians
Nelson, Dana, 68
neocolonialism, 48
neoliberalism, 96, 207
Nevermann, Hans, 112
New York Times, 58–59, 165
Niedenthal, Jack, 3, 143, 148, 193
Nimitz, Chester W., 53, 227
"1954" (song), 118, 122
noise, 177, 197–98, 205, 209–10. *See also* spirited noise
"No Longer Can I Stay, It's True." *See* "I jab pād mol, aet I jab"
North Star. *See* Iju in Eañ
Note, Kessai, 79
nuclear-centered language, 85, 106, 108, 120–21
Nuclear Claims Tribunal, 15–16, 27, 103
nuclear colonialism, 62, 177. *See also* European colonization

nuclear culture, 129; characterized by silence, 5; effort to make the nuclear threat be perceived as real, 20–21; gendering of nuclear colonizing processes, 7; histories of the atomic bomb making the visual primary, 20; loss of health and culture and, 128; nuclear media complex, 46, 54, 131–34; provincializing the bomb, 20, 210; redefined a new world order with the United States leading the West, 6, 9–10; secrecy system and, 21–22; as a sonic culture, 5
nuclear identity, 201
nuclear incorporation, 9, 19, 70–72, 112
nuclear listening, 19, 21, 42, 129, 168
nuclear savage, 70
nuclear silences, 22–23, 43, 52, 67, 72, 95, 209, 251
Nuclear Victims' and Survivors' Remembrance Day, 79, 90, 115–22, 125, 128, 158
nucleation, 137

O'Brien, Patty, 11
Okjenlañ, 82
"177" (song), 115, 120–22
"One Night." *See* "Juon jọtiinin" (song)
one world model, 251
One World or None (film), 10
onomatopoeia, 109
onto-cosmologies, 137, 159
"Onward and Upward" (song), 181
Operation Crossroads, 10, 54
Operation Exodus, 98
Operation Hardtack, 222
Operation Homecoming, 230–32, 239. *See also* Kwajalein; protest
Operation Redwing, 222
oppositional politics, 46, 48
Ostherr, Kirsten, 68

Pacific Proving Grounds, 67–68
parade, 174
party song. *See* al in kamōlo
peace, 188

Pedro, Fred, 42, 79–80
performances, 29
Peters, Glen, 145–46
petition, 76, 85, 89, 108, 126, 129, 139, 222
Petryna, Adriana, 44
physical universalism, 11
piit, 204
Pikeej, 243
"Pilot" (song), 182–83
place-names, 114, 166, 212, 220, 228, 243, 247, 249–50. *See also* Marshall Islands
polio, 229
political protest songs, 108
politics of affect, 36
politics of harmony, 159
prayer, 182
Prinz Eugen, 224, 243
Project 4.1, 2, 15, 57, 93, 114, 228
"Project 4.1" (song), 116
protest, 36, 42, 108, 135, 214, 222–23, 230–34, 237, 251. *See also* Operation Homecoming
Protestantism, 175
proverb, 146
public performances, 25
"Pursuit of Truth" (Graham), 103
Pythagorean, 10–11

Rader, Randall R., 44
radiation: aligned with modern progress, 22; as an opportunity for American middle class, 68; damage wrought on the generational level, 128; effect on women's singing voices of, 87–88, 91–94, 102; as forced labor to make bombs for United States, 62–64; illnesses linked with, 65, 85, 91, 95, 104, 112; international spread of radiation, 127; as a marker of modernization, 49; Marshallese decolonial movement and, 80; radiation affected atoll populations not evacuated, 2; radiation language, 85; radiation treatment for those with cancer due to radiation, 139;

Rongelapese exposure to, 57, 75–76; stigmatization of populations affected by, 59, 91–92, 95–96; unites and divides the Marshal Islands, 18; as a weapon of imperial sensibilities, 251. *See also* Bravo; cancer; thyroid
"Radiation" (song), 76–77, 139–40
radiation songs, Marshallese: with an ear towards the interrelatedness of human and non-human, 37; framing a nuclear reality in which we are all implicated, 35; making senselessness sensible, 13, 19, 111; as nuclear resistance, 81–82, 158; resound remedial efforts, 30; restaging Marshallese against their representations in the nuclear archive, 119; retain memories of US denials of radiation and memories, 78; second generation radiation song, 112; take on the tenor of court cases, 76; used to gesture to their fragmented body parts and voices, 28, 125–27; using the trope of shaking or moving, 47, 191. *See also* bomb songs; "Juon jọtiinin" (song)
radio, 41–42, 45–46, 48, 53, 56, 78–80, 174, 176, 200. *See also* Federal Civil Defense Administration; Marshall Islands; V7AB; V7EMON
radioactive citizenship: allied pursuit of world salvation as the foundation of, 54; definition of, 21; driven by cash economy, 242; in global citizenship, 237; manifests as nuclear nationalism, 77; in the Marshall Islands, 43–44, 64; military occupation and, 218; as a mode of belonging tied to nuclear national security through law, 44; predicated on breaks, 46; territorial appropriation, 214; unsettling, 218. *See also* Federal Civil Defense Administration
radioactive colonization, 137
Radio News, 54
Rainbow Warrior, 98
Rancière, Jacques, 18, 25

Randy, 196–97, 204
Rantak, Katnar, 232–33, 239
rationality, 137
R&B, 3
Reducing Environmental Cancer Risk: What We Can Do Now (report), 129
re-fusals, 29
remediation: of affective alliance, 37; biomedical and biopolitical remediation and, 31; considering songs in terms of, 9; of fragmented temporalities, 105; passing through more than one media as, 32–34; in projects that aim to divest democracy from its Western, capitalist desires, 38; restages the myth of segregation and quarantine, 35–36; singing and, 31, 97, 101, 107, 118, 125, 155; in terms of health and healing, 30, 102; vocal historical, 242
removal songs, 139–40
representational system, 29
reproduction rights, 95
"Republic of the Marshall Islands Supplemental Nuclear Compensation Act of 2008," 62
restricted data, 5, 22, 55, 57, 109–10
rikaki, 180
Ri-Majol, Ainikien, 46
Rita Village, 41
RMI. *See* Marshall Islands
Robie, David, 98
rock 'n' roll, 3, 48
Roi Namur, 224, 243
Ronald Reagan Ballistic Missile Test Site, 228
Rongelapese, 57; Americans taught Rongelapese men how to be viewed in subservient positions, 71–72; denied relocation assistance, 98–100; evacuation of, 2; exposure to radiation, 57, 75–76; feeling of powerlessness of, 121; isolation and, 110; moving back to Rongelap, 4; present day diaspora, 4, 89; relationship with their land since Bravo, 101; relocated to Ejit Island, 58–59; relocation to/ life on Mejato, 98–99; self-determination, 99; stigmatization of, 92; thyroid disease and, 91; unintelligibility of nuclear language Rongelapese had to learn, 120; as US nuclear program test subjects, 57, 59, 66–67, 68–69, 88
Rongelapese women: denied from attending meeting between RMI and DOE, 122, 127; disproportionately affected by nuclear testing, 89, 91; evince the decay that was mapped onto them, 116; nuclear remembrance events, 115; reproductive capacity impacted by radiation, 95; singing voices effected by radiation, 91–94, 102; use their singing practices to appeal for declassification, 88, 127; use their singing practices to draw attention to throat injuries, 88, 97–98
Rongerik, 54–55, 132
roro, 114, 164, 166, 178–79, 191–92, 208, 240, 242
rose, 119
Ruot, 243

S. 1756, 62
sail-in protest, 230
Sakai, Naori, 74
Sarah, 99
savages (trope), 71, 104, 177, 198
schooner song, 114
Schumpeter, Joseph, 21
seascape epistemology, 36, 188–89
secrecy, 5, 21–22, 126
Section 177, 15, 27, 60, 115, 120, 122, 222. *See also* Compact of Free Association
self-determination, 16–17, 44, 99, 127, 135, 172, 239
senses, the, 28, 148, 183, 219
Sensing Law, 218–19
sensory democracy, 38–39, 138, 152, 155, 168, 178, 220
Seremetakis, Nadia C., 27, 29, 160–61

shark, 194–95
Sharlynn, 141–42
"Sh-boom (Life Could Be a Dream)" (song), 3, 18, 218
"Sh'Boom; or, How Early Rock & Roll Taught Us to Stop Worrying and Love the Bomb" (Aquila), 3
Shirley, 85, 211
Shklovsky, Victor, 29
silence: characterizing global nuclear culture, 5, 23; hidden realities of suffering and, 62; of lost generations, 95–96; nuclear silences and, 22–23, 43, 52, 67, 72, 95, 209, 251; of unanswered questions, 122
singing: effect of radiation on women's singing voices, 87–88, 91–94, 102; gendering of singing role assignments, 12, 95; to manifest a unity in which the collective is understood as expressing the singular, 34; Marshallese understanding of the function of, 149; as a means for women to engage in diplomacy, 234; memory songs and, 105, 165; as a point of connection for Marshallese and United States, 11, 167; political protest songs, 108; remediation and, 31, 97, 101, 107, 118, 125, 155; removal songs, 139; silencing some voices in service of sounding others, 18; songs cannot be reduced to the universal, 232; steering songs, 190; timbral singing, 26, 29; Western musical system and, 26. *See also* bomb songs; homecoming songs; throat, the; war songs
Skate Em Lā, 77
skit, 128
slavery, 142
smell, 195
Smith, Andrea, 135
Smith, Linda Tuhiwai, 22
social death, 126
Solomon, Anthony, 45, 229
Solomon Report, 229
"Some People Hate Each Other Because of Money" (song), 240–41
songfest competitions. *See* jepta
sonic histories, 214
soul, 150, 155
soul loss, 151, 153, 157
sound. *See* ainikien
South Pacific Nuclear Free Zone Treaty, 16
spirited noise, 172, 178, 180, 205, 209. *See also* noise
Spongebob Squarepants, 174
Springdale, 143, 177
Standard Man, 68
"Standing on the Promises" (song), 181
status, 72
Stauffer, Jill, 62
steering songs, 190
Stege, Biram, 115
Stege, Kristina, 222
Steingo, Gavin, 18
stick dance, 112, 114
Stras, Laurie, 27, 92
Strategic Defense Initiative, 214
suffering for science, 22, 167, 205
Suffering for Science (Herzig), 22
Sunrise Lib, 42, 242–43
Supreme Court, 4

tabōḷ pile, 219, 242–43, 247–48
"Ta in eṃōkaj aer ba" (song), 99–103
"Take a look." *See* "Bōk mejam" (song)
Tak in al, 198
"Takings Clause," 44
talking story songs, 248
tattoo, 185
Taylor, Jessica, 12
Teaiwa, Katerina, 183
Teaiwa, Teresia K., 6–7, 32
tea rose, 225–26
terra nullius, 62
Territorial Survey of Oceanic Music, 215–16
"These are My Questions for You Now, Still." *See* "Kajjitok in Aō Nan Kew Kiio" (song)

INDEX

throat, the, 26, 28–30, 94, 118, 148, 152, 155. *See also* bomb songs; bōro wot juōn; singing; thyroid
thyroid, 85–86, 91–94, 102, 112, 125–26, 152. *See also* cancer; radiation; throat, the
Tibon, Jorelik, 47–48
Time, 57
Tobin, Jack, 183
tonal harmony, 12
tourism, 224
Traditional Medicine in the Marshall Islands, 150
Treaty of Rarotonga, 16
Treaty on the Prohibition of Nuclear Weapons, 16
Truman, Harry, 15, 53
Trust Territory of the Pacific Islands, 15, 43–45, 114
typhoon, 221
typhoon song, 236

UN Declaration of the Rights of Indigenous Persons, 16
United Democratic Party, 79
United Nations, 10, 57
United States: American and Marshallese postwar positionality, 52–53, 226; American country music, 120; American GIs and, 120; American missionaries in the Marshall Islands, 11–12, 53, 95, 112, 172, 177; Americans' version of freedom impeded Marshallese interconnectedness, 239; avoidance of accountability and compensation by, 15, 44, 49, 59, 61–62, 98, 122, 129, 182, 229–30; Bikinians as America's children, 141, 206; development democracy, 14–15, 44, 46; failed cleanup efforts of, 4, 165; failure to disclose knowledge of nuclear contamination on atolls, 60, 67–68, 72, 75–77; failure to provide explanation to Marshallese about nuclear experimentation, 2, 4, 56–57, 66–67, 87–88; GIs, 120; imposition on inability to hear matrilineage, 220; justification of radiation testing on Marshallese, 22–23, 88; little value Americans have for lives of Marshallese, 64, 70–71; Marshallese adapt American working-class sensibilities, 146, 154; Marshallese songs challenge US American system, 25; Marshall Islands dependence on, 56, 67, 76, 139, 191; media, 55, 70; myth of liberation and, 134, 175, 226, 231; neocolonization and, 48; nuclear culture redefining a new world order with the United States leading the West, 6, 10; ongoing US military weapons testing projects in Kwajalein, 222, 224, 228; racialized hierarchy between Marshallese and US scientists, 71, 103; relationship between Kwajalein and United States deteriorated in the postwar, 222, 227–30; relationship between Marshall Islands and, 4, 15, 32–33; secrecy system around the bomb, 21–22, 126; singing as a point of connection between Marshallese and, 11, 167; US Atomic Age diplomacy promising global harmony, 9–10, 135; US imagination of Marshallese as savage, 22, 104, 177, 198; US professional males vocationally empowered through radiation experiments, 65–66, 68–69. *See also* colonialism; Compact of Free Association; democracy; global harmony; individualism; liberalism
"Upon, upon Those Watchtowers." *See* "Ioon, ioon miadi kan"
US Court of Federal Claims, 44
US Supreme Court, 27, 210
Utrikese, 2, 57, 59, 64
uwaañañ, 173, 192–97, 202, 209–10

V7AB, 41, 50, 78–79, 174, 176, 200
V7EMON, 42, 48, 79–80. *See also* radio
Valentina, 138–41
vocal currency, 137, 155, 234

voice: as a barometer of communal health, 94; democracy's promise to exercise voice, 14, 46, 153; depathologizing the individual voice, 148; equivocality of voicelessness, 159; as guidance in differently gendered spaces, 89; as the means of production and the product of harmony, 22; myth of voicing as freedom or overcoming, 142; political voicelessness can inscribe literal voicelessness, 74; self-determination and, 17; a single person can envoice multiple beings, 34; trope of voice as a gift from United States, 12, 231; used to distinguish the human form nonhuman, 13; voice-based refusals, 138; voice-crossing and, 141; voicelessness herd in terms of voice-based extractions from global harmony, 126

VZAB. *See* radio

Waan Aelōñ in Majel, 184
Walsh, Julianne, 72, 115, 235
war, 190
war songs, 232–33, 240. *See also* "Ioon, ioon miadi kan"; "Koj lum bok at" (song); singing
wave-pattern navigation, 162, 183
Ways of Sensing (Hows and Classen), 23
"We Are the Land, the Land Is Us" (Kabua), 184
"We are the World" (song), 169
weaving, 31
"We Don't Want to Stand Back." *See* "Koj lum bok at" (song)
Weisgall, Jonathan, 54, 132
welcoming/party song. *See* al in kamōlo
Western medicine, 88, 129, 139

"What are they Talking About." *See* "Ta in emṃōkaj aer ba" (song)
"When I Remember My Atoll." *See* "Ñe ij keememej tok aelōñ eo aō" (song)
Wōdjapto, 172, 185–87, 192–97, 202, 209. *See also* Bikinians
Wolfe, Patrick, 24
wombu, 217
women: colonialism suppression of women's voices, 6–7, 32; denigration of women's political participation, 49–51, 89–90, 122, 127, 142, 157, 236; domestic violence and, 49; drumming and, 111–12, 185, 190, 262n38; European men positing Native Pacific women as their opposite, 11; Geiger counters as an extension of male colonial gaze violating, 65; involved in recitation and produce of the canoe, 164; lōrro and, 149–50; radiation's effect on reproductive capacity of, 95–96; radiation's effect on women's singing voices, 87–88, 91–94, 102; role in customary battle, 220, 234; second mom is island in RMI culture, 189; singing as a way for women to engage in diplomacy, 234; vocally soar above the men, 181; women's organizations, 49, 89, 111, 235. *See also* gender; matrilineal; mother, the
Women United Together in the Marshall Islands, 49–50, 79, 90, 111, 235
World War II, 10–11, 50, 52, 225, 227
Wotje, 59
WSZO, 56
Wyatt, Ben, 53–54, 131–33, 178

youth, 156, 159–60
Youth to Youth in Health, 115, 128